CULTURAL PERSPECTIVES

A Sourcebook

Volume II

EDITED BY

Rosemary Mims Fisk
John Mayfield

Samford University

Copley Custom Textbooks

An imprint of XanEdu Publishing, Inc.

ISBN 13: 978-1-58152-237-2
ISBN 10: 1-58152-237-1
Reprinted January 2011

On the Cover: Pablo Picasso (1881–1973). *Guernica*. Paris, June 4, 1937. Oil
on canvas, 349,3x776,6 cm. Museo Nacional Reina Sofia, Madrid, Spain.
Courtesy of Erich Lessing/Art Resource, NY. Copyright © 2002 by the
Estate of Pablo Picasso/Artists Rights Society (ARS), New York. Used by
permission.

Acknowledgments:

pp. 57–62: From *On the Revolutions: Nicholas Copernicus Complete Works*
pp. 18–22, translation and commentary by Edward Rosen. Copyright ©
1978 by Edward Rosen. Reprinted with permission of The Johns Hopkins
University Press.

pp. 178–179: Reprinted by permission of the publishers and the Trustees of
Amherst College from *The Poems of Emily Dickinson*, Thomas H. Johnson,
ed., Cambridge, Mass.: The Belknap Press of Harvard University Press,
Copyright © 1951, 1955, 1979 by the President and Fellows of Harvard
College.

pp. 261–269: From *Civilization and Its Discontents* by Sigmund Freud.
Translated by James Strachey. Translation copyright © 1961 by James
Strachey. © Renewed 1989 by Alix Strachey. Used by permission of W. W.
Norton & Company.

pp. 271–282: Excerpts from *A Room of One's Own* by Virginia Woolf. Copyright © 1929 by Harcourt, Inc. and renewed 1957 by Leonard Woolf.
Reprinted by permission of the publisher.

pp. 283–300: From *Existentialism and Human Emotions* by Jean-Paul Sartre.
Copyright © 1957, 1989 by Regeen Najar. Reprinted by permission.

pp. 301–304: From *The Myth of Sisyphus* by Albert Camus, translated by
Justin O'Brien. Copyright © 1955 by Alfred A. Knopf, a division of Random House, Inc. Reprinted by permission of Alfred A. Knopf, a division
of Random House, Inc.

Editors' Introduction

In the fall of 1997, Samford University introduced an entirely new core curriculum for its undergraduate programs. Called Co-nexus—but usually referred to simply as "the Core"—the new curriculum replaced an outdated and disparate list of general education requirements with an integrated course of study to be completed in the student's first two years. The intent of the new core was to get entering students on the same track, to provide essential skills and cultural literacy early on, to set high academic expectations, and generally to create an "academic culture" where students could make connections intellectually just as they make them socially.

A central element of this core is *Cultural Perspectives*, a two-semester introduction to the humanities. Faculty from English, history, political science, geography, and philosophy collaborated to design a course that would introduce freshmen to their cultural heritage and challenge them to think beyond that heritage—to other times, other cultures, other perspectives. As faculty from many disciplines, we decided to put our diversity to good use to create a course that is interdisciplinary yet interconnected. To that end, all sections of *Cultural Perspectives* share a common chronology and certain common texts, but individual teachers are free to approach the material from many perspectives.

During the first two years, the various instructors experimented with readings that complemented the common texts. Every section's list was different, yet certain works seemed to appear frequently. It seemed advisable to bring these readings together for the sake of convenience and cost. Beyond that, however, was a growing consensus among the faculty that a sourcebook is just that—a book of sources, materials which could be used in class, in research projects, and (we hope) for personal enlightenment. We do not pretend that these readings form a canon of any sort; they represent only a tiny fragment of the thousands of documents that have shaped our culture. They are, however, a starting point, an introduction to our common conversation with the past and with other cultures.

RMF
JM

January, 2011

Contents

1

from Treatise on Christian Liberty

Martin Luther

(1483–1546)

Sometime during October 31, 1517, the eve of the Feast of All Saints, professor of biblical theology and Augustinian monk Martin Luther posted the 95 Theses on the door of the Castle Church in Wittenberg, Germany. Luther primarily wished to call for a debate on the relationship between money and religion. Corruption surrounded the selling of indulgences, or complex permits issued by the Church which supposedly had power to grant forgiveness of sins or even release from punishment in purgatory. Luther's public protest began what would become the Protestant Reformation, creating a third major unit of Christianity along with the Roman Catholic and the Eastern Orthodox churches. The invention of the printing press allowed the new ideas and challenges to reach a wide audience. Sensing the clear threat to the Church's authority, the Pope excommunicated Luther, who refused to recant. By 1521 with the controversy becoming increasingly political, the Emperor of the Holy Roman Empire, Charles V, agreed to hold his own hearing at the Diet of Worms. Again, rather than renounce his own writings and understanding of the Bible, Luther gave his famous response: "I am bound by Scriptures I have cited, for my conscience is captive to the Word of God. I cannot and will not recant anything, since to act against one's conscience is neither safe nor right. I cannot do otherwise. Here I stand, may God help me." The story then becomes tangled with conflicting loyalties as Luther was allowed to escape and be "kidnaped" and held in a private castle before he was condemned to death in absentia, a punishment not carried out in this case. Luther's principled stand gave impetus to a popular movement to reform the Church that spread over much of Europe. It was aided by an increasing desire for political liberty which led to various states breaking away from papal authority. Luther did not approve of all subsequent religious and political experiments his attempt at reform sparked. He, however, broke with the Roman church, married a former nun and raised a family, while continuing to teach, translate the Bible into the German vernacular, and write such notable hymns as "A Mighty Fortress Is Our God."

The Treatise *below reveals the power of Luther's message, that salvation comes through faith in Jesus Christ alone, not through the sacraments. By 1520 Luther announced that baptism is the only indulgence necessary for salvation. Faith is never easy, he argued, when one returns to the essentials of Christianity: faith alone (sola fides), grace alone (sola gratia), Christ alone (solus Christus). The passage below also reveals the difficult paradoxes of the Christian faith and the Protestant emphasis on the primacy of the scriptures and the priesthood of the believer.*

Many people have considered Christian faith an easy thing, and not a few have given it a place among the virtues. They do this because they have not experienced it and have never tasted the great strength there is in faith. It is impossible to write well about it or to understand what has been written about it unless one has at one time or another experienced the courage which faith gives a man when trials oppress him. But he who has had even a faint taste of it can never write, speak, meditate, or hear enough concerning it. It is a living "spring of water welling up to eternal life," as Christ calls it in John 4:[14].

As for me, although I have no wealth of faith to boast of and know how scant my supply is, I nevertheless hope that I have attained to a little faith, even though I have been assailed by great and various temptations; and I hope that I can discuss it, if not more elegantly, certainly more to the point, than those literalists and subtle disputants have previously done, who have not even understood what they have written.

To make the way smoother for the unlearned—for only them do I serve— I shall set down the following two propositions concerning the freedom and the bondage of the spirit:

> A Christian is a perfectly free lord of all, subject to none.
> A Christian is a perfectly dutiful servant of all, subject to all.

These two theses seem to contradict each other. If, however, they should be found to fit together they would serve our purpose beautifully. Both are Paul's own statements, who says in I Cor. 9:[19], "For though I am free from all men, I have made myself a slave to all," and in Rom. 13:[8], "Owe no one anything, except to love one another." Love by its very nature is ready to serve and be subject to him who is loved. So Christ, although he was Lord of all, was "born of woman, born under the law" [Gal. 4:4], and therefore was at the same time a free man and a servant, "in the form of God" and "of a servant" [Phil. 2:6–7].

Let us start, however, with something more remote from our subject, but more obvious. Man has a twofold nature, a spiritual and a bodily one. According to the spiritual nature, which men refer to as the soul, he is called a spiritual, inner, or new man. According to the bodily nature, which men refer to as flesh, he is called a carnal, outward, or old man, of whom the Apostle writes in II Cor. 4:[16], "Though our outer nature is wasting away, our inner nature is being renewed every day." Because of this diversity of nature the Scriptures assert contradictory things concerning the same man, since these two men in the same man contradict each other, "for the desires of the flesh are against the Spirit, and the desires of the Spirit are against the flesh," according to Gal. 5:[17].

First, let us consider the inner man to see how a righteous, free, and pious Christian, that is, a spiritual, new, and inner man, becomes what he is. It is evident that no external thing has any influence in producing Christian righteousness or freedom, or in producing unrighteousness or servitude. A simple argument will furnish the proof of this statement. What can it profit the soul if the body is well, free and active, and eats, drinks and does as it pleases? For in these respects even the most godless slaves of vice may prosper. On the other hand, how will poor health or imprisonment or hunger or thirst or any other external misfortune harm the soul? Even the most godly men, and those who are free because of clear consciences, are afflicted with these things. None of these things touches either the freedom or the servitude of the soul. It does not help the soul if the body is adorned with the sacred robes of priests or dwells in sacred places or is occupied with sacred duties or prays, fasts, abstains from certain kinds of food, or does any work that can be done by the body and in the body. The righteousness and the freedom of the soul require something far different since the things which have been mentioned could be done by any wicked person. Such works produce nothing but hypocrites. On the other hand, it will not harm the soul if the body is clothed in secular dress, dwells in unconsecrated places, eats and drinks as others do, does not pray aloud, and neglects to do all the above-mentioned things which hypocrites can do.

Furthermore, to put aside all kinds of works, even contemplation, meditation, and all that the soul can do, does not help. One thing, and only one thing, is necessary for Christian life, righteousness, and freedom. That one thing is the most holy Word of God, the Gospel of Christ, as Christ says, John 11:[25], "I am the resurrection and the life; he who believes in me, though he die, yet shall he live"; and John 8:[36], "So if the Son makes you free, you will be free indeed"; and Matt. 4:[4], "Man shall not live by bread alone, but by every word that proceeds from the mouth of God." Let us then consider it certain and firmly established that the soul can do without anything except the Word of God and that where the Word of God is missing there is no help at all for the soul. If it has the Word of God it is rich and lacks nothing since it is the Word of life, truth, light, peace, righteousness, salvation, joy, liberty, wisdom, power, grace, glory, and of every incalculable blessing. This is why the prophet in the entire Psalm [119] and in many other places yearns and sighs for the Word of God and uses so many names to describe it.

On the other hand, there is no more terrible disaster with which the wrath of God can afflict men than a famine of the hearing of His Word, as He says in Amos 8:[11]. Likewise there is no greater mercy than when He sends forth His Word, as we read in Psalm 107:[20]: "He sent forth His word, and healed them, and delivered them from destruction." Nor was Christ sent into the world for any other ministry except that of the Word. Moreover, the entire spiritual estate—all the apostles, bishops, and priests—has been called and instituted only for the ministry of the Word.

You may ask, "What then is the Word of God, and how shall it be used, since there are so many words of God?" I answer: The Apostle explains this in Romans 1. The Word is the Gospel of God concerning his Son, Who was made flesh, suffered, rose from the dead, and was glorified through the Spirit who sanctifies. To preach Christ means to feed the soul, make it righteous, set it free and save it, provided it believes the preaching. Faith alone is the saving and efficacious use of the Word of God, according to Rom. 10:[9]: "If you confess with your lips that Jesus is Lord and believe in your heart that God raised Him from the dead, you will be saved." Furthermore, "Christ is the end of the law, that every one who has faith may be justified" [Rom. 10:4]. Again, in Rom. 1:[17], "He who through faith is righteous shall live." The Word of God cannot be received and cherished by any works whatever but only by faith. Therefore it is clear that, as the soul needs only the Word of God for its life and righteousness, so it is justified by faith alone and not any works; for if it could be justified by anything else, it would not need the Word, and consequently it would not need faith. . . .

Should you ask how it happens that faith alone justifies and offers us such a treasure of great benefits without works in view of the fact that so many works, ceremonies, and laws are prescribed in the Scriptures, I answer: First of all, remember what has been said, namely, that faith alone, without works, justifies, frees and saves; we shall make this clearer later on. Here we must point out that the entire Scripture of God is divided into two parts: commandments and promises. Although the commandments teach things that are good, the things taught are not done as soon as they are taught, for the commandments show us what we ought to do but do not give us the power to do it. They are intended to teach man to know himself, that through them he may recognize his inability to do good and may despair of his own ability. That is why they are called the Old Testament and constitute the Old Testament. For example, the commandment, "You shall not covet" [Exod. 20:17], is a command which proves us all to be sinners, for no one can avoid coveting no matter how much he may struggle against it. Therefore, in order not to covet and to fulfill the commandment, a man is compelled to despair of himself, to seek the help which he does not find in himself elsewhere and from someone else, as stated in Hosea 13:[9]: "Destruction is your own, O Israel: your help is only in me." As we fare with respect to one commandment, so we fare with all, for it is equally impossible for us to keep any one of them.

Now when a man has learned through the commandments to recognize his helplessness and is distressed about how he might satisfy the law—since the law must be fulfilled so that not a jot or tittle shall be lost, otherwise man will be condemned without hope—then, being truly humbled and reduced to nothing in his own eyes, he finds in himself nothing whereby he may be justified and saved. Here the second part of Scripture comes to our aid, namely, the promises of God which declare the glory of God, saying, "If you wish to fulfill the law and not covet, as the law demands, come, believe in Christ in whom grace, righteousness, peace, liberty, and all things are promised you. If you believe, you shall have all things; if you do not believe, you shall lack all things." That which is impossible for you to accomplish by trying to fulfill all the works of the law—many and useless as they all are—you will accomplish quickly and easily through faith. God our Father has made all things depend on faith so that whoever has faith will have everything, and whoever does not have faith will have nothing. "For God has consigned all men to disobedience, that he may have mercy upon all," as stated in Rom. 11:[32]. Thus the promises of God give what the commandments of God demand and fulfill what the law prescribes so that all things may be God's alone, both the commandments and the fulfilling of the commandments. He alone commands, He alone fulfills. Therefore the promises of God belong to the New Testament. Indeed, they are the New Testament.

Since these promises of God are holy, true, righteous, free and peaceful words, full of goodness, the soul which clings to them with a firm faith will be so closely united with them and altogether absorbed by them that it not only will share in all their power but will be saturated and intoxicated by them. If a touch of Christ healed, how much more will this most tender spiritual touch, this absorbing of the Word, communicate to the soul all things that belong to the Word. This, then, is how through faith alone without works the soul is justified by the Word of God, sanctified, made true, peaceful and free, filled with every blessing and truly made a child of God, as John 1:[12] says: "But to all who . . . believed in his name, he gave power to become children of God."

From what has been said it is easy to see from what source faith derives such great power and why a good work or all good works together cannot equal it. No good work can rely upon the Word of God or live in the soul, for faith alone and the Word of God rule in the soul. Just as the heated iron glows like fire because of the union of fire with it, so the Word imparts its qualities to the soul. It is clear, then, that a Christian has all that he needs in faith and needs no works to justify him; and if he has no need of works, he has no need of the law; and if he has no need of the law, surely he is free from the law. It is true that "the law is not laid down for the just" [I Tim. 1:[9]]. This is that Christian liberty, our faith, which does not induce us to live in idleness or wickedness but makes the law and works unnecessary for any man's righteousness and salvation. . .

Not only are we the freest of kings, we are also priests forever, which is far more excellent than being kings, for as priests we are worthy to appear before God to pray for others and to teach one another divine things. These are the functions of priests, and they cannot be granted to any unbeliever. Thus Christ has made it possible for us, provided we believe in Him, to be not only His brethren, co-heirs and fellow-kings, but also His fellow-priests. Therefore we may boldly come into the presence of God in the spirit of faith [Heb. 10:19, 22] and cry "Abba, Father!" [We may] pray for one another, and do all things which we see done and foreshadowed in the outer and visible works of priests. . . .

You will ask, "If all who are in the church are priests, how do these whom we now call priests differ from laymen?" I answer: Injustice is done those words "priest," "cleric," "spiritual," "ecclesiastic," when they are transferred from all Christians to those few who are now by a mischievous usage called "ecclesiastics." Holy Scripture makes no distinction between them, although it gives the name "ministers," "servants," "stewards" to those who are now proudly called popes, bishops, and lords and who should according to the ministry of the Word serve others and teach them the faith of Christ and the freedom of believers. Although we are all equally priests, we cannot all publicly minister and teach. We ought not do so even if we could. Paul writes accordingly in I Cor. 4:[1]: "This is how one should regard us, as servants of Christ and stewards of the mysteries of God.". . .

To return to our purpose, I believe that it has now become clear that it is not enough or in any sense Christian to preach the works, life and words of Christ as historical facts, as if the knowledge of these would suffice for the conduct of life; yet this is the fashion among those who must today be regarded as our best preachers. Far less is it sufficient or Christian to say nothing at all about Christ and to teach instead the laws of men and the decrees of the fathers. Now there are not a few who preach Christ and read about Him that they may move men's affections to sympathy with Christ, to anger against the Jews, and such childish and effeminate nonsense. Rather ought Christ to be preached to the end that faith in Him may be established that He may not only be Christ, but be Christ for you and me, and that what is said of Him and is denoted in His name may be effectual in us. Such faith is produced and preserved in us by preaching why Christ came, what He brought and bestowed, what benefit it is to us to accept Him. This is done when that Christian liberty which He bestows is rightly taught and we are told in what way we Christians are all kings and priests and therefore lords of all and may firmly believe that whatever we have done is pleasing and acceptable in the sight of God, as I have already said.

What man is there whose heart, upon hearing these things, will not rejoice to its depth, and when receiving such comfort will not grow tender so that he will love Christ as he never could by means of any laws or works? Who would have the power to harm or frighten such a heart? If the knowledge of sin or the fear of death should break in upon it, it is ready to hope in the Lord. It does not grow afraid when it hears tidings of evil. It is not disturbed when it sees its enemies. This is so because it believes that the righteousness of Christ is its own and that its sin is not its own, but Christ's, and that all sin is swallowed up by the righteousness of

Christ. This, as has been said above, is a necessary consequence. . . of faith in Christ. So the heart learns to scoff at death and sin and to say with the Apostle, "O death, where is thy victory? O death, where is thy sting? The sting of death is sin, and the power of sin is the law. But thanks be to God, who gives us the victory through our Lord Jesus Christ" [I Cor. 15:55–57]. Death is swallowed up not only in the victory of Christ but also by our victory, because through faith His victory has become ours and in that faith we also are conquerors.

Let this suffice concerning the inner man, his liberty, and the source of his liberty, the righteousness of faith. He needs neither laws nor good works but, on the contrary, is injured by them if he believes that he is justified by them.

Now let us turn to the second part, the outer man. Here we shall answer all those who, offended by the word "faith" and by all that has been said, now ask, "If faith does all things and is alone sufficient unto righteousness, why then are good works commanded? We will take our ease and do no works and be content with faith." I answer: not so, you wicked men, not so. That would indeed be proper, if we were wholly inner and perfectly spiritual men. But such we shall be only at the last day, the day of the resurrection of the dead. As long as we live in the flesh we only begin to make some progress in that which shall be perfected in the future life. For this reason the Apostle in Rom. 8:[23] calls all that we attain in this life "the first fruits of the Spirit" because we shall indeed receive the greater portion, even the fullness of the Spirit, in the future. This is the place to assert that which was said above, namely, that a Christian is the servant of all and made subject to all. Insofar as he is free he does no works, but insofar as he is a servant he does all kinds of works. . . .

In doing these works, however, we must not think that a man is justified before God by them, for faith, which alone is righteousness before God, cannot endure that erroneous opinion. We must, however, realize that these works reduce the body to subjection and purify it of its evil lusts, and our whole purpose is to be directed only toward the driving out of lusts. Since by faith the soul is cleansed and made to love God, it desires that all things, and especially its own body, shall be purified so that all things may join with it in loving and praising God. Hence a man cannot be idle, for the need of his body drives him and he is compelled to do many good works to reduce it to subjection. Nevertheless the works themselves do not justify him before God, but he does the works out of spontaneous love in obedience to God and considers nothing except the approval of God, whom he would most scrupulously obey in all things. . . .

The following statements are therefore true: "Good works do not make a good man, but a good man does good works; evil works do not make a wicked man, but a wicked man does evil works." Consequently it is always necessary that the substance or person himself be good before there can be any good works, and that good works follow and proceed from the good person, as Christ also says, "A good tree cannot bear evil fruit, nor can a bad tree bear good fruit" [Matt. 7:18]. It is clear that the fruits do not bear the tree and that the tree does not grow on the fruits; also that, on the contrary, the trees bear the fruits and the fruits grow on the trees. As it is necessary, therefore, that the trees exist before their fruits and the fruits do not make trees either good or bad, but rather as the trees are, so are the fruits they bear; so a man must first be good or wicked before he does a good or wicked work, and his works do not make him good or wicked, but he himself makes his works either good or wicked. . . .

Since human nature and natural reason, as it is called, are by nature superstitious and ready to imagine, when laws and works are prescribed, that righteousness must be obtained through laws and works; and further, since they are trained and confirmed in this opinion by the practice of all earthly lawgivers, it is impossible that they should of themselves escape from the slavery of works and come to a knowledge of the freedom of faith. Therefore there is need of the prayer that the Lord may give us and make us *theodidacti*, that is, those taught by God [John 6:45]; and Himself, as He has promised, write His law in our hearts. Otherwise there is no hope for us. If He Himself does not teach our hearts this wisdom hidden in mystery [I Cor. 2:7], nature can only condemn it and judge it to be heretical because nature is offended by it and regards it as foolishness. So. . . it happened in the old days in the case of the apostles and prophets, and so godless and blind popes and their flatterers do to me and to those who are like me. May God at last be merciful to them and to us and cause His face to shine upon us that we may know His way upon earth [Ps. 67:1–2], His salvation among all nations; God, who is blessed forever [II Cor. 11:31]. Amen.

2

from On the Jews and Their Lies

Martin Luther

In the final decade of his life, Martin Luther found himself involved in yet another controversy. Elector John Frederick had issued a decree in August of 1536 that banished all Jews from his territories and forbade Jews to travel through them. The 15th and 16th centuries in Europe featured waves of such banishments, resulting in an immense population of Jews moving eastward, to Poland and Russia. Scholars still debate the causes of this anti-Semitism that became a mainstay even in the plays of Shakespeare. Luther's earlier writings, such as his 1523 essay "That Jesus Christ Was Born a Jew," hoped for the conversion of the Jews now that the gospel could be read and debated by all. When the Jews—along with the Papists, Sacramentarians, Anabaptists, Turks, and other groups—refused to convert even though the gospel had been preached to them for two decades, Luther actively advocated their banishment. Any opposition to the gospel was a poisonous yeast in the Christian loaf. Regrettable as Luther's views were, even in the context of his time, because of his position as a revered religious leader to later generations of Germans and many others, these views had tragic consequences when they were cited by anti-Semites such as the Nazis as a justification for their own savage persecutions and executions of millions of Jews in the past century.

. . . First, their synagogues or churches should be set on fire, and whatever does not burn up should be covered or spread over with dirt so that no one may ever be able to see a cinder or stone of it. And this ought to be done for the honour of God and of Christianity in order that God may see that we are Christians, and that we have not wittingly tolerated or approved of such public lying, cursing, and blaspheming of His Son and His Christians. . . .

Secondly, their homes should likewise be broken down and destroyed. For they perpetrate the same things there that they do in their synagogues. For this reason they ought to be put under one roof or in a stable, like gypsies, in order that they may realize that they are not masters in

11

our land, as they boast, but miserable captives, as they complain of us incessantly before God with bitter wailing.

Thirdly, they should be deprived of their prayerbooks and Talmuds in which such idolatry, lies, cursing, and blasphemy are taught.

Fourthly, their rabbis must be forbidden under threat of death to teach any more. . . .

Fifthly, passport and travelling privileges should be absolutely forbidden to the Jews. For they have no business in the rural districts since they are not nobles, nor officials, nor merchants, nor the like. Let them stay at home. . . .

Sixthly, they ought to be stopped from usury. All their cash and valuables of silver and gold ought to be taken from them and put aside for safe-keeping. For this reason, as said before, everything that they possess they stole and robbed from us through their usury, for they have no other means of support. . . . Such evilly acquired money is cursed, unless, with God's blessing, it is put to some good and necessary use. . . .

Seventhly, let the young and strong Jews and Jewesses be given the flail, the axe, the hoe, the spade, the distaff, and spindle and let them earn their bread by the sweat of their noses as is enjoined upon Adam's children. For it is not proper that they should want us cursed *Goyyim* to work in the sweat of our brow and that they, pious crew, idle away their days at the fireside in laziness, feasting, and display. And in addition to this, they boast impiously that they have become masters of the Christians at our expense. We ought to drive the rascally lazy bones out of our system.

If, however, we are afraid that they might harm us personally, or our wives, children, servants, cattle, etc., when they serve us or work for us—since it is surely to be presumed that such noble lords of the world and poisonous bitter worms are not accustomed to any work and would very unwillingly humble themselves to such a degree among the cursed *Goyy-im*—then let us apply the same cleverness (expulsion) as the other nations, such as France, Spain, Bohemia, etc., and settle with them for that which they have extorted usuriously from us, and after having divided it up fairly let us drive them out of the country for all time. For, as has been said, God's rage is so great against them that they only become worse and worse through mild mercy, and not much better through severe mercy. Therefore away with them. . . .

To sum up, dear princes and nobles who have Jews in your domains, if this advice of mine does not suit you, then find a better one so that you and we may be free of this insufferable devilish burden—the Jews. . . .

3

Women's Speaking

Margaret Fell

(ca. 1666)

*M*argaret Fell came to Quakerism through the teaching of founder George *Fox. Her home in England, Swarthmore Hall, became the organizational center of the Friends movement. Fox (who later became Fell's husband) recorded that in 1650 a Justice Bennet called the group Quakers because before his court they exhorted him to "tremble at the word of God." Although the name Quaker was originally derisive, it was taken up by the early Society of Friends as a sign of their religious emotion. Friends are part of the Anabaptist tradition which stresses the guidance of the Holy Spirit over external authorities or ordained ministries and has a long tradition of actively working for peace and humanitarian causes. In the sixteenth and seventeenth centuries women were barred from preaching and from holding office in "established" churches (but not in many anti-establishment churches), although they frequently outnumbered men in the congregation. Roman Catholics, Anglicans, and churches in the Reformed tradition focused primarily on two passages by St. Paul to exclude women from church leadership: I Corinthians 14:34–35 ("Let your women keep silence in the churches. . . .") and I Timothy 2:1–12 ("But I suffer not a woman to teach, nor to usurp authority over the man, but to be in silence."). With the rise of sects, however, women began to challenge the interpretations of the Pauline prohibition by suggesting that Paul was dealing with specific historical problems. They asked male leaders to reread Galatians 3:28: "There is neither Jew nor Greek, there is neither bond nor free, there is neither male nor female: for ye are all one in Christ Jesus."*

Margaret Fell's Women's Speaking Justified *appeared just ten years after two women had been arrested for preaching and publicly tortured at Oxford and Cambridge. Fell herself was confined for several years in prison because she held Quaker meetings in her home, refused to take an oath, and protested compulsory tithes. From prison she wrote this rational, biblically based, and at times emotional argument for the right of women to preach. She herself never preached, but her daughter Sarah Fell became an influential preacher who used Hebrew to debate her male opponents.*

WOMEN'S SPEAKING

Justified, Proved, and Allowed of by the Scriptures.

All Such as Speak by the Spirit and Power of the Lord Jesus.

And How Women Were the First that Preached the Tidings of the Resurrection of Jesus, and Were Sent by Christ's Own Command, before He Ascended to the Father, John 20.17.

Originally Printed in the Year, 1666, in London

And it shall come to pass in the 14 dayes, saith the Lord, I Will pour out my Spirit upon all Flesh; your Son and Daughters shall Prophesie, Acts 2. 27. Joel 2.28.

It is written in the Prophets, They shall be all thought of God, saith Christ, John 6.45.

And all thy Children shall be taught of the Lord, and great shall be the Peace of thy Children. Isa. 54.13.

And they shall teach no more every man his Neighbbour, and every man his Brother, saying, Know the Lord; for they shall all know me, from the least to the greatest of them, saith the Lord. Jer. 31.34.

Whereas it hath been an Objection in the minds of many, and several times hath been objected by the Clergy, or Ministers, and others, against Women's speaking in the Church; and so consequently may be taken, that, they are condemned for medling in the things of God; the ground of which Objection, is taken from the Apostle's words, which he Writ in his first Epistle to the *Corinthians*, chap. 14. vers. 34, 35. And also what he writ to *Timothy* in the first Epistle, chap. 2. vers. 11, 12. But how far they wrong the Apostle's intentions in these Scriptures, we shall shew clearly when we come to them in their course and order. But first let me lay down how God himself hath manifested his Will and Mind concerning Women, and unto Women.

And first, When *God created Man in his own Image, in the Image of God created he them, Male and Female; and God blessed them; and God said unto them, Be fruitful, and multiply: and God said, Behold, I have given you of every Herb,* etc. *Gen.* 1. Here God joyns them together in his own Image, and makes no such distinctions and differences as men do; for though they be weak, he is strong; and as he said to the Apostle, *His Grace is sufficient,* and his *strength is made manifest in weakness,* II Cor. 12.9. And such hath the Lord chosen, even *the weak things of the world, to confound the things which are mighty; and things which are despised, hath God chosen, to bring to nought things that are,* I Cor. 1. And God hath put no such difference between the Male and Female as men would make.

It is true, *The Serpent that was more subtile then any* other *Beast of the Field,* came unto the Woman, with his Temptations, and with a lie; his subtilty discerning her to be more inclinable to hearken to him, when he said, *If ye eat, your eyes shall be opened;* and the Woman saw that t*he Fruit was good to make one wise;* there the temptation got into her, and *she did eat, and gave to her Husband, and he did eat* also, and so they were both tempted into the transgression and disobedience; and therefore God said unto *Adam,* when that he hid himself when he heard his voice, *Hast thou eaten of the Tree which I commanded thee that thou shouldst not eat?* And *Adam* said, *The Woman which thou gavest me, she gave me of the Tree, and I did eat. And the Lord said unto the Woman, What is this that thou hast done?* and the Woman said, *The Serpent beguiled me, and I did eat.* Here the Woman spoke the truth unto the Lord. See what the Lord saith, verse 15, after he had pronounced Sentence on the Serpent; *I will put enmity between thee and the Woman, and between thy Seed and her Seed, it shall bruise thy head, and thou shalt bruise his heel,* Gen. 3.

Let this Word of the Lord, which was from the beginning, stop the mouths of all that oppose Women's Speaking in the Power of the Lord; for he hath put enmity between the Woman and the Serpent; and if the Seed of the Woman speak not, the Seed of the Serpent speaks; for God hath put enmity between the two Seeds, and it is manifest, that those that speak against the Woman and her Seed's Speaking, speak out of the envy of the old Serpents Seed; and God hath fulfilled his Word and his Promise, *When the fullness of time was come, he hath sent forth his Son, made of a Woman, made under the Law, that we might receive the adoption of Sons,* Gal. 4.4,5.

Moreover, the Lord is pleased, when he mentions his Church, to call her by the name of *Woman,* by his Prophets, saying, *I have called thee as a Woman forsaken, and grieved in Spirit, and as a Wife of Youth,* Isa. 54. Again, *How long wilt thou go about, thou back-sliding Daughter? For the Lord hath created a new thing in the earth, a Woman shall compass a Man,* Jer. 31.22. And *David,* when he was speaking of Christ and his Church, he saith, *The*

Kings Daughter is all glorious within, her cloathing is of wrought Gold, she shall be brought unto the King: with gladness and rejoycing shall they be brought; they shall enter into the Kings Pallace, Psal. 45. And also King *Solomon* in his Song, where he speaks of Christ and his Church, where she is complaining and calling for Christ, he saith, *If thou knowest not, O thou fairest among women, go thy way by the footsteps of the Flock,* Cant. [Song of Solomon] 1.8;5.9. And *John,* when he saw the wonder that was in Heaven, he saw a *Woman clothed with the Sun, and the Moon under her feet, and upon her head a Crown of twelve Stars; and there appeared another wonder in Heaven, a great red Dragon stood ready to devour her Child:* here the envy appears that God put between the Woman and the Dragon, *Revelations* 12.

Thus much may prove that the Church of Christ is a Woman, and those that speak against the Woman's speaking, speak against the Church of Christ, and the Seed of the Woman, which Seed is Christ; that is to say, Those that speak against the Power of the Lord, and the Spirit of the Lord speaking in a Woman, simply, by reason of her Sex, or because she is a Woman, not regarding the Seed, and Spirit, and Power that speaks in her; such speak against Christ, and his Church, and are of the Seed of the Serpent, wherein lodgeth the enmity. And as God the Father made no such difference in the first Creation, nor never since between the Male and the Female, but always out of his Mercy and loving kindness, had regard unto the weak. So also, his Son, Christ Jesus, confirms the same thing; when the *Pharisees* came to him, and asked him, *if it were lawful for a man to put away his Wife?* He answered and said unto them, *Have you not read, That he that made them in the beginning, made them Male and Female,* and said, *For this cause shall a Man leave Father and Mother, and shall cleave unto his Wife, and they twain shall be one flesh, wherefore they are no more twain but one flesh; What therefore God hath joyned together, let no Man put asunder,* Mat. 19.

Again, Christ Jesus, when he came to the City of *Samaria,* where *Jacobs* Well was, where the Woman of *Samaria* was; you may read, in *John* 4 how he was pleased to preach the Everlasting Gospel to her; and when the Woman said unto him, *I know that when the Messiah cometh,* (which is called Christ) *when he cometh, he will tell us all things;* Jesus saith unto her, *I that speak unto thee am he;* This is more than ever he said in plain words to Man or Woman (that we read of) before he suffered. Also he said unto *Martha,* when she said, *she knew that her Brother should rise again in the last day,* Jesus said unto her, *I am the Resurrection and the Life: he that believeth on me, though he were dead, yet shall he live; and whosoever liveth and believeth shall never die. Believest thou this?* she answered, *Yea Lord, I believe thou art the Christ, the Son of God.* Here she manifested her true and saving Faith, which few at that day believed so on him, *John* 11. 25, 26. . . . .

Thus we see that Jesus owned the Love and Grace that appeared in Women, and did not despise it; and by what is recorded in the Scriptures, he received as much love, kindness, compassion, and tender dealing towards him from Women, as he did from any others, both in his life time, and also after they had exercised their cruelty upon him; for *Mary Magdalene,* and *Mary* the Mother of *James,* beheld where he was laid; *And when the Sabbath was past,* Mary Magdalene, *and* Mary *the Mother of* James, *and* Salome, *had brought sweet spices that they might annoint him: And very early in the morning, the first day of the week, they came unto the Sepulchre at the rising of the Sun; And they said among themselves, Who shall roll us away the stone from the door of the Sepulchre? And when they looked, the stone was rolled away, for it was very great;* Mark 16.1,2,3,4. Luke 24.1,2; *and they went down into the Sepulchre;* and as *Matthew* saith, *The Angel rolled away the stone, and he said unto the Women, Fear not, I know whom ye seek, Jesus which was Crucified; he is not here, he is risen,* Mat. 28. Now *Luke* saith thus, *That there stood two men by them in shining apparel, and as they were perplexed and afraid, the men said unto them, He is not here; remember how he said unto you when he was in Galilee, That the Son of Man must be delivered into the hands of sinful men, and be crucified, and the third day rise again; and they remembred his words, and returned from the Sepulchre, and told all these things to the eleven, and to all the rest.*

It was *Mary Magdalene,* and *Joanna,* and *Mary* the Mother of *James,* and the other Women that were with them, which told these things to the Apostles, *And their words seemed unto them as idle tales, and they believed them not.* Mark this, ye despisers of the weakness of Women, and look upon your selves to be so wise; but Christ Jesus doth not so, for he makes use of the weak: for when he met the Women after he was risen he said unto them, *All Hail,* and they came and held him by the Feet, and worshipped him; then said Jesus unto them, *Be not afraid; go tell my Brethren that they go into Gallilee, and there they shall see me,* Mat. 28. 10. Mark 16.9. And *John* saith, when *Mary* was weeping at the Sepulchre, that Jesus said unto her, *Woman, why weepest thou? what seekest thou? And when she supposed him to be the Gardner, Jesus saith unto her,* Mary; *she turned her self, and saith unto him,* Rabboni, *which is to say Master; Jesus saith unto her, Touch me not, for I am not yet ascended to my Father, but go to my Brethren, and say unto them, I*

ascend unto my Father, and your Father, and to my God, and your God, John
20.16,17.

Mark this, you that despise and oppose the Message of the Lord God that
he sends by Women; what had become of the Redemption of the whole
Body of Mankind, if they had not believed the Message that the Lord
Jesus sent by these Women, of and concerning his Resurrection? And if
these Women had not thus, out of their tenderness and bowels of love,
who had received Mercy, and Grace, and forgiveness of sins, and Virtue,
and Healing from him; which many men also had received the like, if
their hearts had not been so united and knit unto him in love, that they
could not depart as the men did, but sat watching, and waiting, and
weeping about the Sepulchre until the time of his Resurrection, and so
were ready to carry his Message, as is manifested; else how should his
Disciples have known, who were not there? . . .

And now to the Apostle's words, which is the ground of the great Objection against Women's Speaking. And first, I *Cor.* 14, let the Reader seriously read that Chapter, and see the end and drift of the Apostle in speaking
these words: for the Apostle is there exhorting the *Corinthians* unto charity,
and to desire Spiritual gifts, and not to speak in an unknown tongue; and
not to be Children in understanding, but to be children in malice, but in
understanding to be men; and that the Spirits of the Prophets should be
subject to the Prophets; for God is not the Author of Confusion, but of
Peace: And then he saith, *Let your Women keep silence in the church,* etc.

Where it doth plainly appear that the Women, as well as others, that were
among them, were in confusion; for he saith, *How is it Brethren? when ye
come together, every one of you hath a Psalm, hath a Doctrine, hath a Tongue,
hath a Revelation, hath an Interpretation? Let all things be done to edifying.* Here
was no edifying, but all was in confusion speaking together; Therefore he
saith, *If any man speak in an unknown Tongue, let it be by two, or at most by
three, and that by course, and let one Interpret, but if there be no Interpreter, let
him keep silence in the Church.* Here the Man is commanded to keep silence
as well as the Woman, when they are in confusion and out of order.

But the Apostle saith further, *They are commanded to be in Obedience,* as also
saith the Law; and *if they will learn any thing, let them ask their Husbands at
home; for it is a shame for a Woman to speak in the Church.*

Here the Apostle clearly manifests his intent; for he speaks of Women that
were under the Law, and in that Transgression as *Eve* was, and such as

were to learn, and not to speak publickly, but they must first ask their Husbands at home; and it was a shame for such to speak in the Church: And it appears clearly, that such Women were speaking among the *Corinthians*, by the Apostles exhorting them from malice and strife, and confusion, and he preacheth the Law unto them, and he saith, in the law it is written, *With men of other tongues, and other lips, will I speak unto this people,* verse 21.

And what is all this to Women's Speaking? that have the Everlasting Gospel to preach, and upon whom the Promise of the Lord is fulfilled, and his Spirit poured upon them according to his Word? *Acts* 2.16,17,18. And if the Apostle would have stopped such as had the Spirit of the Lord poured upon them, why did he say just before, *If any thing be revealed to another that sitteth by, let the first hold his peace?* and *you may all prophesie one by one.* Here he did not say that such Women should not Prophesy as had the Revelation and Spirit of God poured upon them; but their Women that were under the Law, and in the Transgression, and were in strife, confusion & malice in their speaking; for if he had stopt Women's praying or prophesying, why doth he say, *Every man praying or prophesying, having his head covered, dishonoureth his head, but every Woman that prayeth or prophesieth with her head uncovered, dishonoureth her head? Judge in your selves, Is it comely that a Women pray or prophesie uncovered? For the Woman is not without the Man, neither is the Man without the Woman, in the Lord,* I Cor. 11.3,4,13.

Also that other Scripture, in *I Tim.* 2 where he is exhorting that Prayer and Supplication be made every where, lifting up holy Hands without wrath and doubting; he saith in the like manner also, That *Women must adorn themselves in modest apparel, with shamefastness and sobriety, not with broidered hair, or gold, or pearl, or costly array;* He saith, *Let Women learn in silence with all subjection, but I suffer not a Woman to teach, nor to usurp authority over the Man, but to be in silence, for* Adam *was first formed, then* Eve; *and* Adam *was not deceived, but the Woman being deceived was in the transgression.*

Here the Apostle speaks particularly to a Woman in Relation to her Husband, to be in subjection to him, and not to teach, nor usurp authority over him, and therefore he mentions *Adam* and *Eve;* But let it be strained to the utmost, as the opposers of Women's Speaking would have it, that is, that they should not preach nor speak in the Church, of which there is nothing here; Yet the Apostle is speaking to such as he is teaching to wear their apparel, what to wear, and what not to wear; such as were not come to wear modest apparel, and such as were not come to shamefastness and sobriety, but he was exhorting them from broidered hair, gold, and pearls, and costly array; and such are not to usurp authority over the Man, but to learn in silence with all subjection, as it becometh Women professing Godliness with good works.

And what is all this to such as have the Power and Spirit of the Lord Jesus poured upon them, and have the Message of the Lord Jesus given unto them? Must not they speak the Word of the Lord because of these undecent and unreverent Women that the Apostle speaks of, and to, in these two Scriptures? And how are the men of this Generation blinded, that bring these Scriptures, and pervert the Apostles Words, and corrupt his intent in speaking of them? and by these Scriptures, endeavour to stop the Message and Word of the Lord God in Women, by contemning and despising of them. If the Apostle would have had Women's speaking stopt; and did not allow of them, why did he entreat his true Yoak-Fellow to help those Women who labored with him in the Gospel? *Phil.* 4.3. And why did the Apostles joyn together in Prayer and Supplication with the Women, and *Mary* the Mother of Jesus, and with his Brethren, *Acts* 1.14 if they had not allowed, and had union and fellowship with the Spirit of God, wherever it was revealed in Women as well as others? But all this opposing and gainsaying of Womens Speaking, hath risen out of the bottomless Pit, and spirit of Darkness that hath spoken for these many hundred years together in this night of Apostacy, since the Revelations have ceased and been hid: and so that spirit hath limited and bound all up within its bond and compass, and so would suffer none to speak, but such as that spirit of Darkness approved of, Man or Woman.

And so here hath been the misery of these last Ages past, in the time of the Reign of the Beast, that *John* saw when he stood upon the Sand of the Sea, rising out of the Sea, and out of the Earth, having seven Heads and ten Horns, *Rev.* 13. In this great City of *Babylon*, which is the Woman that hath sitten so long upon the Scarlet-coloured Beast, full of names of Blasphemy, having seven Heads and ten Horns; and this Woman hath been arrayed and decked with gold, and pearls, and precious stones; and she hath had a golden Cup in her hand, full of Abominations, and hath made all Nations drunk with the Cup of her Fornication; and all the world hath wondred after the Beast, and hath worshiped the Dragon that gave power to the Beast; and this woman hath been drunk with the blood of the Saints, and with the blood of the Martyrs of Jesus; and this hath been the woman that hath been speaking and usurping authority for many hundred years together: And let the times and ages past testifie how many have been murdered and slain, in Ages and Generations past; every Religion and Profession (as it hath been called) killing and murdering one another, that would not joyn one with another: And thus the Spirit of Truth, and the Power of the Lord Jesus Christ hath been quite lost among them that have done this; and this mother of Harlots hath sitten as a Queen, and said, *She should see no sorrow*; but though her days have been long, even many hundred of years, for there was power given unto the Beast, to continue forty and two months, and to make war with the Saints, and to overcome them; and all that have dwelt upon the earth have worshiped him, whose names are not written in the Book of the Life of the Lamb, slain from the foundation of the world.

But blessed be the Lord, his time is over, which was above twelve hundred years, and the darkness is past, and the night of Apostacy draws to an end, and the true Light now shines, the morning-Light, the bright morning-Star, the Root and Off-spring of *David*, he is risen, he is risen, glory to the highest for evermore; and the joy of the morning is come, and the Bride, the Lambs Wife, is making her self ready, as a Bride that is adorning for her Husband, and to her is granted that she shall be arrayed in fine linnen, clean and white, and the fine linnen is the Righteousness of the Saints; The *Holy Jerusalem* is descending out of Heaven from God, having the Glory of God, and her Light is like a Jasper stone, clear as Christal.

And this is that free Woman that all the Children of the Promise are born of; not the Children of the bond-woman, which is *Hagar*, which genders to strife and to bondage, and which answers to *Jerusalem* which is in bondage with her Children; but this is *the Jerusalem which is free, which is the Mother of us all*; And so this bond-woman and her children, that are born after the flesh, have persecuted them that are born after the Spirit, even until now; but now the bond-woman and her Seed is to be cast out, that hath kept so long in bondage and in slavery; and under limits; this bond-woman and her brood is to be cast out, and our Holy City, the *New Jerusalem*, is coming down from Heaven, and her Light will shine throughout the whole earth, even as a *Jasper stone, clear as Christal*, which brings freedom and liberty, and perfect Redemption to her whole Seed; and this is that Woman and Image of the Eternal God, that God hath owned, and doth own, and will own for evermore.

More might be added to this purpose, both out of the Old Testament and New, where it is evident that God made no difference, but gave his good Spirit, as it pleased him, both to Man and Woman, as *Deborah, Huldah, & Sarah*. The Lord calls by his *prophet Isaiah, Harken unto me, ye that follow after Righteousness, ye that seek the Lord, look unto the Rock from whence ye were hewen, and to the hole of the Pit from whence ye were digged; look unto* Abraham *your Father, and to Sarah that bare you; for the Lord will comfort Sion, etc.* Isa. 5. *And* Anna *the Prophetess, who was a Widow of four-score and four years of age, which departed not from the Temple, but served God with fastings and prayers night and day, she coming in at that instant,* (when old *Simeon* took the Child Jesus in his arms, and) *she gave thanks unto the Lord, and spake of him to all them who looked for Redemption in* Jerusalem, *Luke* 2.36,37,38. And *Philip* the Evangelist, into whose house the Apostle *Paul* entered, who was one of the Seven, *Acts* 6.3. He had four Daughters which were Virgins, that did prophesie, *Acts* 21.

And so let this serve to stop that opposing Spirit that would limit the Power and Spirit of the Lord Jesus, whose Spirit is poured upon all flesh, both Sons and Daughters, now in his Resurrection; and since that the Lord God in the Creation, when he made man in his own Image, he made them *male* and *female;* and since that Christ Jesus, as the Apostle saith, was made of a Woman, and the power of the Highest overshadowed her, and the holy Ghost came upon her, and the holy thing that was born of her, was called *the Son of God,* and when he was upon the Earth, he manifested his *love,* and his *will,* and his *mind,* both to the Woman of *Samaria,* and *Martha,* and *Mary* her Sister, and several others, as hath been shewed; and after his Resurrection also manifested himself unto them first of all, even before he ascended unto his Father. *Now when Jesus was risen, the first day of the week, he appeared first unto Mary Magdalene,* Mark 16.9. And thus the Lord Jesus hath manifested himself and his Power, without respect of Persons; and so let all mouths be stopt that would limit him, whose Power and Spirit is infinite, that is pouring it upon all flesh.

And thus much in answer to these two Scriptures,[1] which have been such a stumbling block, that the ministers of Darkness have made such a mountain of. But the Lord is removing all this, and taking it out of the way.

Note

[1] I Corinthians 14:34–35 and 1 Timothy 2:1–12.

4

from Canons and Decrees of the Council of Trent

(1563)

*L*uther's challenge sparked calls for reform and reorganization in the Roman
Catholic Church. Many reformers hoped that the Church might meet the
Protestants halfway and open the door to reunion. More conservative elements
wanted to strengthen leadership and practices in the Church itself. In response,
Pope Paul III convened the Council of Trent. The Council met for three sessions
over eighteen years and ranged widely. Dominated by conservatives, the Council's work fell into two broad areas: it clarified the Church's theological foundations, and it streamlined and rationalized its administration. Theologically, the
Council reaffirmed the authority of tradition as well as scripture and declared
good works to be prerequisites to, not simply the outcome of, salvation—a direct
rebuff to Luther. It affirmed the Nicene Creed, fixed the canon of books in the
Bible, authorized the Vulgate edition of St. Jerome as a true text of the Bible, set
the number of sacraments at seven, and so on. Administratively, the Council
demanded that church leaders take on a more active and responsive role, ordering bishops to reside in their dioceses, requiring the creation of seminaries to
instruct parish clergy, and encouraging the laity to participate in the sacraments.
The work of the Council can hardly be overestimated. It essentially set the pattern of Catholic belief and practice for the next four hundred years.

The Second Vatican Council (1962–1965) inaugurated a new era in Catholic history. Roman Catholics began to worship in English, Spanish, and other languages, not just in Latin. The Council affirmed the reading and critical study of
the Bible as central to Christian life. Catholics also began to work with other
Christians to promote Christian unity. In 1999 the Roman Catholic Church and
the Lutheran World Federation issued the Joint Declaration on the Doctrine
of Justification. While acknowledging that Lutherans and Catholics emphasized
different things, it articulated a theology of justification that both groups agreed
upon. In 2006 the World Methodist Council joined this affirmation.

The Necessity of Preparation for Justification in Adults, and Whence It Proceeds

It is furthermore declared that in adults the beginning of that justification must proceed from the predisposing grace of God through Jesus Christ, that is, from His vocation, whereby, without any merits on their part, they are called; that they who by sin had been cut off from God, may be disposed through His quickening and helping grace to convert themselves to their own justification by freely assenting to and cooperating with that grace; so that, while God touches the heart of man through the illumination of the Holy Ghost, man himself neither does absolutely nothing while receiving that inspiration, since he can also reject it, nor yet is he able by his own free will and without the grace of God to move himself to justice in His sight. Hence, when it is said in the sacred writings: *Turn ye to me, and I will turn to you* [Zach. 1:3], we are reminded of our liberty; and when we reply: *Convert us, O Lord, to thee, and we shall be converted* [Lam. 5:21], we confess that we need the grace of God. . . .

How the Gratuitous Justification of the Sinner by Faith Is to Be Understood

But when the Apostle [Paul] says that man is justified by faith and freely, these words are to be understood in that sense in which the uninterrupted unanimity of the Catholic Church has held and expressed them, namely, that we are therefore said to be justified by faith, because faith is the beginning of human salvation, the foundation and root of all justification, *without which it is impossible to please God* [Heb. 11:6] and to come to the fellowship of His sons; and we are therefore said to be justified gratuitously, because none of those things that precede justification, whether faith or works, merit the grace of justification. For, if *by grace, it is not now by works, otherwise*, as the Apostle says, *grace is no more grace* [Rom. 11:6]. . . .

In What the Justification of the Sinner Consists, and What Are Its Causes

. . . For though no one can be just except he to whom the merits of the passion of our Lord Jesus Christ are communicated, yet this takes place in that justification of the sinner, when by the merit of the most holy passion, *the charity of God is poured forth by the Holy Ghost in the hearts* [Rom. 5:5] of those who are justified and inheres in them; whence man through Jesus Christ, [with] whom he is [now one], receives in that justification, together with the remission of sins, all these infused at the same time, namely, faith, hope and charity. For faith, unless hope and charity be added to it, neither unites man perfectly with Christ nor makes him a living member of His body. For which reason it is most truly said that *faith without works is dead* [James 2:17, 20] and of no profit, and in *Christ Jesus neither circumcision availeth anything nor uncircumcision, but faith that worketh by charity* [Gal. 5:6, 6:15].

This faith, conformably to Apostolic tradition, catechumens ask of the Church before the sacrament of baptism, when they ask for the faith that gives eternal life, which without hope and charity faith cannot give. Whence also they hear immediately the word of Christ: *If thou wilt enter into life, keep the commandments* [Matt. 19:17]. . . .

Furthermore, to check unbridled spirits, it [the council] decrees that no one relying on his own judgement shall, in matters of faith and morals pertaining to the edification of Christian doctrine, distorting the Holy Scriptures in accordance with his own conceptions, presume to interpret them contrary to that sense which holy mother Church, to whom it belongs to judge of their true sense and interpretation, has held and holds, or even contrary to the unanimous teaching of the Fathers, even though such interpretations should never at any time be published. Those who act contrary to this shall be made known by the ordinaries[1] and punished in accordance with the penalties prescribed by the law.

And wishing, as is proper, to impose a restraint in this matter on printers also, who, now without restraint, thinking what pleases them is permitted them, print without the permission of ecclesiastical superiors the books of the Holy Scriptures and the notes and commentaries thereon of all persons indiscriminately, often with the name of the press omitted, often also under a fictitious press name, and what is worse, without the name of the author, and also indiscreetly have for sale such books printed elsewhere, [this council] decrees and ordains that in the future the Holy Scriptures, especially the old Vulgate Edition, be printed in the most correct manner possible, and that it shall not be lawful for anyone to print or to have printed any books whatsoever dealing with sacred doctrinal matters without the name of the author, or in the future to sell them, or even to have them in possession, unless they have first been examined and approved by the ordinary, under penalty of anathema[2] and fine. . . .

On the Invocation, Veneration, and Relics of Saints, and on Sacred Images

The holy council commands all bishops and others who hold the office of teaching and have charge of the *cura animarum*,[3] that in accordance with the usage of the Catholic and Apostolic Church, received from the primitive times of the Christian religion, and with the unanimous teaching of the holy Fathers and the decrees of sacred councils, they above all instruct the faithful diligently in matters relating to intercession and invocation of the saints, the veneration of relics, and the legitimate use of images, teaching them that the saints who reign together with Christ offer up their prayers to God for men, that it is good and beneficial suppliantly to invoke them and to have recourse to their prayers, assistance and support in order to obtain favors from God through His Son, Jesus Christ our Lord, who alone is our redeemer and savior. . . . Also, that the holy bodies of the holy martyrs and of others living with Christ, which were the living members of Christ and the temple of the Holy Ghost, to be awakened by Him to eternal life and to be glorified, are to be venerated by the faithful, through which many benefits are bestowed by God on men. . . . Moreover, that the images of Christ, of the Virgin Mother of God, and of the other saints are to be placed and retained especially in the churches, and that due honor and veneration is to be given them. . . .

Canons on the Sacraments in General

Canon 1. If anyone says that the sacraments of the New Law were not all instituted by our Lord Jesus Christ, or that there are more or less than seven, namely, baptism, confirmation, Eucharist, penance, extreme unction, order and matrimony, or that any one of these seven is not truly and intrinsically a sacrament, let him be anathema. . . .

Can. 10. If anyone says that all Christians have the power to administer the word and all the sacraments, let him be anathema. . . .

Canons on the Sacrament of Order

Canon 1. If anyone says that there is not in the New Testament a visible and external priesthood, or that there is no power of consecrating and offering the true body and blood of the Lord and of forgiving . . . sins, but only the office and bare ministry of preaching the Gospel; or that those who do not preach are not priests at all, let him be anathema. . . .

Can. 4. If anyone says that by sacred ordination the Holy [Spirit] is not imparted and that therefore the bishops say in vain: *Receive ye the Holy [Spirit]*, or that by it a character is not imprinted, or that he who has once been a priest can again become a layman, let him be anathema.

Can. 5. If anyone says that the holy unction which the Church uses in ordination is not only not required but is detestable and pernicious, as also are the other ceremonies of Order, let him be anathema.

Can. 6. If anyone says that in the Catholic Church there is not instituted a hierarchy by divine ordinance, which consists of bishops, priests and ministers, let him be anathema.

Can. 7. If anyone says that bishops are not superior to priests, or that they have not the power to confirm and ordain, or that the power which they have is common to them and to priests, or that orders conferred by them without the consent or call of the people or of the secular power are invalid, or that those who have been neither rightly ordained nor sent by ecclesiastical and canonical authority, but come from elsewhere, are lawful ministers of the word and of the sacraments, let him be anathema.

Notes

1 bishops
2 Condemnation and excommunication
3 "Care of souls"

5

from Institutes of the Christian Religion

John Calvin

(1509–1564)

*John Calvin ranks alongside Luther as a central architect of the Protestant Refor-
mation. Born in Picardy in France, Calvin initially went to Paris to study for
the priesthood; later, his father moved him to Orleans to prepare for a career in
law. Calvin seems to have been readying himself for the life of a classical scholar,
but about 1534 he experienced a conversion, cut his ties with the Church, and
fled to Switzerland. In 1536 he published the first edition of the* Institutes of the
Christian Religion, *the most ambitious explication of belief since Thomas
Aquinas'* Summa Theologica. *Protestants in Geneva urged him to move there,
which he did. He was never formally part of the political structure, but his influence in matters of government was extensive. He wrote a set of "ecclesiastical
ordinances" which the town council adopted as law, he encouraged prohibitions
against such behavior as card-playing or dancing, and he sanctioned the burning of witches and the exile or execution of dissidents.*

*Calvin's theology borrowed elements of Renaissance humanism, legal reasoning,
traditional theology, and intense emotionalism. Convinced that humans must act
to change their world, but at the same time believing in human depravity, Calvin
made the omnipotence of God and the infallibility of the scriptures his starting
points. He expanded Augustinian notions of predestination, challenged the validity of the Sacraments, rethought the place of women (and authority generally),
and advocated the doctrine of Christian calling. His beliefs were fundamental to
Presbyterians and the many variations of European and American Puritans.
Beyond that, Calvin's concept of the calling and his reformulation of authority
have been associated with the rise of merchant capitalism and the bourgeoisie.*

The Authority of the Scripture

Before I proceed any further, it is proper to introduce some remarks on
the authority of the Scripture, not only to prepare the mind to regard it
with due reverence, but also to remove every doubt. For, when it is admitted to be a declaration of the word of God, no man can be so deplorably

presumptuous, unless he be also destitute of common sense and of the common feelings of men, as to dare to derogate from the credit due to the speaker. But since we are not favoured with daily oracles from heaven, and since it is only in the Scriptures that the Lord hath been pleased to preserve his truth in perpetual remembrance, it obtains the same complete credit and authority with believers, when they are satisfied of its divine origin, as if they heard the very words pronounced by God himself. The subject, indeed, merits a diffuse discussion, and a most accurate examination. But the reader will pardon me, if I attend rather to what the design of this work admits, than to what the extensive nature of the present subject requires. But there has very generally prevailed a most pernicious error, that the Scriptures have only so much weight as is conceded to them by the suffrages of the Church; as though the eternal and inviolable truth of God depended on the arbitrary will of men. For thus, with great contempt of the Holy Spirit, they inquire, Who can assure us that God is the author of them? Who can with certainty affirm, that they have been preserved safe and uncorrupted to the present age? Who can persuade us that this book ought to be received with reverence, and that expunged from the sacred number, unless all these things were regulated by the decisions of the Church? It depends, therefore, (say they) on the determination of the Church, to decide both what reverence is due to the Scripture, and what books are to be comprised in its canon. Thus sacrilegious men, while they wish to introduce an unlimited tyranny, under the name of the Church, are totally unconcerned with what absurdities they embarrass themselves and others, provided they can extort from the ignorant this, one admission, that the Church can do every thing. But if this be true, what will be the condition of those wretched consciences, which are seeking a solid assurance of eternal life, if all the promises extant concerning it rest only on the judgment of men? Will the reception of such an answer cause their fluctuations to subside, and their terrors to vanish? Again, how will the impious ridicule our faith, and all men call it in question, if it be understood to possess only a precarious authority depending on the favour of men!

But such cavillers are completely refuted even by one word of the Apostle. He testifies that the Church is "built upon the foundation of the apostles and prophets." If the doctrine of the prophets and apostles be the foundation of the Church, it must have been certain, antecedently to the existence of the Church. Nor is there any foundation for this cavil, that though the Church derive its origin from the Scriptures, yet it remains doubtful what writings are to be ascribed to the prophets and apostles, unless it be determined by the Church. For if the Christian Church has been from the beginning founded on the writings of the prophets and the preaching of the apostles, wherever that doctrine is found, the approbation of it has certainly preceded the formation of the Church; since without it the Church itself had never existed. It is a very false notion, therefore, that the power of judging of the Scripture belongs to the Church, so as to make the certainty of it dependent on the Church's will. Wherefore, when the Church receives it, and seals it with her suffrage, she does not authenticate a thing otherwise dubious or controvertible; but, knowing it to be the truth of her God, performs a duty of piety, by treating it with immediate veneration. But, with regard to the question, How shall we be persuaded of its Divine original, unless we have recourse to the decree of the Church? this is just as if any one should inquire, How shall we learn to distinguish light from darkness, white from black, sweet from bitter? For the Scripture exhibits as clear evidence of its truth, as white and black things do of their colour, or sweet and bitter things of their taste.

• • •

Innate Depravity

I shall be content with citing a single passage, which, however, will resemble a very lucid mirror, in which we may behold at full length the image of our nature. For the Apostle, when he wishes to demolish the arrogance of mankind, does it by these testimonies: "There is none righteous, no, not one; there is none that understandeth, there is none that seeketh after God. They are all gone out of the way, they are together become unprofitable; there is none that doeth good, no, not one. Their throat is an open sepulchre; with their tongues they have used deceit; the poison of asps is under their lips; whose mouth is full of cursing and bitterness; their feet are swift to shed blood; destruction and misery are in their ways; there is no fear of God before their eyes." In this terrible manner he inveighs, not against particular individuals, but against all the posterity of Adam. He does not declaim against the depraved manners of one or another age, but accuses the perpetual corruption of our nature. For his design in that passage is not simply to rebuke men, in order that they may repent, but rather to teach us that all men are overwhelmed with an inevitable calamity, from which they can never emerge unless they are extricated by the mercy of God. As this could not be proved unless it were evinced by the ruin and destruction of our nature, he has adduced these testimonies, which demonstrate our nature to be totally ruined. Let this, then, be admitted, that men are such as they are here described, not only by corrupt habits, but also by a depravity of nature; for otherwise the reasoning of the Apostle could not be supported, "that there is no salvation for man but from the mercy of God; since in himself he is in a ruined and desperate condition." Here I shall not attempt to establish the application of the testimonies, to preclude the appearance of their being improperly introduced. I shall treat them just as if they had been originally uttered by Paul, and not quoted from the Prophets. He divests man first of righteousness, that is, integrity and purity, and then of understanding. Defect of understanding is proved by apostasy from God, the seeking of whom is the first step in the path of wisdom; but this loss must necessarily befall those who have revolted from God. He adds, that all have gone out of the way, and are become altogether corrupt, that there is not one that does good. Then he subjoins the flagitious crimes, with which they, who are once abandoned to iniquity, contaminate all members of their bodies. Lastly, he declares them to be destitute of the fear of God, the rule by which all our steps ought to be directed. If these are the hereditary characters of mankind, in vain do we seek in our nature for any thing that is good. I grant, indeed, that all these crimes are not exhibited in every individual; yet it cannot be denied that this monster lurks in the hearts of all. For as the body, which already contains within itself the cause and matter of a disease, although it has yet no sensation of pain, cannot be said to enjoy good health, neither can the soul be esteemed healthy, while it is full of such moral maladies; although this similitude will not correspond in every particular; for in the body, however diseased, there remains the vigour of life; but the soul, immersed in this gulf of iniquity, is not only the subject of vices, but totally destitute of every thing that is good.

• • •

Eternal Election or God's Predestination of some to Salvation, and of others to Destruction

The covenant of life not being equally preached to all, and among those to whom it is preached not always finding the same reception, this diversity discovers the wonderful depth of the Divine judgment. Nor is it to be doubted that this variety also follows, subject to the decision of God's eternal election. If it be evidently the result of the Divine will, that salvation is freely offered to some, and others are prevented from attaining it,—this immediately gives rise to important and difficult questions, which are incapable of any other explication, than by the establishment of pious minds in what ought to be received concerning election and predestination—a question, in the opinion of many, full of perplexity; for they consider nothing more unreasonable, than that, of the common mass of mankind, some should be predestinated to salvation, and others to destruction. But how unreasonably they perplex themselves will afterwards appear from the sequel of our discourse. Besides, the very obscurity which excites such dread, not only displays the utility of this doctrine, but shows it to be productive of the most delightful benefit. We shall never be clearly convinced as we ought to be, that our salvation flows from the fountain of God's free mercy, till we are acquainted with his eternal election, which illustrates the grace of God by this comparison, that he adopts not all promiscuously to the hope of salvation, but gives to some what he refuses to others. Ignorance of this principle evidently detracts from the Divine glory, and diminishes real humility. But according to Paul, what is so necessary to be known, never can be known, unless God, without any regard to works, chooses those whom he has decreed. "At this present time also, there is a remnant according to the election of grace. And if by grace, then it is no more of works; otherwise, grace is no more grace. But if it be of works, then it is no more grace; otherwise, work is no more work." If we need to be recalled to the origin of election, to prove that we obtain salvation from no other source than the mere goodness of God, they who desire to extinguish this principle, do all they can to obscure what ought to be magnificently and loudly celebrated, and to pluck humility by the roots. In ascribing the salvation of the remnant of the people to the election of grace, Paul clearly testifies, that it is then only known that God saves whom he will of his mere good pleasure, and does not dispense a reward to which there can be no claim. They who shut the gates to prevent any one from presuming to approach and taste the doctrine, do no less injury to man than to God; for nothing else will be sufficient to produce in us suitable humility, or to impress us with a due sense of our great obligations to God. Nor is there any other basis for solid confidence, even according to the authority of Christ, who, to deliver us from all fear, and render us invincible amidst so many dangers, snares, and deadly conflicts, promises to preserve in safety all whom the Father has committed to his care. Whence we infer, that they who know not themselves to be God's peculiar people will be tortured with continual anxiety; and therefore, that the interest of all believers, as well as their own, is very badly consulted by those who, blind to the three advantages we have remarked, would wholly remove the foundation of our salvation. And hence the Church rises to our view, which otherwise, as Bernard justly observes, could neither be discovered nor recognized among creatures, being in two respects wonderfully concealed in the bosom of a blessed predestination, and in the mass of a miserable damnation. But before I enter on the subject itself, I must address some preliminary observations to two sorts of persons. The discussion of predestination—a subject of itself rather intricate—is made very perplexed and therefore dangerous, by human curiosity, which no barriers can restrain from wandering into forbidden labyrinths, and soaring beyond its sphere, as if determined to leave none of the Divine secrets unscrutinized or unexplored. As we see multitudes every where guilty of this arrogance and presumption, and among them some who are not censurable in other respects, it is proper to admonish them of the bounds of their duty on this subject. First, then, let them remember that when they inquire into predestination, they penetrate the inmost recess of Divine wisdom, where the careless and confident intruder will obtain no satisfaction to his curiosity, but will enter a labyrinth from which he will find no way to depart. For it is unreasonable that man should scrutinize with impunity those things which the Lord has determined to be hidden in himself; and investigate, even from eternity, that sublimity of wisdom which God would have us to adore and not comprehend, to promote our admiration of his glory. The secrets of his will which he determined to reveal to us, he discovers in his word; and these are all that he foresaw would concern us or conduce to our advantage.

• • •

Predestination, by which God adopts some to the hope of life, and adjudges others to eternal death, no one, desirous of the credit of piety, dares absolutely to deny. But it is involved in many cavils, especially by those who make foreknowledge the cause of it. We maintain, that both belong to God; but it is preposterous to represent one as dependent on the other. When we attribute foreknowledge to God, we mean that all things have ever been, and perpetually remain, before his eyes, so that to his knowledge nothing is future or past, but all things are present; and present in such a manner, that he does not merely conceive of them from ideas formed in his mind, as things remembered by us appear present to our minds, but really beholds and sees them as if actually placed before him. And this foreknowledge extends to the whole world, and to all the creatures. Predestination we call the eternal decree of God, by which he has determined in himself, what he would have to become of every individual of mankind. For they are not all created with a similar destiny; but eternal life is foreordained for some, and eternal damnation for others. Every man, therefore, being created for one or the other of these ends, we say, he is predestinated either to life or to death. This God has not only testified in particular persons, but has given a specimen of it in the whole posterity of Abraham, which should evidently show the future condition of every nation to depend upon his decision.

• • •

The True Church and the Necessity of Our Union with Her, Being the Mother of all the Pious

. . . Here we must regard both the secret election of God, and his internal vocation; because he alone "knoweth them that are his"; and keeps them enclosed under his "seal" to use the expression of Paul; except that they bear his impression, by which they may be distinguished from the reprobate. But because a small and contemptible number is concealed among a vast multitude, and a few grains of wheat are covered with a heap of chaff, we must leave to God alone the knowledge of his Church whose foundation is his secret election. Nor is it sufficient to include in our thoughts and minds the whole multitude of the elect, unless we conceive of such a unity of the Church, into which we know ourselves to be truly ingrafted. For unless we are united with all the other members under Christ our Head, we can have no hope of the future inheritance. Therefore the Church is called *Catholic,* or universal; because there could not be two or three churches, without Christ being divided, which is impossible. But all the elect of God are so connected with each other in Christ, that as they depend upon one head, so they grow up together as into one body, compacted together like members of the same body; being made truly one, as living by one faith, hope, and charity, through the same Divine Spirit, being called not only to the same inheritance of eternal life, but also to a participation of one God and Christ. Therefore, though the melancholy desolation which surrounds us, seems to proclaim that there is nothing left of the Church, let us remember that the death of Christ is fruitful, and that God wonderfully preserves his Church as it were in hiding-places; according to what he said to Elijah: "I have reserved to myself seven thousand men, who have not bowed the knee to Baal."

This article of the creed, however, relates in some measure to the external Church, that every one of us may maintain a brotherly agreement with all the children of God, may pay due deference to the authority of the

Church, and in a word, may conduct himself as one of the flock. Therefore we add *The Communion of Saints*—a clause which, though generally omitted by the ancients, ought not to be neglected, because it excellently expresses the character of the Church; as though it had been said that the saints are united in the fellowship of Christ on this condition, that whatever benefits God confers upon them, they should mutually communicate to each other. This destroys not the diversity of grace, for we know that the gifts of the Spirit are variously distributed; nor does it disturb the order of civil polity, which secures to every individual the exclusive enjoyment of this property, as it is necessary for the preservation of the peace of society that men should have peculiar and distinct possessions.

• • •

Here are three things, therefore, worthy of our observation. First, that whatever holiness may distinguish the children of God, yet such is their condition as long as they inhabit a mortal body, that they cannot stand before God without remission of sins. Secondly, that this benefit belongs to the Church; so that we cannot enjoy it unless we continue in its communion. Thirdly, that it is dispensed to us by the ministers and pastors of the Church, either in the preaching of the gospel, or in the administration of the sacraments; and that this is the principal exercise of the power of the keys, which the Lord has conferred on the society of believers. Let every one of us, therefore, consider it as his duty, not to seek remission of sins anywhere but where the Lord has placed it. Of public reconciliation, which is a branch of discipline, we shall speak in its proper place.

• • •

On Civil Government

Having already stated that man is the subject of two kinds of government, and having sufficiently discussed that which is situated in the soul, or the inner man, and relates to eternal life,—we are, in this chapter, to say something of the other kind, which relates to civil justice, and the regulation of the external conduct. For, though the nature of this argument seems to have no connection with the spiritual doctrine of faith which I have undertaken to discuss, the sequel will show that I have sufficient reason for connecting them together, and, indeed, that necessity obliges me to it; especially since, on the one hand, infatuated and barbarous men madly endeavour to subvert this ordinance established by God, and, on the other hand, the flatterers of princes, extolling their power beyond all just bounds, hesitate not to oppose it to the authority of God himself. Unless both these errors be resisted, the purity of the faith will be destroyed. Besides, it is of no small importance for us to know what benevolent provision God has made for mankind in this instance, that we may be stimulated by a greater degree of pious zeal to testify our gratitude. In the first place, before we enter on the subject itself, it is necessary for us to recur to the distinction which we have already established, lest we fall into an error very common in the world, and injudiciously confound together these two things, the nature of which is altogether different. For some men when they hear that the Gospel promises a liberty which acknowledges no king or magistrate among men, but submits to Christ alone, think they can enjoy no advantage of their liberty, while they see any power exalted above them. They imagine, therefore, that nothing will prosper, unless the whole world be modeled in a new form, without any tribunals, or laws, or magistrates, or anything of a similar kind, which they consider injurious to their liberty. But he who knows how to distinguish between the body and the soul, between this present transitory life and the future eternal one, will find no difficulty in understanding, that the spiritual kingdom of Christ and civil government are things very different and remote from each other. Since it is a Jewish folly, therefore, to seek and include the kingdom of Christ under the elements of this world, let us, on the contrary, considering what the Scripture clearly inculcates, that the benefit which is received from the grace of Christ is spiritual; let us, I say, remember to confine within its proper limits all this liberty which is promised and offered to us in him. For why is it that the same apostle, who, in one place, exhorts to "stand fast in the liberty wherewith Christ hath made us free, and be not entangled again with the yoke of bondage," in another, enjoins servants to "care not for" their servile condition; except that spiritual liberty may very well consist with civil servitude? In this sense we are likewise to understand him in these passages: "There is neither Jew nor Greek, there is neither bond nor free, there is neither male nor female." Again: "There is neither Greek nor Jew, circumcision nor uncircumcision, Barbarian, Scythian, bond nor free; But Christ is all, and in all"; in which he signifies, that it is of no importance, what is our condition among men, or under the laws of what nation we live, as the kingdom of Christ consists not in these things.

Yet this distinction does not lead us to consider the whole system of civil government as a polluted thing, which has nothing to do with Christian men. Some fanatics, who are pleased with nothing but liberty, or rather licentiousness without any restraint, do indeed boast and vociferate, that since we are dead with Christ to the elements of this world, and being translated into the kingdom of God, sit among the celestials, it is a degradation to us, and far beneath our dignity, to be occupied with those secular and impure cares which relate to things altogether uninteresting to a Christian man. Of what use, they ask, are laws without judgments and tribunals? But what have judgments to do with a Christian man? And if it be unlawful to kill, of what use are laws and judgments to us? But as we have just suggested that this kind of government is distinct from that spiritual and internal reign of Christ, so it ought to be known that they are in no respect at variance with each other. For that spiritual reign, even now upon earth, commences within us some preludes of the heavenly kingdom, and in this mortal and transitory life affords us some prelibations of immortal and incorruptible blessedness; but this civil government is designed, as long as we live in this world, to cherish and support the external worship of God, to preserve the pure doctrine of religion, to defend the constitution of the Church, to regulate our lives in a manner requisite for the society of men, to form our manners to civil justice, to promote our concord with each other, and to establish general peace and tranquillity; all which I confess to be superfluous if the kingdom of God, as it now exists in us, extinguishes the present life. But if it is the will of God, that while we are aspiring toward our true country, we be pilgrims on the earth, and if such aids are necessary to our pilgrimage, they who take them from man deprive him of his human nature. They plead that there should be so much perfection in the Church of God, that its order would suffice to supply the place of all laws; but they foolishly imagine a perfection which can never be found in any community of men. For since the insolence of the wicked is so great, and their iniquity so obstinate that it can scarcely be restrained by all the severity of the laws, what may we expect they would do, if they found themselves at liberty to perpetrate crimes with impunity, whose outrages even the arm of power cannot altogether prevent?

But for speaking of the exercise of civil polity, there will be another place more suitable. At present we only wish it to be understood, that to entertain a thought of its extermination, is inhuman barbarism; it is equally as necessary to mankind as bread and water, light and air, and far more excellent. For it not only tends to secure the accommodations arising from all these things, that men may breathe, eat, drink and be sustained in life, though it comprehends all these things while it causes them to live together, yet I say this is not its only tendency; its objects also are that idolatry, sacrileges against the name of God, blasphemies against his truth, and other offences against religion may not openly appear and be disseminated among the people; that the public tranquillity may not be disturbed; that every person may enjoy his property without molestation; that men may transact their business together without fraud or injustice; that integrity and modesty may be cultivated among them; in short, that there may be a public form of religion among Christians, and that humanity may be maintained among men. Nor let any one think it strange that I now refer to human polity the charge of the due maintenance of religion, which I may appear to have placed beyond the jurisdiction of men. For I do not allow men to make laws respecting religion and the worship of God now, any more than I did before, though I approve of civil government which provides that the true religion which is contained in the law of God be not violated and polluted by public blasphemies with impunity. But the perspicuity of order will assist the readers to attain a clearer understanding of what sentiments ought to be entertained respecting the whole system of civil administration, if we enter on a discussion of each branch of it. These are three: The magistrate, who is the guardian and conservator of the laws; the laws, according to which he governs; the people, who are governed by the laws and obey the magistrate. Let us, therefore, examine, first, the function of a magistrate, whether it be a legitimate calling and approved by God, the nature of the duty, and the extent of the power; secondly, by what laws Christian government ought to be regulated; and lastly, what advantage the people derive from the laws, and what obedience they owe to the magistrate.

The Lord has not only testified that the function of magistrates has his approbation and acceptance, but has eminently commended it to us, by dignifying it with the most honourable titles. We will mention a few of them. When all who sustain the magistracy are called "gods," it ought not to be considered as an appellation of trivial importance, for it implies, that they have their command from God, that they are invested with his authority and are altogether his representatives, and act as his vicegerents. This is not an invention of mine, but the interpretation of Christ, who says, "If he called them gods, unto whom the word of God came, and the Scripture cannot be broken." What is the meaning of this, but that their commission has been given to them by God, to serve him in their office, and, as Moses and Jehoshaphat said to the judges whom they appointed, to "judge not for man, but for the Lord?" To the same purpose is the declaration of the wisdom of God by the mouth of Solomon: "By me kings reign, and princes degree justice. By me princes rule, and nobles, even all the judges of the earth." This is just as if it had been affirmed that the authority possessed by kings and other governors over all things upon earth is not a consequence of the perverseness of men but of the providence and holy ordinance of God, who has been pleased to regulate human affairs in this manner; forasmuch as he is present, and also presides among them, in making laws and in executing equitable judgments. This is clearly taught by Paul, when he enumerates governments among the gifts of God, which being variously distributed according to the diversity of grace, ought to be employed by the servants of Christ to the edification of the Church. For though in that place he is properly speaking of the council of elders, who were appointed in the primitive Church to preside over the regulation of the public discipline, the same office which in writing to the Corinthians he calls "governments," yet, as we see that civil government tends to promote the same object, there is no doubt that he recommends to us every kind of just authority. But he does this in a manner much more explicit, where he enters on a full discussion of that subject. For he says, "There is no power but of God; the powers that be are ordained of God. Rulers are ministers of God, revengers to execute wrath upon him that doeth evil. Do that which is good, and thou shalt have praise of the same." This is corroborated by the examples of holy men, of whom some have been kings, as David, Josiah, Hezekiah; some have been viceroys, as Joseph and Daniel; some have held civil offices in a common wealth, as Moses, Joshua, and the Judges; whose functions God declared to be approved by him. Wherefore no doubt ought now to be entertained by any person that civil magistracy is a calling not only holy and legitimate, but far the most sacred and honourable in human life.

• • •

And for private men, who have no authority to deliberate on the regulation of any public affairs, it would surely be a vain occupation to dispute which would be the best form of government in the place where they live. Besides, this could not be simply determined, as an abstract question, without great impropriety, since the principle to guide the decision must depend on circumstances. And even if we compare the different forms together, without their circumstances, their advantages are so nearly equal, that it will not be easy to discover of which the utility preponderates. The forms of civil government are considered to be of three kinds:

Monarchy, which is the dominion of one person, whether called a king or a duke, or any other title; Aristocracy, or the dominion of the principal persons of a nation; and Democracy, or popular government, in which the power resides in the people at large. It is true that the transition is easy from monarchy to despotism; it is not much more difficult from aristocracy to oligarchy or the faction of a few; but it is most easy of all from democracy to sedition. Indeed, if these three forms of government which are stated by philosophers be considered in themselves, I shall by no means deny that either aristocracy or a mixture of aristocracy and democracy far excels all others; and that indeed not of itself, but because it very rarely happens that kings regulate themselves so that their will is never at variance with justice and rectitude; or, in the next place, that they are endued with such penetration and prudence as in all cases to discover what is best. The vice or imperfection of men therefore renders it safer and more tolerable for the government to be in the hands of many, that they may afford each other mutual assistance and admonition, and that if any one arrogate to himself more than is right, the many may act as censors and masters to restrain his ambition. This has always been proved by experience, and the Lord confirmed it by his authority when he established a government of this kind among the people of Israel, with a view to preserve them in the most desirable condition, till he exhibited in David a type of Christ. And as I readily acknowledge that no kind of government is more happy than this where liberty is regulated with becoming moderation and properly established on a durable basis, so also I consider those as the most happy people who are permitted to enjoy such a condition; and if they exert their strenuous and constant efforts for its preservation and retention, I admit that they act in perfect consistence with their duty. And to this object the magistrates likewise ought to apply their greatest diligence, that they suffer not the liberty, of which they are constituted guardians, to be in any respect diminished, much less to be violated; if they are inactive and unconcerned about this, they are perfidious to their office, and traitors to their country. But if those to whom the will of God has assigned another form of government transfer this to themselves so as to be tempted to desire a revolution, the very thought will be not only foolish and useless, but altogether criminal. If we limit not our views to one city, but look round and take a comprehensive survey of the whole world, or at least extend our observations to distant lands, we shall certainly find it to be a wise arrangement of Divine Providence that various countries are governed by different forms of civil polity, for they are admirably held together with a certain inequality, as the elements are combined in very unequal proportions. All these remarks, however, will be unnecessary to those who are satisfied with the will of the Lord. For if it be his pleasure to appoint kings over kingdoms, and senators or other magistrates over free cities, it is our duty to be obedient to any governors whom God has established over the places in which we reside.

• • •

But here, it seems, arises an important and difficult question. If by the law of God all Christians are forbidden to kill, and the prophet predicts respecting the Church that "they shall not hurt nor destroy in all my holy mountain, saith the Lord," how can it be compatible with piety for magistrates to shed blood? But if we understand, that in the infliction of punishments, the magistrate does not act at all from himself, but merely executes the judgments of God, we shall not be embarrassed with his scruple. The law of the Lord commands, "Thou shalt not kill"; but that homicide may not go unpunished, the legislator himself puts the sword into the hands of his ministers, to be used against all homicides. *To hurt* and *to destroy* are incompatible with the character of the godly; but to avenge the afflictions of the righteous at the command of God, is neither *to hurt* nor *to destroy*. Therefore it is easy to conclude that in this respect magistrates are not subject to the common law, by which, though the Lord binds the hands of men, he does not bind his own justice, which he exercises by the hands of magistrates. So, when a prince forbids all his subjects to strike or wound anyone, he does not prohibit his officers from executing that justice which is particularly committed to them. I sincerely wish that this consideration were constantly in our recollection, that nothing is done here by the temerity of men, but everything by the authority of God, who commands it, and under whose guidance we never err from the right way. For we can find no valid objection to the infliction of public vengeance unless the justice of God be restrained from the punishment of crimes.

• • •

But in the obedience which we have shown to be due to the authority of governors, it is always necessary to make one exception, and that is entitled to our first attention—that it do not seduce us from obedience to him to whose will the desires of all kings ought to be subject, to whose decrees all their commands ought to yield, to whose majesty all their sceptres ought to submit. And, indeed, how preposterous it would be for us, with a view to satisfy men, to incur the displeasure of him on whose account we yield obedience to men! The Lord, therefore, is the King of kings; who, when he has opened his sacred mouth, is to be heard alone above all, for all, and before all; in the next place, we are subject to those men who preside over us, but no otherwise than in him. If they command any thing against him, it ought not to have the least attention nor, in this case, ought we to pay any regard to all that dignity attached to magistrates, to which no injury is done when it is subjected to the unrivalled and supreme power of God. On this principle Daniel denied that he had committed any crime against the king in disobeying his impious decree; because the king had exceeded the limits of his office, and had not only done an injury to men, but, by raising his arm against God, had degraded his own authority. On the other hand, the Israelites are condemned for having been too submissive to the impious edict of their king. For when Jeroboam had made his golden calves, in compliance with his will, they deserted the temple of God and revolted to new superstitions. Their posterity conformed to the decrees of their idolatrous kings with the same facility. The prophet severely condemns them for having "willingly walked after the commandment"; So far is any praise from being due to the pretext of humility with which courtly flatterers excuse themselves and deceive the unwary, when they deny that it is lawful for them to refuse compliance with any command of their kings, as if God had resigned his right to mortal men when he made them rulers of mankind, or as if earthly power were diminished by being subordinated to its author before whom even the principalities of heaven tremble with awe. I know what great and present danger awaits this constancy, for kings cannot bear to be disregarded without the greatest indignation; and "the wrath of a king," says Solomon, "is as messengers of death." But since this edict has been proclaimed by that celestial herald, Peter, "We ought to obey God rather than men,"—let us console ourselves with this thought, that we truly perform the obedience which God requires of us when we suffer anything rather than deviate from piety. And that our hearts may not fail us, Paul stimulates us with another consideration— that Christ has redeemed us at the immense price which our redemption cost him, that we may not be submissive to the corrupt desires of men, much less be slaves to their impiety.

6

Selected Poems

Anne Bradstreet

(1612–1672)

*I*n 1630 the Arbella *sailed into Massachusetts Bay carrying many passengers who would become famous in American history and literature. On board was eighteen-year-old Anne Bradstreet, who had listened to John Winthrop preach his legendary* Model of Christian Charity *sermon where he reminded his Puritan followers of their covenant theology: "We shall be as a city upon a hill. The eyes of all people are upon us." Certainly no woman was better connected to the political hierarchy of Puritan New England than was Anne Bradstreet, for her father and husband each served as governor. Anne herself followed her culture's expectations for a woman's role, as she worked to raise eight children and in private wrote poetry, often as a kind of journal of her inner thoughts. In 1650 her brother-in-law took her poems to England without her knowledge, where they appeared anonymously as the book* The Tenth Muse Lately Sprung Up in America. *Her wish not to draw attention to herself apparently worked, for as late as the 1970s the site of her home in Salem bore the simple plaque: "Former home of Simon Bradstreet, Governor of the Bay Colony. . . . " Yet today she is recognized, along with Walt Whitman and Emily Dickinson, as one of America's greatest lyric poets, and the first American poet to be published. Her poem* The Prologue *stood at the beginning of* The Tenth Muse *and subtly questions the status quo of sexual politics and aesthetics, a seeming apology for writing at all.* The Author to Her Book *follows the formal tradition of the English metaphysical poets with its extended metaphor of her book as a child. The poems invite the reader to deconstruct their surface meaning for the underlying ones the author could not talk about overtly. To view her poems as completely subversive of the dominant ideologies is to miss their real difficulty, however. Bradstreet clearly wanted to believe in a Calvinist theology that promised "the perseverance of the Saints," that worldly sufferings were a sign of divine Election. The poems capture her struggle to reconcile her harsh theology with the earthly concerns of a woman, wife, and mother.*

A Letter to Her Husband, Absent upon Public Employment

My head, my heart, mine eyes, my life, nay more,
My joy, my magazine of earthly store,
If two be one, as surely thou and I,
How stayest thou there, whilst I at Ipswich lie?   4
So many steps, head from the heart to sever,
If but a neck, soon should we be together:
I, like the earth this season, mourn in black,
My sun is gone so far in's zodiac,   8
Whom whilst I 'joy'd, nor storms, nor frosts I felt,
His warmth such frigid colds did cause to melt.
My chilled limbs now numbed lie forlorn;
Return, return sweet Sol from Capricorn;   12
In this dead time, alas, what can I more
Then view those fruits which through thy heat I bore?
Which sweet contentment yield me for a space,
True living pictures of their father's face.   16
O strange effect! now thou art southward gone,
I weary grow, the tedious day so long;
But when thou northward to me shalt return,
I wish my sun may never set, but burn   20
Within the Cancer of my glowing breast,
The welcome house of him my dearest guest.
Where ever, ever stay, and go not thence,
Till nature's sad decree shall call thee hence;   24
Flesh of thy flesh, bone of thy bone,
I here, thou there, yet both but one.

The Author to Her Book

Thou ill-form'd offspring of my feeble brain,
Who after birth did'st by my side remain,
Till snatcht from thence by friends, less wise than true
Who thee abroad, expos'd to public view,   4
Made thee in rags halting to th' press to trudge,
Where errors were not lessened (all may judge).

At thy return my blushing was not small,
My rambling brat (in print) should mother call; 8
I cast thee by as one unfit for light,
Thy visage was so irksome in my sight;
Yet being mine own, at length affection would
Thy blemishes amend, if so I could: 12
I wash'd thy face, but more defects I saw,
And rubbing off a spot, still made a flaw.
I stretcht thy joints to make thee even feet,
Yet still thou run'st more hobbling than is meet; 16
In better dress to trim thee was my mind,
But nought save homespun cloth i' th' house I find
In this array, 'mongst vulgars may'st thou roam
In critic's hands, beware thou does not come; 20
And take thy way where yet thou art not known
If for thy father asked, say thou had'st none:
And for thy mother, she alas is poor,
Which caus'd her thus to send thee out of door. 24

BEFORE THE BIRTH OF ONE OF HER CHILDREN

All things within this fading world hath end,
Adversity doth still our joys attend;
No ties so strong, no friends so dear and sweet,
But with death's parting blow is sure to meet. 4
The sentence past is most irrevocable,
A common thing, yet oh inevitable;
How soon, my dear, death may my steps attend,
How soon't may be thy lot to lose thy friend, 8
We both are ignorant, yet love bids me
These farewell lines to recommend to thee,
That when that knot's untied that made us one,
I may seem thine, who in effect am none. 12
And if I see not half my days that's due,
What nature would, God grant to yours and you;
The many faults that well you know I have,
Let be interr'd in my oblivion's grave; 16

If any worth or virtue were in me,
Let that live freshly in thy memory
And when thou feel'st no grief, as I no harms,
Yet love thy dead, who long lay in thine arms: 20
And when thy loss shall be repaid with gains
Look to my little babes, my dear remains.
And if thou love thy self, or loved'st me,
These O protect from step-dame's injury.   24
And if chance to thine eyes shall bring this verse,
With some sad sighs honor my absent hearse;
And kiss this paper for thy love's dear sake,
Who with salt tears this last farewell did take.   28

THE PROLOGUE [TO HER BOOK]

1

To sing of wars, of captains, and of kings,
Of cities founded, commonwealth begun,
For my mean pen are too superior things:
Or how they all, or each their dates have run   4
Let poets and historians set these forth,
My obscure lines shall not so dim their worth.

2

But when my wond'ring eyes and envious heart
Great Bartas' sugar'd lines do but read o'er,   8
Fool I do grudge the Muses did not part
'Twixt him and me that overfluent store;
A Bartas can do what a Bartas will
But simple I according to my skill.   12

3

From schoolboy's tongue no rhet'ric we expect,
Nor yet a sweet consort from broken strings,
Nor perfect beauty where's a main defect:
My foolish, broken, blemish'd Muse so sings,   16
And this to mend, alas, no art is able,
'Cause nature made it so irreparable.

4

Nor can I, like that fluent sweet tongu'd Greek
Who lisp'd at first, in future times speak plain.　　20
By art he gladly found what he did seek,
A full requital of his striving pain.
Art can do much, but this maxim's most sure:
A weak or wounded brain admits no cure.　　24

5

I am obnoxious to each carping tongue
Who says my hand a needle better fits,
A poet's pen all scorn I should thus wrong,
For such despite they cast on female wits;　　28
If what I do prove well, it won't advance,
They'll say it's stol'n, or else it was by chance.

6

But sure the antique Greeks were far more mild
Else of our sex, why feigned they those nine　　32
And poesy made Calliope's own child;
So 'mongst the rest they placed the arts divine;
But this weak knot they will full soon untie,
The Greeks did nought, but play the fools and lie.　　36

7

Let Greeks be Greeks, and women what they are
Men have precedency and still excel,
It is but vain unjustly to wage war;
Men can do best, and women know it well.　　40
Preeminence in all and each is yours;
Yet grant some small acknowledgment of ours.

8

And oh ye high flown quills that soar the skies,
And ever with your prey still catch your praise,　　44
If e'er you deign these lowly lines your eyes,
Give thyme or parsley wreath, I ask no bays;
This mean and unrefined ore of mine
Will make your glist'ring gold but more to shine.　　48

Upon the Burning of Our House
July 10, 1666

In silent night when rest I took,
For sorrow near I did not look,
I waken'd was with thund'ring noise
And Piteous shrieks of dreadful voice.   4
That fearful sound of fire and fire,
Let no man know is my Desire.
I, starting up, the light did spy,
And to my God my heart did cry   8
To strengthen me in my Distress
And not to leave me succorless.
Then, coming out, beheld a space
The flame consume my dwelling place.   12

And when I could no longer look,
I blest His name that gave and took,
That laid my goods now in the dust:
Yea so it was, and so 'twas just.   16
It was his own: it was not mine;
Far be it that I should repine.

He might of All justly bereft,
But yet sufficient for us left.   20
When by the ruins oft I past,
My sorrowing eyes aside did cast,
And here and there the places spy
Where oft I sat and long did lie.   24

Here stood that Trunk, and there that chest,
There lay that store I counted best:
My pleasant things in ashes lie,
And them behold no more shall I.   28
Under thy roof no guest shall sit,
Nor at thy table eat a bit.

No pleasant tale shall e'er be told,
Nor things recounted done of old.　　　　32
No Candle e'er shall shine in Thee,
Nor bridegroom's voice e'er heard shall be.
In silence ever shall thou lie;
Adieu, Adieu; All's vanity.　　　　36

Then straight I gin my heart to chide,
And did thy wealth on earth abide?
Didst fix thy hope on mold'ring dust,
The arm of flesh didst make thy trust?　　　　40
Raise up thy thoughts above the sky
That dunghill mists away may fly.

Thou hast an house on high erect
Fram'd by that mighty Architect,　　　　44
With glory richly furnished,
Stands permanent tho' this be fled.
It's purchased, and paid for too
By him who hath enough to do.　　　　48

A Price so vast as is unknown
Yet by his Gift, is made thine own.
There's wealth enough, I need no more;
Farewell, my Pelf, farewell my Store.　　　　52
The world no longer let me Love,
My hope and Treasure lies Above.

7

Letter to the Town of Providence

Roger Williams

(ca. 1603?–1683)

*R*oger Williams was born in London, the son of a "merchant taylor." In his *youth he was employed by the jurist Sir Edward Coke, who later sponsored his entrance into Cambridge, where Williams graduated in 1627. Three years later Williams with his new wife (the daughter of a Puritan minister) sailed for Massachusetts. Between 1630 and 1635 Williams found himself frequently at odds with the government of Massachusetts Bay over two key issues. The political rulers assumed that civil authority enforced religious law and that the land of the New World was the property of English colonials. Williams countered that civil authority was absolutely separate from that of the church; he also maintained that Indians owned the land and should be compensated for it. Banished in 1635, Williams founded the separatist colony of Rhode Island, where he befriended the natives, learned their language, and became a valuable negotiator between them and the English. He also refined his arguments regarding the separation of church and state and the issue of religious tolerance, most notably in his landmark work,* The Bloudy Tenet of Persecution *(1644) where he contended that no nation, since Christ, had enjoyed divine favor. All governments, then, were civil, no more. A metaphoric statement of his position is contained in this letter to the town of Providence. In 1639, Williams joined the Baptists, who strongly endorsed his separatist views. The union was more one of form than substance, however; Williams's theology remained fairly orthodox throughout his life.*

January, 1655

That ever I should speak or write a tittle that tends to such an infinite liberty of conscience is a mistake, and which I have ever disclaimed and abhorred. To prevent such mistakes, I shall at present only propose this case: There goes many a ship to sea, with many hundred souls in one ship, whose weal and woe is common, and is a true picture of a commonwealth, or a human combination or society. It hath fallen out sometimes, that both Papists and Protestant, Jews or Turks, may be embarked in one ship; upon which supposal I affirm, that all the liberty of conscience, that ever I pleaded for, turns upon these two hinges—that none of the Papists, Protestants, Jews, or Turks, be forced to come to the ship's prayers or worship, nor compelled from their own particular prayers or worship, if they practice any. I further add, that I never denied, that notwithstanding this liberty, the commander of this ship ought to command the ship's course, yea, and also command that justice, peace, and sobriety, be kept and practiced, both among the seamen and all the passengers. If any of the seamen refuse to perform their services, or passengers to pay their freight; if any refuse to help, in person or purse, toward the common charges or defence; if any refuse to obey the common laws and orders of the ship, concerning their common peace or preservation; if any shall mutiny and rise up against their commanders or officers; if any should preach or write that there ought to be no commanders or officers, because all are equal in Christ, therefore no masters nor officers, no laws nor orders, nor correction nor punishments; I say, I never denied, but in such cases, whatever is pretended, the commander or commanders may judge, resist, compel, and punish such transgressors, according to their deserts and merits. This if seriously and honestly minded, may, if it so please the Father of lights, let in some light to such as willingly shut not their eyes.

I remain studious of your common peace and liberty.

Roger Williams

8

from De Revolutionibus

Nicolaus Copernicus

(1473–1543)

*N*icolaus Copernicus was born into a prosperous merchant family in Poland
in 1473. Under the sponsorship of an uncle, he studied at several universities in Poland and Italy, dabbling in law, medicine, astrology, and astronomy. His
astronomical inquiries began with Aristotle's concept of the heavenly spheres, a
universe divided into earthly and heavenly realms with the planets and stars
revolving in fixed spheres around a motionless Earth. Ptolemy had later refined
the system, adding spheres-within-spheres, or epicycles, to account for the seemingly erratic motion of the planets (which to the eye appear to slow down, stop,
back up, and move again). Biblical evidence, such as Joshua's command that the
sun "stand still" gave the system a certain theological tidiness, but it was a nav-
igator's headache and a scientific problem. Copernicus postulated a simpler system that used complex mathematical proofs to argue that the Sun, not the Earth
was the center of the universe and that the Earth not only moved around the Sun
but rotated on its own axis. While Copernicus's theories were not much more
accurate than some of the ones they replaced, his book De Revolutionibus was a
decisive step in shattering the medieval view of the cosmos and advancing the Scientific Revolution. Galileo and Johannes Kepler both used the heliocentric model
as a starting point for their more sophisticated observations. Copernicus himself
was aware of the potential impact of his argument and refrained from publishing
it until late in his life. Legend has it that he received the first copy on his deathbed
in 1543.

Chapter 10

Of all things visible, the highest is the heaven of the fixed stars. This, I see,
is doubted by nobody. But the ancient philosophers wanted to arrange
the planets in accordance with the duration of the revolutions. Their principle assumes that of objects moving equally fast, those farther away
seem to travel more slowly, as is proved in Euclid's *Optics*. The moon
revolves in the shortest period of time because, in their opinion, it runs

on the smallest circle as the nearest to the earth. The highest planet, on the other hand, is Saturn, which completes the biggest circuit in the longest time. Below it is Jupiter, followed by Mars. With regard to Venus and Mercury, however, differences of opinion are found. For, these planets do not pass through every elongation from the sun, as the other planets do. Hence Venus and Mercury are located above the sun by some authorities, like Plato's *Timaeus*, but below the sun by others, like Ptolemy and many of the moderns. Al-Bitruji places Venus above the sun, and Mercury below it.

According to Plato's followers, all the planets, being dark bodies other-wise, shine because they receive sunlight. If they were below the sun, therefore, they would undergo no great elongation from it, and hence they would be seen halved or at any rate less than fully round. For, the light which they receive would be reflected mostly upward, that is, toward the sun, as we see in the new or dying moon. In addition, they argue, the sun must sometimes be eclipsed by the interposition of these planets, and its light cut off in proportion to their size. Since this is never observed, these planets do not pass beneath the sun at all, according to those who follow Plato.

On the other hand, those who locate Venus and Mercury below the sun base their reasoning on the wide space which they notice between the sun and the moon. For the moon's greatest distance from the earth is 64⅙ earth-radii. This is contained, according to them, about 18 times in the sun's least distance from the earth, which is 1160 earth-radii. Therefore between the sun and the moon there are 1096 earth-radii. Consequently, to avoid having so vast a space remain empty, they announce that the same numbers almost exactly fill up the apsidal distances, by which they com-pute the thickness of those spheres. Thus the moon's apogee is followed by Mercury's perigee. Mercury's apogee is succeeded by the perigee of Venus, whose apogee, finally, almost reaches the sun's perigee. For between the apsides of Mercury they calculate about 177½ earth radii. Then the remaining space is very nearly filled by Venus' interval of 910 earth-radii.

Therefore they do not admit that these heavenly bodies have any opacity like the moon's. On the contrary, these shine either with their own light or with the sunlight absorbed throughout their bodies. Moreover, they do not eclipse the sun, because it rarely happens that they interfere with our view of the sun, since they generally deviate in latitude. Besides, they are tiny bodies in comparison with the sun. Venus, although bigger than Mercury, can occult barely a hundredth of the sun. So says Al-Battani of Raqqa, who thinks that the sun's diameter is ten times larger [than Venus'], and therefore so minute a speck is not easily descried in the most brilliant light. Yet in his Paraphrase of Ptolemy, Ibn Rushd reports having seen something blackish when he found a conjunction of the sun and Mercury indicated in the tables. And thus these two planets are judged to be moving below the sun's sphere.

But this reasoning also is weak and unreliable. This is obvious from the fact that there are 38 earth-radii to the moon's perigee, according to Ptolemy, but more than 49 according to a more accurate determination, as will be made clear below. Yet so great a space contains, as we know, nothing but air and, if you please, also what is called "the element of fire." Moreover, the diameter of Venus' epicycle which carries it 45° more or less to either side of the sun, must be six times longer than the line drawn from the earth's center to Venus' perigee, as will be demonstrated in the proper place. In this entire space which would be taken up by that huge epicycle of Venus and which, moreover, is so much bigger than what would accommodate the earth, air, aether, moon, and Mercury, what will they say is contained if Venus revolved around a motionless earth?

Ptolemy argues also that the sun must move in the middle between the planets which show every elongation from it and those which do not. This argument carries no conviction because its error is revealed by the fact that the moon too shows every elongation from the sun.

Now there are those who locate Venus and then Mercury below the sun, or separate these planets [from the sun] in some other sequence. What reason will they adduce to explain why Venus and Mercury do not likewise traverse separate orbits divergent from the sun, like the other planets, without violating the arrangement [of the planets] in accordance with their [relative] swiftness and slowness? Then one of two alternatives will have to be true. Either the earth is not the center to which the order of the planets and spheres is referred, or there really is no principle of arrangement nor any apparent reason why the highest place belongs to Saturn rather than to Jupiter or any other planet.

In my judgement, therefore, we should not in the least disregard what was familiar to Martianus Capella, the author of an encyclopedia, and to certain other Latin writers. For according to them, Venus and Mercury revolve around the sun as their center. This is the reason, in their opinion, why these planets diverge no farther from the sun than is permitted by the curvature of their revolutions. For they do not encircle the earth, like the other planets, but "have opposite circles." Then what else do these authors mean but that the center of their spheres is near the sun? Thus Mercury's sphere will surely be enclosed within Venus', which by common consent is more than twice as big, and inside that wide region it will occupy a space adequate for itself. If anyone seizes this opportunity to link Saturn, Jupiter, and Mars also to that center, provided he understands their spheres to be so large that together with Venus and Mercury the earth too is enclosed inside and encircled, he will not be mistaken, as is shown by the regular pattern of their motions.

For [these outer planets] are always closest to the earth, as is well known, about the time of their evening rising, that is, when they are in opposition to the sun, with the earth between them and the sun. On the other hand, they are at their farthest from the earth at the time of their evening setting, when they become invisible in the vicinity of the sun, namely, when we have the sun between them and the earth. These facts are enough to show that their center belongs more to the sun, and is identical with the center around which Venus and Mercury likewise execute their revolutions.

But since all these planets are related to a single center, the space between Venus' convex sphere and Mars' concave sphere must be set apart as also a sphere or spherical shell, both of whose surfaces are concentric with those spheres. This [intercalated sphere] receives the earth together with its attendant, the moon, and whatever is contained within the moon's sphere. Mainly for the reason that in this space we find quite an appropriate and adequate place for the moon, we can by no means detach it from the earth, since it is incontrovertibly nearest to the earth.

Hence I feel no shame in asserting that this whole region engirdled by the moon, and the center of the earth, traverse this grand circle amid the rest of the planets in an annual revolution around the sun. Near the sun is the center of the universe. Moreover, since the sun remains stationary, whatever appears as a motion of the sun is really due rather to the motion of the earth. In comparison with any other spheres of the planets, the distance from the earth to the sun has a magnitude which is quite appreciable in proportion to those dimensions. But the size of the universe is so great that the distance earth-sun is imperceptible in relation to the sphere of the fixed stars. This should be admitted, I believe, in preference to perplexing the mind with an almost infinite multitude of spheres, as must be done by those who kept the earth in the middle of the universe. On the contrary, we should rather heed the wisdom of nature. Just as it especially avoids producing anything superfluous or useless, so it frequently prefers to endow a single thing with many effects.

All these statements are difficult and almost inconceivable, being of course opposed to the beliefs of many people. Yet, as we proceed, with God's help I shall make them clearer than sunlight, at any rate to those who are not unacquainted with the science of astronomy. Consequently, with the first principle remaining intact, for nobody will propound a more suitable principle than that the size of the spheres is measured by the length of the time, the order of the spheres is the following, beginning with the highest.

The first and the highest of all is the sphere of the fixed stars, which contains itself and everything, and is therefore immovable. It is unquestionably the place of the universe, to which the motion and position of all the other heavenly bodies are compared. Some people think that it also shifts in some way. A different explanation of why this appears to be so will be adduced in my discussion of the earth's motion.

[The sphere of the fixed stars] is followed by the first of the planets, Saturn, which completes its circuit in thirty years. After Saturn, Jupiter accomplishes its revolution in twelve years. Then Mars revolves in two years. The annual revolution takes the series' fourth place, which contains the earth, as I said, together with the lunar sphere as an epicycle. In the fifth place Venus returns in 9 months. Lastly, the sixth place is held by Mercury, which revolves in a period of 80 days.

At rest, however, in the middle of everything is the sun. For in this most beautiful temple, who would place this lamp in another or better position than that from which it can light up the whole thing at the same time? For, the sun is not inappropriately called by some people the lantern of the universe, its mind by others, and its ruler by still others. [Hermes] the Thrice Greatest labels it a visible god, and Sophocles' Electra, the all-seeing. Thus indeed, as though seated on a royal throne, the sun governs the family of planets revolving around it. Moreover, the earth is not deprived of the moon's attendance. On the contrary, as Aristotle says in a work on animals, the moon has the closest kinship with the earth. Meanwhile the earth has intercourse with the sun, and is impregnated for its yearly parturition.

In this arrangement, therefore, we discover a marvelous symmetry of the universe, and an established harmonious linkage between the motion of the spheres and their size, such as can be found in no other way. For this permits a not inattentive student to perceive why the forward and backward arcs appear greater in Jupiter than in Saturn and smaller than in Mars, and on the other hand greater in Venus than in Mercury. This reversal in direction appears more frequently in Saturn than in Jupiter, and also more rarely in Mars and Venus than in Mercury. Moreover, when Saturn, Jupiter, and Mars rise at sunset, they are nearer to the earth than when they set in the evening or appear at a later hour. But Mars in particular, when it shines all night, seems to equal Jupiter in size, being distinguished only by its reddish color. Yet in the other configurations it is found barely among the stars of the second magnitude, being recognized by those who track it with assiduous observations. All these phenomena proceed from the same cause, which is in the earth's motion.

Yet none of these phenomena appears in the fixed stars. This proves their immense height, which makes even the sphere of the annual motion, or its reflection, vanish from before our eyes. For, every visible object has some measure of distance beyond which it is no longer seen, as is demonstrated in optics. From Saturn, the highest of the planets, to the sphere of the fixed stars there is an additional gap of the largest size. This is shown by the twinkling lights of the stars. By this token in particular they are distinguished from the planets, for there had to be a very great difference between what moves and what does not move. So vast, without any question, is the divine handiwork of the most excellent Almighty.

9

from Letter to the
Grand Duchess Christina

Galileo Galilei

(1564–1642)

A native of northern Italy, Galileo Galilei became a founder of modern experi-mental science as he ushered in one of the most important, and least under-stood, moments in the history of the scientific revolution. A mathematician and philosopher by training—and a tireless inventor and experimenter by habit—Galileo became interested in the movement of the heavens when he purchased a telescope in 1609. As he improved the lenses he began to see things in the heav-ens that contradicted accepted beliefs. For instance, according to Aristotle the heavens were perfect and thus the moon had to be perfectly round and smooth, yet Galileo noticed that the moon had craters and mountains. After later discov-ering that Venus goes through stages—and determining that this was possible only if it were revolving around the sun—Galileo began to think that Nicolas Copernicus (1473–1543) was right: the Sun, and not the Earth, was the center of the universe.

Because this heliocentric view appeared to contradict scripture (in Joshua 10:12–14, Joshua commands the sun to stand still), Galileo had to proceed cau-tiously, ever convinced he was right even though his evidence was not complete. At first the Catholic Church accepted, even encouraged, his ideas because the Church assumed Galileo was proposing his model as theory, not fact. In 1613 one of his students reported attending a dinner party hosted by the Grand Duchess Christina where he overheard Galileo's ideas being attacked as unscriptural and thus erroneous. Galileo fired off an angry letter to his student suggesting that on matters of planetary motion he, Galileo, was right and scripture was wrong. Inaccurate copies of this letter managed to circulate among scientists and churchmen, and Galileo had to retrieve and revise it; the result is the infamous "Letter" (1615) excerpted below. When he was about sixty years old, Galileo compiled his ideas in the form of a pretended dialogue, or debate, between the opposing theories of the solar system. This 1632 work, Dialogue Concerning the Two Chief World Systems, *caused him to be summoned to Rome to stand trial before the Inquisition. Galileo received life imprisonment for heresy, and his books were included on* The Index, *the list of books banned by the Church.*

To the Most Serene Grand Duchess Mother:

Some years ago, as Your Serene Highness well knows, I discovered in the heavens many things that had not been seen before our own age. The novelty of these things, as well as some consequences which followed from them in contradiction to the physical notions commonly held among academic philosophers, stirred up against me no small number of professors—as if I had placed these things in the sky with my own hands in order to upset nature and overturn the sciences. They seemed to forget that the increase of known truths stimulates the investigation, establishment, and growth of the arts; not their diminution or destruction.

Showing a greater fondness for their own opinions than for truth, they sought to deny and disprove the new things which, if they had cared to look for themselves, their own senses would have demonstrated to them. To this end they hurled various charges and published numerous writings filled with vain arguments, and they made the grave mistake of sprinkling these with passages taken from places in the Bible which they had failed to understand properly, and which were ill suited to their purposes. . . .

Persisting in their original resolve to destroy me and everything mine by any means they can think of, these men are aware of my views in astronomy and philosophy. They know that as to the arrangement of the parts of the universe, I hold the sun to be situated motionless in the center of the revolution of the celestial orbs while the earth rotates on its axis and revolves about the sun. They know also that I support this position not only by refuting the arguments of Ptolemy and Aristotle, but by producing many counter-arguments; in particular, some which relate to physical effects whose causes can perhaps be assigned in no other way. In addition there are astronomical arguments derived from many things in my new celestial discoveries that plainly confute the Ptolemaic system while admirably agreeing with and confirming the contrary hypothesis. Possibly because they are disturbed by the known truth of other propositions of mine which differ from those commonly held, and therefore mistrusting their defense so long as they confine themselves to the field of philosophy, these men have resolved to fabricate a shield for their fallacies out of the mantle of pretended religion and the authority of the Bible. These they apply, with little judgment, to the refutation of arguments that they do not understand and have not even listened to.

First they have endeavored to spread the opinion that such propositions in general are contrary to the Bible and are consequently damnable and heretical. . . .

Next, becoming bolder, and hoping (though vainly) that this seed which first took root in their hypocritical minds would send out branches and ascend to heaven, they began scattering rumors among the people that before long this doctrine would be condemned by the supreme authority. They know, too, that official condemnation would not only suppress the two propositions which I have mentioned, but would render damnable all other astronomical and physical statements and observations that have any necessary relation or connection with these. . . .

Now as to the false aspersions which they so unjustly seek to cast upon me, I have thought it necessary to justify myself in the eyes of all men, whose judgment in matters of religion and of reputation I must hold in great esteem. I shall therefore discourse of the particulars which these men produce to make this opinion detested and to have it condemned not merely as false but as heretical. To this end they make a shield of their hypocritical zeal for religion. They go about invoking the Bible, which they would have minister to their deceitful purposes. Contrary to the sense of the Bible and the intention of the holy Fathers, if I am not mistaken, they would extend such authorities until even in purely physical matters—where faith is not involved—they would have us altogether abandon reason and the evidence of our senses in favor of some biblical passage, though under the surface meaning of its words this passage may contain a different sense.

I hope to show that I proceed with much greater piety than they do, when I argue not against condemning this book, but against condemning it in the way they suggest—that is, without understanding it, weighing it, or so much as reading it. . . .

The reason produced for condemning the opinion that the earth moves and the sun stands still is that in many places in the Bible one may read that the sun moves and the earth stands still. Since the Bible cannot err, it follows as a necessary consequence that anyone takes an erroneous and heretical position who maintains that the sun is inherently motionless and the earth movable.

With regard to this argument, I think in the first place that it is very pious to say and prudent to affirm that the holy Bible can never speak untruth—

whenever its true meaning is understood. But I believe nobody will deny that it is often very abstruse, and may say things which are quite different from what its bare words signify. Hence in expounding the Bible if one were always to confine oneself to the unadorned grammatical meaning, one might fall into error. Not only contradictions and propositions far from true might thus be made to appear in the Bible, but even grave heresies and follies. Thus it would be necessary to assign to God feet, hands, and eyes, as well as corporeal and human affections, such as anger, repentance, hatred, and sometimes even the forgetting of things past and ignorance of those to come. These propositions uttered by the Holy Ghost were set down in that manner by the sacred scribes in order to accommodate them to the capacities of the common people, who are rude and unlearned. . . .

This being granted, I think that in discussions of physical problems we ought to begin not from the authority of scriptural passages, but from sense-experiences and necessary demonstrations; for the holy Bible and the phenomena of nature proceed alike from the divine Word, the former as the dictate of the Holy Ghost and the latter as the observant executrix of God's commands. It is necessary for the Bible, in order to be accommodated to the understanding of every man, to speak many things which appear to differ from the absolute truth so far as the bare meaning of the words is concerned. But Nature, on the other hand, is inexorable and immutable; she never transgresses the laws imposed upon her, or cares a whit whether her abstruse reasons and methods of operation are understandable to men. For that reason it appears that nothing physical which sense-experience sets before our eyes, or which necessary demonstrations prove to us, ought to be called in question (much less condemned) upon the testimony of biblical passages which may have some different meaning beneath their words. For the Bible is not chained in every expression to conditions as strict as those which govern all physical effects; nor is God any less excellently revealed in Nature's actions than in the sacred statements of the Bible. . . .

Let us grant . . . that theology is conversant with the loftiest divine contemplation, and occupies the regal throne among sciences by dignity. But acquiring the highest authority in this way, if she does not descend to the lower and humbler speculations of the subordinate sciences and has no regard for them because they are not concerned with blessedness, then her professors should not arrogate to themselves the authority to decide on controversies in professions which they have neither studied nor practiced. Why, this would be as if an absolute despot, being neither a physician nor an architect but knowing himself free to command, should undertake to administer medicines and erect buildings according to his whim—at grave peril of his poor patients' lives, and the speedy collapse of his edifices.

Again, to command that the very professors of astronomy themselves see to the refutation of their own observations and proofs as mere fallacies and sophisms is to enjoin something that lies beyond any possibility of accomplishment. For this would amount to commanding that they must not see what they see and must not understand what they know, and that in searching they must find the opposite of what they actually encounter. Before this could be done they would have to be taught how to make one mental faculty command another, and the inferior powers the superior, so that the imagination and the will might be forced to believe the opposite of what the intellect understands. I am referring at all times to merely physical propositions, and not to supernatural things which are matters of faith.

I entreat those wise and prudent Fathers to consider with great care the difference that exists between doctrines subject to proof and those subject to opinion. Considering the force exerted by logical deductions, they may ascertain that it is not in the power of the professors of demonstrative sciences to change their opinions at will and apply themselves first to one side and then to the other. There is a great difference between commanding a mathematician or a philosopher and influencing a lawyer or a merchant, for demonstrated conclusions about things in nature or in the heavens cannot be changed with the same facility as opinions about what is or is not lawful in a contract, bargain, or bill of exchange. This difference was well understood by the learned and holy Fathers, as proven by their having taken great pains in refuting philosophical fallacies. This may be found expressly in some of them; in particular, we find the following words of St. Augustine:

> It is to be held as an unquestionable truth that whatever the sages of this world have demonstrated concerning physical matters is in no way contrary to our Bibles, hence whatever the sages teach in their books that is contrary to the holy Scriptures may be concluded without any hesitation to be quite false. And according to our ability let us make this evident, and let us keep the faith of our Lord, in whom are hidden all the treasures of wisdom so that we neither become seduced by the verbiage of false philosophy nor frightened by the superstition of counterfeit religion.

From the above words I conceive that I may deduce this doctrine: that in the books of the sages of this world there are contained some physical truths which are soundly demonstrated, and others that are merely stated; as to the former, it is the office of wise divines to show that they do not contradict the holy Scriptures. And as to the propositions which are stated but not rigorously demonstrated, anything contrary to the Bible involved by them must be held undoubtedly false and should be proved so by every possible means.

Now if truly demonstrated physical conclusions need not be subordinated to biblical passages, but the latter must rather be shown not to interfere with the former, then before a physical proposition is condemned it must be shown to be not rigorously demonstrated—and this is to be done not by those who hold the proposition to be true, but by those who judge it to be false. This seems very reasonable and natural, for those who believe an argument to be false may much more easily find the fallacies in it than men who consider it to be true and conclusive. . . .

Your Highness may thus see how irregularly those persons proceed who in physical disputes arrange scriptural passages (and often those ill understood by them) in the front rank of their arguments. If these men really believe themselves to have the true sense of a given passage, it necessarily follows that they believe they have in hand the absolute truth of the conclusion they intend to debate. Hence they must know that they enjoy a great advantage over their opponents, whose lot it is to defend the false position; and he who maintains the truth will have many sense experiences and rigorous proofs on his side, whereas his antagonist cannot make use of anything but illusory appearances, quibbles, and fallacies. Now if these men know they have such advantages over the enemy even when they stay within proper bounds and produce no weapons other than those proper to philosophy, why do they, in the thick of the battle, betake themselves to a dreadful weapon which cannot be turned aside, and seek to vanquish the opponent by merely exhibiting it? If I may speak frankly, I believe they have themselves been vanquished, and, feeling unable to stand up against the assaults of the adversary, they seek ways of holding him off. To that end they would forbid him the use of reason, divine gift of Providence, and would abuse the just authority of holy Scripture—which, in the general opinion of theologians, can never oppose manifest experiences and necessary demonstrations when rightly understood and applied. If I am correct, it will stand them in no stead to go running to the Bible to cover up their inability to understand (let alone resolve) their opponents' arguments, for the opinion which they fight has never been condemned by the holy Church. If they wish to proceed in sincerity, they should by silence confess themselves unable to deal with such matters. . . .

Therefore let these men begin to apply themselves to an examination of the arguments of Copernicus and others, leaving condemnation of the doctrine as erroneous and heretical to the proper authorities. Among the circumspect and most wise Fathers, and in the absolute wisdom of one who cannot err, they may never hope to find the rash decisions into which they allow themselves to be hurried by some particular passion or personal interest. With regard to this opinion, and others which are not directly matters of faith, certainly no one doubts that the Supreme Pontiff has always an absolute power to approve or condemn; but it is not in the power of any created being to make things true or false, for this belongs to their own nature and to the fact. Therefore in my judgment one should first be assured of the necessary and immutable truth of the fact, over which no man has power. This is wiser counsel than to condemn either side in the absence of such certainty, thus depriving oneself of continued authority and ability to choose by determining things which are now undetermined and open and still lodged in the will of supreme authority. And in brief, if it is impossible for a conclusion to be declared heretical while we remain in doubt as to its truth, then these men are wasting their time clamoring for condemnation of the motion of the earth and stability of the sun, which they have not yet demonstrated to be impossible or false. . . .

10

from The Novum Organum

Francis Bacon

(1561–1626)

*O*ne of the most controversial figures of his time, Francis Bacon seemed to
lead two lives. Highly ambitious, always in debt, Bacon shrewdly and often
unscrupulously worked his way up the ranks of London society under Queen
Elizabeth and James I. He was a court politician of the first order who sincerely
believed in the divine right of kings yet seemed able to take dispassionate stands
on the many constitutional and religious controversies that plagued his times.
For that, he made as many enemies as friends. Having risen to the post of lord
chancellor, he was disgraced and demoted on charges of corruption and influ-
ence-peddling.

Bacon's other, more enduring life sprang from his great love of books and knowledge. While he was not a scientist per se, Bacon's contribution to the scientific
revolution of the 17th century is considerable. Fearlessly taking issue with
scholasticism, Bacon argued for a new, more aggressively scientific approach to
knowledge. His Novum Organum, excerpted below, makes compelling arguments for the need to separate knowledge from faith and base what we know on
precise experiments and observation of nature itself. Bacon also anticipated the
English fascination with technology and practical applications of science.
Knowledge, he argues, is power, and power is the agent of progress.

Aphorisms Concerning the Interpretation of Nature and the Kingdom of Man

I. Man, being the servant and interpreter of Nature, can do and understand so much and so much only as he has observed in fact or in thought
in the course of nature: beyond this he neither knows anything nor can
do anything.

II. Neither the naked hand nor the understanding left to itself can effect
much. It is by instruments and helps that the work is done, which are as

much wanted for the understanding as for the hand. And as the instruments of the hand either give motion or guide it, so the instruments of the mind supply either suggestions for the understanding or cautions.

III. Human knowledge and human power meet in one; for where the cause is not known the effect cannot be produced. Nature to be commanded must be obeyed; and that which in contemplation is as the cause is in operation as the rule.

IV. Toward the effecting of works, all that man can do is to put together or put asunder natural bodies. The rest is done by nature working within.

• • •

VI. It would be an unsound fancy and self-contradictory to expect that things which have never yet been done can be done except by means which have never yet been tried.

• • •

XI. As the sciences which we now have do not help us in finding out new works, so neither does the logic which we now have help us in finding out new sciences.

XII. The logic now in use[1] serves rather to fix and give stability to the errors which have their foundation in commonly received notions than to help the search after truth. So it does more harm than good.

• • •

XVIII. The discoveries which have hitherto been made in the sciences are such as lie close to vulgar notions, scarcely beneath the surface. In order to penetrate into the inner and further recesses of nature, it is necessary that both notions and axioms be derived from things by a more sure and guarded way, and that a method of intellectual operation be introduced altogether better and more certain.

XIX. There are and can be only two ways of searching into and discovering truth. The one flies from the senses and particulars to the most general axioms, and from these principles, the truth of which it takes for settled and immovable, proceeds to judgment and to the discovery of middle axioms. And this way is now in fashion. The other derives axioms from the senses and particulars, rising by a gradual and unbroken ascent, so that it arrives at the most general axioms last of all. This is the true way, but as yet untried.

• • •

XXII. Both ways set out from the senses and particulars, and rest in the highest generalities; but the difference between them is infinite. For the one just glances at experiment and particulars in passing, the other dwells duly and orderly among them.

The one, again, begins at once by establishing certain abstract and useless generalities, the other rises by gradual steps to that which is prior and better known in the order of nature.

• • •

XXXI. It is idle to expect any great advancement in science from the superinducing and engrafting of new things upon old. We must begin anew from the very foundations, unless we would revolve forever in a circle with mean and contemptible progress.

• • •

XXXV. It was said by Borgia of the expedition of the French into Italy, that they came with chalk in their hands to mark out their lodgings, not with arms to force their way in. I in like manner would have my doctrine enter quietly into the minds that are fit and capable of receiving it; for confutations cannot be employed when the difference is upon first principles and very notions, and even upon forms of demonstration.

XXXVI. One method of delivery alone remains to us which is simply this: we must lead men to the particulars themselves, and their series and order; while men on their side must force themselves for a while to lay their notions by and begin to familiarize themselves with facts.

XXXVII. The doctrine of those who have denied that certainty could be attained at all has some agreement with my way of proceeding at the first setting out; but they end in being infinitely separated and opposed. For the holders of that doctrine assert simply that nothing can be known; I also assert that not much can be known in nature by the way which is now in use. But then they go on to destroy the authority of the senses and understanding; whereas I proceed to devise and supply helps for the same.

XXXVIII. The idols and false notions which are now in possession of the human understanding, and have taken deep root therein, not only so beset men's minds that truth can hardly find entrance, but even after entrance is obtained, they will again in the very instauration of the sciences meet and trouble us, unless men being forewarned of the danger fortify themselves as far as may be against their assaults.

XXXIX. There are four classes of Idols which beset men's minds. To these for distinction's sake I have assigned names, calling the first class *Idols of the Tribe;* the second, *Idols of the Cave;* the third, *Idols of the Marketplace;* the fourth, *Idols of the Theatre.*

XL. The formation of ideas and axioms by true induction is no doubt the proper remedy to be applied for the keeping off and clearing away of idols. To point them out, however, is of great use; for the doctrine of Idols is to the interpretation of nature what the doctrine of the refutation of sophisms is to common logic.

XLI. The Idols of the Tribe have their foundation in human nature itself, and in the tribe or race of men. For it is a false assertion that the sense of man is the measure of things. On the contrary, all perceptions as well of the sense as of the mind are according to the measure of the universe. And the human understanding is like a false mirror, which, receiving rays irregularly, distorts and discolors the nature of things by mingling its own nature with it.

XLII. The Idols of the Cave are the idols of the individual man. For everyone (besides the errors common to human nature in general) has a cave or den of his own, which refracts and discolors the light of nature; owing either to his own proper and peculiar nature; or to his education and conversation with others; or to the reading of books, and the authority of those whom he esteems and admires; or to the differences of impressions, accordingly as they take place in a mind preoccupied and predisposed or in a mind indifferent and settled; or the like. So that the spirit of man (according as it is meted out to different individuals) is in fact a thing variable and full of perturbation, and governed as it were by chance. Whence it was well observed by Heraclitus that men look for sciences in their own lesser worlds, and not in the greater or common world.

XLIII. There are also Idols formed by the intercourse and association of men with each other, which I call Idols of the Marketplace, on account of the commerce and consort of men there. For it is by discourse that men associate; and words are imposed according to the apprehension of the vulgar. And therefore the ill and unfit choice of words wonderfully obstructs the understanding. Nor do the definitions or explanations wherewith in some things learned men are wont to guard and defend themselves, by any means set the matter right. But words plainly force and overrule the understanding, and throw all into confusion, and lead men away into numberless empty controversies and idle fancies.

XLIV. Lastly, there are Idols which have immigrated into men's minds from the various dogmas of philosophies, and also from wrong laws of demonstration. These I call Idols of the Theatre, because in my judgment all the received systems are but so many stage plays, representing worlds of their own creation after an unreal and scenic fashion. Nor is it only of the systems now in vogue, or only of the ancient sects and philosophies, that I speak; for many more plays of the same kind may yet be composed and in like artificial manner set forth; seeing that errors the most widely different have nevertheless causes for the most part alike. Neither again do I mean this only of entire systems, but also of many principles and axioms in science, which by tradition, credulity, and negligence have come to be received. . . .

Note

1 Scholasticism.

11

from Discourse on Method

René Descartes

(1596–1650)

René Descartes was born to a well-to-do family in central France and educated at the elite Jesuit school at La Fleche. He grew up in a particularly messy era in French history, when religious wars, regicide, and general instability made all life chaotic and unsettled. As if in reply to his times, he began searching for some design that would bring unity to mathematical and scientific knowledge. The effort led him down many paths, and Descartes's legacy includes physiology, physics, psychology, philosophy, and notably mathematics. He invented analytical geometry.

While many of his conclusions have been superseded or discredited, Descartes's influence was profound. Like Bacon and others, he rejected the scholasticism of Thomas Aquinas and the Aristotelian method of syllogistic reasoning. Unlike the English scholars, Descartes was unwilling to rely primarily on sensory experience because senses, he argued, could be misled. He posited instead a duality between mind and body (Cartesian dualism), wherein reason was intuitively capable of seizing truths that the senses missed. God, he argued, had graced the human mind, and only the human, with the ability to make sense of a cosmos that itself was mechanistic, not mystical. His most famous dictum, cogito ergo sum *(I think, therefore I am), is a revolutionary assertion of the importance of the individual mind. His method is an approach to knowledge that makes doubt absolutely essential to critical awareness.*

Part I

Good sense is of all things in the world the most equally distributed, for everybody thinks himself so abundantly provided with it, that even those most difficult to please in all other matters do not commonly desire more of it than they already possess. It is unlikely that this is an error on their part; it seems rather to be evidence in support of the view that the power of forming a good judgment and of distinguishing the true from the false, which is properly speaking what is called Good Sense or Reason, is by nature equal in all men. Hence too it will show that the diversity of our opinions does not proceed from some men being more rational than others, but solely from the fact that our thoughts pass through diverse channels and the same objects are not considered by all. For to be possessed of good mental powers is not sufficient; the principal matter is to apply them well. The greatest minds are capable of the greatest vices as well as of the greatest virtues, and those who proceed very slowly may, provided they always follow the straight road, really advance much faster than those who, though they run, forsake it.

For myself I have never ventured to presume that my mind was in any way more perfect than that of the ordinary man; I have even longed to possess thought as quick, or an imagination as accurate and distinct, or a memory as comprehensive or ready, as some others. And besides these I do not know any other qualities that make for the perfection of the human mind. For as to reason or sense, inasmuch as it is the only thing that constitutes us men and distinguishes us from the brutes, I would fain believe that it is to be found complete in each individual, and in this I follow the common opinion of the philosophers, who say that the question of more or less occurs only in the sphere of the *accidents* and does not affect the *forms* or *natures* of the *individuals* in the same *species*.

But I shall not hesitate to say that I have had great good fortune from my youth up, in lighting upon and pursuing certain paths which have conducted me to considerations and maxims from which I have formed a Method, by whose assistance it appears to me I have the means of gradually increasing my knowledge and of little by little raising it to the highest point which the mediocrity of my talents and the brief duration of my life can permit me to reach. For I have already reaped from it fruits of such a nature that, even though I always try in the judgments I make on myself to lean to the side of self-depreciation rather than to that of arrogance, and though, looking with the eye of a philosopher on the diverse actions and enterprises of all mankind, I find scarcely any which do not seem to me vain and useless, I do not cease to receive extreme satisfaction in the progress which I seem to have already made in the search after truth, and to form such hopes for the future as to venture to believe that, if amongst the occupations of men, simply as men, there is some one in particular that is excellent and important, that is the one which I have selected.

It must always be recollected, however, that possibly I deceive myself, and that what I take to be gold and diamonds is perhaps no more than copper and glass. I know how subject we are to delusion in whatever touches ourselves, and also how much the judgments of our friends ought to be suspected when they are in our favor. But in this Discourse I shall be very happy to show the paths I have followed, and to set forth my life as in a picture, so that everyone may judge of it for himself; and thus in learning from the common talk what are the opinions which are held of it, a new means of obtaining self-instruction will be reached, which I shall add to those which I have been in the habit of using.

• • •

Part II

I was then in Germany, to which country I had been attracted by the wars which are not yet at an end [the Thirty Years War]. And as I was returning from the coronation of the Emperor to join the army, the setting in of winter detained me in a quarter where, since I found no society to divert me, while fortunately I had also no cares or passions to trouble me, I remained the whole day shut up alone in a stove-heated room, where I had complete leisure to occupy myself with my own thoughts. One of the first of the considerations that occurred to me was that there is very often less perfection in works composed of several portions, and carried out by the hands of various masters, than in those on which one individual alone has worked. Thus we see that buildings planned and carried out by one architect alone are usually more beautiful and better proportioned than those which many have tried to put in order and improve, making use of old walls which were built with other ends in view. In the same way also, those ancient cities which, originally mere villages, have become in the process of time great towns, are usually badly constructed in comparison with those which are regularly laid out on a plain by a surveyor who is free to follow his own ideas. Even though, considering their buildings each one apart, there is often as much or more display of skill in the one case than in the other, the former have large buildings and small buildings indiscriminately placed together, thus rendering the streets crooked and irregular, so that it might be said that it was chance rather than the will of men guided by reason that led to such an arrangement. And if we consider that this happens despite the fact that from all time there have been certain officials who have had the special duty of looking after the buildings of private individuals in order that they may be public ornaments, we shall understand how difficult it is to bring about much that is satisfactory in operating only upon the works of others. Thus I imagined that those people who were once half-savage, and who have become civilized only by slow degrees, merely forming their laws as the disagreeable necessities of their crimes and quarrels constrained them, could not succeed in establishing so good a system of government as those who, from the time they first came together as communities, carried into effect the constitution laid down by some prudent legislator. Thus it is quite certain that the constitution of the true Religion whose ordinances are of God alone is incomparably better regulated than any other. And, to come down to human affairs, I believe that if Sparta was very flourishing in former times, this was not because of the excellence of each and every one of its laws, seeing that many were very strange and even contrary to good morals, but because, being drawn up by one individual, they all tended towards the same end. And similarly I thought that the sciences found in books—in those at least whose reasonings are only probable and which have no demonstrations, composed as they are of the gradually accumulated opinions of many different individuals—do not approach so near to the truth as the simple reasoning which a man of common sense can quite naturally carry out respecting the things which come immediately before him. Again I thought that since we have all been children before being men, and since it has for long fallen to us to be governed by our appetites and by our teachers (who often enough contradicted one another, and none of whom perhaps counseled us always for the best), it is almost impossible that our judgments should be so excellent or solid as they should have been had we had complete use of our reason since our birth, and had we been guided by its means alone.

It is true that we do not find that all the houses in a town are razed to the ground for the sole reason that the town is to be rebuilt in another fashion, with streets made more beautiful; but at the same time we see that many people cause their own houses to be knocked down in order to rebuild them, and that sometimes they are forced so to do where there is danger of the houses falling of themselves, and when the foundations are not secure. From such examples I argued to myself that there was no plausibility in the claim of any private individual to reform a state by altering everything, and by overturning it throughout, in order to set it right again.

Nor is it likewise probable that the whole body of the Sciences, or the order of teaching established by the Schools, should be reformed. But as regards all the opinions which up to this time I had embraced, I thought I could not do better than endeavor once for all to sweep them completely away, so that they might later on be replaced, either by others which were better, or by the same, when I had made them conform to the uniformity of a rational scheme. And I firmly believed that by this means I should succeed in directing my life much better than if I had only on principles of which I allowed myself to be in youth persuaded without built on old foundations and relied having inquired into their truth. For although in so doing I recognized various difficulties, these were at the same time not insurmountable, nor comparable to those which are found in reformation of the most insignificant kind in matters which concern the public. In the case of great bodies it is too difficult a task to raise them again when they are once thrown down, or even to keep them in their places when once thoroughly shaken; and their fall cannot be otherwise than very violent. Then as to any imperfections that they may possess (and the very diversity that is found between them is sufficient to tell us that these in many cases exist) custom has doubtless greatly mitigated them, while it has also helped us to avoid, or insensibly corrected a number against which mere foresight would have found it difficult to guard. And finally the imperfections are almost always more supportable than would be the process of removing them, just as the great roads which wind about amongst the mountains become, because of being frequented, little by little so well-beaten and easy that it is much better to follow them than to try to go more directly by climbing over rocks and descending to the foot of precipices.

This is the reason why I cannot in any way approve of those turbulent and unrestful spirits who, being called neither by birth nor fortune to the management of public affairs, never fail to have always in their minds some new reforms. And if I thought that in this treatise there was contained the smallest justification for this folly, I should be very sorry to allow it to be published. My design has never extended beyond trying to reform my own opinion and to build on a foundation which is entirely my own. If my work has given me a certain satisfaction, so that I here present to you a draft of it, I do not so do because I wish to advise anybody to imitate it. Those to whom God has been most beneficent in the bestowal of His graces will perhaps form designs which are more elevated; but I fear much that this particular one will seem too venturesome for many. The simple resolve to strip oneself of all opinions and beliefs formerly received is not to be regarded as an example that each man should follow, and the world may be said to be mainly composed of two classes of minds neither of which could prudently adopt it. There are those who, believing themselves to be cleverer than they are, cannot restrain themselves from being precipitate in judgment and have not sufficient patience to arrange their thoughts in proper order; hence, once a man of this description had taken the liberty of doubting the principles he formerly accepted, and had deviated from the beaten track, he would never be able to maintain the path which must be followed to reach the appointed end more quickly, and he would hence remain wandering astray all through his life. Secondly, there are those who having reason or modesty enough to judge that they are less capable of distinguishing truth from falsehood than some others from whom instruction might be obtained, are right in contenting themselves with following the opinions of these others rather than in searching better ones for themselves.

For myself I should doubtless have been of these last if I had never had more than a single master, or had I never known the diversities which have from all time existed between the opinions of men of the greatest learning. But I had been taught, even in my College days, that there is nothing imaginable so strange or so little credible that it has not been maintained by one philosopher or other, and I further recognized in the course of my travels that all those whose sentiments are very contrary to ours are yet not necessarily barbarians or savages, but may be possessed of reason in as great or even a greater degree than ourselves. I also considered how very different the self-same man, identical in mind and spirit, may become, according as he is brought up from childhood amongst the French or Germans, or has passed his whole life amongst Chinese or cannibals. I likewise noticed how even in the fashions of one's clothing the same thing that pleased us ten years ago, and which will perhaps please us once again before ten years are passed, seems at the present time extravagant and ridiculous. I thus concluded that it is much more custom and example that persuade us than any certain knowledge, and yet in spite of this the voice of the majority does not afford a proof of any value in truths a little difficult to discover, because such truths are much more likely to have been discovered by one man than by a nation. I could not, however, put my finger on a single person whose opinions seemed preferable to those of others, and I found that I was, so to speak, constrained myself to undertake the direction of my procedure.

But like one who walks alone and in the twilight I resolved to go so slowly, and to use so much circumspection in all things, that if my advance was but very small, at least I guarded myself well from falling. I did not wish to set about the final rejection of any single opinion which might formerly have crept into my beliefs without having been introduced there by means of Reason, until I had first of all employed sufficient time in planning out the task which I had undertaken, and in seeking the true Method of arriving at a knowledge of all the things of which my mind was capable.

Among the different branches of Philosophy, I had in my younger days to a certain extent studied Logic; and in those of Mathematics, Geometrical Analysis and Algebra—three arts or sciences which seemed as though they ought to contribute something to the design I had in view. But in examining them I observed in respect to Logic that the syllogisms and the greater part of the other teaching served better in explaining to others those things that one knows (or like the art of Lully, in enabling one to speak without judgment of those things of which one is ignorant) than in learning what is new. And although in reality Logic contains many precepts which are very true and very good, there are at the same time mingled with them so many others which are hurtful or superfluous, that it is almost as difficult to separate the two as to draw a Diana or a Minerva out of a block of marble which is not yet roughly hewn. And as to the Analysis of the ancients and the Algebra of the moderns, besides the fact that they embrace only matters the most abstract, such as appear to have no actual use, the former is always so restricted to the consideration of symbols that it cannot exercise the Understanding without greatly fatiguing the Imagination; and in the latter one is so subjected to certain rules and formulas that the result is the construction of an art which is confused and obscure, and which embarrasses the mind, instead of a science which contributes to its cultivation. This made me feel that some other Method must be found, which, comprising the advantages of the three, is yet exempt from their faults. And as a multiplicity of laws often furnishes excuses for evildoing, as a State is hence much better ruled when, having but very few laws, these are most strictly observed; so, instead of the great number of precepts of which Logic is composed, I believed that I should find the four which I shall state quite sufficient, provided that I adhered to a firm and constant resolve never on any single occasion to fail in their observance.

The *first* of these was to accept nothing as true which I did not clearly recognize to be so: that is to say, carefully to avoid precipitation and prejudice in judgments, and to accept in them nothing more than what was presented to my mind so clearly and distinctly that I could have no occasion to doubt it.

The *second* was to divide up each of the difficulties which I examined into as many parts as possible, and as seemed requisite in order that it might be resolved in the best manner possible.

The *third* was to carry on my reflections in due order, commencing with objects that were the most simple and easy to understand, in order to rise little by little, or by degrees, to knowledge of the most complex, assuming an order, even if a fictitious one, among those which do not follow a natural sequence relatively to one another.

The *last* was in all cases to make enumerations so complete and reviews so general that I should be certain of having omitted nothing.

• • •

Part IV

For a long time I had remarked that it is sometimes requisite in common life to follow opinions which one knows to be most uncertain, exactly as though they were indisputable, as has been said above. But because in this case I wished to give myself entirely to the search after Truth, I thought that it was necessary for me to take an apparently opposite course, and to reject as absolutely false everything as to which I could imagine the least ground of doubt, in order to see if afterwards there remained anything in my belief that was entirely certain. Thus, because our senses sometimes deceive us, I wished to suppose that nothing is just as they cause us to imagine it to be; and because there are men who deceive themselves in their reasoning and fall into paralogisms, even concerning the simplest matters of geometry, and judging that I was as subject to error as was any other, I rejected as false all the reasons formerly accepted by me as demonstrations. And since all the same thoughts and conceptions which we have while awake may also come to us in sleep, without any of them being at that time true, I resolved to assume that everything that ever entered into my mind was no more true than the illusions of my dreams. But immediately afterwards I noticed that whilst I thus wished to think all things false, it was absolutely essential that the 'I' who thought this should be somewhat, and remarking that this truth *I think, therefore I am* was so certain and so assured that all the most extravagant suppositions brought forward by the skeptics were incapable of shaking it, I came to the conclusion that I could receive it without scruple as the first principle of the Philosophy for which I was seeking.

And then, examining attentively that which I was, I saw that I could conceive that I had no body, and that there was no world nor place where I might be; but yet that I could not for all that conceive that I was not. On the contrary, I saw from the very fact that I thought of doubting the truth of other things, I very evidently and certainly followed that I was; on the other hand if I had only ceased from thinking, even if all the rest of what I had ever imagined had really existed, I should have no reason for thinking that I had existed. From that I knew that I was a substance the whole essence or nature of which is to think, and that for its existence there is no need of any place, nor does it depend on any material thing; so that this 'me,' that is to say, the soul by which I am what I am, is entirely distinct from body, and is even more easy to know than is the latter; and even if body were not, the soul would not cease to be what it is.

After this I considered generally what in a proposition is requisite in order to be true and certain; for since I had just discovered one which I knew to be such, I thought that I ought also to know in what this certainty consisted. And having remarked that there was nothing at all in the statement *I think, therefore I am* which assures me of having thereby made a true assertion, excepting that I see very clearly that to think it is necessary to be, I came to the conclusion that I might assume, as a general rule, that the things which we conceive very clearly and distinctly are all true—remembering, however, that there is some difficulty in ascertaining which are those that we distinctly conceive.

Following upon this, and reflecting on the fact that I doubted, and that consequently my existence was not quite perfect (for I saw clearly that it was a greater perfection to know than to doubt), I resolved to inquire whence I had learnt to think of anything more perfect than I myself was; and I recognized very clearly that this conception must proceed from some nature which was really more perfect. As to the thoughts which I had of many other things outside of me, like the heavens, the earth, light, heart, and a thousand others, I had not so much difficulty in knowing whence they came, because, remarking nothing in them which seemed to render them superior to me, I could believe that, if they were true, they were dependencies upon my nature, in so far as it possessed some perfection; and if they were not true, that I held them from nought, that is to say, that they were in me because I had something lacking in my nature. But this could not apply to the idea of a Being more perfect than my own, for to hold it from nought would be manifestly impossible; and because it is no less contradictory to say of the more perfect that it is what results from and depends on the less perfect, than to say that there is something which proceeds from nothing, it was equally impossible that I should hold it from myself. In this way it could but follow that it had been placed in me by a Nature which was really more perfect than mine could be and which even had within itself all the perfections of which I could form any idea—that is to say, to put it in a word, which was God. . . .

12

from An Essay Concerning Human Understanding

John Locke

(1632–1704)

*W*here Isaac Newton's innovations in physics and mathematics set down the scientific bases for the Enlightenment, John Locke's inquiries into human nature and the origins of knowledge opened new paths in politics and philosophy. As a student and then tutor at Christ Church, Oxford, Locke was fascinated by experimental science and later helped found the Royal Society for the Promotion of Natural Knowledge, one of the key agents in the English scientific revolution. At the same time, Locke was politically involved. His family had supported the Parliamentarians during the English Civil War, and although Locke welcomed the restoration of the Stuart monarch in 1660 he remained contemptuous of the doctrine of the "divine right of kings." Both his scientific pursuits and his political activism were to produce germinal works.

One of these is An Essay Concerning Human Understanding, *published in 1690. Like many others, Locke was impressed with Descartes's glorification of human reason and the power of the mind. Like Descartes, he looked beyond the syllogistic and argumentative tenets of scholasticism. But Locke mostly rejected Descartes's notion of intuitive knowledge and focused, like Bacon, on the world of sensory experience. The* Essay *originates the view of the mind as a blank slate (tabula rasa); it also opens the way to consider how environment shapes human nature and how humans can, in turn, manipulate nature to improve society.*

No Innate Principles in the Mind

The way shown how we come by any knowledge, sufficient to prove it not innate.—It is an established opinion among some men, that there are in the understanding certain inborn principles; some primary notions, characters, as it were stamped upon the mind of man; which the soul receives in its very first being, and brings into the world with it. It would be sufficient to convince unprejudiced readers of the falseness of this supposition, if I

87

should only show (as I hope I shall in the following parts of this discourse) how men, barely by the use of their natural faculties, may attain to all the knowledge they have, without the help of any inborn impressions; and may arrive at certainty, without any such original notions or principles. For I imagine anyone will easily grant that it would be impertinent to suppose the ideas of colors innate in a creature to whom God has given sight, and a power to receive them by the eyes from external objects: and no less unreasonable would it be to attribute several truths to the impressions of nature, and inborn characters, when we may observe in ourselves faculties fit to attain as easy and certain knowledge of them as if they were originally imprinted on the mind. . . .

Of Ideas in General and Their Origin

Idea is the object of thinking.—Every man being conscious that he thinks, and that which his mind is applied to while thinking being the ideas that are there, it is without a doubt that men have in their minds several ideas,—such as are those expressed by the words whiteness, hardness, sweetness, thinking, motion, man, elephant, army, drunkenness, and others. It is in the first place then to be inquired, how he comes by them? I know it is an accepted doctrine that men have inborn ideas, stamped upon their minds in their very beginning. This opinion I have at large examined already; and, I suppose what I have already said . . . will be much more easily admitted, when I have shown whence the understanding may get all the ideas it has; and by what ways and degrees they may come into the mind;—for which I shall appeal to every one's own observation and experience.

All ideas come from sensation or reflection.—Let us then suppose the mind to be, as we say, white paper, void of all characters, without any ideas.—How comes it to be furnished? From where comes that vast store which the busy and boundless fancy of man has painted on it with an almost endless variety? From where has it all the materials of reason and knowledge? To this I answer, in one word, from *experience*. On that all our knowledge is founded; and from that it is ultimately derived. Our observation, turned upon either external objects, or upon the internal operations of our minds, is that which supplies our understanding with all the materials of thinking. These two are the fountains of knowledge, from where come all the ideas we have, or naturally can have.

The objects of sensation one source of ideas.—First, our senses, acquainted with particular sensible objects, convey to the mind several distinct perceptions of things, according to those various ways wherein those objects do affect them. And thus we come by those ideas we have of yellow, white, heat, cold, soft, hard, bitter, sweet, and all those which we call sensible qualities; which when I say the senses convey to the mind, I mean, they from external objects convey to the mind what produces there those perceptions. This great source of most of the ideas we have, depending wholly upon our senses, and derived by them to the understanding, I call *sensation.*

The operations of our minds, the other source of them.—Secondly, the other fountain from which experience furnishes the understanding with ideas is, the perception of the operations of our own mind within us, when it considers the ideas it has got. These operations, as the soul comes to reflect on and consider, furnish the understanding with another set of ideas, which could not be had from external things. And such are perception, thinking, doubting, believing, reasoning, knowing, willing, and all the different notions of our own minds;—which we being conscious of, and observing in ourselves, do from these receive into our understandings as distinct ideas as we do from bodies affecting our senses. This source of ideas every man has wholly in himself; and though it be not sense, as having nothing to do with external objects, yet it is very like it, and might properly enough be called internal sense. But as I call the other *sensation,* so I call this *reflection,* the ideas being such only as the mind gets by reflecting on its own operations within itself. By reflection then, in the following part of this discourse, I would have understood to mean that observation which the mind takes of its own operations. . . . These two, I say, namely, external material things, as the objects of *sensation,* and the operations of our own minds within, as the objects of *reflection,* are to me the only origin from where all our ideas take their beginnings. The term operations here I use in a large sense, as including not merely the actions of the mind about its ideas, but some sort of passions arising sometimes from them, such as is the satisfaction or uneasiness arising from any thought.

All our ideas are of the one or the other of these.—The understanding seems to me not to have the least glimmering of any ideas which it does not receive from one of these two. External objects furnish the mind with the ideas of sensible qualities, which are all those different perceptions they produce in us; and the mind furnishes the understanding with ideas of its own operations.

These, when we have taken a full survey of them, and their several modes, combinations, and relations, we shall find to contain all our whole stock of ideas; and that we have nothing in our minds which did not come in one of these two ways. Let anyone examine his own thoughts, and thoroughly search into his understanding; and then let him tell me, whether all the original ideas he has there, are any other than of the objects of his senses, or of the operations of his mind, considered as objects of his reflection. And how great a mass of knowledge soever he imagines to be lodged there, he will, upon taking a strict view, see that he has not any idea in his mind but what one of these two have imprinted;— though perhaps, with infinite variety compounded and enlarged by the understanding, as we shall see hereafter. . . .

The soul begins to have ideas when it begins to perceive.—To ask, at what time a man has first any ideas, is to ask, when he begins to perceive;—having ideas, and perception, being the same thing. I know it is an opinion, that the soul always thinks, and that it has the actual perception of ideas in itself constantly, as long as it exists; and that actual thinking is as inseparable from the soul as actual extension is from the body; which if true, to inquire about the beginning of a man's ideas is the same as to inquire after the beginning of his soul. For, by this account, soul and its ideas, as body and its extension, will begin to exist both at the same time. . . .

No ideas but from sensation and reflection, evident, if we observe children.—I see no reason, therefore, to believe that the soul thinks before the senses have furnished it with ideas to think about. And as those are increased and retained, so it comes, by exercise, to improve its faculty of thinking in the several parts of it; as well as, afterwards, by compounding those ideas, and reflecting on its own operations, it increases its stock, as well as facility in remembering, imagining, reasoning, and other modes of thinking.

State of a child in the mother's womb.—He that will suffer himself to be informed by observation and experience, and not make his own theory the rule of nature, will find few signs of a soul accustomed to much thinking in a newborn child, and much fewer of any reasoning at all. And yet it is hard to imagine that the rational soul should think so much, and not reason at all. And he that will consider that infants newly come into the world spend the greatest part of their time in sleep, and are seldom awake but when either hunger calls, or some pain (the most demanding of all sensations), or some other violent impression on the body forces the mind to perceive and attend to it;—he, I say, who considers this, will perhaps find reason to imagine that a fetus in the mother's womb differs not much from the state of a vegetable. It passes the greatest part of its time without perception or thought; doing very little but sleeping in a place where it needs not seek food, and is surrounded by liquid, always equally soft, and nearly of the same temperature. There the eyes have no light and the ears are so shut up as to hear few sounds, and there is little or no variety or change of objects to stimulate the senses.

The mind thinks in proportion to the matter it gets from experience to think about.—Follow a child from its birth, and observe the alterations that time makes, and you shall find, as the mind by the senses comes more and more to be furnished with ideas, it comes to be more and more awake. It thinks more, the more it has matter to think about. After some time it begins to know the objects which, being most familiar with it, have made lasting impressions. Thus it comes by degrees to know the persons it daily converses with, and distinguishes them from strangers. . . . And so we may observe how the mind, by degrees, improves; and it advances to the exercise of those other faculties by enlarging, compounding, and abstracting its ideas, and of reasoning about them, and reflecting upon all these. . . .

A man begins to have ideas when he first has sensation. What sensation is.—If it is asked, when does a man begin to have any ideas, I think the true answer is,—when he first has any sensation. For, since there appear not to be any ideas in the mind before the senses have conveyed any in, I conceive that ideas in the understanding are concurrent with sensation—which is such an impression or motion made in some part of the body, that produces some perception in the understanding. It is about these impressions made on our senses by outward objects that the mind seems first to engage itself, in such operations as we call perception, remembering, consideration, reasoning, and so forth.

The origin of all our knowledge.—In time the mind comes to reflect on its own operations about the ideas gotten by sensation, and thereby stores itself with a new set of ideas, which I call ideas of reflection. These are the impressions that are made on our senses by outward objects that are external to the mind; and its own operations, proceeding from powers internal and belonging to itself, which, when reflected on by the mind, become also objects of its thought. They are, as I have said, the origin of all knowledge. Thus the first capacity of human intellect is—that the mind is fitted to receive the impressions made on it; either through the senses by outward objects, or by its own operations when it reflects on them. This is the first step a man makes toward the discovery of anything, and the groundwork whereon to build all those notions which ever he shall have naturally in this world. All those sublime thoughts which tower above the clouds, and reach as high as heaven itself, take their rise and footing here. In all that vast space wherein the mind wanders, in those far-out speculations it may seem to be occupied with, it matters not one bit beyond those ideas which sense or reflection have offered for its consideration.

In the reception of simple ideas, the understanding is for the most part passive.— In this part the understanding is merely passive; and whether or not it will have these beginnings and, as it were, materials of knowledge, is not in its own power. For the objects of our senses do, many of them, thrust their particular ideas upon our minds whether we will or not; and the operations of our minds will not let us be without, at least, some obscure notions of them. No man can be wholly ignorant of what he does when he thinks. These simple ideas, when offered to the mind, the understanding can no more refuse to have, nor alter when they are imprinted, nor blot them out and make new ones itself, than a mirror can refuse, alter, or obliterate the images or ideas which the objects set before it produce. As the bodies that surround us variously affect our organs, the mind is forced to receive the impressions; and cannot avoid the perception of those ideas that are joined to them.

Of Simple Ideas

Uncompounded appearances.—The better to understand the nature, manner, and extent of our knowledge, one thing is carefully to be observed concerning the ideas we have; and that is, that some of them are simple and some complex.

Though the qualities that affect our senses are, in the things themselves, so united and blended, that there is no separation, no distance between them; yet it is plain, the ideas they produce in the mind enter by the senses simple and unmixed. For, though the sight and touch often take in from the same object, at the same time, different ideas;—as a man sees at once motion and color; the hand feels softness and warmth in the same piece of wax; yet the simple ideas thus united in the same subject are as perfectly distinct as those that come in by different senses. The coldness and hardness which a man feels in a piece of ice are as distinct ideas in the mind as the smell and whiteness of a lily; or as the taste of sugar, and smell of a rose. And nothing can be plainer to a man than the clear and distinct perception he has of those simple ideas; which, being each in itself uncompounded, contains in it nothing but one uniform appearance in the mind, and is not distinguishable into different ideas.

The mind can neither make nor destroy them.—These simple ideas, the materials of all our knowledge, are suggested and furnished to the mind only by those two ways above mentioned, which are sensation and reflection. When the understanding is once stored with these simple ideas, it has the power to repeat, compare, and unite them, even to an almost infinite variety, and so can make at pleasure new complex ideas. But it is not in the power of the most exalted wit, or enlarged understanding, by any quickness or variety of thought, to invent or frame even one new simple idea in the mind, which is not taken in by the ways before mentioned: nor can any force of the understanding destroy those that are there. The power of man, in this little world of his own understanding being much the same as it is in the great world of visible things: wherein his power, however managed by art and skill, reaches no farther than to compound and divide the materials that are at his hand. He can do nothing toward making the least particle of new matter, or destroying one atom of what is already in existence. The same inability everyone will find in himself, if he tries to fashion in his understanding one simple idea, not received by his senses from external objects, or by reflection from the operations of his own mind about them. I would have anyone try to imagine any taste which had never touched his palate; or frame the idea of a scent he had never smelled. If he can do this, I will also conclude that a blind man has ideas of colors, and a deaf man true distinct notions of sounds. . . .

Of Complex Ideas

Made by the mind out of simple ones.—We have up to now considered those ideas, in the reception of which the mind is only passive, and which come from sensation and reflection. . . . But as the mind is wholly passive in the reception of all its simple ideas, so it exerts several acts of its own whereby out of its simple ideas, as the materials and foundations of the rest, the others are framed. The acts of the mind, wherein it exerts its power over its simple ideas, are chiefly these three: (1) Combining several simple ideas into one compound one; and thus all complex ideas are made. (2) The bringing of two ideas, whether simple or complex, together, and setting them by one another, so as to take a view of them at once, without uniting them into one; by which way it gets all its ideas of relations. (3) Separating them from all other ideas that accompany them in their real existence: this is called abstraction; and thus all its general ideas are made. This shows man's power, and its ways of operation, to be much the same in the material and intellectual world. For the materials in both being such as he has no power over, either to make or destroy, all that man can do is either to unite them together, or to set them by one another, or wholly separate them. I shall here begin with the first of these in the consideration of complex ideas, and come to the other two in their due places. As simple ideas are observed to exist in several combinations united together, so the mind has the power to consider several of them united together as one idea; and that not only as they are united in external objects, but as the mind has joined them together. Ideas thus made up of several simple ones put together, I call complex;—such as are beauty, gratitude, a man, an army, the universe; which, though consisting of various simple ideas, or complex ideas made up of simple ones, yet are, when the mind pleases, considered each by itself, as one entire thing, and called by one name.

Made voluntarily.—In this capacity for repeating and joining together its ideas, the mind has great power in varying and multiplying the objects of its thoughts, infinitely beyond what sensation or reflection furnished it with; but all this is still confined to those simple ideas which it received from those two sources, and which are the ultimate materials of all its compositions. For simple ideas are all from things themselves, and of these the mind can have no more, nor other than what are suggested to it. It can have no other ideas of sensible qualities than what come from without by the senses; nor any ideas of other kind of operations of thinking than what it finds in itself. But when it has once got these simple ideas, it is not confined barely to observation, and what offers itself from without; it can, by its own power, put together those ideas it has, and make new complex ones, which it never received so united. . . .

13

from Second Treatise of Civil Government

John Locke

(1632–1704)

John Locke never confined himself to abstract speculation; he was politically active in a time of profound change. In 1666, after a brief stint in the diplomatic mission to Brandenburg, Locke fell into the company of Anthony Ashley Cooper, the first Lord Shaftesbury. The latter was a hard-driving, controversial man who argued for civil liberty, religious toleration, the rule of Parliament, and a constitutional monarchy; he simultaneously promoted English colonization and economic development. The two became fast friends, with Locke adding a thoughtful studiousness to Shaftesbury's energy and commitment. Shaftesbury fell in and out of favor under Charles II, and when he died in 1683 Locke wisely exiled himself to Holland for five years. During that time England underwent another transformation. Charles died, and his brother—James II—took the throne as an extreme monarchist and a Catholic. This was too much for a country moving steadily towards toleration and Parliamentary supremacy, so James was sent packing in 1689 and replaced with his daughter, Mary, and her husband, the Dutch Prince William of Orange. This Glorious Revolution permanently limited the power of the monarchy in England.

The Revolution also prompted Locke to release his Two Treatises on Government. *The first treatise was an attack on absolute monarchy; the second, more innovative (excerpted below) sets down most of the basics of classical liberalism, or the theory of limited, representative government based on the sovereignty of the people and the rights of the individual. Few documents in political theory have had more impact than this second treatise.*

Chapter I

. . . I think it may not be amiss to set down what I take to be political power; that the power of a magistrate over a subject may be distinguished from that of a father over his children, a master over his servant, a husband over his wife, and a lord over his slave. All which distinct powers happening sometimes together in the same man, if he be considered under these different relations, it may help us to distinguish these powers one from another, and show the difference betwixt a ruler of a commonwealth, a father of a family, and captain of a galley.

Political power, then, I take to be a right of making laws with penalties of death, and consequently all less penalties, for the regulating and preserving of property, and of employing the force of the community, in the execution of such laws, and in the defense of the common-wealth from foreign injury; and all this only for the public good.

Chapter II

Of the State of Nature

To understand political power right, and derive it from its original, we must consider what state all men are naturally in, and that is, a state of perfect freedom to order their actions and dispose of their possessions and persons, as they think fit, within the bounds of the law of nature; without asking leave, or depending upon the will of any other man.

A state also of equity, wherein all the power and jurisdiction is reciprocal, no one having more than another; there being nothing more evident, than that creatures of the same species and rank, promiscuously born to all the same advantages of nature, and the use of the same faculties, should also be equal one amongst another without subordination or subjection; unless the lord and master of them all should, by any manifest declaration of his will, set one above another, and confer on him, by an evident and clear appointment, an undoubted right to dominion and sovereignty. . . .

But though this be a state of liberty, yet it is not a state of license: though man in that state have an uncontrollable liberty to dispose of his person or possessions, yet he has not liberty to destroy himself, or so much as any creature in his possession, but where some nobler use than its bare preservation calls for it. The state of nature has a law of nature to govern it, which obliges every one: and reason, which is that law, teaches all mankind, who will but consult it, that being all equal and independent, no one ought to harm another in his life, health, liberty, or possessions: for men being all the workmanship of one omnipotent and infinitely wise Maker; all the servants of one sovereign master, sent into the world by his order, and about his business; they are his property, whose workmanship they are, made to last during his, not another's pleasure: and being furnished with like faculties, sharing all in one community of nature, there cannot be supposed any such subordination among us, that may authorize us to destroy another, as if we were made for one another's uses, as the inferior ranks of creatures are for ours. Every one, as he is bound to preserve himself, and not to quit his station willfully, so by the like reason, when his own preservation comes not in competition, ought he, as much as he can, to preserve the rest of mankind, and may not, unless it be to do justice to an offender, take away or impair the life, or what tends to the preservation of life, the liberty, health, limb, or goods of another.

And that all men may be restrained from invading others' rights, and from doing hurt to one another, and the law of nature be observed, which willeth the peace and preservation of all mankind, the execution of the law of nature is, in that state, put into every man's hands, whereby every one has a right to punish the transgressors of that law to such a degree as may hinder its violation: for the law of nature would, as all other laws that concern men in this world, be in vain, if there were nobody that in the state of nature had a power to execute the law, and thereby preserve the innocent and restrain offenders. And if any one in the state of nature may punish another for any evil he has done, every one may do so: for in that state of perfect equality, where naturally there is no superiority or jurisdiction of one over another, what any may do in prosecution of that law, every one must needs have a right to do.

And thus, in the state of nature, "one man comes by a power over another"; but yet no absolute or arbitrary power, to use a criminal, when he has got him in his hands, according to the passionate heats, or boundless extravagancy of his own will; but only to retribute to him, so far as calm reason and conscience dictate, what is proportionate to his transgression; which is so much as may serve for reparation and restraint; for these two are the only reasons, why one man may lawfully do harm to another, which is that we call punishment. In transgressing the law of nature, the offender declares himself to live by another rule than that of reason and common equity, which is that measure God has set to the actions of men, for their mutual security; and so he becomes dangerous to mankind, the tie, which is to secure them from injury and violence, being slighted and broken by him. Which being a trespass against the whole species, and the peace and safety of it, provided for by the law of nature; every man upon this score, by the right he hath to preserve mankind in general, may restrain, or, where it is necessary, destroy things noxious to them, and so may bring such evil on any one, who hath transgressed that law, as may make him repent the doing of it, and thereby deter him, and by his example others, from doing the like mischief. And in this case, and upon this ground, "every man hath a right to punish the offender, and be executioner of the law of nature." . . .

Chapter III

Of the State of War

The state of war is a state of enmity and destruction: and therefore declaring by word or action, not a passionate and hasty, but a sedate settled design upon another man's life, puts him in a state of war with him against whom he has declared such an intention, and so has exposed his life to the other's power to be taken away by him, or any one that joins with him in his defence, and espouses his quarrel; it being reasonable and just, I should have a right to destroy that which threatens me with destruction; for, by the fundamental law of nature, man being to be preserved as much as possible, when all cannot be preserved, the safety of the innocent is to be preferred: and one may destroy a man who makes war upon him, or has discovered an enmity to his being, for the same reason that he may kill a wolf or a lion; because such men are not under the ties of the common law of reason, have no other rule, than that of force and violence, and so may be treated as beasts of prey, those dangerous and noxious creatures, that will be sure to destroy him whenever he falls into their power.

And hence it is, that he who attempts to get another man in to his absolute power, does thereby put himself into a state of war with him; it being to be understood as a declaration of a design upon his life: for I have reason to conclude, that he who would get me into his power without my consent, would use me as he pleased when he got me there, and destroy me too when he had a fancy to it; for nobody can desire to have me in his absolute power, unless it be to compel me by force to that which is against the right of my freedom, i.e., make me a slave. To be free from such force is the only security of my preservation; and reason bids me look on him, as an enemy to my preservation, who would take away that freedom which is the fence to it; so that he who makes an attempt to enslave me, thereby puts himself into a state of war with me. He that, in the state of nature, would take away the freedom that belongs to any one in that state, must necessarily be supposed to have a design to take away everything else, that freedom being the foundation of all the rest; as he that, in the state of society, would take away the freedom belonging to those of that society or commonwealth, must be supposed to design to take away from them every thing else, and so be looked on as in a state of war.

This makes it lawful for a man to kill a thief, who has not in the least hurt him, nor declared any design upon his life, any farther than, by the use of force, so to get him in his power, as to take away his money, or what he pleases, from him; because using force, where he has no right, to get me into his power, let his pretence be what it will, I have no reason to suppose, that he, who would take away my liberty, would not, when he had me in his power, take away every thing else. And therefore it is lawful for me to treat him as one who has put himself into a state of war with me, i.e., kill him if I can; for to that hazard does he justly expose himself, whoever introduces a state of war, and is aggressor in it.

And here we have the plain "difference between the state of nature and the state of war," which however some men have confounded, are as far distant as a state of peace, goodwill, mutual assistance and preservation, and a state of enmity, malice, violence and mutual destruction, are one from another. Men living together according to reason, without a common superior on earth, with authority to judge between them, is properly the state of nature. But force, or a declared design of force, upon the person of another where there is no common superior on earth to appeal to for relief, is the state of war: and it is the want of such an appeal gives a man the right of war even against an aggressor, though he be in society and a fellow-subject. . . .

Chapter IV

Of Slavery

The natural liberty of man is to be free from any superior power on earth, and not to be under the will or legislative authority of man, but to have only the law of nature for his rule. The liberty of man, in society, is to be under no other legislative power, but that established, by consent, in the commonwealth; nor under the dominion of any will, or restraint of any law, but what that legislative shall enact, according to the trust put in it. Freedom then is not what Sir Robert Filmer tells us, "a liberty for every one to do what he lists, to live as he pleases, and not be tied by any laws":

but freedom of men under government is, to have a standing rule to live by, common to every one of that society, and made by the legislative power erected in it; a liberty to follow my own will in all things, where the rule prescribes not; and not to be subject to the inconstant, uncertain, unknown, arbitrary will of another man: as freedom of nature is, to be under no other restraint but the law of nature.

This freedom from absolute, arbitrary power, is so necessary to, and closely joined with a man's preservation, that he cannot part with it, but by what forfeits his preservation and life together. . . .

Chapter V

Of Property

. . . God, who hath given the world to men in common, hath also given them reason to make use of it to the best advantage of life, and convenience. The earth, and all that is therein, is given to men for the support and comfort of their being. And though all the fruits it naturally produces, and beasts it feeds, belong to mankind in common, as they are produced by the spontaneous hand of nature; and nobody has originally a private dominion, exclusive of the rest of mankind, in any of them, as they are thus in their natural state; yet being given for the use of men there must of necessity be a means to appropriate them some way or other, before they can be of any use, or at all beneficial to any particular man. The fruit, or venison, which nourishes the wild Indian, who knows no enclosure, and is still a tenant in common, must be his, and so his, i.e., a part of him, that another can no longer have any right to it, before it can do him any good for the support of his life.

Though the earth, and all inferior creatures, be common to all men, yet every man has a property in his own person: this nobody has any right to but himself. The labour of his body, and the work of his hands, we may say, are properly his. Whatsoever then he removes out of the state that nature hath provided, and left it in, he hath mixed his labour with, and joined it to something that is his own, and thereby makes it his property. It being by him removed from the common state nature hath placed it in, it hath by his labour something annexed to it, that excludes the common right of other men. For this labour being the unquestionable property of the labourer, no man but he can have a right to what that is once joined to, at least where there is enough, and as good, left in common for others.

He that is nourished by the acorns he picked up under an oak, or the apples he gathered by the trees in the wood, has certainly appropriated them to himself. Nobody can deny but the nourishment is his. I ask then, when did they begin to be his? when he digested? or when he eat? or when he boiled? or when he brought them home? or when he picked them up? and it is plain, if the first gathering made them not his, nothing else could. That labour put a distinction between them and common: that added something to them more than nature, the common mother of all, had done and so they became his private right. And will any one say he had no right to those acorns or apples he thus appropriated, because he had not the consent of all mankind to make them his? was it a robbery thus to assume to himself what belonged to all in common? If such a consent as that was necessary, man had starved, notwithstanding the plenty God had given him. We see in commons, which remain so by compact, that it is the taking any part of what is common, and removing it out of the state nature leaves it in, which begins the property; without which the common is of no use. And the taking of this or that part does not depend on the express consent of all the commoners. Thus the grass my horse has bit; the turfs my servant has cut; and the ore I have digged in any place, where I have a right to them in common with others, become my property, without the assignation or consent of any body. The labour that was mine, removing them out of that common state they were in, hath fixed my property in them.

• • •

Nor is it so strange, as perhaps before consideration it may appear, that the property of labour should be able to over-balance the community of land; for it is labour indeed that put the difference of value on every thing; and let any one consider what the difference is between an acre of land planted with tobacco or sugar, sown with wheat or barley, and an acre of the same land lying in common, without any husbandry upon it, and he will find, that the improvement of labour makes the far greater part of the value. I think it will be but a very modest computation to say, that of the products of the earth useful to the life of man, nine tenths are the effects of labour; nay, if we will rightly estimate things as they come to our use, and cast up the several expenses about them, what in them is purely owing to nature, and what to labour, we shall find, that in most of them ninety-nine hundredths are wholly to be put on the account of labour. . . .

Chapter VII

Of Political or Civil Society

. . . Where-ever . . . any number of men are so united into one society, as to quit every one his executive power of the law of nature, and to resign it to the public, there and there only is a political, or civil society. And this is done, where-ever any number of men, in the state of nature, enter into society to make one people, one body politic, under one supreme government; or else when any one joins himself to, and incorporates with any government already made: for hereby he authorizes the society, or, which is all one, the legislative thereof, to make laws for him, as the public good of the society shall require; to the execution whereof, his own assistance, (as to his own degrees) is due. And this puts men out of a state of nature into that of a common-wealth, by setting up a judge on earth, with authority to determine all the controversies, and redress the injuries that may happen to any member of the common-wealth: which judge is the legislative, or magistrate appointed by it. And where-ever there are any number of men, however associated, that have no such decisive power to appeal to, there they are still in the state of nature.

Hence it is evident, that absolute monarchy, which by some men is counted the only government in the world, is indeed inconsistent with civil society, and so can be no form of civil government at all; for the end of civil society being to avoid and remedy these inconveniences of the state of nature, which necessarily follow from every man being judge in his own case, by setting up a known authority, to which every one of that society may appeal upon any injury received, or controversy that may arise, and which every one of the society ought to obey; where-ever any persons are, who have not such an authority to appeal to for the decision of any difference between them, there those persons are still in the state of nature and so is every absolute prince, in respect of those who are under his dominion. . . .

For he being supposed to have all, both legislative and executive power in himself alone, there is no judge to be found, no appeal lies open to any one, who may fairly and indifferently, and with authority decide, and from whose decision relief and redress may be expected of any injury or inconveniency that may be suffered from the prince, or by his order: so that such a man, however entitled, Czar, or Grand Seignior, or how you please, is as much in the state of nature, with all under his dominion, as he is with the rest of mankind: for where-ever any two men are, who have no standing rule, and common judge of appeal to on earth, for the determination of controversies of right betwixt them, there they are still in the state of nature, and under all the inconveniences of it, with only this woeful difference to the subject, or rather slave of an absolute prince; that whereas in the ordinary state of nature he has a liberty to judge of his right, and, according to the best of his power, to maintain it; now whenever his property is invaded by the will and order of his monarch, he has not only no appeal, as those in society ought to have, but, as if he were degraded from the common state of rational creatures, is denied a liberty to judge of, or to defend his right; and so is exposed to all the misery and inconveniences, that a man can fear from one, who being in the unrestrained state of nature, is yet corrupted with flattery, and armed with power. . . .

For he that thinks absolute power purifies men's blood, and corrects the baseness of human nature, need read but the history of this or any other age, to be convinced of the contrary. . . .

Chapter VIII

Of the Beginning of Political Societies

Men being, as has been said, by nature, all free, equal, and independent, no one can be put out of this estate, and subjected to the political power of another, without his own consent. The only way, whereby any one divests himself of his natural liberty, and puts on the bonds of civil society, is by agreeing with other men to join and unite into a community, for their comfortable, safe, and peaceable living one amongst another, in a secure enjoyment of their properties, and a greater security against any, that are not of it. This any number of men may do, because it injures not the freedom of the rest; they are left as they were in the liberty of the state of nature. When any number of men have so consented to make one community or government, they are thereby presently incorporated, and make one body politic, wherein the majority have a right to act and conclude the rest.

For when any number of men have, by the consent of every individual, made a community, they have thereby made that community one body, with a power to act as one body, which is only by the will and determination of the majority: for that which acts any community, being only the consent of the individuals of it, and it being necessary to that which is one body to move one way; it is necessary the body should move that way whither the greater force carries it, which is the consent of the majority: or else it is impossible it should act or continue one body, one community, which the consent of every individual that united into it, agreed that it should; and so every one is bound by that consent to be concluded by the majority. And therefore we see, that in assemblies, empowered to act by positive laws, where no number is set by that positive law which empowers them, the act of the majority passes for the act of the whole, and of course determines; as having, by the law of nature and reason, the power of the whole.

And thus every man, by consenting with others to make one body politic under one government, puts himself under an obligation, to every one of that society, to submit to the determination of the majority, and to be concluded by it; or else this original compact, whereby he with others incorporates into one society, would signify nothing, and be no compact, if he be left free, and under no other ties than he was in before in the state of nature. . . .

Chapter IX

Of the Ends of Political Society and Government

If man in the state of nature be so free, as has been said; if he be absolute lord of his own person and possessions, equal to the greatest, and subject to nobody, why will he part with his freedom? why will he give up his empire, and subject himself to the dominion and control of any other power? To which it is obvious to answer, that though in the state of nature he hath such a right, yet the enjoyment of it is very uncertain, and constantly exposed to the invasion of others; for all being kings as much as he, every man his equal, and the greater part no strict observers of equity and justice, the enjoyment of the property he has in this state is very unsafe, very unsecure. This makes him willing to quit a condition, which however free, is full of fears and continual dangers: and it is not without reason, that he seeks out, and is willing to join in society with others, who are already united, or have a mind to unite, for the mutual preservation of their lives, liberties, and estates, which I call by the general name, property.

The great and chief end, therefore, of men's uniting into commonwealths, and putting themselves under government, is the preservation of their property. To which in the state of nature there are many things wanting.

First, There wants an established, settled, known law, received and allowed by common consent to be the standard of right and wrong, and the common measure to decide all controversies between them; for though the law of nature be plain and intelligible to all rational creatures; yet men being biased by their interest, as well as ignorant for want of studying it, are not apt to allow of it as a law binding to them in the application of it to their particular cases.

Secondly, In the state of nature there wants a known and indifferent judge, with authority to determine all differences according to the established law: for every one in that state being both judge and executioner of the law of nature, men being partial to themselves, passion and revenge is very apt to carry them too far, and with too much heat, in their own cases; as well as negligence and unconcernedness, to make them too remiss in other men's.

Thirdly, In the state of nature, there often wants power to back and support the sentence when right, and to give it due execution. They who by any injustice offended, will seldom fail, where they are able, by force to make good their injustice; such resistance many times makes the punishment dangerous, and frequently destructive, to those who attempt it.

Thus mankind, notwithstanding all the privileges of the state of nature, being but in an ill condition, while they remain in it, are quickly driven into society. Hence it comes to pass that we seldom find any number of men live any time together in this state. The inconveniences that they are therein exposed to, by the irregular and uncertain exercise of the power every man has of punishing the transgressions of others, make them take sanctuary under the established laws of government, and therein seek the preservation of their property. It is this makes them so willingly give up every one his single power of punishing, to be exercised by such alone, as shall be appointed to it amongst them; and by such rules as the community, or those authorized by them to that purpose, shall agree on. And in this we have the original right of both the legislative and executive power, as well as of the governments and societies themselves.

• • •

But though men, when they enter into society, give up the equality, liberty, and executive power they had in the state of nature, into the hands of the society, to be so far disposed of by the legislature, as the good of the

society shall require; yet it being only with an intention in every one the
better to preserve himself, his liberty and property; (for no rational creature can be supposed to change his condition with an intention to be
worse) the power of the society, or legislative constituted by them, can
never be supposed to extend farther, than the common good; but is obliged to secure every one's property, by providing against those three defects
above mentioned, that made the state of nature so unsafe and uneasy. And
so whoever has the legislative or supreme power of any commonwealth,
is bound to govern by established standing laws, promulgated and known
to the people, and not by extemporary decrees; by indifferent and upright
judges, who are to decide controversies by those laws; and to employ the
force of the community at home, only in the execution of such laws; or
abroad to prevent or redress foreign injuries, and secure the community
from inroads and invasion. And all this to be directed to no other end, but
the peace, safety, and public good of the people.

Chapter XIII

Of the Subordination of the Powers of the Commonwealth

Though in a constituted commonwealth, standing upon its own basis,
and acting according to its own nature, that is, acting for the preservation
of the community, there can be but one supreme power, which is the legislative, to which all the rest are and must be subordinate; yet the legislative being only a fiduciary power to act for certain ends, there remains
still "in the people a supreme power to remove or alter the legislative,"
when they find the legislative act contrary to the trust reposed in them:
for all power given with trust for the attaining an end, being limited by
that end; whenever that end is manifestly neglected or opposed, the trust
must necessarily be forfeited, and the power devolve into the hands of
those that gave it, who may place it anew where they shall think best for
their safety and security. And thus the community perpetually retains a
supreme power of saving themselves from the attempts and designs of
any body, even of their legislators, whenever they shall be so foolish, or
so wicked, as to try and carry on designs against the liberties and properties of the subject: for no man, or society of men, having a power to deliver up their preservation, or consequently the means of it, to the absolute
will and arbitrary dominion of another; whenever any one shall go about
to bring them into such a slavish condition, they will always have a right
to preserve what they have not a power to part with; and to rid themselves

of those who invade this fundamental, sacred, and unalterable law of self-preservation, for which they entered into society. And thus the community may be said in this respect to be always the supreme power. . . .

Chapter XIX

Of the Dissolution of Government

. . . The reason why men enter into society, is the preservation of their property; and the end why they choose and authorize a legislative is, that there may be laws made, and rules set, as guards and fences to the properties of all the members of the society: to limit the power, and moderate the dominion, of every part and member of the society: for since it can never be supposed to be the will of the society, that the legislature should have a power to destroy that which every one designs to secure by entering into society, and for which the people submitted themselves to legislators of their own making; whenever the legislators endeavor to take away and destroy the property of the people, or to reduce them to slavery under arbitrary power, they put themselves into a state of war with the people, who are thereupon absolved from any farther obedience, and are left to the common refuge, which God hath provided for all men, against force and violence. Whensoever therefore the legislative shall transgress this fundamental rule of society; and either by ambition, fear, folly or corruption, endeavour to grasp themselves or put into the hands of any other, an absolute power over the lives, liberties, and estates of the people, by this breach of trust they forfeit the power the people had put into their hands for quite contrary ends, and it devolves to the people, who have a right to resume their original liberty, and, by the establishment of a new legislative, (such as they shall think fit) provide for their own safety and security, which is the end for which they are in society. What I have said here, concerning the legislative in general holds true also concerning the supreme executor, who having a double trust put in him, both to have a part in the legislative, and the supreme execution law, acts against both, when he goes about to set up his own arbitrary will as the law of the society. He acts also contrary to his trust, when he either employs the force, treasure, and offices of the society to corrupt the representatives, and gain them to his purposes; or openly preengages the electors, and prescribes to their choice, such, whom he has, by solicitations, threats, promises, or otherwise, won to his designs: and employs them to bring in such, who have promised beforehand what to vote, and what to enact. Thus to regulate candidates and electors, and new-model the ways of election, what is it but to cut up the government by the roots, and poison the very fountain of public security? . . .

But it will be said, this hypothesis lays a ferment for frequent rebellion. To which I answer,

First, no more than any other hypothesis: for when the people are made miserable, and find themselves exposed to the ill-usage of arbitrary power, cry up their governors as much as you will, for sons of Jupiter; let them be sacred or divine, descended, or authorized from heaven; give them out for whom or what you please, the same will happen. The people generally ill-treated, and contrary to right, will be ready upon any occasion to ease themselves of a burden that sits heavy upon them. They will wish, and seek for the opportunity, which in the change, weakness, and accidents of human affairs, seldom delays long to offer itself. He must have lived but a little while in the world, who has not seen examples of this in his time; and he must have read very little, who cannot produce examples of it in all sorts of governments in the world.

Secondly, I answer, such revolutions happen not upon every little mismanagement in public affairs. Great mistakes in the ruling part, many wrong and inconvenient laws, and all the slips of human frailty, will be borne by the people without mutiny or murmur. But if a long train of abuses, prevarications, and artifices, all tending the same way, make the design visible to the people, and they cannot but feel what they lie under, and see whither they are going; it is not to be wondered, that they should then rouse themselves, and endeavor to put the rule into such hands which may secure to them the ends for which government was at first erected . . . .

Whosoever uses force without right, as every one does in society, who does it without law, puts himself into a state of war with those against whom he so used it; and in that state all former ties are cancelled, all other rights cease, and every one has a right to defend himself, and to resist the aggressor. . . .

14

from Common Sense

Thomas Paine

(1737–1809)

*T*homas Paine began his checkered career as a corset-maker, itinerant preacher, and schoolmaster in England. For a time he worked as a customs inspector, charged with hunting for smugglers. Having lost the latter job for publicly denouncing corruption, he met Benjamin Franklin (who agreed to write him a letter of introduction) and then moved to the American colonies in 1774. Within months the battles of Lexington and Concord, and the battle of Bunker Hill, had worked the colonies to the brink of revolution. In January, 1776, Paine responded with Common Sense, one of the most influential political pamphlets of all time. He later drifted back to England, then to France when revolution broke out in that country. He served for a time in the National Assembly, where he was a moderate who voted against the execution of Louis XVI. That stance cost him a year in prison and a near-trip to the guillotine. Ultimately Paine moved back to America, where he died, broke as usual. Only nine people attended his funeral.

Paine's best-known work is Common Sense. Over 100,000 copies (estimates go as high as a half-million) were printed in less than three months—enough to ensure that virtually every literate colonial would have access to a copy. In it, Paine combined wit and a shrewd use of biblical allusions with Lockean liberalism to argue for American independence. The pamphlet provided critical momentum for the convention that issued the Declaration of Independence later that year. Paine also wrote The Crisis, whose first line ("These are the times that try men's souls") is one of the most-cited phrases in the English language. Washington read from it to his troops at Valley Forge. In 1791 Paine wrote The Rights of Man, a radical reply to the conservative Edmund Burke and a vigorous defense of the French Revolution. While in prison in France, he wrote his statement on religion and faith, The Age of Reason (see the next selection).

Introduction

Perhaps the sentiments contained in the following pages, are not *yet* sufficiently fashionable to procure them general favor; a long habit of not thinking a thing *wrong*, gives it a superficial appearance of being *right*, and raises at first a formidable outcry in defense of custom. But the tumult soon subsides: Time makes more converts than reason. . . .

The cause of America is in a great measure the cause of all mankind. Many circumstances hath, and will arise, which are not local, but universal, and through which the principles of all Lovers of Mankind are affected, and in the Event of which, their Affections are interested. The laying a Country desolate with Fire and Sword, declaring War against the natural rights of all Mankind, and extirpating the Defenders thereof from the Face of the Earth, is the Concern of every Man to whom Nature hath given the Power of feeling; of which Class, regardless of Party Censure, is the *author*.

Of the Origin and Design of Government in General with Concise Remarks on the English Constitution.

Some writers have so confounded society with government, as to leave little or no distinction between them; whereas they are not only different, but have different origins. Society is produced by our wants, and government by our wickedness; the former promotes our happiness *positively* by uniting our affections, the latter *negatively* by restraining our vices. The one encourages intercourse, the other creates distinctions. The first a patron, the last a punisher.

Society in every state is a blessing, but government even in its best state is but a necessary evil; in its worst state an intolerable one; for when we suffer, or are exposed to the same miseries *by a government*, which we might expect in a country *without government*, our calamity is heightened by reflecting that we furnish the means by which we suffer. Government, like dress, is the badge of lost innocence; the palaces of kings are built on the ruins of the bowers of paradise. For were the impulses of conscience clear, uniform, and irresistibly obeyed, man would need no other lawgiver; but that not being the case, he finds it necessary to surrender up a part of his property to furnish means for the protection of the rest; and this he is induced to do by the same prudence which in every other case advises him out of two evils to choose the least. *Wherefore*, security being the true design and end of government, it unanswerably follows, that whatever *form* thereof appears most likely to ensure it to us, with the least expense and greatest benefit, is preferable to all others.

In order to gain a clear and just idea of the design and end of government, let us suppose a small number of persons settled in some sequestered part of the earth, unconnected with the rest, they will then represent the first peopling of any country, or of the world. In this state of natural liberty, society will be their first thought. A thousand motives will excite them thereto, the strength of one man is so unequal to his wants, and his mind so unfitted for perpetual solitude, that he is soon obliged to seek assistance and relief of another, who in his turn requires the same. Four or five united would be able to raise a tolerable dwelling in the midst of a wilderness, but *one* man might labour out the common period of life without accomplishing any thing; when he had felled his timber he could not remove it, not erect it after it was removed; hunger in the mean time would urge him from his work, and every different want call him a different way. Disease, nay even misfortune would be death, for though neither might be mortal, yet either would disable him from living, and reduce him to a state in which he might rather be said to perish than to die.

Thus necessity, like a gravitating power, would soon form our newly arrived emigrants into society, the reciprocal blessings of which, would supersede, and render the obligations of law and government unnecessary while they remained perfectly just to each other; but as nothing but heaven is impregnable to vice, it will unavoidably happen, that in proportion as they surmount the first difficulties of emigration, which bound them together in a common cause, they will begin to relax in their duty and attachment to each other; and this remissness will point out the necessity of establishing some form of government to supply the defect of moral virtue.

Some convenient tree will afford them a State-House, under the branches of which, the whole colony may assemble to deliberate on public matters. It is more than probable that their first laws will have the title only of *regulations*, and be enforced by no other penalty than public disesteem. In this first parliament every man, by natural right, will have a seat.

But as the colony increases, the public concerns will increase likewise, and the distance at which the members may be separated, will render it too inconvenient for all of them to meet on every occasion as at first, when their number was small, their habitations near, and the public concerns few and trifling. This will point out the convenience of their consenting to leave the legislative part to be managed by a select number chosen from the whole body, who are supposed to have the same concerns at stake which those who have appointed them, and who will act in the same manner as the whole body would act, were they present. If the colony continues to increase, it will become necessary to augment the number of the representatives, and that the interest of every part of the colony may be attended to, it will be found best to divide the whole into convenient parts, each part sending its proper number; and that the *elected* might never form to themselves an interest separate from the *electors*, prudence will point out the propriety of having elections often; because as the *elected* might by that means return and mix again with the general body of the *electors* in a few months, their fidelity to the public will be secured by the prudent reflexion of not making a rod for themselves. And as this frequent interchange will establish a common interest with every part of the community, they will mutually and naturally support each other, and on this (not on the unmeaning name of king) depends the *strength of government, and the happiness of the governed.*

Here then is the origin and rise of government; namely, a mode rendered necessary by the inability of moral virtue to govern the world; here too is the design and end of government, viz. freedom and security. And however our eyes may be dazzled with show, or our ears deceived by sound; however prejudice may warp our wills, or interest darken our understanding, the simple voice of nature and of reason will say, it is right.

I draw my idea of the form of government from a principle in nature, which no art can overturn, viz. that the more simple any thing is, the less liable it is to be disordered, and the easier repaired when disordered; and with this maxim in view, I offer a few remarks on the so much boasted constitution of England.[1] That it was noble for the dark and slavish times in which it was erected, is granted. When the world was overrun with tyranny the least remove therefrom was a glorious rescue. But that it is imperfect, subject to convulsions, and incapable of producing what it seems to promise, is easily demonstrated.

Absolute governments (tho' the disgrace of human nature) have this advantage with them, that they are simple; if the people suffer, they know the head from which their suffering springs, know likewise the remedy, and are not bewildered by a variety of causes and cures. But the constitution of England is so exceedingly complex, that the nation may suffer for years together without being able to discover in which part the fault lies; some will say in one and some in another, and every political physician will advise a different medicine.

I know it is difficult to get over local or long standing prejudices, yet if we will suffer ourselves to examine the component parts of the English constitution, we shall find them to be the base remains of two ancient tyrannies, compounded with some new republican materials.

First—The remains of monarchical tyranny in the person of the king.

Secondly—The remains of aristocratical tyranny in the persons of the peers.

Thirdly—The new republican materials in the persons of the commons, on whose virtue depends the freedom of England. . . .

That the crown is this overbearing part in the English constitution, needs not be mentioned, and that it derives its whole consequence merely from being the giver of places and pensions, is self-evident, wherefore, though we have been wise enough to shut and lock a door against absolute monarchy, we at the same time have been foolish enough to put the crown in possession of the key.

The prejudice of Englishmen in favour of their own government by king, lords and commons, arises as much or more from national pride than reason. Individuals are undoubtedly safer in England than in some other countries, but the *will* of the king is as much the *law* of the land in Britain as in France, with this difference, that instead of proceeding directly from his mouth, it is handed to the people under the more formidable shape of an act of parliament. For the fate of Charles the First[2] hath only made kings more subtle—not more just.

Wherefore, laying aside all national pride and prejudice in favour of the modes and forms, the plain truth is, that *it is wholly owing to the constitution of the people, and not to the constitution of the government*, that the crown is not as oppressive in England as in Turkey. . . .

Of Monarchy and Hereditary Succession

Mankind being originally equals in the order of creation, the equality could only be destroyed by some subsequent circumstance; the distinctions of rich, and poor, may in a great measure be accounted for, and that without having recourse to the harsh, ill-sounding names of oppression and avarice. Oppression is often the *consequence*, but seldom or never the *means* of riches; and though avarice will preserve a man from being necessitously poor, it generally makes him too timorous to be wealthy.

But there is another and greater distinction, for which no truly natural or religious reason can be assigned, and that is, the distinction of men into *kings and subjects*. Male and female are the distinctions of nature, good and bad the distinctions of heaven; but how a race of men came into the world so exalted above the rest, and distinguished like some new species, is worth inquiring into, and whether they are the means of happiness or of misery to mankind.

In the early ages of the world, according to the scripture chronology, there were not kings; the consequence of which was, there were no wars; it is the pride of kings which throw mankind into confusion. Holland without a king hath enjoyed more peace for this last century than any of the monarchical governments in Europe. Antiquity favours the same remark; for the quiet and rural lives of the first patriarchs hath a happy something in them, which vanishes away when we come to the history of Jewish royalty.

Government by kings was first introduced into the world by the Heathens, from whom the children of Israel copied the custom. It was the most prosperous invention the Devil ever set on foot for the promotion of idolatry. The Heathens paid divine honors to their deceased kings, and the Christian world hath improved on the plan, by doing the same to their living ones. How impious is the title of sacred majesty applied to a worm, who in the midst of his splendor is crumbling to dust!

As the exalting one man so greatly above the rest cannot be justified on the equal rights of nature, so neither can it be defended on the authority of scripture; for the will of the Almighty, as declared by Gideon and the prophet Samuel, expressly disapproves of government by kings. All anti-monarchical parts of scripture have been very smoothly glossed over in monarchical governments, but they undoubtedly merit the attention of countries which have their governments yet to form. *"Render unto Caesar the things which are Caesar's"* is the scripture doctrine of courts, yet it is no support of monarchial government, for the Jews at that time were without a king, and in a state of vassalage to the Romans.

Near three thousand years passed away from the Mosaic account of the creation, till the Jews under a national delusion requested a king. Till then their form of government (except in extraordinary cases, where the

Almighty interposed) was a kind of republic administered by a judge and the elders of the tribes. Kings they had none, and it was held sinful to acknowledge any being under that title but the Lord of Hosts. And when a man seriously reflects on the idolatrous homage which is paid to the persons of kings, he need not wonder that the Almighty, ever jealous of his honour, should disapprove of a form of government which so impiously invades the prerogative of heaven.

Monarchy is ranked in scripture as one of the sins of the Jews, for which a curse in reserve is denounced against them. The history of that transaction is worth attending to.

The children of Israel being oppressed by the Midianites, Gideon marched against them with a small army, and victory, thro' the divine interposition, decided in his favour. The Jews, elated with success, and attributing it to the generalship of Gideon, proposed making him a king, saying, *Rule thou over us, thou and thy son and thy son's son.* Here was temptation in its fullest extent; not a kingdom only, but an hereditary one, but Gideon in the piety of his soul replied, *I will not rule over you, neither shall my son rule over you, the Lord shall rule over you.* Words need not be more explicit; Gideon doth not decline the honor, but denieth their right to give it; neither doth he compliment them with invented declarations of his thanks, but in the positive style of a prophet charges them with disaffection to their proper Sovereign, the King of heaven. . . .

That the Almighty hath here entered his protest against monarchical government, is true, or the scripture is false. And a man hath good reason to believe that there is as much of kingcraft, as priestcraft, in withholding the scripture from the public in Popish countries. For monarchy in every instance is the Popery of government.

To the evil of monarchy we have added that of hereditary succession; and as the first is a degradation and lessening of ourselves, so the second, claimed as a matter of right, is an insult and an imposition on posterity. For all men being originally equals, no *one* by *birth* could have a right to set up his own family in perpetual preference to all others for ever, and though himself might deserve *some* decent degree of honors of his contemporaries, yet his descendants might be far too unworthy to inherit them. One of the strongest *natural* proofs of the folly of hereditary right in kings, is, that nature disapproves it, otherwise she would not so frequently turn it into ridicule by giving mankind an *ass for a lion*.

Secondly, as no man at first could possess any other public honours than were bestowed upon him, so the givers of those honours could have no power to give away the right of posterity. And though they might say, "We choose you for *our* head," they could not, without manifest injustice to their children, say "that your children and your children's children shall reign over *ours* for ever." Because such an unwise, unjust, unnatural compact might (perhaps) in the next succession put them under the government of a rogue or a fool. Most wise men, in their private sentiments, have ever treated hereditary right with contempt; yet it is one of those evils, which when once established is not easily removed; many submit from fear, others from superstition, and the more powerful part shares with the king the plunder of the rest.

This is supposing the present race of kings in the world to have had an honorable origin; whereas it is more than probable, that could we take off the dark covering of antiquity, and trace them to their first rise, that we should find the first of them nothing better than the principal ruffian of some restless gang, whose savage manners or pre-eminence in subtlety obtained him the title of chief among plunderers. . . .

England, since the conquest,[3] hath known some few good monarchs, but groaned beneath a much larger number of bad ones; yet no man in his senses can say that their claim under William the Conqueror is a very honourable one. A French bastard landing with an armed banditti, and establishing himself king of England against the consent of the natives, is in plain terms a very paltry rascally original. It certainly hath no divinity in it. However, it is needless to spend much time in exposing the folly of hereditary right; if there are any so weak as to believe it, let them promiscuously worship the ass and lion, and welcome. I shall neither copy their humility, nor disturb their devotion.

Yet I should be glad to ask how they suppose kings came at first? The question admits but of three answers, viz. either by lot, by election, or by usurpation. If the first king was taken by lot, it establishes a precedent for the next, which excludes hereditary succession. . . . If the first king of any country was by election, that likewise establishes a precedent for the next; for to say, that the *right* of all future generations is taken away, by the act of the first electors, in their choice not only of a king, but of a family of kings for ever, hath no parallel in or out of scripture but the doctrine of original sin, which supposes the free will of all men lost in Adam; and from such comparison, and it will admit of no other, hereditary succession can derive no glory. For as in Adam all sinned, and as in the first electors all men obeyed; as in the one all mankind were subjected to Satan, and in the other to Sovereignty; as our innocence was lost in the first, and our authority in the last; and as both disable us from reassuming some former state and privilege, it unanswerably follows that original sin and hereditary succession are parallels. Dishonorable rank! Inglorious connection! Yet the most subtle sophist cannot produce a juster simile.

As to usurpation, no man will be so hardy as to defend it; and that William the Conqueror was an usurper is a fact not to be contradicted. The plain truth is, that the antiquity of English monarchy will not bear looking into.

But it is not so much the absurdity as the evil of hereditary succession which concerns mankind. Did it ensure a race of good and wise men it would have the seal of divine authority, but as it opens a door to the *foolish,* the *wicked,* and the *improper,* it hath in it the nature of oppression. Men who look upon themselves born to reign, and others to obey, soon grow insolent; selected from the rest of mankind their minds are early poisoned by importance; and the world they act in differs so materially from the world at large, that they have but little opportunity of knowing its true interests, and when they succeed to the government are frequently the most ignorant and unfit of any throughout the dominions.

Another evil which attends hereditary succession is, that the throne is subject to be possessed by a minor at any age; all which time the regency, acting under the cover of a king, have every opportunity and inducement to betray their trust. The same national misfortune happens, when a king, worn out with age and infirmity, enters the last stage of human weakness. In both these cases the public becomes a prey to every miscreant, who can tamper successfully with the follies either of age or infancy.

The most plausible plea, which hath ever been offered in favour of hereditary succession, is, that it preserves a nation from civil wars; and were this true, it would be weighty; whereas, it is the most barefaced falsity ever imposed upon mankind. The whole history of England disowns the fact. Thirty kings and two minors have reigned in that distracted kingdom since the conquest, in which time there have been (including the Revolution) no less than eight civil wars and nineteen rebellions. Wherefore instead of making for peace, it makes against it, and destroys the very foundation it seems to stand on. . . .

In short, monarchy and succession have laid (not this or that kingdom only) but the world in blood and ashes. 'Tis a form of government which the word of God bears testimony against, and blood will attend it.

If we inquire into the business of a king, we shall find that in some countries they have none; and after sauntering away their lives without pleasure to themselves or advantage to the nation, withdraw from the scene, and leave their successors to tread the same idle ground. In absolute monarchies the whole weight of business, civil and military, lies on the king; the children of Israel in their request for a king, urged this plea "that he may judge us, and go out before us and fight our battles." But in countries where he is neither a judge nor a general, as in England, a man would be puzzled to know what *is* his business. . . .

In England a king hath little more to do than to make war and give away places; which in plain terms, is to impoverish the nation and set it together by the ears. A pretty business indeed for a man to be allowed eight hundred thousand sterling a year for, and worshiped into the bargain! Of more worth is one honest man to society and in the sight of God, than all the crowned ruffians that ever lived. . . .

Notes

1   The "constitution" of England is not a single document, as is the Constitution of the United States. Rather, it is the cumulative body of common law, tradition, and mixed estates (monarchy, peerage, commons) which "constitute" civil society in England.

2   Charles I of England was beheaded in 1649 at the height of the English Civil War.

3   The victory of William the Conqueror and the Normans over the Anglo-Saxons in 1066.

15

from The Age of Reason

Thomas Paine

(1737–1809)

Thomas Paine's radicalism was no sham. In Common Sense *(1776) he expanded the colonists' complaints about taxation into a full-fledged call for independence. In* The Rights of Man *(1791) Paine bore down on the inequities of class, poverty, illiteracy, and war. Going far beyond even the classical liberalism of his day (for which he was one of the most popular and quoted spokesmen), he called for a progressive income tax and direct government aid to the poor and aged. English officials promptly pronounced his work seditious, labeled him a traitor, and spurred him to flee for France. Ironically, Paine was not radical enough there; his republicanism did not extend to regicide, and he spent months in jail.*

Ever active, Paine spent the time writing. Having called for American independence, abolition of the monarchy, and a wholesale reform of European society, Paine turned to religion. The Age of Reason *(1794) is part statement of faith, part diatribe against prejudice, and part deistic theology. Benjamin Franklin read an early draft of the work and advised him not to publish it even though Franklin himself agreed with Paine's deism (as did Thomas Jefferson and others). Wrote Franklin, "He that spits against the wind, spits in his own face."*

PART I

Chapter I

The Author's Profession of Faith

It has been my intention, for several years past, to publish my thoughts upon religion; I am well aware of the difficulties that attend the subject, and from that consideration, had reserved it to a more advanced period of life. I intended it to be the last offering I should make to my fellow citizens of all nations, and that at a time when the purity of the motive that induced me to it could not admit of a question, even by those who might disapprove the work.

The circumstance that has now taken place in France, of the total abolition of the whole national order of priesthood, and of everything appertaining to compulsive systems of religion, and compulsive articles of faith, has not only precipitated my intention, but rendered a work of this kind exceedingly necessary, lest, in the general wreck of superstition, of false systems of government, and false theology, we lose sight of morality, of humanity, and of the theology that is true. As several of my colleagues, and others of my fellow-citizens of France, have given me the example of making their voluntary and individual profession of faith, I also will make mine; and I do this with all that sincerity and frankness with which the mind of man communicates with itself.

I believe in one God, and no more; and I hope for happiness beyond this life.

I believe the equality of man, and I believe that religious duties consist in doing justice, loving mercy, and endeavoring to make our fellow-creatures happy.

But, lest it should be supposed that I believe many other things in addition to these, I shall, in the progress of this work, declare the things I do not believe, and my reasons for not believing them.

I do not believe in the creed professed by the Jewish church, by the Roman church, by the Greek church, by the Turkish church, by the Protestant church, nor by any church that I know of. My own mind is my own church.

All national institutions of churches, whether Jewish, Christian, or Turkish, appear to me no other than human inventions set up to terrify and enslave mankind, and monopolize power and profit.

I do not mean by this declaration to condemn those who believe otherwise; they have the same right to their belief as I have to mine. But it is necessary to the happiness of man, that he be mentally faithful to himself. Infidelity does not consist in believing, or in disbelieving; it consists in professing to believe what he does not believe.

It is impossible to calculate the moral mischief, if I may so express it, that mental lying has produced in society. When a man has so far corrupted and prostituted the chastity of his mind, as to subscribe his professional belief to things he does not believe, he has prepared himself for the commission of every other crime. He takes up the trade of a priest for the sake of gain, and, in order to qualify himself for that trade, he begins with a perjury. Can we conceive anything more destructive to morality than this?

Soon after I had published the pamphlet *Common Sense*, in America, I saw the exceeding probability that a revolution in the system of government would be followed by a revolution in the system of religion. The adulterous connection of church and state, wherever it had taken place, whether Jewish, Christian, or Turkish, had so effectually prohibited, by pains and penalties, every discussion upon established creeds, and upon first principles of religion, that until the system of government should be changed, those subjects could not be brought fairly and openly before the world; but that whenever this should be done, a revolution in the system of religion would follow. Human inventions and priestcraft would be detected; and man would return to the pure, unmixed, and unadulterated belief of one God, and no more.

Chapter II

Of Missions and Revelations

Every national church or religion has established itself by pretending some special mission from God, communicated to certain individuals. The Jews have their Moses; the Christians their Jesus Christ, their apostles and saints; and the Turks their Mahomet; as if the way to God was not open to every man alike.

Each of those churches shows certain books, which they call *revelation*, or the Word of God. The Jews say that their Word of God was given by God to Moses face to face; the Christians say, that their Word of God came by divine inspiration; and the Turks say, that their Word of God (the Koran) was brought by an angel from heaven. Each of those churches accuses the other of unbelief; and, for my own part, I disbelieve them all.

As it is necessary to affix right ideas to words, I will, before I proceed further into the subject, offer some observations on the word *revelation*. Revelation when applied to religion, means something communicated *immediately* from God to man.

No one will deny or dispute the power of the Almighty to make such a communication if he pleases. But admitting, for the sake of a case, that something has been revealed to a certain person, and not revealed to any other person, it is revelation to that person only. When he tells it to a second person, a second to a third, a third to a fourth, and so on, it ceases to be a revelation to all those persons. It is revelation to the first person only, and *hearsay* to every other, and, consequently, they are not obliged to believe it.

It is a contradiction in terms and ideas to call anything a revelation that comes to us at second hand, either verbally or in writing. Revelation is necessarily limited to the first communication. After this, it is only an account of something which that person says was a revelation made to him; and though he may find himself obliged to believe it, it cannot be incumbent on me to believe it in the same manner, for it was not a revelation made to *me*, and I have only his word for it that it was made to *him*.

When Moses told the children of Israel that he received the two tables of the commandments from the hand of God, they were not obliged to believe him, because they had no other authority for it than his telling them so; and I have no other authority for it than some historian telling me so, the commandments carrying no internal evidence of divinity with them. They contain some good moral precepts such as any man qualified to be a lawgiver or a legislator could produce himself, without having recourse to supernatural intervention.

When I am told that the Koran was written in Heaven, and brought to Mahomet by an angel, the account comes to near the same kind of hearsay evidence and second hand authority as the former. I did not see the angel myself, and therefore I have a right not to believe it.

When also I am told that the woman, called the Virgin Mary, said, or gave out, that she was with child without any cohabitation with a man, and that her betrothed husband, Joseph, said that an angel told him so, I have a right to believe them or not: such a circumstance required a much stronger evidence than their bare word for it: but we have not even this; for neither Joseph nor Mary wrote any such matter themselves. It is only reported by others that *they said so*. It is hearsay upon hearsay, and I do not choose to rest my belief upon such evidence.

It is, however, not difficult to account for the credit that was given to the story of Jesus Christ being the Son of God. He was born when the heathen mythology had still some fashion and repute in the world, and that mythology had prepared the people for the belief of such a story. Almost all the extraordinary men that lived under the heathen mythology were reputed to be the sons of some of their gods. It was not a new thing at that time to believe a man to have been celestially begotten; the intercourse of gods with women was then a matter of familiar opinion. Their Jupiter, according to their accounts, had cohabited with hundreds; the story therefore had nothing in it either new, wonderful, or obscene; it was conformable to the opinions that then prevailed among the people called Gentiles, or mythologists, and it was those people only that believed it. The Jews, who had kept strictly to the belief of one God, and no more, and who had always rejected the heathen mythology, never credited the story.

It is curious to observe how the theory of what is called the Christian Church sprang out of the tail of the heathen mythology. A direct incorporation took place in the first instance, by making the reputed founder to be celestially begotten. The trinity of gods that then followed was no other than a reduction of the former plurality, which was about twenty or thirty thousand. The statue of Mary succeeded the statue of Diana of Ephesus. The deification of heroes changed into the canonization of saints. The Mythologists had gods for everything; the Christian Mythologists had saints for everything. The church became as crowded with the one, as the pantheon had been with the other; and Rome was the place of both. The Christian theory is little else than the idolatry of the ancient mythologists, accommodated to the purposes of power and revenue; and it yet remains to reason and philosophy to abolish the amphibious fraud.

Chapter III

Concerning the Character of Jesus Christ, and His History

Nothing that is here said can apply, even with the most distant disrespect, to the *real* character of Jesus Christ. He was a virtuous and an amiable man. The morality that he preached and practiced was of the most benevolent kind; and though similar morality had been preached by Confucius, and by some of the Greek philosophers, many years before, by the Quakers since, and by many good men in all ages, it has not been exceeded by any.

Jesus Christ wrote no account of himself, of his birth, parentage, or anything else. Not a line of what is called the New Testament is of his writing. The history of him is altogether the work of other people; and as to the account given of his resurrection and ascension, it was the necessary counterpart to the story of his birth. His historians, having brought him into the world in a supernatural manner, were obliged to take him out again in the same manner, or the first part of the story must have fallen to the ground.

The wretched contrivance with which this latter part is told, exceeds everything that went before it. The first part, that of the miraculous conception, was not a thing that admitted of publicity; and therefore the tellers of this part of the story had this advantage, that though they might not be credited, they could not be detected. They could not be expected to prove it, because it was not one of those things that admitted of proof, and it was impossible that the person of whom it was told could prove it himself.

But the resurrection of a dead person from the grave, and his ascension through the air, is a thing very different, as to the evidence it admits of, to the invisible conception of a child in the womb. The resurrection and ascension, supposing them to have taken place, admitted of public and ocular demonstration, like that of the ascension of a balloon, or the sun at noon day, to all Jerusalem at least. A thing which everybody is required to believe, requires that the proof and evidence of it should be equal to all, and universal; and as the public visibility of this last related act was the only evidence that could give sanction to the former part, the whole of it falls to the ground, because that evidence never was given. Instead of this, a small number of persons, not more than eight or nine, are introduced as proxies for the whole world, to say they saw it, and all the rest of the world are called upon to believe it. But it appears that Thomas did not believe the resurrection; and, as they say, would not believe without having ocular and manual demonstration himself. *So neither will I;* and the reason is equally as good for me, and for every other person, as for Thomas.

It is in vain to attempt to palliate or disguise this matter. The story, so far as relates to the supernatural part, has every mark of fraud and imposition stamped upon the face of it. Who were the authors of it is as impossible for us now to know, as it is for us to be assured that the books in which the account is related were written by the persons whose names they bear. The best surviving evidence we now have respecting this affair is the Jews. They are regularly descended from the people who lived in the time this resurrection and ascension is said to have happened, and they say, *it is not true.* It has long appeared to me a strange inconsistency to cite the Jews as a proof of the truth of the story. It is just the same as if a man were to say, I will prove the truth of what I have told you, by producing the people who say it is false.

That such a person as Jesus Christ existed, and that he was crucified, which was the mode of execution at that day, are historical relations strictly within the limits of probability. He preached most excellent morality, and the equality of man; but he preached also against the corruptions and avarice of the Jewish priests, and this brought upon him the hatred and vengeance of the whole order of priesthood. The accusation which those priests brought against him was that of sedition and conspiracy against the Roman government, to which the Jews were then subject and tributary; and it is not improbable that the Roman government might have some secret apprehension of the effects of his doctrine as well as the Jewish priests; neither is it improbable that Jesus Christ had in contemplation the delivery of the Jewish nation from bondage of the Romans. Between the two, however, this virtuous reformer and revolutionist lost his life.

Chapter IV

Of the Bases of Christianity

It is upon this plain narrative of facts, together with another case I am going to mention, that the Christian mythologists, calling themselves the Christian Church, have erected their fable, which for absurdity and extravagance is not exceeded by anything that is to be found in the mythology of the ancients.

The ancient mythologists tell us that the race of Giants made war against Jupiter, and that one of them threw a hundred rocks against him at one throw; that Jupiter defeated him with thunder, and confined him afterwards under Mount Etna; and that every time the Giant turns himself, Mount Etna belches fire. It is here easy to see that the circumstance of the mountain, that of its being a volcano, suggested the idea of the fable; and that the fable is made to fit and wind itself up with that circumstance.

The Christian mythologists tell that their Satan made war against the Almighty, who defeated him, and confined him afterwards, not under a mountain, but in a pit. It is here easy to see that the first fable suggested the idea of the second; for the fable of Jupiter and the Giants was told many hundred years before that of Satan.

Thus far the ancient and the Christian mythologists differ very little from each other. But the latter have contrived to carry the matter much farther. They have contrived to connect the fabulous part of the story of Jesus

Christ with the fable originating from Mount Etna; and, in order to make all the parts of the story tye together, they have taken to their aid the traditions of the Jews; for the Christian mythology is made up partly from the ancient mythology, and partly from the Jewish traditions.

The Christian mythologists, after having confined Satan in a pit, were obliged to let him out again to bring on the sequel of the fable. He is then introduced into the garden of Eden in the shape of a snake, or a serpent, and in that shape he enters into familiar conversation with Eve, who is no ways surprised to hear a snake talk; and the issue of this tete-a-tete is, that he persuades her to eat an apple, and the eating of that apple damns all mankind.

After giving Satan this triumph over the whole creation, one would have supposed that the church mythologists would have been kind enough to send him back again to the pit, or, if they had not done this, that they would have put a mountain upon him, (for they say that their faith can remove a mountain) or have put him under a mountain, as the former mythologists had done, to prevent his getting again among the women, and doing more mischief. But instead of this, they leave him at large, without even obliging him to give his parole. The secret of which is, that they could not do without him; and after being at the trouble of making him, they bribed him to stay. They promised him all the Jews, all the Turks by anticipation, nine-tenths of the world beside, and Mahomet into the bargain. After this, who can doubt the bountifulness of the Christian Mythology?

Having thus made an insurrection and a battle in heaven, in which none of the combatants could be either killed or wounded—put Satan into the pit—let him out again—given him a triumph over the whole creation—damned all mankind by the eating of an apple, these Christian mythologists bring the two ends of their fable together. They represent this virtuous and amiable man, Jesus Christ, to be at once both God and man, and also the Son of God, celestially begotten, on purpose to be sacrificed, because they say that Eve in her longing had eaten an apple.

Chapter V

Examination in Detail of the Preceding Bases

Putting aside everything that might excite laughter by its absurdity, or detestation by its profaneness, and confining ourselves merely to an examination of the parts, it is impossible to conceive a story more derogatory to the Almighty, more inconsistent with his wisdom, more contradictory to his power, than this story is.

In order to make for it a foundation to rise upon, the inventors were under the necessity of giving to the being whom they call Satan a power equally as great, if not greater, than they attribute to the Almighty. They have not only given him the power of liberating himself from the pit, after what they call his fall, but they have made that power increase afterwards to infinity. Before this fall they represent him only as an angel of limited existence, as they represent the rest. After his fall, he becomes, by their account, omnipresent. He exists everywhere, and at the same time. He occupies the whole immensity of space.

Not content with this deification of Satan, they represent him as defeating by stratagem, in the shape of an animal of the creation, all the power and wisdom of the Almighty. They represent him as having compelled the Almighty to the *direct necessity* either of surrendering the whole of the creation to the government and sovereignty of this Satan, or of capitulating for its redemption by coming down upon earth, and exhibiting himself upon a cross in the shape of a man.

Had the inventors of this story told it the contrary way, that is, had they represented the Almighty as compelling Satan to exhibit *himself* on a cross in the shape of a snake, as a punishment for his new transgression, the story would have been less absurd, less contradictory. But, instead of this they make the transgressor triumph, and the Almighty fall.

That many good men have believed this strange fable, and lived very good lives under that belief (for credulity is not a crime) is what I have no doubt of. In the first place, they were educated to believe it, and they would have believed anything else in the same manner. There are also many who have been so enthusiastically enraptured by what they conceived to be the infinite love of God to man, in making a sacrifice of himself, that the vehemence of the idea has forbidden and deterred them from examining into the absurdity and profaneness of the story. The more unnatural anything is, the more is it capable of becoming the object of dismal admiration.

Chapter IX

In What the True Revelation Consists

But some perhaps will say—Are we to have no word of God—no revelation? I answer yes. There is a Word of God; there is a revelation.

THE WORD OF GOD IS THE CREATION WE BEHOLD: And it is in *this word*, which no human invention can counterfeit or alter, that God speaketh universally to man.

Human language is local and changeable, and is therefore incapable of being used as the means of unchangeable and universal information. The idea that God sent Jesus Christ to publish, as they say, the glad tidings to all nations, from one end of the earth unto the other, is consistent only with the ignorance of those who know nothing of the extent of the world, and who believed, as those world saviours believed, and continued to believe for several centuries, (and that in contradiction to the discoveries of philosophers and the experience of navigators,) that the earth was flat like a trencher; and that a man might walk to the end of it.

But how was Jesus Christ to make anything known to all nations? He could speak but one language, which was Hebrew; and there are in the world several hundred languages. Scarcely any two nations speak the same language, or understand each other; and as to translations, every man who knows anything of languages, knows that it is impossible to translate from one language into another, not only without losing a great part of the original, but frequently of mistaking the sense; and besides all this, the art of printing was wholly unknown at the time Christ lived.

It is always necessary that the means that are to accomplish any end be equal to the accomplishment of that end, or the end cannot be accomplished. It is in this that the difference between finite and infinite power and wisdom discovers itself. Man frequently fails in accomplishing his end, from a natural inability, of the power to the purpose; and frequently from the want of wisdom to apply power properly. But it is impossible for infinite power and wisdom to fail as man faileth. The means it useth are always equal to the end: but human language, more especially as there is not an universal language, is incapable of being used as an universal means of unchangeable and uniform information; and therefore it is not the means that God useth in manifesting himself universally to man.

It is only in the CREATION that all our ideas and conceptions of a *word of God* can unite. The Creation speaketh an universal language, independently of human speech or human language, multiplied and various as they be. It is an ever existing original, which every man can read. It cannot be forged; it cannot be counterfeited; it cannot be lost; it cannot be altered; it cannot be suppressed. It does not depend upon the will of man whether it shall be published or not; it publishes itself from one end of the earth to the other. It preaches to all nations and to all worlds; and this *word of God* reveals to man all that is necessary for man to know of God.

Do we want to contemplate his power? We see it in the immensity of the creation. Do we want to contemplate his wisdom? We see it in the unchangeable order by which the incomprehensible Whole is governed. Do we want to contemplate his munificence? We see it in the abundance with which he fills the earth. Do we want to contemplate his mercy? We see it in his not withholding that abundance even from the unthankful. In fine, do we want to know what God is? Search not the book called the scripture, which any human hand might make, but the scripture called the Creation.

16

from Fundamental Principles of the Metaphysic of Morals

Immanuel Kant

(1724–1804)

The two most important ethical philosophers of the Enlightenment were arguably David Hume (1711–1776) and Immanuel Kant (1724–1804). Hume, an urbane and skeptical English aristocrat, took John Locke's emphasis on the role of sensation and experience to its ethical conclusion. Moral knowledge, argued Hume, proceeds from human desires and sentiments; what we regard as ethical systems are the conventions of society and have no universal foundation in reason or logic. We behave "morally" from our attachment to society and our need to be happy in it. Kant, a rather private man who never ventured more than sixty miles from his home in Konigsberg, took precisely the opposite view. Morality and happiness, he countered, are not the same things. The mind is more than a receptor; it is a creative, ordering force capable of moving beyond sensation to an appreciation of higher truths. Thus it responds to duty and discipline, which are not always pleasurable. Kant's challenge to humanity was the "categorical imperative": Judge an individual action as if it would be extended as a universal moral law.

Nothing can possibly be conceived in the world, or even out of it, which can be called good without qualification, except a GOOD WILL. Intelligence, wit, judgment, and the other *talents* of the mind, however they may be named, or courage, resolution, perseverance, as qualities of temperament, are undoubtedly good and desirable in many respects. But these gifts of nature may also become extremely bad and mischievous if the will which is to make use of these gifts, and which therefore constitutes what is called *character*, is not good. It is the same with the *gifts of fortune*. Power, riches, honor, even health, and the general well-being and contentment with one's condition which is called *happiness*, inspire pride and often presumption if there is not a good will to correct the influence of these things on the mind, and with this to rectify also the whole principle of acting and adapt it to its end. . . .

A good will is good not because of what it performs or effects, nor by its aptness for attaining some proposed end, but simply by virtue of the volition; that is, it is good in itself and when considered by itself is to be esteemed much higher than all that it can bring about in pursuing any inclination, nay even in pursuing the sum total of all inclinations. It might happen that, owing to special misfortune, or to the niggardly provision of a step-motherly nature, this will should wholly lack power to accomplish its purpose. If with its greatest efforts this will should yet achieve nothing and there should remain only good will . . . , then, like a jewel, good will would still shine by its own light as a thing having its whole value in itself. Its usefulness or fruitlessness can neither add to nor detract anything from this value. . . .

. . . [W]e assume, as a fundamental principle, that no organ [designed] for any purpose will be found in the physical constitution of an organized being, except one which is also the fittest and best adapted for that purpose. Now if the proper object of nature for a being with reason and a will was its *preservation*, its *welfare*, in a word its *happiness*, then nature would have hit upon a very bad arrangement when it selected the reason of the creature to carry out this function. For all the actions which the creature has to perform with a view to this purpose, and the whole rule of its conduct would be far more surely prescribed by [its own] instinct, and that end [happiness] would have been attained by instinct far more certainly than it ever can be by reason. Should reason have been attributed to this favored creature over and above [such instinct], reason would only have served this creature for contemplating the happy constitution of its nature, for admiring it and congratulating itself thereon, and for feeling thankful for it to the beneficent cause. But [certainly nature would not have arranged it so that] such a creature should subject its desires to that weak and deceptive guidance, and meddle with nature's intent. In a word, nature would have taken care that reason should not turn into *practical* exercise, nor have the presumption, with its feeble insight, to figure out for itself a plan of happiness and the means for attaining it.

In fact, we find that the more cultivated reason applies itself with deliberate purpose to enjoying life and happiness, so much more does the man lack true satisfaction. From this circumstance there arises in many men, if they are candid enough to confess it, a certain degree of *misology*; that is, hatred of reason, especially in the case of those who are more experienced in the use of reason. For, after calculating all the advantages they derive, not only from the invention of all the arts of common luxury, but even from the sciences . . . , they find that they have actually only brought more trouble upon themselves, rather than gaining in happiness. They end by envying, rather than despising, the common run of men who keep closer to the guidance of mere instinct and who do not allow their reason to have much influence on their conduct. . . .

. . . Nay, it may even reduce happiness to nothing without nature failing thereby in her purpose. For reason recognizes the establishment of a good will as its highest practical destination, and is capable of only satisfying its own proper kind in attaining this purpose: the attainment of an end determined only by reason, even when such an attainment may involve many a disappointment over otherwise desirable purposes. . . .

To be beneficent when we can is a duty; besides this, there are many minds so sympathetically constituted that without any other motive of vanity or self-interest, they find a pleasure in spreading joy and can take delight in the satisfaction of others so far as it is their own work. But I maintain that in such a case, however proper, however amiable an action of this kind may be, it nevertheless has no true moral worth, but is on a level with other inclinations; e.g. the inclination to honor which, if it is happily directed to that which is actually of public utility and accordant with duty and consequently honorable, deserves praise and encourage-ment but not respect. For the maxim lacks the moral ingredient that such actions be done *out of duty*, not from inclination. Put the case [another way and suppose] that the mind of that philanthropist were clouded by sorrow of his own, extinguishing all sympathy with the lot of others, and that while he still has the power to benefit others in distress he is not touched by their trouble because he is absorbed with his own; suppose that he now tears himself out of this deadening insensibility, and per-forms the action without any inclination for it, but simply from duty; only then has his action genuine moral worth. Furthermore, if nature has put little sympathy into the heart of this or that man, if a supposedly upright man is by temperament cold and indifferent to the sufferings of others, perhaps because in respect of his own sufferings, he is provided with the special gift of patience and fortitude so that he supposes or even requires that others should have the same; such a man would certainly not be the meanest product of nature. But if nature had not specially shaped him to be a philanthropist, would he not find cause in himself for attributing to himself a value far higher than the value of a good-natured temperament could be? Unquestionably. It is just in this that there is brought out the moral worth of the character which is incomparably the highest of all; namely, that he is beneficent, not from inclination, but from duty. . . .

The second proposition is: That an action done from duty derives its moral worth, *not from the purpose* which is to be attained by it, but from the maxim by which it is determined. Therefore the action does not depend on the realization of its objective, but merely on the *principle* of volition by which the action has taken place, without regard to any object of desire. . . .

The third proposition, which is a consequence of the preceding two, I would express thus: *Duty is the necessity of an action, resulting from respect for the law.* I may have an *inclination* for an object as the effect of my proposed action, but I cannot have *respect* for an object just for this reason: that it is merely an effect and not an action of will. Similarly, I cannot have respect for an inclination, whether my own or another's; I can at most, if it is my own, approve it; if it is another's I can sometimes even cherish it; that is, look on it as favorable to my own interest. Only the law itself which is connected with my will by no means as an effect but as a principle which does not serve my inclination but outweighs it, or at least in case of choice excludes my inclination from its calculation; only such a law can be an object of respect and hence a command. Now an action done from duty must wholly exclude the influence of inclination, and with it every object of the will, so that nothing remains which can determine the will objectively except the *law*, and [determine the will] subjectively except *pure respect* for this practical law, and hence [pure respect] for the maxim to follow this law even to the thwarting of all my inclinations.

Thus the moral worth of an action does not consist of the effect expected from it, nor from any principle of action which needs to borrow its motive from this expected effect. . . . Therefore the pre-eminent good which we call moral can consist in nothing other than the *concept of law* in itself, *which is certainly only possible in a rational being,* in so far as this conception, and not the expected effect, determines the will. . . .

But what sort of law can it be the conception of which must determine the will, even without our paying any attention to the effect expected from it, in order that this will may be called good absolutely and without qualification? As I have stripped the will of every impulse which could arise from it from obedience to any law, there remains nothing but the general conformity of the will's actions to law in general. Only this conformity to law is to serve the will as a principle; that is, I am never to act in any way other than *so I could want my maxim also to become a general law.* It is the simple conformity to law in general, without assuming any particular law applicable to certain actions, that serves the will as its principle, and must so serve it, if duty is not to be a vain delusion and a chimerical notion. The common reason of men in their practical judgments agrees perfectly with this and always has in view the principle suggested here. For example, let the question be: When in distress may I make a promise with the intention of not keeping it? I readily distinguish here between the two meanings which the question may have: Whether it is prudent, or whether it is in accordance with duty, to make a false promise. The former undoubtedly may often be the case. I [may] see clearly that it is not enough to extricate myself from a present difficulty by means of this subterfuge, but that it must be carefully considered whether there may not result from such a lie a much greater inconvenience than that from which I am now freeing myself. But, since in spite of all my supposed *cunning* the consequences cannot be foreseen easily; the loss of credit may be much more injurious to me than any mischief which I seek to avoid at present. That being the case, one might consider whether it would not be more *prudent* to act according to a general maxim, and make it a habit to give no promise except with the intention of keeping it. But, it is soon clear that such a maxim is still only based on the fear of consequences. It is a wholly different thing to be truthful from a sense of duty, than to be so from apprehension of injurious consequences. In the first case, the very conceiving of the action already implies a law for me; in the second case, I must first look about elsewhere to see what results may be associated with it which would affect me. For it is beyond all doubt wicked to deviate from the principle of duty; but to be unfaithful to my maxim of prudence may often be very advantageous to me, although it is certainly wiser to abide by it. However, the shortest way, and an unerring one, to discover the answer to this question of whether a lying promise is consistent with duty, is to ask myself, "Would I be content if this maxim of extricating myself from difficulty by a false promise held good as a general law for others as well as for myself?" Would I care to say to myself, "Everyone may make a deceitful promise when he finds himself in a difficulty from which he cannot extricate himself otherwise"? Then I would presently become aware that while I can decide in favor of the lie, I can by no means decide that lying should be a general law. For under such a law there would be no promises at all, since I would state my intentions in vain in regard to my future actions to those who would not believe my allegation, or, if they did so too hastily, they would pay me back in my own coin. Hence, as soon as such a maxim was made a universal law, it would necessarily destroy itself. . . .

Thus we have arrived at the principle of moral knowledge of common human reason. Although common men no doubt do not conceive this principle in such an abstract and universal form, yet they really always have it before their eyes and use it as the standard for their decision. It would be easy to show here how, with this compass in hand, men are well able to distinguish, in every case that occurs, what is good, bad, conformable to duty or inconsistent with it. Without teaching them anything at all new, we are only, like Socrates, directing their attention to the principle they employ themselves and [showing] that we therefore do not need science and philosophy to know what we should do to be honest and good and even wise and virtuous. Indeed, we might well have understood before that the knowledge of what every man ought to do, and hence also [what he ought] to know is within the reach of every man, even the commonest. . . .

Innocence is indeed a glorious thing, only it is a pity that it cannot maintain itself well and is easily seduced. On this account even wisdom, which otherwise consists more in conduct than in knowledge, yet has need of science, not in order to learn from it, but to secure for its own precepts acceptance and permanence. In opposition to all the commands of duty that reason represents to man as so greatly deserving respect, man feels within himself a powerful counterpoise in his wants and inclinations, the entire satisfaction of which he sums up under the name of happiness. Reason issues its commands unyieldingly, without promising anything to the inclinations and with disregard and contempt, as it were, for these demands which are so impetuous and at the same time so plausible and which will not allow themselves to be suppressed by any command. Hence there arises a natural *dialectic*; that is, a disposition to argue against these strict laws of duty and to question their validity, or at least to question their purity and strictness. [There is also a disposition] to make them more accordant, if possible, with our wishes and inclinations; that is to say, to corrupt them at their very source and to destroy their value entirely, an act that even common practical reason cannot ultimately approve.

Thus the *common reason of man* is compelled to leave its proper sphere and to take a step into the field of a *practical philosophy*, but not for satisfying any desire to speculate, which never occurs to it as long as it is content to be mere sound reason. But the purpose is to secure on practical ground information and clear instruction respecting the source of the principle [of common sense] and the correct definition of this principle as contrasted with the maxims which are based on wants and inclinations, so that common sense may escape from the perplexity of opposing claims, and not run the risk of losing all genuine moral principles through the equivocation into which it easily falls. . . .

If hitherto we have drawn our concept of duty from the common use of our practical reason it is by no means to be inferred that we have treated it as an empirical concept. On the contrary, if we attend to the experience of men's conduct, we meet frequent and, as we admit ourselves, just complaints that there is not to be found a single certain example of the disposition to act from pure duty. Although many things are done *in conformity* to what duty prescribes, it is nevertheless always doubtful whether they are done strictly *out of duty* [which would have to be the case if they are to have a moral value]. Hence, in all ages there have been philosophers who have denied altogether that this disposition actually exists in human actions at all, and who have ascribed everything to a more or less refined self-love. Not that they have on that account questioned the soundness of the conception of morality; on the contrary they have spoken with sincere regret of the frailty and corruption of human nature, which though noble enough to take as its law an idea so worthy of respect, is yet too weak to follow it, and employs reason, which ought to give it the purpose of accommodating the inclinations, whether single, or, at best, in the greatest possible harmony with one another. In fact it is absolutely impossible to ascertain by experience with complete certainty a single case in which the maxim of an action, however right in itself, rested simply on moral grounds and on the conception of duty. Sometimes it happens that with the sharpest self examination, we can find nothing, beside the moral principle of duty, powerful enough to move us to this or that action and to such a great sacrifice; yet we cannot infer from this with certainty that it was not some really secret impulse of self-love, under the false appearance of that idea [of the moral principle of duty] that was the actual determining cause of the will. We then like to flatter ourselves by falsely taking credit for a more noble motive. In fact we can never, even by the strictest self-examination, penetrate completely [to the causes] behind the secret springs of action, since when we ask about moral worth, we are not concerned with actions but with their inward principles which we do not see. . . .

Moral concepts cannot be obtained by abstraction from any empirical and hence merely contingent knowledge. It is exactly this purity in origin that makes them worthy of serving our supreme practical principle [for right action] and, as we add anything empirical, we detract in proportion from their genuine influence and from the absolute value of actions. It is not only very necessary from a purely speculative point of view, but it is also of the greatest practical importance to derive those notions and laws from pure reason, to present them pure and unmixed, and even to determine the entire faculty of pure practical reason. In doing so we must not make the principles of pure practical reason dependent on the particular nature of human reason, though in speculative philosophy they may be permitted and even necessary at times. Since moral laws ought to hold true for every rational creature we must derive them from the general concept of a rational being. Although morality has need of anthropology for its application to man, yet in this way, as in the first step, we must treat morality independently as pure philosophy; that is, metaphysics, complete in itself. . . .

Everything in nature works according to laws. Rational beings alone have the faculty for acting according to *the concept* of laws; that is, according to principles. [In other words, rational beings alone] have a will. Since deriving actions from principles requires *reason*, the will is nothing more than practical reason. If reason infallibly determines the will, then the actions of such a being that are recognized as objectively necessary are also subjectively necessary. The will is a faculty for choosing *only that* which reason, independent of inclination, recognizes as practically necessary; that is, as good. But if reason does not sufficiently determine the will by itself, if the latter is also subject to the subjective conditioning of particular impulses which do not always coincide with the objective conditions; in a word, if the will *in itself* does not completely accord with reason, as is actually the case with men, then the actions which are objectively recognized as necessary are subjectively contingent. Determining such a will according to objective laws is compulsory. . . . This means that the relation of objective laws to a will not thoroughly good is conceived as the determination of the will of a rational being by principles of reason which the will, because of its nature, does not necessarily follow.

The concept of an objective principle, in so far as it is compulsory for a will, is called a command of reason and the formulation of such a command is called an IMPERATIVE. . . .

Consequently no imperative holds true for a Divine will, or in general for a *holy* will. *Ought* is out of place here because the act of willing is already necessarily in unison with the law. Therefore imperatives are only formulations for expressing the relation of the objective laws of all volition to the subjective imperfections of the will of this or that rational being; that is, the human will.

All *imperatives* command either *hypothetically* or *categorically*. . . . Since every practical law represents a possible action as good, and on this account as necessary for a subject who can determine practically by reason, all imperatives are formulations determining an action which is necessary according to the principle of a will in some respects good. If the action is good only as a means to *something else*, then the imperative is *hypothetical*. If the action is conceived as good *in itself* and consequently as necessarily being the principle of a will which of itself conforms to reason, then it is *categorical*. . . .

Whatever is possible through the ability of some rational being may also be considered as a possible purpose of some will. Therefore the principles of action concerning the means needed to attain some possible purpose are really infinitely numerous. All sciences have a practical aspect consisting of problems expressing that some end is possible for us, and of imperatives directing how it may be attained. Therefore, these may, in general, be called imperatives of *skill*. There is no question as to whether the end is rational and good, but only as to what one must do in order to attain it. The precepts for the physician to make his patient thoroughly healthy, and for a poisoner to ensure certain death, are equivalent in that each serves to effect its purpose perfectly. Since in early youth it cannot be known what purposes are likely to occur to us in the course of life, parents seek to have their children taught a *great many things* and provide for their *skill* in using means for all sorts of purposes. They cannot be sure whether any particular purpose may perhaps hereafter be an objective for their pupil; it is possible that he might aim at any of them. This anxiety is so great that parents commonly neglect to form and correct their judgment on the value of the things which may be chosen as ends.

However, there is *one* end which may actually be assumed to be an end for a rational beings, there is one purpose which they not only *may* have, but which we may assume with certainty that they all actually *do have* by natural necessity; that is *happiness.* . . . Now a man's skill in choosing the means to his own greatest well-being may be called *prudence* in the most specific sense. Thus the imperative which refers to the choice of means to one's own happiness, that is, the precept of prudence, is still hypothetical. This action is not commanded absolutely but only as a means to another purpose. Whereas, the categorical imperative directly commands a certain conduct without being conditioned by any other attainable purpose. . . . This imperative may be called the imperative of morality. . . .

. . . [U]nfortunately the notion of happiness is so indefinite that although every man wishes to attain it, he can never say definitely and consistently what it is that he really wishes and wills. The reason is that the elements belonging to the notion of happiness are altogether empirical; that is, they must be borrowed from experience. Nevertheless, the idea of happiness implies something absolute and whole; a maximum of well-being in my present and all future circumstances. Now, it is impossible for even the most clear-sighted and most powerful being, as long as it is supposedly finite, to frame for itself a definite concept of what it really wills [when it wants to be happy]. If he wills riches, how much anxiety, envy, and snares might not be drawn upon his shoulders thereby? If he wills knowledge and discernment, perhaps such knowledge might only prove to be so much sharper sight showing him much more fearfully the unavoidable evils now concealed from him, or suggesting more wants for his desires which already give him concern enough. . . . In short, a human being is unable with certainty to determine by any principle what would make him truly happy, because to do so he would have to be omniscient. Therefore, we cannot act on any definite principles to secure happiness, but only on counsels derived from experience; e.g., the frugality, courtesy, reserve, etc., which experience teaches us will promote well-being, for the most part. Hence it follows that the imperatives of prudence do not command at all, strictly speaking; that is, they cannot present actions objectively as practically *necessary*, so that they are to be regarded as *counsels (consilia)* or reason rather than precepts *(praecepta)*. The problem of determining certainly and generally which action would most promote the happiness of a rational being is completely insoluble. Consequently, no imperative respecting happiness is possible, for such a command should, in a strict sense, command men to do what makes them happy. Happiness is an ideal, not of reason, but of imagination resting solely on empirical grounds. . . .

On the other hand, the question of how the imperative of *morality* is possible is undoubtedly the only question demanding a solution as this imperative is not at all hypothetical, and the objective necessity it presents cannot rest on any hypothesis, as is the case with hypothetical imperatives. Only we must never leave out of consideration the fact that we *cannot* determine *by any example*, i.e., empirically, whether there is any such imperative at all. Rather it is to be feared that all those apparently categorical imperatives may actually be hypothetical. For instance, when you have a precept such as: thou shalt not promise deceitfully, and it is assumed that the [normative] necessity of this is not a mere counsel to avoid some other evil, it might mean: you shall not make a lying promise lest it become known and your credit would be destroyed. On the contrary, an action of this kind should be regarded as evil in itself so that the imperative of the prohibition is categorical. Yet we cannot show with certainty in any instance that the will is determined merely by the law without any other source of action, although this may appear to be so. It is always possible that fear of disgrace, also perhaps obscure dread of other dangers, may have a secret influence on the will. Who can prove by experience the nonexistence of a cause when all that experience tells is that we do not perceive it? In such a case the so-called moral imperative, which appears to be categorical and unconditional, would really only be a pragmatic precept, drawing our attention to our own interests, and merely teaching us to take these interests into consideration.

Therefore we shall have to investigate *a priori* the possibility of a *categorical imperative*, since, in this case, we do not have the advantage that the imperative's reality is given in experience, so that the elucidation of its possibility would be needed only for explaining it, not for establishing it. It can be discerned that the categorical imperative has the purport of a practical law. All the rest may certainly be called *principles* of the will but not laws, since whatever is merely necessary for attaining some casual purpose may be considered contingent in itself, and at any time we can be free from the precept if we give up the purpose. However, the unconditional command leaves the will no liberty to choose the opposite, and consequently only the will carries with it that necessity we require in law. . . .

When I conceive of a hypothetical imperative at all, I do not know previously what it will contain until I am given the condition. But when I conceive of a categorical imperative I know at once what it contains. In addition to the law, the imperative contains only the necessity that the maxim conform to this law. As the maxim contains no condition restricting the maxim, nothing remains but the general statement of the law to which the maxim of the action should conform, and it is only this conformity that the imperative properly represents as necessary.

Therefore there is only one categorical imperative, namely this: *Act only on a maxim by which you can will that it, at the same time, should become a general law.* . . .

17

from A Vindication of the Rights of Woman

Mary Wollstonecraft

(1759–1797)

*M*ary Wollstonecraft grew up without the security of a stable family or dependable finances, for her father was a heavy drinker whose abusive personality and imprudent spending left Mary and her sisters to support themselves. She tried the only respectable occupations available to women—taking in needlework, becoming a governess, and teaching—before settling on writing. The revolutionary climate drew her to the finest minds of the day. Her social and intellectual circles included the American patriot Thomas Paine, writer Dr. Samuel Johnson, and philosopher William Godwin, whom she later married when she became pregnant. Mary Wollstonecraft died just twelve days after giving birth to this daughter, also named Mary, who grew up to write the novel Frankenstein (1816). Mary married the famous poet Percy Bysshe Shelley. The scandals of the family's personal lives caused many readers to reject their romantic ideas of freedom and justice even though these ideas formed the backdrop of the Enlightenment and particularly the French Revolution.

Wollstonecraft's writings are decidedly political. She chose to write in the most masculine genre of the time—the political treatise—to argue that human happiness is a political concern. Her two great works of human rights both argue that moral virtue is the most important right of all and can flourish only where there is freedom of choice. Her book A Vindication of the Rights of Men *(1790) denounced the slave trade as an abuse of the property rights that conservatives wanted to protect. With* A Vindication of the Rights of Woman *in 1792, she extended the discussion of slavery to include the relations between men and women. Because she knew that her audience would not be easily convinced, she abandoned the more confrontational persuasive rhetorical mode in favor of what she called "episodical observations," anecdotes and thoughts that guide readers to identify the source of evil for themselves. Rich metaphors and learned allusions supply hidden structures to her argument. The excerpt below from* A Vindication of the Rights of Woman *is lifted from its larger context that argues that women's oppression is largely due*

to their deficient education. In an age that promised unprecedented human possi-
bility, her Enlightenment liberal feminism simply asks that the rights won by the
American and French Revolutions be extended to women as well.

Chapter IX

Of the Pernicious Effects Which Arise from the Unnatural Distinction Established in Society

From the respect paid to property flow, as from a poisoned fountain, most of the evils and vices which render this world such a dreary scene to the contemplative mind. For it is in the most polished society that noisome reptiles and venomous serpents lurk under the rank herbage; and there is voluptuousness pampered by the still sultry air, which relaxes every good disposition before it ripens into virtue.

One class presses on another; for all are aiming to procure respect on account of their property: and property, once gained, will procure the respect due only to talents and virtue. Men neglect the duties incumbent on man, yet are treated like demi-gods; religion is also separated from morality by a ceremonial veil, yet men wonder that the world is almost, literally speaking, a den of sharpers or oppressors.

There is a homely proverb, which speaks a shrewd truth, that whoever the devil finds idle he will employ. And what but habitual idleness can hereditary wealth and titles produce? For man is so constituted that he can only attain a proper use of his faculties by exercising them, and will not exercise them unless necessity, of some kind, first set the wheels in motion. Virtue likewise can only be acquired by the discharge of relative duties; but the importance of these sacred duties will scarcely be felt by the being who is cajoled out of his humanity by the flattery of sycophants.[1] There must be more equality established in society, or morality will never gain ground, and this virtuous equality will not rest firmly even when founded on a rock, if one half of mankind be chained to its bottom by fate, for they will be continually undermining it through ignorance or pride.

It is vain to expect virtue from women till they are, in some degree, independent of men; nay, it is vain to expect that strength of natural affection, which would make them good wives and mothers. Whilst they are absolutely dependent on their husbands they will be cunning, mean, and selfish, and the men who can be gratified by the fawning fondness of spaniel-like affection, have not much delicacy, for love is not to be bought, in any sense of the words, its silken wings are instantly shriveled up when any thing beside a return in kind is sought. Yet whilst wealth enervates men; and women live, as it were, by their personal charms, how can we expect them to discharge those ennobling duties which equally require exertion and self-denial. Hereditary property sophisti-cates[2] the mind, and the unfortunate victims to it, if I may so express myself, swathed from their birth, seldom exert the locomotive faculty of body or mind; and, thus viewing every thing through one medium, and that a false one, they are unable to discern in what true merit and happi-ness consist. False, indeed, must be the light when the drapery of situation hides the man, and makes him stalk in masquerade, dragging from one scene of dissipation to another the nerveless limbs that hang with stupid listlessness, and rolling round the vacant eye which plainly tells us that there is no mind at home.

I mean, therefore, to infer that the society is not properly organized which does not compel men and women to discharge their respective duties, by making it the only way to acquire that countenance from their fellow-creatures, which every human being wishes some way to attain. The respect, consequently, which is paid to wealth and mere personal charms, is a true north-east blast, that blights the tender blossoms of affection and virtue. Nature has wisely attached affections to duties, to sweeten toil, and to give that vigor to the exertions of reason which only the heart can give. But, the affection which is put on merely because it is the appropri-ated insignia of a certain character, when its duties are not fulfilled, is one of the empty compliments which vice and folly are obliged to pay to virtue and the real nature of things.

To illustrate my opinion, I need only observe, that when a woman is admired for her beauty, and suffers herself to be so far intoxicated by the admiration she receives, as to neglect to discharge the indispensable duty of a mother, she sins against herself by neglecting to cultivate an affection that would equally tend to make her useful and happy. True happiness, I mean all the contentment, and virtuous satisfaction, that can be snatched in this imperfect state, must arise from well regulated affections; and an affection includes a duty. Men are not aware of the misery they cause, and the vicious weakness they cherish, by only inciting women to render themselves pleasing; they do not consider that they thus make natural and artificial duties clash, by sacrificing the comfort and respectability of a woman's life to voluptuous notions of beauty, when in nature they all harmonize.

Cold would be the heart of a husband, were he not rendered unnatural by early debauchery, who did not feel more delight at seeing his child suckled by its mother, than the most artful wanton tricks could ever raise; yet this natural way of cementing the matrimonial tie, and twisting esteem with fonder recollections, wealth leads women to spurn. To preserve their beauty, and wear the flowery crown of the day, which gives them a kind of right to reign for a short time over the sex, they neglect to stamp impressions on their husbands' hearts, that would be remembered with more tenderness when the snow on the head began to chill the bosom, than even their virgin charms. The maternal solicitude of a reasonable affectionate woman is very interesting, and the chastened dignity with which a mother returns the caresses that she and her child receive from a father who has been fulfilling the serious duties of his station, is not only a respectable, but a beautiful sight. So singular, indeed, are my feelings, and I have endeavored not to catch factitious ones, that after having been fatigued with the sight of insipid grandeur and the slavish ceremonies that with cumbrous pomp supplied the place of domestic affections, I have turned to some other scene to relieve my eye, by resting it on the refreshing green every where scattered by nature. I have then viewed with pleasure a woman nursing her children, and discharging the duties of her station with, perhaps, merely a servant maid to take off her hands the servile part of the household business. I have seen her prepare herself and children, with only the luxury of cleanliness, to receive her husband, who returning weary home in the evening found smiling babes and a clean hearth. My heart has loitered in the midst of the group, and has even throbbed with sympathetic emotion, when the scraping of the well known foot has raised a pleasing tumult.

Whilst my benevolence has been gratified by contemplating this artless picture, I have thought that a couple of this description, equally necessary and independent of each other, because each fulfilled the respective duties of their station, possessed all that life could give.—Raised sufficiently above abject poverty not to be obliged to weigh the consequence of every farthing they spend, and having sufficient to prevent their attending to a frigid system of economy,[3] which narrows both heart and mind. I declare, so vulgar are my conceptions, that I know not what is wanted to render this the happiest as well as the most respectable situation in the world, but a taste for literature, to throw a little variety and interest into social converse, and some superfluous money to give to the needy and to buy books. For it is not pleasant when the heart is opened by compassion and the head active in arranging plans of usefulness, to have a prim urchin continually twitching back the elbow to prevent the hand from drawing out an almost empty purse, whispering at the same time some prudential maxim about the priority of justice.

Destructive, however, as riches and inherited honors are to the human character, women are more debased and cramped, if possible, by them, than men, because men may still, in some degree, unfold their faculties by becoming soldiers and statesmen.

As soldiers, I grant, they can now only gather, for the most part, vain glorious laurels, whilst they adjust to a hair the European balance, taking especial care that no bleak northern nook or sound incline the beam.[4] But the days of true heroism are over, when a citizen fought for his country like a Fabricius or a Washington, and then returned to his farm to let his virtuous fervor run in a more placid, but not a less salutary, stream. No, our British heroes are oftener sent from the gaming table than from the plow; and their passions have been rather inflamed by hanging with dumb suspense on the turn of a die, then sublimated by panting after the adventurous march of virtue in the historic page.

The statesman, it is true, might with more propriety quit the Faro Bank, or card-table, to guide the helm, for he has still but to shuffle and trick.[5] The whole system of British politics, if system it may courteously be called, consisting in multiplying dependents and contriving taxes which grind the poor to pamper the rich; thus a war, or any wild goose chase, is, as the vulgar use the phrase, a lucky turn-up of patronage for the minister, whose chief merit is the art of keeping himself in place.

It is not necessary then that he should have bowels for[6] the poor, so he can secure for his family the odd trick. Or should some shew of respect, for what is termed with ignorant ostentation an Englishman's birth-right, be expedient to bubble the gruff mastiff[7] that he has to lead by the nose, he can make an empty shew, very safely, by giving his single voice, and suffering his light squadron to file off to the other side. And when a question of humanity is agitated he may dip a sop in the milk of human kindness, to silence Cerberus,[8] and talk of the interest which his heart takes in an attempt to make the earth no longer cry for vengeance as it sucks in its children's blood, though his cold hand may at the very moment rivet their chains, by sanctioning the abominable traffic. A minister is no longer a minister than while he can carry a point, which he is determined to carry.—Yet it is not necessary that a minister should feel like a man, when a bold push might shake his seat.

But, to have done with these episodical observations, let me return to the more specious[9] slavery which chains the very soul of woman, keeping her for ever under the bondage of ignorance.

The preposterous distinctions of rank, which render civilization a curse, by dividing the world between voluptuous tyrants, and cunning envious dependents, corrupt, almost equally, every class of people, because respectability is not attached to the discharge of the relative duties of life, but to the station, and when the duties are not fulfilled the affections cannot gain sufficient strength to fortify the virtue of which they are the natural reward. Still there are some loop-holes out of which a man may creep, and dare to think and act for himself; but for a woman it is an Herculean task, because she has difficulties peculiar to her sex to overcome, which require almost superhuman powers.

A truly benevolent legislator always endeavors to make it the interest of each individual to be virtuous; and thus private virtue becoming the cement of public happiness, an orderly whole is consolidated by the tendency of all the parts towards a common centre. But, the private or public virtue of woman is very problematical; for Rousseau, and a numerous list of male writers, insist that she should all her life be subjected to a severe restraint, that of propriety. Why subject her to propriety—blind propriety, if she be capable of acting from a nobler spring, if she be an heir of immortality? Is sugar always to be produced by vital blood? Is one half of the human species, like the poor African slaves, to be subject to prejudices that brutalize them, when principles would be a surer guard, only to sweeten the cup of man? Is not this indirectly to deny woman reason? for a gift is a mockery, if it be unfit for use.

Women are, in common with men, rendered weak and luxurious by the relaxing pleasures which wealth procures; but added to this they are made slaves to their persons, and must render them alluring, that man may lend them his reason to guide their tottering steps aright. Or should they be ambitious, they must govern their tyrants by sinister tricks, for without rights there cannot be any incumbent duties. The laws respecting woman, which I mean to discuss in a future part, make an absurd unit of a man and his wife;[10] and then, by the easy transition of only considering him as responsible, she is reduced to a mere cipher.

The being who discharges the duties of its station is independent; and, speaking of women at large, their first duty is to themselves as rational creatures, and the next, in point of importance, as citizens, is that, which includes so many, of a mother. The rank in life which dispenses with their fulfilling this duty, necessarily degrades them by making them mere dolls. Or, should they turn to something more important than merely fitting drapery upon a smooth block, their minds are only occupied by some soft platonic attachment; or, the actual management of an intrigue may keep their thoughts in motion; for when they neglect domestic duties, they have it not in their power to take the field and march and counter-march like soldiers, or wrangle in the senate to keep their faculties from rusting.

I know that, as a proof of the inferiority of the sex, Rousseau[11] has exultingly exclaimed, How can they leave the nursery for the camp!—And the camp has by some moralists been termed the school of the most heroic virtues; though, I think, it would puzzle a keen casuist to prove the reasonableness of the greater number of wars that have dubbed heroes. I do not mean to consider this question critically; because, having frequently viewed these freaks of ambition as the first natural mode of civilization, when the ground must be torn up, and the woods cleared by fire and sword, I do not choose to call them pests; but surely the present system of war has little connection with virtue of any denomination, being rather the school of *finesse* and effeminacy, than of fortitude.

Yet, if defensive war, the only justifiable war, in the present advanced state of society, where virtue can shew its face and ripen amidst the rigors which purify the air on the mountain's top, were alone to be adopted as just and glorious, the true heroism of antiquity might again animate female bosoms.—But fair and softly, gentle reader, male or female, do not alarm thyself, for though I have compared the character of a modern soldier with that of a civilized woman, I am not going to advise them to turn their distaff[12] into a musket, though I sincerely wish to see the bayonet converted into a pruning-hook. I only recreated an imagination, fatigued by contemplating the vices and follies which all proceed from a feculent stream of wealth that has muddied the pure rills of natural affection, by supposing that society will some time or other be so constituted, that man must necessarily fulfil the duties of a citizen, or be despised, and that while he was employed in any of the departments of civil life, his wife, also an active citizen, should be equally intent to manage her family, educate her children, and assist her neighbors.

But, to render her really virtuous and useful, she must not, if she discharge her civil duties, want, individually, the protection of civil laws; she must not be dependent on her husband's bounty for her subsistence during his life, or support after his death—for how can a being be generous who has nothing of its own? or, virtuous, who is not free? The wife, in the present state of things, who is faithful to her husband, and neither suckles nor educates[13] her children, scarcely deserves the name of a wife, and has no right to that of a citizen. But take away natural rights, and duties become null.

Women then must be considered as only the wanton solace of men, when they become so weak in mind and body, that they cannot exert themselves, unless to pursue some frothy pleasure, or to invent some frivolous fashion. What can be a more melancholy sight to a thinking mind, than to look into the numerous carriages that drive helter-skelter about this metropolis in a morning full of pale-faced creatures who are flying from themselves. I have often wished, with Dr. Johnson,[14] to place some of them in a little shop with half a dozen children looking up to their languid countenances for support. I am much mistaken, if some latent vigor would not soon give health and spirit to their eyes, and some lines drawn by the exercise of reason on the blank cheeks, which before were only undulated by dimples, might restore lost dignity to the character, or rather enable it to attain the true dignity of its nature. Virtue is not to be acquired even by speculation, much less by the negative supineness that wealth naturally generates.

Besides, when poverty is more disgraceful than even vice, is not morality cut to the quick? Still to avoid misconstruction, though I consider that women in the common walks of life are called to fulfil the duties of wives and mothers, by religion and reason, I cannot help lamenting that women of a superior cast have not a road open by which they can pursue more extensive plans of usefulness and independence. I may excite laughter, by dropping an hint, which I mean to pursue, some future time, for I really think that women ought to have representatives, instead of being arbitrarily governed without having any direct share allowed them in the deliberations of government.

But, as the whole system of representation is now, in this country, only a convenient handle for despotism, they need not complain, for they are as well represented as a numerous class of hard working mechanics, who pay for the support of royalty when they can scarcely stop their children's mouths with bread. How are they represented, whose very sweat supports the splendid stud of an heir apparent, or varnishes the chariot of some female favorite who looks down on shame? Taxes on the very necessaries of life, enable an endless tribe of idle princes and princesses to pass with stupid pomp before a gaping crowd, who almost worship the very parade which costs them so dear. This is mere gothic grandeur, something like the barbarous, useless parade of having sentinels[15] on horseback at Whitehall, which I could never view without a mixture of contempt and indignation.

How strangely must the mind be sophisticated when this sort of state impresses it! But, till these monuments of folly are leveled by virtue, similar follies will leaven the whole mass. For the same character, in some degree, will prevail in the aggregate of society: and the refinements of luxury, or the vicious repinings of envious poverty, will equally banish virtue from society, considered as the characteristic of that society, or only allow it to appear as one of the stripes of the harlequin coat, worn by the civilized man.

In the superior ranks of life, every duty is done by deputies, as if duties could ever be waved, and the vain pleasures which consequent idleness forces the rich to pursue, appear so enticing to the next rank, that the numerous scramblers for wealth sacrifice every thing to tread on their heels. The most sacred trusts are then considered as sinecures, because they were procured by interest, and only sought to enable a man to keep *good company*. Women, in particular, all want to be ladies. Which is simply to have nothing to do, but listlessly to go they scarcely care where, for they cannot tell what.

But what have women to do in society? I may be asked, but to loiter with easy grace; surely you would not condemn them all to suckle fools and chronicle small beer![16] No. Women might certainly study the art of healing, and be physicians as well as nurses. And midwifery, decency seems to allot to them, though I am afraid the word midwife, in our dictionaries, will soon give place to *accoucheur*,[17] and one proof of the former delicacy of the sex be effaced from the language.

They might, also, study politics, and settle their benevolence on the broadest basis; for the reading of history will scarcely be more useful than the perusal of romances, if read as mere biography; if the character of the times, the political improvements, arts, &c. be not observed. In short, if it be not considered as the history of man; and not of particular men, who filled a niche in the temple of fame, and dropped into the black rolling stream of time, that silently sweeps all before it, into the shapeless void called eternity.—For shape, can it be called, "that shape hath none?"[18]

Business of various kinds, they might likewise pursue, if they were educated in a more orderly manner, which might save many from common and legal prostitution. Women would not then marry for a support, as men accept of places under government, and neglect the implied duties; nor would an attempt to earn their own subsistence, a most laudable one! sink them almost to the level of those poor abandoned creatures who live by prostitution. For are not milliners and mantua-makers[19] reckoned the next class? The few employments open to women, so far from being liberal, are menial; and when a superior education enables them to take charge of the education of children as governesses, they are not treated like the tutors of sons, though even clerical tutors are not always treated in a manner calculated to render them respectable in the eyes of their pupils, to say nothing of the private comfort of the individual. But as women educated like gentlewomen, are never designed for the humiliating situation which necessity sometimes forces them to fill; these situations are considered in the light of a degradation; and they know little of the human heart, who need to be told, that nothing so painfully sharpens sensibility as such a fall in life.

Some of these women might be restrained from marrying by a proper spirit or delicacy, and others may not have had it in their power to escape in this pitiful way from servitude; is not that government then very defective, and very unmindful of the happiness of one half of its members, that does not provide for honest, independent women, by encouraging them to fill respectable stations? But in order to render their private virtue a public benefit, they must have a civil existence in the state, married or single; else we shall continually see some worthy woman, whose sensibility has been rendered painfully acute by undeserved contempt, droop like "the lily broken down by a plowshare."

It is a melancholy truth; yet such is the blessed effect of civilization! the most respectable women are the most oppressed; and, unless they have understandings far superior to the common run of understandings, taking in both sexes, they must, from being treated like contemptible beings, become contemptible. How many women thus waste life away, the prey of discontent, who might have practiced as physicians, regulated a farm, managed a shop, and stood erect, supported by their own industry, instead of hanging their heads surcharged with the dew of sensibility, that consumes the beauty to which it at first gave lustre; nay, I doubt whether pity and love are so near akin as poets feign, for I have seldom seen much compassion excited by the helplessness of females, unless they were fair; then, perhaps, pity was the soft handmaid of love, or the harbinger of lust.

How much more respectable is the woman who earns her own bread by fulfilling any duty, than the most accomplished beauty!—beauty did I say?—so sensible am I of the beauty of moral loveliness, or the harmonious propriety that attunes the passions of a well-regulated mind, that I blush at making the comparison; yet I sigh to think how few women aim at attaining this respectability by withdrawing from the giddy whirl of pleasure, or the indolent calm that stupefies the good sort of women it sucks in.

Proud of their weakness, however, they must always be protected, guarded from care, and all the rough toils that dignify the mind.—If this be the fiat of fate, if they will make themselves insignificant and contemptible, sweetly to waste "life away," let them not expect to be valued when their beauty fades, for it is the fate of the fairest flowers to be admired and pulled to pieces by the careless hand that plucked them. In how many ways do I wish, from the purest benevolence, to impress this truth on my sex; yet I fear that they will not listen to a truth, that dear-bought experience has brought home to many an agitated bosom, nor willingly resign the privileges of rank and sex for the privileges of humanity, to which those have no claim who do not discharge its duties.

Those writers are particularly useful, in my opinion, who make man feel for man, independent of the station he fills, or the drapery of factitious sentiments. I then would fain convince reasonable men of the importance of some of my remarks, and prevail on them to weigh dispassionately the whole tenor of my observations.—I appeal to their understandings, and, as a fellow-creature, claim, in the name of my sex, some interest in their hearts. I entreat them to assist to emancipate their companion, to make her a *help meet* for them!

Would men but generously snap our chains, and be content with rational fellowship instead of slavish obedience, they would find us more observant daughters, more affectionate sisters, more faithful wives, more reasonable mothers—in a word, better citizens. We should then love them with true affection, because we should learn to respect ourselves; and the peace of mind of a worthy man would not be interrupted by the idle vanity of his wife, nor the babes sent to nestle in a strange bosom, having never found a home in their mother's.

Notes

1 False flatterers.

2 Ruins or corrupts.

3 Associated with common people.

4 "incline the beam": the scale that representations of blind justice hold up. Wollstonecraft's metaphor for balance suggests that soldiers now fight to prevent the slightest changes in power, not in heroic wars with heroic consequences.

5 "shuffle and trick": puns on card gambling and devious politics.

6 Feelings for.

7 To fool even the guard dog.

8 The guard dog of Hades, the Greek hell or underworld.

9 Seemingly attractive but deceptive.

10 Under English law man and wife were legally one; the man spoke for both.

11 French philosopher Jean Jacques Rousseau's (1712–1778) fictional Emile argues against female equality by complaining that women cannot leave a nursery to go to war.

12 An instrument used in spinning to wind wool; a job fit only for women.

13 These duties are hired out to the wetnurse and governess, respectively.

14 Dr. Samuel Johnson (1709–1784), one of the most respected authors in 18th-century England and compiler of the first widely-used English dictionary. His *Rambler* essays discussed many of the same issues that concerned Wollstonecraft.

15 The expensive showmanship that continues today as the Changing of the Guard at Buckingham Palace.

16 Allusion to Shakespeare's *Othello* (II.i.158); the phrase means to keep household accounts.

17 Male version of the female midwife.

18 Allusion to death, from Milton's *Paradise Lost* (II.667).

19 Dressmakers, usually women (as tailors were usually men).

18

from Remember the Ladies

Abigail Adams (1744–1818)

John Adams (1735–1826)

The American Revolution was one of three watershed events in the late 18th century. A rather limited colonial protest against taxation in the 1760s became transformed into a call for independence, and then a full-scale re-evaluation of social relationships. This remarkable shift, combined with the French Revolution and the Industrial Revolution, challenged virtually every facet of life in the trans-Atlantic community and, ultimately, the world.

Yet this revolutionary potential was not fully apparent at the time; indeed it is still being debated. Those who supported the American Revolution usually had limited goals and an essentially conservative vision. A few, however, could see beyond the immediate crisis and perceive the logical implications of liberal ideology. One such person was Abigail Adams, the talented, witty, and often acerbic wife of John Adams. Her correspondence with her husband is an engaging blend of intellectual challenge and tender affection. The letters below (including one written on the eve of independence to James Sullivan) suggest the explosive volatility of revolutionary rhetoric.

Abigail Adams to John Adams
Braintree March 31, 1776

. . . I long to hear that you have declared an independancy—and by the way in the new Code of Laws which I suppose it will be necessary for you to make I desire you would Remember the Ladies, and be more generous and favourable to them than your ancestors. Do not put such unlimited power into the hands of the Husbands. Remember all Men would be tyrants if they could. If perticular care and attention is not paid to the Laidies we are determined to foment a Rebelion, and will not hold ourselves bound by any Laws in which we have no voice, or Representation.

That your Sex are Naturally Tyrannical is a Truth so thoroughly established as to admit of no dispute, but such of you as wish to be happy willingly give up the harsh title of Master for the more tender and endearing one of Friend. Why then, not put it out of the power of the vicious and the Lawless to use us with cruelty and indignity with impunity. Men of Sense in all Ages abhor those customs which treat us only as the vassals of your Sex. Regard us then as Beings placed by providence under your protection and in imitation of the Supreme Being make use of that power only for our happiness. . . .

John Adams to Abigail Adams
Ap. 14, 1776

. . . As to your extraordinary Code of Laws, I cannot but laugh. We have been told that our Struggle has loosened the bands of Government every where. That Children and Apprentices were disobedient—that schools and Colleges were grown turbulent—that Indians slighted their Guardians and Negroes grew insolent to their Masters. But your Letter was the first Intimation that another Tribe more numerous and powerfull than all the rest were grown discontented.—This is rather too coarse a Compliment but you are so saucy, I wont blot it out.

Depend upon it, We know better than to repeal our Masculine systems. Altho they are in full Force, you know they are little more than Theory. We dare not exert our Power in its full Latitude. We are obliged to go fair, and softly, and in Practice you know We are the subjects. We have only the Name of Masters, and rather than give up this, which would completely subject Us to the Despotism of the Peticoat, I hope General Washington, and all our brave Heroes would fight. . . . I begin to think the Ministry as deep as they are wicked. After stirring up Tories, Landjobbers, Trimmers, Bigots, Canadians, Indians, Negroes, Hanoverians, Hessians, Russians, Irish Roman Catholicks, Scotch Renegadoes, at last they have stimulated the Ladies to demand new Priviledges and threaten to rebell. . . .

Abigail Adams to John Adams
B[raintre]e May 7, 1776

. . . I can not say that I think you very generous to the Ladies, for whilst you are proclaiming peace and good will to Men, Emancipating all Nations, you insist upon retaining an absolute power over Wives. But you must remember that Arbitrary power is like most other things which are very hard, very liable to be broken—and notwithstanding all your wise Laws and Maxims we have it in our power not only to free ourselves but to subdue our Masters, and without violence throw both your natural and legal authority at our feet—

> Charm by accepting, by submitting sway
> Yet have our Humour most when we obey.

I thank you for several Letters which I have received since I wrote Last. They alleviate a tedious absence, and I long earnestly for a Saturday Evening, and experience a similar pleasure to that which I used to find in the return of my Friend upon that day after a weeks absence. The Idea of a year dissolves all my Phylosophy. . . .

Johnny and Charls have the Mumps, a bad disorder, but they are not very bad. Pray be kind enough to remember me at all times and write as often as you possibly can.

John Adams to James Sullivan
Philadelphia May 26, 1776

Dear Sir

. . . Our worthy Friend, Mr. Gerry has put into my Hand, a Letter from you, of the Sixth of May, in which you consider the Principles of Representation and Legislation, and give us Hints of Some Alterations, which you Seem to think necessary, in the Qualification of Voters. . . .

It is certain in Theory, that the only moral Foundation of Government is the Consent of the People. But to what an Extent Shall We carry this Principle? Shall We Say, that every Individual of the Community, old and young, male and female, as well as rich and poor, must consent, expressly to every Act of Legislation? No, you will Say. This is impossible. How then does the Right arise in the Majority to govern the Minority, against their Will? Whence arises the Right of the Men to govern Women, without their Consent? Whence the Right of the old to bind the Young, without theirs.

But let us first Suppose, that the whole Community of every Age, Rank, Sex, and Condition, has a Right to vote. This Community, is assembled— a Motion is made and carried by a Majority of one Voice. The Minority will not agree to this. Whence arises the Right of the Majority to govern, and the Obligation of the Minority to obey? from Necessity, you will Say, because there can be no other Rule. But why exclude Women? You will

Say, because their Delicacy renders them unfit for Practice and Experience, in the great Business of Life, and the hardy Enterprizes of War, as well as the arduous Cares of State. Besides, their attention is So much engaged with the necessary Nurture of their Children, that Nature has made them fittest for domestic Cares. And Children have not judgment or Will of their own. True. But will not these Reasons apply to others? Is it not equally true, that Men in general in every Society, who are wholly destitute of Property, are also too little acquainted with public Affairs to form a Right Judgment, and too dependent upon other Men to have a Will of their own? If this is a Fact, if you give to every Man, who has no Property, a Vote, will you not make a fine encouraging Provision for Corruption by your fundamental Law? Such is the Frailty of the human Heart, that very few Men, who have no Property, have any judgment of their own. They talk and vote as they are directed by Some Man of Property, who has attached their Minds to his Interest. . . .

Harrington has Shewn that Power always follows Property. This I believe to be as infallible a Maxim, in Politicks, as, that Action and Re-action are equal, is in Mechanicks. Nay I believe We may advance one Step farther and affirm that the Ballance of Power in a Society, accompanies the Ballance of Property in Land. The only possible Way then of preserving the Ballance of Power on the side of equal Liberty and public Virtue, is to make the Acquisition of Land easy to every Member of Society: to make a Division of the Land into Small Quantities, So that the Multitude may be possessed of landed Estates. If the Multitude is possessed of the Ballance of real Estate, the Multitude will have the Ballance of Power, and in that Case the Multitude will take Care of the Liberty, Virtue, and Interest of the Multitude in all Acts of Government. . . .

The Same Reasoning, which will induce you to admit all Men, who have no Property, to vote, with those who have, for those Laws, which affect the Person will prove that you ought to admit Women and Children: for generally Speaking, Women and Children, have as good Judgment, and as independent Minds as those Men who are wholly destitute of Property: these last being to all Intents and Purposes as much dependent upon others, who will please to feed, cloath, and employ them, as Women are upon their Husbands, or Children on their Parents.

As to your Idea, of proportioning the Votes of Men in Money Matters, to the Property they hold, it is utterly impracticable. There is no possible Way of Ascertaining, at any one Time, how much every Man in a Community, is worth; and if there is, So fluctuating is Trade and Property, that this State of it, would change in half an Hour. The Property of the whole Community, is Shifting every Hour, and no Record can be kept of the Changes.

Society can be governed only by general Rules. Government cannot accommodate itself to every particular Case, as it happens, nor to the Circumstances of particular Persons. It must establish general, comprehensive Regulations for Cases and Persons. The only Question is, which general Rule, will accommodate most Cases and most Persons.

Depend upon it, sir, it is dangerous to open So fruitfull a Source of Controversy and Altercation, as would be opened by attempting to alter the Qualifications of Voters. There will be no End of it. New Claims will arise. Women will demand a Vote. Lads from 12 to 21 will think their Rights not enough attended to, and every Man, who has not a Farthing, will demand an equal Voice with any other in all Acts of State. It tends to confound and destroy all Distinctions, and prostrate all Ranks, to one common Levell.

19

Declaration of Sentiments; Seneca Falls Convention, 1848

Elizabeth Cady Stanton

The seeds of the first American women's rights convention occurred not in America but in London in 1840, when the World Anti-Slavery Convention refused to seat two American women as delegates simply because of their gender. Elizabeth Cady Stanton (1815–1902) had received the best formal education available to American women, graduating from the Troy Female Seminary at age seventeen, and had taught herself law in the offices of her father (a U.S. Congressman and later a New York Supreme Court judge) and her husband, a dedicated abolitionist. Lucretia Mott (1793–1880) had attended public school in Boston for two years and a Friends' boarding school for two more before being hired as a teacher at half the salary of the male teachers. Her interest in women's rights and her role as minister in the Society of Friends caused her to travel around the country lecturing on issues of social reform. In 1833 Mott attended the founding convention of the American Anti-Slavery Society and became president of the Philadelphia Female Anti-Slavery Society. Although a mob attacked her home after the burning of Pennsylvania Hall, Philadelphia, where the convention had been meeting in 1838, it was the rebuff of herself, Stanton, and other women from the World's convention in London that radicalized her to move from abolition to women's rights as a primary cause, although the two issues remained linked. In 1848 the two women called a convention "to discuss the social, civil, and religious rights of women" at Seneca Falls, New York, the home of Stanton. Here Stanton read the Declaration of Sentiments, a document of grievances and demands patterned on the Declaration of Independence. The convention passed twelve resolutions; all were unanimous except the ninth—the most radical of all—which called for the right to vote and passed only narrowly. The older Mott had guessed correctly that the sheer radicalism of this demand might make the entire work of the convention seem ridiculous, and in fact many withdrew their support from women's rights over this issue.

When, in the course of human events, it becomes necessary for one portion of the family of man to assume among the people of the earth a position different from that which they have hitherto occupied, but one to which the laws of nature and of nature's God entitle them, a decent respect to the opinions of mankind requires that they should declare the causes that impel them to such a course.

We hold these truths to be self-evident: that all men and women are created equal; that they are endowed by their Creator with certain inalienable rights; that among these are life, liberty, and the pursuit of happiness; that to secure these rights governments are instituted, deriving their just powers from the consent of the governed. Whenever any form of government becomes destructive of these ends, it is the right of those who suffer from it to refuse allegiance to it, and to insist upon the institution of a new government, laying its foundation on such principles, and organizing its powers in such form, as to them shall seem most likely to effect their safety and happiness. Prudence, indeed, will dictate that governments long established should not be changed for light and transient causes; and accordingly all experience hath shown that mankind are more disposed to suffer, while evils are sufferable, than to right themselves by abolishing the forms to which they were accustomed. But when a long train of abuses and usurpations, pursuing invariably the same object, evinces a design to reduce them under absolute despotism, it is their duty to throw off such government, and to provide new guards for their future security. Such has been the patient sufferance of the women under this government, and such is now the necessity which constrains them to demand the equal situation to which they are entitled.

The history of mankind is a history of repeated injuries and usurpations on the part of man toward woman, having in direct object the establishment of an absolute tyranny over her. To prove this, let facts be submitted to a candid world.

He has never permitted her to exercise her inalienable right to the elective franchise.

He has compelled her to submit to laws, in the formation of which she had no voice.

He has withheld from her rights which are given to the most ignorant and degraded men—both natives and foreigners.

Having deprived her of this first right of a citizen, the elective franchise, thereby leaving her without representation in the halls of legislation, he has oppressed her on all sides.

He has made her, if married, in the eye of the law, civilly dead.

He has taken from her all right in property, even to the wages she earns.

He has made her, morally, an irresponsible being, as she can commit many crimes with impunity, provided they be done in the presence of her husband. In the covenant of marriage, she is compelled to promise obedience to her husband, he becoming, to all intents and purposes, her master—the law giving him power to deprive her of her liberty, and to administer chastisement.

He has so framed the laws of divorce, as to what shall be the proper causes, and in case of separation, to whom the guardianship of the children shall be given, as to be wholly regardless of the happiness of women—the law, in all cases, going upon a false supposition of the supremacy of man, and giving all power into his hands.

After depriving her of all rights as a married woman, if single, and the owner of property, he has taxed her to support a government which recognizes her only when her property can be made profitable to it.

He has monopolized nearly all the profitable employments, and from those she is permitted to follow, she receives but a scanty remuneration. He closes against her all the avenues to wealth and distinction which he considers most honorable to himself. As a teacher of theology, medicine, or law, she is not known.

He has denied her the facilities for obtaining a thorough education, all colleges being closed against her.

He allows her in Church, as well as State, but a subordinate position, claiming Apostolic authority for her exclusion from the ministry, and, with some exceptions, from any public participation in the affairs of the Church.

He has created a false public sentiment by giving to the world a different code of morals for men and women, by which moral delinquencies which exclude women from society, are not only tolerated, but deemed of little account in man.

He has usurped the prerogative of Jehovah himself, claiming it as his right to assign for her a sphere of action, when that belongs to her conscience and to her God.

He has endeavored, in every way that he could, to destroy her confidence in her own powers, to lessen her self-respect, and to make her willing to lead a dependent and abject life.

Now, in view of this entire disfranchisement of one-half the people of this country, their social and religious degradation—in view of the unjust laws above mentioned, and because women do feel themselves aggrieved, oppressed, and fraudulently deprived of their most sacred rights, we insist that they have immediate admission to all the rights and privileges which belong to them as citizens of the United States.

In entering upon the great work before us, we anticipate no small amount of misconception, misrepresentation, and ridicule; but we shall use every instrumentality within our power to effect our object. We shall employ agents, circulate tracts, petition the State and National legislatures, and endeavor to enlist the pulpit and the press in our behalf. We hope this Convention will be followed by a series of Conventions embracing every part of the country.

20

Romantic Poetry

William Wordsworth

(1770–1850)

*A*lthough William Wordsworth graduated from St. John's College, Cambridge, his travels and memories of childhood losses influenced the themes of his writings more than did his studies. A summer walking tour of France in 1790, a year after the fall of the Bastille, drew him into the revolutionary spirit until the increasing violence and a liaison with an aristocratic Catholic girl caused a crisis of loyalties. With England's declaration of war against France, Wordsworth began to look not to politics but to nature for spiritual regeneration. With poet Samuel Taylor Coleridge he collaborated on the poems that became Lyrical Ballads, *published anonymously in 1798. Readers and reviewers sensed a new style and spirit in these poems that appeared deceptively simple at first reading. In 1800 Wordsworth published a second edition under his own name and added a new Preface that defended his poetic principles and introduced readers to an art which treats experiences beyond the grasp of the rational mind. In Wordsworth we see the beginnings of what later would be called Romanticism, a movement that valued human subjectivity in the face of cold, scientific Enlightenment rationalism. For the Victorians, however, Wordsworth was simply the poet of nature, childhood, memory, and consolation, whose popularity made the Lake District a tourist spot. A return visit to the Wye valley with his sister Dorothy on July 13, 1798 (significantly the eve of Bastille Day) prompted the meditation on the ruined Abbey which became a poem not about Tintern Abbey at all but about the poet's own inner thoughts. This poem, almost an ode, concludes the 1798* Lyrical Ballads.

LINES WRITTEN A FEW MILES ABOVE TINTERN ABBEY
On Revisiting the Banks of the Wye during a Tour, July 13, 1798

Five years have passed; five summers, with the length
Of five long winters! and again I hear
These waters, rolling from their mountain-springs
With a sweet inland murmur.—Once again

5   Do I behold these steep and lofty cliffs,
Which on a wild secluded scene impress
Thoughts of more deep seclusion; and connect
The landscape with the quiet of the sky.
The day is come when I again repose
10   Here, under this dark sycamore, and view
These plots of cottage-ground, these orchard-tufts,
Which, at this season, with their unripe fruits,
Among the woods and copses lose themselves,
Nor, with their green and simple hue, disturb
15   The wild green landscape. Once again I see
These hedge-rows, hardly hedge-rows, little lines
Of sportive wood run wild; these pastoral farms
Green to the very door; and wreathes of smoke
Sent up, in silence, from among the trees,
20   With some uncertain notice, as might seem,
Of vagrant dwellers in the houseless woods,
Or of some hermit's cave, where by his fire
The hermit sits alone.
                  Though absent long,
These forms of beauty have not been to me,
25   As is a landscape to a blind man's eye:
But oft, in lonely rooms, and mid the din
Of towns and cities, I have owed to them,
In hours of weariness, sensations sweet,
Felt in the blood, and felt along the heart,
30   And passing even into my purer mind
With tranquil restoration:—feelings too
Of unremembered pleasure; such, perhaps,
As may have had no trivial influence
On that best portion of a good man's life;
35   His little, nameless, unremembered acts

Of kindness and of love. Nor less, I trust,
To them I may have owed another gift,
Of aspect more sublime; that blessed mood,
In which the burthen of the mystery,
40   In which the heavy and the weary weight
Of all this unintelligible world
Is lighten'd:—that serene and blessed mood,

In which the affections gently lead us on,
Until, the breath of this corporeal frame,
45   And even the motion of our human blood
Almost suspended, we are laid asleep
In body, and become a living soul:
While with an eye made quiet by the power
Of harmony, and the deep power of joy,
50   We see into the life of things.
                                  If this
Be but a vain belief, yet, oh! how oft,
In darkness, and amid the many shapes
Of joyless day-light; when the fretful stir
Unprofitable, and the fever of the world,
55   Have hung upon the beatings of my heart,
How oft, in spirit, have I turned to thee
O sylvan Wye! Thou wanderer through the wood
How often has my spirit turned to thee!

And now, with gleams of half-extinguish'd thought.
60   With many recognitions dim and faint,
And somewhat of a sad perplexity,
The picture of the mind revives again:
While here I stand, not only with the sense
Of present pleasure, but with pleasing thoughts
65   That in this moment there is life and food
For future years. And so I dare to hope
Though changed, no doubt, from what I was, when first
I came among these hills; when like a roe
I bounded o'er the mountains, by the sides
70   Of the deep rivers, and the lonely streams,
Wherever nature led; more like a man
Flying from something that he dreads, than one
Who sought the thing he loved. For nature then
(The coarser pleasures of my boyish days,
75   And their glad animal movements all gone by,)
To me was all in all.—I cannot paint
What then I was. The sounding cataract
Haunted me like a passion: the tall rock,
The mountain, and the deep and gloomy wood,

80 Their colours and their forms, were then to me
    An appetite: a feeling and a love,
    That had no need of a remoter charm,
    By thought supplied, or any interest
    Unborrowed from the eye.—That time is past,
85 And all its aching joys are now no more,
    And all its dizzy raptures. Not for this
    Faint I, nor mourn nor murmur; other gifts
    Have followed, for such loss, I would believe,
    Abundant recompence. For I have learned
90 To look on nature, not as in the hour
    Of thoughtless youth, but hearing oftentimes
    The still, sad music of humanity,
    Not harsh nor grating, though of ample power
    To chasten and subdue. And I have felt
95 A presence that disturbs me with the joy
    Of elevated thoughts; a sense sublime
    Of something far more deeply interfused,
    Whose dwelling is the light of setting suns,
    And the round ocean, and the living air,
100 And the blue sky, and in the mind of man,
    A motion and a spirit, that impels
    All thinking things, all objects of all thought,
    And rolls through all things. Therefore am I still
    A lover of the meadows and the woods,
105 And mountains; and of all that we behold
    From this green earth; of all the mighty world
    Of eye and ear, both what they half-create,
    And what perceive; well pleased to recognize
    In nature and the language of the sense,
110 The anchor of my purest thoughts, the nurse,
    The guide, the guardian of my heart, and soul
    Of all my moral being.

                              Nor, perchance,
    If I were not thus taught, should I the more
    Suffer my genial spirits to decay:
115 For thou art with me, here, upon the banks
    Of this fair river; thou, my dearest Friend,
    My dear, dear Friend, and in thy voice I catch

The language of my former heart, and read
My former pleasures in the shooting lights
120 Of thy wild eyes. Oh! yet a little while
May I behold in thee what I was once,
My dear, dear Sister! And this prayer I make,
Knowing that Nature never did betray
The heart that loved her; 'tis her privilege,
125 Through all the years of this our life, to lead
From joy to joy: for she can so inform
The mind that is within us, so impress
With quietness and beauty, and so feed
With lofty thoughts, that neither evil tongues,
130 Rash judgments, nor the sneers of selfish men,
Nor greetings where no kindness is, nor all
The dreary intercourse of daily life,
Shall e'er prevail against us, or disturb
Our chearful faith that all which we behold
135 Is full of blessings. Therefore let the moon
Shine on thee in thy solitary walk;
And let the misty mountain winds be free
To blow against thee: and in after years,
When these wild ecstasies shall be matured
140 Into a sober pleasure, when thy mind
Shall be a mansion for all lovely forms,
Thy memory be as a dwelling-place
For all sweet sounds and harmonies; Oh! then,
If solitude, or fear, or pain, or grief,
145 Should be thy portion with what healing thoughts
Of tender joy wilt thou remember me,
And these my exhortations! Nor, perchance,
If I should be, where I no more can hear
Thy voice, nor catch from thy wild eyes these gleams
150 Of past existence, wilt thou then forget

That on the banks of this delightful stream
We stood together; and that I, so long
A worshipper of Nature, hither came,
Unwearied in that service: rather say
155 With warmer love, oh! with far deeper zeal

Of holier love. Nor wilt thou then forget,
That after many wanderings, many years
Of absence, these steep woods and lofty cliffs,
And this green pastoral landscape, were to me
160   More dear, both for themselves, and for thy sake.

                                                    1798

from PREFACE TO LYRICAL BALLADS (1800, 1802)

The First Volume of these Poems has already been submitted to general perusal. It was published, as an experiment which, I hoped, might be of some use to ascertain how far, by fitting to metrical arrangement a selection of the real language of men in a state of vivid sensation, that sort of pleasure and that quantity of pleasure may be imparted, which a Poet may rationally endeavour to impart.

. . . They who have been accustomed to the gaudiness and inane phraseology of many modern writers, if they persist in reading this book to its conclusion, will, no doubt, frequently have to struggle with feelings of strangeness and aukwardness: they will look round for poetry, and will be induced to inquire by what species of courtesy these attempts can be permitted to assume that title. I hope, therefore, the Reader will not censure me, if I attempt to state what I have proposed to myself to perform. . . .

[The Principal Object of the Poems. Humble and Rustic Life]

The principal object, then, proposed in these poems was to chuse incidents and situations from common life, and to relate or describe them, throughout, as far as was possible, in a selection of language really used by men, and, at the same time, to throw over them a certain colouring of imagination, whereby ordinary things should be presented to the mind in an unusual way; and further, and above all, to make these incidents and situations interesting by tracing in them, truly though not ostentatiously, the primary laws of our nature: chiefly, as far as regards the manner in which we associate ideas in a state of excitement. Low and rustic life was generally chosen, because in that condition the essential passions of the heart find a better soil in which they can attain their maturity, are less under restraint, and speak a plainer and more emphatic language; because in that condition of life our elementary feelings coexist in a state of greater simplicity and consequently may be more accurately contemplated and more forcibly communicated; because the manners of rural life germinate from those elementary feelings; and from the necessary character of rural occupations, are more easily comprehended, and are more durable; and, lastly, because in that condition the passions of men are incorporated with the beautiful and permanent forms of nature. The language, too, of these men has been adopted (purified indeed from what appear to be its real defects, from all lasting and rational causes of dislike or disgust) because such men hourly communicate with the best objects from which the best part of language is originally derived; and because, from their rank in society and the sameness and narrow circle of their intercourse, being less under the influence of social vanity they convey their feelings and notions in simple and unelaborated expressions. Accordingly, such a language, arising out of repeated experience and regular feelings, is a more permanent, and a far more philosophical language, than that which is frequently substituted for it by Poets, who think that they are conferring honour upon themselves and their art, in proportion as they separate themselves from the sympathies of men, and indulge in arbitrary and capricious habits of expression, in order to furnish food for fickle tastes, and fickle appetites of their own creation.

"The Spontaneous Overflow of Powerful Feelings"

. . . [A]ll good poetry is the spontaneous overflow of powerful feelings: but though this be true, Poems to which any value can be attached, were never produced on any variety of subjects but by a man who, being possessed of more than usual organic sensibility, had also thought long and deeply. For our continued influxes of feeling are modified and directed by our thoughts, which are indeed the representatives of all our past feelings; and, as by contemplating the relation of these general representatives to each other we discover what is really important to men, so, by the repetition and continuance of this act, our feelings will be connected with important subjects, till at length, if we be originally possessed of much sensibility, such habits of mind will be produced that, by obeying blindly and mechanically the impulses of those habits, we shall describe objects, and utter sentiments, of such a nature, and in such connection with each other, that the understanding of the reader must necessarily be in some degree enlightened, and his affections ameliorated.

I have said that each of these poems has a purpose. . . . I should mention one other circumstance which distinguishes these Poems from the popular Poetry of the day; it is this, that the feeling therein developed gives importance to the action and situation, and not the action and situation to the feeling. . . .

I will not suffer a sense of false modesty to prevent me from asserting, that I point my Reader's attention to this mark of distinction, far less for the sake of these particular Poems than from the general importance of the subject. The subject is indeed important! For the human mind is capable of being excited without the application of gross and violent stimulants; and he must have a very faint perception of its beauty and dignity who does not know this, and who does not further know, that one being is elevated above another in proportion as he possesses this capability. It has therefore appeared to me, that to endeavor to produce or enlarge this capability is one of the best services in which, at any period, a Writer can be engaged; but this service, excellent at all times, is especially so at the present day. For a multitude of causes, unknown to former times, are now acting with a combined force to blunt the discriminating powers of the mind, and, unfitting it for all voluntary exertion to reduce it to a state of almost savage torpor. The most effective of these causes are the great national events which are daily taking place, and the encreasing accumulation of men in cities, where the uniformity of their occupations produces a craving for extraordinary incident, which the rapid communication of intelligence hourly gratifies. To this tendency of life and manners the literature and theatrical exhibitions of the country have conformed themselves. The invaluable works of our elder writers, I had almost said the works of Shakespeare and Milton, are driven into neglect by frantic novels, sickly and stupid German Tragedies, and deluges of idle and extravagant stories in verse.—When I think upon this degrading thirst after outrageous stimulation, I am almost ashamed to have spoken of the feeble effort with which I have endeavoured to counteract it; and, reflecting upon the magnitude of the general evil, I should be oppressed with no dishonorable melancholy, had I not a deep impression of certain inherent and indestructible qualities of the human mind, and likewise of certain powers in the great and permanent objects that act upon it which are equally inherent and indestructible; and did I not further add to this impression a belief, that the time is approaching when the evil will be systematically opposed, by men of greater powers, and with far more distinguished success.

[The Language of Poetry]

Having dwelt thus long on the subjects and aim of these Poems, I shall request the Reader's permission to apprize him of a few circumstances relating to their *style*, in order, among, other reasons, that he may not censure me for not having performed what I never attempted. The reader will find that personifications of abstract ideas rarely occur in these volumes; and, I hope, are utterly rejected as an ordinary device to elevate the style, and raise it above prose. I have proposed to myself to imitate, and, as far as is possible, to adopt the very language of men; and assuredly such personifications do not make any natural or regular part of that language. They are, indeed, a figure of speech occasionally prompted by passion, and I have made use of them as such; but have endeavoured utterly to reject them as a mechanical device of style, or as a family language which Writers in metre seem to lay claim to by prescription. I have wished to keep my Reader in the company of flesh and blood, persuaded that by so doing I shall interest him. Others who pursue a different track will interest him likewise; I do not interfere with their claim, I only wish to prefer a claim of my own. There will also be found in these volumes little of what is usually called poetic diction; as much pains has been taken to avoid it as others ordinarily take to produce it; this I have done for the reason already alleged, to bring my language near to the language of men, and further, because the pleasure which I have proposed to myself to impart is of a kind very different from that which is supposed by many persons to be the proper object of poetry. I do not know how without being culpably particular I can give my Reader a more exact notion of the style in which I wished these poems to be written, than by informing him that I have at all times endeavoured to look steadily at my subject; consequently, I hope that there is in these Poems little falsehood of description, and my ideas are expressed in language fitted to their respective importance. Something I must have gained by this practice, as it is friendly to one property of all good poetry, namely, good sense; but it has necessarily cut me off from a large portion of phrases and figures of speech which from father to son have long been regarded as the common inheritance of Poets. . . .

. . . [T]o illustrate the subject in a general manner, I will here adduce a short composition of Gray, who was at the head of those who, by their reasonings, have attempted to widen the space of separation betwixt Prose and

Metrical composition, and was more than any other man curiously elaborate in the structure of his own poetic diction.

> In vain to me the smiling mornings shine,
> And reddening Phoebus lifts his golden fire:
> The birds in vain their amorous descant join,
> Or chearful fields resume their green attire:
> These ears alas! for other notes repine;
> *A different object do these eyes require;*
> *My lonely anguish melts no heart but mine;*
> *And in my breast the imperfect joys expire;*
> Yet Morning smiles the busy race to cheer,
> And new-born pleasure brings to happier men;
> The fields to all their wonted tribute bear;
> To warm their little loves the birds complain.
> *I fruitless mourn to him that cannot hear*
> *And weep the more because I weep in vain.*

[Thomas Gray, "Sonnet on the Death of Mr. Richard West" (1742)]

It will easily be perceived, that the only part of this Sonnet which is of any value is the lines printed in Italics; it is equally obvious, that, except in the rhyme, and in the use of the single word "fruitless" for fruitlessly, which is so far a defect, the language of these lines does in no respect differ from that of prose.

By the foregoing quotation I have shewn that the language of Prose may yet be well adapted to Poetry; and I have previously asserted that a large portion of the language of every good poem can in no respect differ from that of good Prose. I will go further. I do not doubt that it may be safely affirmed, that there neither is, nor can be, any essential difference between the language of prose and metrical composition. . . .

[What Is a Poet?]

. . . What is a Poet? To whom does he address himself? And what language is to be expected from him? He is a man speaking to men: a man, it is true, endued with more lively sensibility, more enthusiasm and tenderness, who has a greater knowledge of human nature, and a more comprehensive soul, than are supposed to be common among mankind; a man pleased with his own passions and volitions, and who rejoices more than other men in the spirit of life that is in him; delighting to contemplate similar volitions and passions as manifested in the goings-on of the Universe, and habitually impelled to create them where he does not find them. To these qualities he has added a disposition to be affected more than other men by absent things as if they were present; an ability of conjuring up in himself passions, which are indeed far from being the same as those produced by real events, yet (especially in those parts of the general sympathy which are pleasing and delightful) do more nearly resemble the passions produced by real events, than anything, which, from the motions of their own minds merely, other men are accustomed to feel in themselves; whence, and from practice, he has acquired a greater readiness and power in expressing what he thinks and feels, and especially those thoughts and feelings which, by his own choice, or from the structure of his own mind, arise in him without immediate external excitement.

But, whatever portion of this faculty we may suppose even the greatest Poet to possess, there cannot be a doubt that the language which it will suggest to him, must in liveliness and truth, fall far short of that which is uttered by men in real life, under the actual pressure of those passions, certain shadows of which the Poet thus produces, or feels to be produced, in himself. However exalted a notion we would wish to cherish of the character of a Poet, it is obvious, that while he describes and imitates passions, his situation is altogether slavish and mechanical, compared with the freedom and power of real and substantial action and suffering. So that it will be the wish of the Poet to bring his feelings near to those of the persons whose feelings he describes, nay, for short spaces of time perhaps, to let himself slip into an entire delusion, and even confound and identify his own feelings with theirs; modifying only the language which is thus suggested to him, by a consideration that he describes for a particular purpose, that of giving pleasure. Here, then, he will apply the principle on which I have so much insisted, namely, that of selection; on this he will depend for removing what would otherwise be painful or disgusting in the passion; he will feel that there is no necessity to trick out or to elevate nature: and, the more industriously he applies this principle, the deeper will be his faith that no words which his fancy or imagination can suggest, will be to be compared with those which are the emanations of reality and truth. . . .

["Emotion Recollected in Tranquillity"]

I have said that Poetry is the spontaneous overflow of powerful feelings; it takes its origin from emotion recollected in tranquillity: the emotion is contemplated till, by a species of reaction, the tranquillity gradually disappears, and an emotion, kindred to that which was before the subject of contemplation, is gradually produced, and does itself actually exist in the mind. In this mood successful composition generally begins. . . .

William Blake

(1757–1827)

Villiam Blake was a brilliant poet and innovative artist, but his imaginative eccentricities seemed like madness to many of his contemporaries, and he died impoverished and almost unknown. His popularity today comes chiefly from his more accessible works from the 1790s, particularly his Songs of Innocence and of Experience. The collection focuses on the different ways children and adults see and understand their world (the seeing/perceiving, or I/eye dualities that concerned Wordsworth and other Romantics), but also on the social and political injustices of his age. For Blake these contraries are never simple distinctions; they coexist in the soul at any given moment.

THE CHIMNEY SWEEPER [INNOCENCE]

When my mother died I was very young,
And my father sold me while yet my tongue
Could scarcely cry "'weep! 'weep! 'weep! 'weep!"[1]
So your chimneys I sweep & in soot I sleep.

There's little Tom Dacre, who cried when his head
That curl'd like a lamb's back, was shav'd, so I said,
"Hush, Tom! never mind it, for when your head's bare,
You know that the soot cannot spoil your white hair."

And so he was quiet, & that very night,
As Tom was a-sleeping he had such a sight!
That thousands of sweepers, Dick, Joe, Ned, & Jack,
Were all of them lock'd up in coffins of black;

And by came an Angel who had a bright key,
And he open'd the coffins & set them all free;
Then down a green plain, leaping, laughing they run,
And wash in a river and shine in the Sun.

Then naked & white, all their bags left behind,
They rise upon clouds, and sport in the wind.
And the Angel told Tom, if he'd be a good boy,
He'd have God for his father & never want joy.

And so Tom awoke; and we rose in the dark
And got with our bags & our brushes to work.
Tho' the morning was cold, Tom was happy & warm;
So if all do their duty, they need not fear harm.

THE CHIMNEY SWEEPER [EXPERIENCE]

A little black thing among the snow
Crying "'weep, 'weep," in notes of woe!
"Where are thy father & mother? say?"
"They are both gone up to the church to pray.

"Because I was happy upon the heath,
And smil'd among the winter's snow;
They clothed me in the clothes of death,
And taught me to sing the notes of woe.

"And because I am happy, & dance & sing,
They think they have done me no injury,
And are gone to praise God & his Priest & King,
Who make up a heaven of our misery."

1794

Note

1 The lisping child's call to advertise his trade—"sweep! sweep!"— becomes a relevant pun.

Emily Dickinson

(1830–1886)

*O*nly eight of Emily Dickinson's poems were published while she lived; the remaining 1,800 she left tied up in little bundles in her upstairs bedroom of the family home in Amherst, Massachusetts. The poems reveal that this woman who lived in near seclusion had in fact a very passionate and complex inner life. Her poetry's irregular rhythms and rhymes and use of words in startling new ways expressed a spiritual unrest that defies easy categories. Lyric poetry is defined as the poet's own thoughts and feelings. Dickinson's highly subjective "I" suggests that her imagination was at its most intense when she contemplated themes of love and especially death.

I HEARD A FLY BUZZ—WHEN I DIED—

I heard a Fly buzz—when I died—
The Stillness in the Room
Was like the Stillness in the Air—
Between the Heaves of Storm—

The Eyes around—had wrung them dry—
And Breaths were gathering firm
For that last Onset—when the King
Be witnessed—in the Room—

I willed my Keepsakes—Signed away
What portion of me be
Assignable—and then it was
There interposed a Fly—

With Blue—uncertain stumbling Buzz—
Between the light—and me—
And then the Windows failed—and then
I could not see to see—

c. 1862, 1896

THIS WORLD IS NOT CONCLUSION

This World is not Conclusion.
A Species stands beyond—
Invisible, as Music—
But positive, as Sound—
It beckons, and it baffles—
Philosophy—dont know—
And through a Riddle, at the last—
Sagacity, must go—
To guess it, puzzles scholars—
To gain it, Men have borne
Contempt of Generations
And Crucifixion, shown—
Faith slips—and laughs, and rallies—
Blushes, if any see—
Plucks at a twig of Evidence—
And asks a Vane, the way—
Much Gesture, from the Pulpit—
Strong Hallelujahs roll—
Narcotics cannot still the Tooth
That nibbles at the soul—

c. 1862, 1896

21

from An Inquiry into the Nature and Causes of the Wealth of Nations

Adam Smith

(1723–1790)

While Adam Smith is best known as an economist, the patron of classical liberalism in the marketplace, he considered himself foremost a moral philosopher. He was born in Scotland and educated at the University of Glasgow and later at Oxford. Smith's first major work was The Theory of Modern Sentiments *(1759), in which he explored human nature for the roots of moral decision-making. In true Enlightenment style, Smith found them in immutable, natural laws that applied to all humans in all places. We are, he argued, a duality of appetites and passions on the one hand and reason and sympathy on the other, all mediated by an "inner man" of moral judgment. Smith used much the same approach when he turned to the community at large. His* An Inquiry into the Nature and Causes of the Wealth of Nations *(1776) applied liberal theory to economics with much the same impact that Locke's work had done for politics. Smith's natural man is rational, competitive, driven by a desire for economic well-being. Too often Smith has been categorized as an apologist for unregulated capitalism and laissez-faire economic policies. In fact, he was critical of monopoly in any guise, whether state-sponsored or not. Smith's analysis of market forces, the laws of supply and demand, and the division of labor were seminal to the thinking of later social theorists, including Karl Marx.*

Of the Division of Labor

The greatest improvement in the productive powers of labor, and the greater part of the skill, dexterity, and judgment with which it is anywhere directed, or applied, seem to have been the effects of the division of labor. . . .

This great increase of the quantity of work, which, in consequence of the division of labor, the same number of people are capable of performing, is owing to three different circumstances: first, to the increase of dexterity in every particular workman; secondly, to the saving of the time which is commonly lost in passing from one kind of work to another; and lastly, to the invention of a great number of machines which facilitate and reduce labor, and enable one man to do the work of many.

First, the improvement of the dexterity of the workman necessarily increases the quantity of the work he can perform; and the division of labor, by reducing every man's business to some one simple operation, and by making this operation the sole employment of his life, necessarily increases very much the dexterity of the workman. A common smith, who, though accustomed to handle the hammer, has never been used to make nails, if upon some particular occasion is obliged to attempt it, will scarce be able to make above two or three hundred nails in a day, and those very bad ones. A smith who has been accustomed to make nails, but whose sole or principal business has not been that of making nails, can seldom make more than eight hundred or a thousand nails in a day. I have seen several boys under twenty years of age who had never exercised any other trade but that of making nails, and who, when they exerted themselves, could make, each of them, upwards of two thousand three hundred nails in a day. The making of a nail, however, is by no means one of the simplest operations. The same person blows the bellows, stirs or tends the fire as there is occasion, heats the iron, and forges every part of the nail; forging the head too he is obliged to change his tools. The different operations into which the making of a pin, or of a metal button, is subdivided, are all of them much more simple, and the dexterity of the person, of whose life it has been the sole business to perform them, is usually much greater. The rapidity with which some of the operations of those manufactures are performed, exceeds what the human hand could be supposed capable of acquiring.

Secondly, the advantage which is gained by saving the time commonly lost in passing from one sort of work to another, is much greater than we should at first imagine. It is impossible to pass very quickly from one kind of work to another, that is carried on in a different place, and with quite different tools. A country weaver, who cultivates a small farm, must lose a good deal of time in passing from his loom to the field, and from the field to his loom. When the two trades can be carried on in the same workhouse, the loss of time is no doubt much less. It is even in this case, however, very considerable. A man commonly delays a little in turning his hand from one sort of employment to another. When he first begins the new work he is seldom very quick and steady; his mind, as they say, does not go to it, and for some time he rather trifles than applies to good purpose. The habit of delaying and of careless application, which is naturally acquired by every country workman obliged to change his work and tools every half hour, and to apply his hand in twenty different ways almost every day of his life, renders him almost always slothful and lazy, and incapable of any vigorous application even on the most pressing occasions. Independent, therefore, of his deficiency in point of dexterity, this cause alone must always reduce considerably the quantity of work which he is capable of performing.

Thirdly, and lastly, everybody must realize how much labor is facilitated and reduced by the application of proper machinery. It is unnecessary to give any example. I shall only observe, therefore, that the invention of all those machines by which labor is so much aided, seems to have been originally owing to the division of labor. Men are much more likely to discover easier and readier methods of attaining any object, when the whole attention of their minds is directed toward that single object, than when it is dissipated among a great variety of things. But in consequence of the division of labor, the whole of every man's attention comes naturally to be directed toward some one very simple object. It is naturally to be expected, therefore, that some one or other of those who are employed in each particular branch of labor should soon find out easier and readier methods of performing their own particular work, wherever the nature of it admits of such improvement. A great part of the machines made use of in those manufactures in which labor is most subdivided, were originally the inventions of common workmen, who, being employed in some very simple operation, naturally turned their thoughts toward finding out easier and readier methods of performing it. Whoever has been much accustomed to visit such manufactures, must frequently have been shown very pretty machines, which were the inventions of such workmen, in order to speed up their own particular part of the work. In the first fire engines, a boy was constantly employed to open and shut alternately the communication between the boiler and the cylinder, according as the piston either ascended or descended. One of those boys, who loved to play with his companions, observed that, by tying a string from the handle of the valve which opened this communication to another part of the machine, the valve would open and shut without his assistance, and leave him at liberty to amuse himself with his playmates. One of the greatest improvements that has been made upon this machine, since it was first invented, was in this manner the discovery of a boy who wanted to save his own labor.

All the improvements in machinery, however, have by no means been the inventions of those who had occasion to use the machines. Many improvements have been made by the ingenuity of the makers of the machines, when to make them became the business of a peculiar trade; and some by those who are called philosophers or men of speculation, whose trade it is not to do anything, but to observe everything; and who, upon that account, are often capable of combining together the powers of the most distant and dissimilar objects. In the progress of society, philosophy or speculation becomes, like every other employment, the principal or sole trade and occupation of a particular class of citizens. Like every other employment too, it is subdivided into a great number of different branches, each of which affords occupation to a special class of philosophers; and this subdivision of employment in philosophy, as well as in every other business, improves dexterity, and saves time. Each individual becomes more expert in his own branch, more work is done upon the whole, and the quantity of science is considerably increased by it.

It is the great multiplication of the productions of all the different arts, as a consequence of the division of labor, which occasions, in a well-governed society, that universal wealth extends itself to the lowest ranks of the people. Every workman has a great quantity of his own work to dispose of beyond what he himself has need for; and every other workman being exactly in the same situation is enabled to exchange a great quantity of his own goods for a great quantity, or, what comes to the same thing, for the price of a great quantity of theirs. He supplies them abundantly with what they have need of, and they accommodate him as amply with what he needs, and a general plenty spreads through all the various ranks of the society. . . .

Of the Principle which Gives Rise to the Division of Labor

This division of labor, from which so many advantages are derived, is not originally the effect of any human wisdom, which foresees and intends that general wealth to which it gives rise. It is the necessary, though very slow and gradual, consequence of a certain disposition in human nature which has in view no such extensive purpose; the disposition to barter and exchange one thing for another. . . .

In a tribe of hunters or shepherds a particular person makes bows and arrows, for example, with more readiness and dexterity than any other.

He frequently exchanges them for cattle or for venison with his companions; and he finds at last that he can in this manner get more cattle and venison, than if he himself went to the field to catch them. From a regard to his own interest, therefore, the making of bows and arrows grows to be his chief business, and he becomes a sort of armorer. Another excels in making the frames and covers of their little huts or moveable houses. He is accustomed to be of use in this way to his neighbors, who reward him in the same manner with cattle and with venison, till at last he finds it in his interest to dedicate himself entirely to this employment, and to become a sort of house-carpenter. In the same manner a third becomes a blacksmith or a brass-worker; a fourth a tanner or dresser of hides or skins, the principal part of the clothing of savages. And thus the certainty of being able to exchange all that surplus produce of his own labor, which is over and above his own consumption, for such parts of the produce of other men's labor as he may have need of, encourages every man to apply himself to a particular occupation—and to cultivate and bring to perfection whatever talent or genius he may possess for that particular kind of business.

The difference of natural talents in different men is, in reality, much less than we are aware of, and the very different genius which appears to distinguish men of different professions, when grown to maturity, is not upon many occasions so much the cause, as the effect of the division of labor. The difference between the most dissimilar characters, between a philosopher and a common street porter, for example, seems to arise not so much from nature, as from habit, custom, and education. When they came into the world, and for the first six or eight years of their existence, they were, perhaps, very much alike, and neither their parents nor playmates could see any noticeable difference. About that age, or soon after, they come to be employed in very different occupations. The difference of talents comes then to be taken notice of, and widens by degrees, till at last the pride of the philosopher is willing to acknowledge scarce any resemblance. But without the disposition to barter and exchange, every man must have procured to himself every necessity and convenience of life which he wanted. All must have had the same duties to perform, and the same work to do, and there could have been no such difference of employment as could alone give rise to any great difference of talents.

As it is this disposition which forms that difference of talents, so remarkable among men of different professions, so it is this same disposition which renders that difference useful. Many breeds of animals acknowledged to be all of the same species, derive from nature a much more noticeable distinction of genius, than what, prior to custom and education, appears to take place among men. By nature a philosopher is not in genius and disposition half so different from a street porter, as a mastiff is from a greyhound, or a greyhound from a spaniel, or this last from a shepherd's dog. Those different breeds of animals, however, though all of the same species, are of scarce any use to one another. The strength of the mastiff is not in the least supported either by the swiftness of the greyhound, or by the sagacity of the spaniel, or by the docility of the shepherd's dog. The effects of those different geniuses and talents, for lack of power or disposition to barter and exchange, cannot be brought into a common stock—and do not in the least contribute to the better accommodation and convenience of the species. Each animal is still obliged to support and defend itself, separately and independently, and derives no sort of advantage from that variety of talents with which nature has endowed its fellows. Among men, on the contrary, the most dissimilar geniuses are of use to one another. The different products of their respective talents, by the general disposition to barter and exchange, are brought, as it were, into a common stock, where every man may purchase whatever part of the product of other men's talents he has need of.

• • •

Of the Natural and Market Price of Commodities

There is in every society or neighborhood an ordinary or average rate both of wages and profit in every different employment of labor and capital. This rate is naturally regulated . . . partly by the general circumstances of the society, their riches or poverty, their advancing, stationary, or declining condition; and partly by the particular nature of each employment.

There is likewise in every society or neighborhood an ordinary or average rate of rent, which is regulated too . . . partly by the general circumstances of the society or neighborhood in which the land is situated, and partly by the natural or improved fertility of the land.

These ordinary or average rates may be called the natural rates of wages, profit, and rent, at the time and place in which they commonly prevail.

When the price of any commodity is neither more nor less than what is sufficient to pay the rent of the land, the wages of the labor, and the profits of the capital employed in raising, preparing, and bringing it to market, according to their natural rates, the commodity is then sold for what may be called its natural price.

The commodity is then sold precisely for what it is worth, or for what it really costs the person who brings it to market; for though in common language what is called the prime cost of any commodity does not include the profit of the person who is to sell it, yet if he sells it at a price which does not allow him the ordinary rate of profit in his neighborhood, he is evidently a loser by the trade—since by employing his capital in some other way he might have made that profit. His profit, besides, is his revenue, the proper fund of his subsistence. As while he is preparing and bringing the goods to market, he advances to his workmen their wages, or their subsistence; so he advances to himself, in the same manner, his own subsistence, which is generally suitable to the profit which he may reasonably expect from the sale of his goods. Unless they yield him this profit, therefore, they do not repay him what they may very properly be said to have really cost him.

Though the price, therefore, which leaves him this profit, is not always the lowest at which a dealer may sometimes sell his goods, it is the lowest at which he is likely to sell them for any considerable time; at least where there is perfect liberty, or where he may change his trade as often as he pleases.

The actual price at which any commodity is commonly sold is called its market price. It may either be above, or below, or exactly the same with its natural price. . . .

When the quantity brought to market is just sufficient to supply the effectual demand and no more, the market price naturally comes to be either exactly, or as nearly as can be judged of, the same with the natural price. The whole quantity on hand can be disposed of for this price, and cannot be disposed of for more. The competition of the different dealers obliges them all to accept this price, but does not oblige them to accept less.

The quantity of every commodity brought to market naturally adjusts itself to the effectual demand. It is in the interest of all those who employ their land, labor, or capital, in bringing any commodity to market, that the quantity never should exceed the effectual demand; and it is in the interest of all other people that it never should fall short of that demand.

If at any time it exceeds the effectual demand, some of the component parts of its price must be paid below their natural rate. If it is rent, the interest of the landlords will immediately prompt them to withdraw a part of their land; and if it is wages or profit, the interest of the laborers in the one case, and of their employers in the other, will prompt them to withdraw a part of their labor or capital from this employment. The quantity brought to market will soon be no more than sufficient to supply the effectual demand. All the different parts of its price will rise to their natural rate, and the whole price to its natural price.

If, on the contrary, the quantity brought to market should at any time fall short of the effectual demand, some of the component parts of its price must rise above their natural rate. If it is rent, the interest of all other landlords will naturally prompt them to prepare more land for the raising of this commodity, if it is wages or profit, the interest of all other laborers and dealers will soon prompt them to employ more labor and capital in preparing and bringing it to market. The quantity brought there will soon be sufficient to supply the effectual demand. All the different parts of its price will soon sink to their natural rate, and the whole price to its natural price.

The natural price, therefore, is, as it were, the central price, to which the prices of all commodities are continually moving. Different factors may sometimes keep them suspended a good deal above it, and sometimes force them down even somewhat below it. But whatever may be the obstacles which hinder them from settling on this center, they are constantly tending toward it.

The whole quantity of industry annually employed in order to bring any commodity to market, naturally adjusts itself in this manner to the effectual demand. It naturally aims at bringing always that precise quantity there which may be sufficient to supply, and no more than supply, that demand. . . .

Of the Wages of Labor

The product of labor constitutes the natural compensation or wages of labor.

In that original state of things, which precedes both the ownership of land and the accumulation of capital, the whole product of labor belongs to the laborer. He has neither landlord nor master to share with him.

Had this state continued, the wages of labor would have grown with all those improvements in its productive powers, to which the division of labor gives rise. All things would gradually have become cheaper. They would have been produced by a smaller quantity of labor; and as the commodities produced by equal quantities of labor would naturally in this state of things be exchanged for one another, they would have been purchased likewise with the product of a smaller quantity. . . .

But this original state of things, in which the laborer enjoyed the whole product of his own labor, could not last beyond the first introduction of the ownership of land and the accumulation of capital. It was at an end, therefore, long before the most considerable improvements were made in the productive powers of labor, and it would be to no purpose to trace further what might have been its effects upon the compensation or wages of labor.

As soon as land becomes private property, the landlord demands a share of almost all the products which the laborer can either raise, or collect from it. His rent makes the first deduction from the product of the labor which is employed upon land.

It seldom happens that the person who tills the ground has the means to support himself till he reaps the harvest. His support is generally advanced to him from the capital of a master, the farmer who employs him, and who would have no interest to employ him, unless he was to share in the produce of his labor, or unless his capital was to be returned to him with a profit. This profit makes a second deduction from the yield of the labor which is employed upon land.

The product of almost all other labor is liable to the like deduction of profit. In all arts and manufactures the greater part of the workmen stand in need of a master to advance them the materials of their work, and their wages and support till it is completed. He shares in the product of their labor, or in the value which it adds to the materials used; and in this share consists his profit.

It sometimes happens, indeed, that a single independent workman has capital sufficient both to purchase the materials for his work, and to support himself till it is completed. He is both master and workman, and enjoys the whole product of his own labor, or the whole value which it adds to the materials used. It includes what are usually two distinct revenues, belonging to two distinct persons: the profits of capital, and the wages of labor.

Such cases, however, are not very frequent, and in every part of Europe, twenty workmen serve under a master for one that is independent; and the wages of labor are everywhere understood to be what they usually are when the laborer is one person, and the owner of the capital which employs him another.

What the common wages of labor are depends everywhere upon the contract usually made between those two parties, whose interests are by no means the same. The workmen desire to get as much as possible, the masters to give as little as possible. The formers are likely to combine in order to raise, the latter in order to lower the wages of labor.

It is not, however, difficult to foresee which of the two parties must, upon all ordinary occasions, have the advantage in the dispute, and force the other into a compliance with their terms. The masters, being fewer in number, can combine much more easily; and the law authorizes, or at least does not prohibit, their combinations—while it prohibits those of the workmen. We have no acts of parliament against combining to lower the price of work; but many against combining to raise it. In all such disputes the masters can hold out much longer. A landlord, a farmer, a master manufacturer, or merchant, though they did not employ a single workman, could generally live a year or two upon the capital which they have already acquired. Many workmen could not subsist a week, few could subsist a month, and scarcely any a year without employment. In the long run the workman may be as necessary to his master as his master is to him, but the necessity is not so immediate.

We rarely hear, it has been said, of the associations of masters, though frequently of those of workmen. But whoever imagines, upon this account, that masters rarely combine, is as ignorant of the world as of the subject. Masters are always and everywhere in a sort of unspoken, but constant and uniform association, not to raise the wages of labor above their actual rate. To violate this combination is everywhere a most unpopular action, and a sort of reproach to a master among his neighbors and equals. We seldom, indeed, hear of this combination, because it is the usual, and one may say, the natural state of things which nobody ever hears of. Masters, too, sometimes enter into particular associations to lower the wages of labor even below this rate. These are always conducted with the utmost silence and secrecy, until the moment of execution; and when the workmen yield, as they sometimes do, without resistance, though severely felt by them, they are never heard of by other people.

Such associations, however, are frequently resisted by a contrary defensive union of the workmen who sometimes too, without any provocation of this kind, combine of their own accord to raise the price of their labor. Their usual justifications are, sometimes, the high price of foodstuff, sometimes the great profit which their masters make by their work. But whether their unions be offensive or defensive, they are always abundantly heard of. In order to bring the point to a speedy decision, they take always recourse to the loudest clamor, and sometimes to the most shocking violence and outrage. They are desperate, and act with the folly and extravagance of desperate men, who must either starve or frighten their masters into an immediate compliance with their demands. The masters upon these occasions are just as noisy and never cease to call aloud for the assistance of the civil authorities, and the rigorous execution of those laws which have been enacted with so much severity against the unions of servants, laborers, and journeymen. The workmen, accordingly, very seldom derive any advantage from the violence of those tumultuous unions, which, partly from the actions of the civil officials, partly from the superior steadiness of the masters, partly from the necessity which the greater part of the workmen are under of submitting for the sake of present subsistence, generally end in nothing but the punishment or ruin of the ring leaders.

But though in disputes with their workmen, masters must generally have the advantage, there is however a certain rate below which it seems impossible to reduce, for any considerable time, the ordinary wages even of the lowest kind of labor. . . .

There are certain circumstances, however, which sometimes give the laborers an advantage, and enable them to raise their wages considerably above this rate, evidently the lowest which is consistent with common humanity.

When in any country the demand for those who live by wages is continually increasing; when every year furnishes employment for a greater number than had been employed the year before, the workmen have no reason to combine in order to raise their wages. The scarcity of hands gives rise to competition among masters, who bid against one another in order to get workmen, and thus voluntarily break through the natural combination of masters not to raise wages. The demand for those who live by wages, it is evident, cannot increase but in proportion to the increase of the funds which arc destined for the payment of wages. These funds are of two kinds: first, the revenue which is over and above what is necessary for the maintenance; and, secondly, the capital which is over and above what is necessary for the employment of their masters.

When the landlord or monied man has a greater income than what he judges sufficient to maintain his own family, he employs either the whole or a part of the surplus in maintaining one or more household servants. Increase this surplus, and he will naturally increase the number of those servants.

When an independent workman, such as a weaver or shoemaker, has more capital than what is sufficient to purchase the materials for his own work, and to maintain himself till he can sell it, he naturally employs one or more assistants with the surplus, in order to make a profit by their work. Increase this surplus, and he will naturally increase the number of his assistants.

The demand for those who live by wages, therefore, necessarily increases with the increase of the revenue and capital of every country, and cannot possibly increase without it. The increase of revenue and capital is the increase of national wealth. The demand for those who live by wages, therefore, naturally increases with the increase of national wealth, and cannot possibly increase without it. . . .

22

from The Origin of Species *and* The Descent of Man

Charles Darwin

(1809–1882)

After two years of medical study at the University of Edinburgh convinced him he would never be a physician, Charles Darwin transferred to Cambridge University to study for a ministry in the Church of England. Darwin's family could afford such ventures, for his maternal grandfather was the wealthy factory owner Josiah Wedgwood, and his paternal grandfather the great horticulturist Erasmus Darwin. Upon graduation but before Charles accepted his official orders in the church, he signed on as a naturalist aboard the H.M.S. Beagle, *engaged in scientific explorations around South America from 1831–1836. His observations on this voyage caused him to note variations of species of animals and plants in various locales, particularly on remote islands, and to publish his findings in a popular journalistic book* Voyage of the Beagle *(1845). The idea of evolution had been discussed in scientific circles for many years, but in 1858 the news that scientist Alfred Russel Wallace was about to propose a similar theory of evolution as Darwin caused the two men to present their theories jointly. The next year Darwin brought out his thorough but cautious* The Origin of Species on the Basis of Natural Selection *(1859), in many ways a model of nineteenth-century scientific argument. Here Darwin supplemented his work aboard the* Beagle *with knowledge gathered from English breeders of livestock, dogs, etc. If man could cause changes in a species, surely nature — through the process of natural selection — could do the same. The first passage below begins as Darwin concludes his evidence for a grand "battle of life" and then moves to the evidence of "an interminable number of indeterminate forms," or the existence of missing links that would prove that man and other species are part of a grand algorithm of life (a mathematical phrase modern scientists use to explain Darwinian biology). The phrase "survival of the fittest" soon had sweeping implications for society, moving way beyond its context here of a biological struggle for food or reproduction. Darwin's companion work* The Descent of Man *in 1871 applied his theories to human beings, partly in response to adverse reactions from conservative theologians. Not since 1632 when Galileo disproved the Church's teachings of a geocentric universe had there been such a conflict between science and religion. By the time of his death the Church of England recognized Darwin's importance to scientific thought and allowed him to be buried at Westminster Abbey in London.*

from THE ORIGIN OF SPECIES

As this whole volume is one long argument, it may be convenient to the reader to have the leading facts and inferences briefly recapitulated.

That many and serious objections may be advanced against the theory of descent with modification through variation and natural selection, I do not deny. I have endeavored to give to them their full force. Nothing at first can appear more difficult to believe than that the more complex organs and instincts have been perfected, not by means superior to, though analogous with, human reason, but by the accumulation of innumerable slight variations, each good for the individual possessor. Nevertheless, this difficulty, though appearing to our imagination insuperably great, cannot be considered real if we admit the following propositions, namely, that all parts of the organization and instincts offer, at least, individual differences—that there is a struggle for existence leading to the preservation of profitable deviations of structure or instinct—and, lastly, that gradations in the state of perfection of each organ may have existed, each good of its kind. The truth of these propositions cannot, I think, be disputed.

It is, no doubt, extremely difficult even to conjecture by what gradations many structures have been perfected, more especially among broken and failing groups of organic beings, which have suffered much extinction; but we see so many strange gradations in nature, that we ought to be extremely cautious in saying that any organ or instinct, or any whole structure, could not have arrived at its present state by many graduated steps. There are, it must be admitted, cases of special difficulty opposed to the theory of natural selection; and one of the most curious of these is the existence in the same community of two or three defined castes of workers or sterile female ants; but I have attempted to show how these difficulties can be mastered. . . .

As according to the theory of natural selection, an interminable number of intermediate forms must have existed, linking together all the species in each group by gradations as fine as are our existing varieties, it may be asked: Why do we not see these linking forms all around us? Why are not all organic beings blended together in an inextricable chaos? With respect to existing forms, we should remember that we have no right to expect (excepting in rare cases) to discover *directly* connecting links between them, but only between each and some extinct and supplanted form. Even on a wide area, which has during a long period remained continuous, and of which the climatic and other conditions of life change insensibly in proceeding from a district occupied by one species into another district occupied by a closely allied species, we have no just right to expect often to find intermediate varieties in the intermediate zones. For we have reason to believe that only a few species of a genus ever undergo change; the other species becoming utterly extinct and leaving no modified progeny. Of the species which do change, only a few within the same country change at the same time; and all modifications are slowly effected. I have also shown that the intermediate varieties which probably at first existed in the intermediate zones, would be liable to be supplanted by the allied forms on either hand; for the latter, from existing in greater numbers, would generally be modified and improved at a quicker rate than the intermediate varieties, which existed in lesser numbers; so that the intermediate varieties would, in the long run, be supplanted and exterminated.

On this doctrine of the extermination of an infinity of connecting links, between the living and extinct inhabitants of the world, and at each successive period between the extinct and still older species, why is not every geological formation charged with such links? Why does not every collection of fossil remains afford plain evidence of the gradation and mutation of the forms of life? Although geological research has undoubtedly revealed the former existence of many links, bringing numerous forms of life much closer together, it does not yield the infinitely many fine gradations between past and present species required on the theory; and this is the most obvious of the many objections which may be urged against it. Why, again, do whole groups of allied species appear, though this appearance is often false, to have come in suddenly on the successive geological stages? Although we now know that organic beings appeared on this globe, at a period incalculably remote, long before the lowest bed of the Cambrian system was deposited, why do we not find beneath this system great piles of strata stored with the remains of the progenitors of the Cambrian fossils? For on the theory, such strata must somewhere have been deposited at these ancient and utterly unknown epochs of the world's history.

I can answer these questions and objections only on the supposition that the geological record is far more imperfect than most geologists believe. The number of specimens in all our museums is absolutely as nothing compared with the countless generations of countless species which have certainly existed. The parent-form of any two or more species would not be in all its characters directly intermediate between its modified offspring, any more than the rock-pigeon is directly intermediate in crop and tail between its descendants, the pouter and fantail pigeons. We should not be able to recognize a species as the parent of another and modified species, if we were to examine the two ever so closely, unless we possessed most of the intermediate links; and owing to the imperfection of the geological record, we have no just right to expect to find so many links. If two or three, or even more linking forms were discovered, they would simply be ranked by many naturalists as so many new species, more especially if found in different geological sub-stages, let their differences be ever so slight. Numerous existing doubtful forms could be named which are probably varieties; but who will pretend that in future ages so many fossil links will be discovered, that naturalists will be able to decide whether or not these doubtful forms ought to be called varieties? Only a small portion of the world has been geologically explored. Only organic beings of certain classes can be preserved in a fossil condition, at least in any great number. Many species when once formed never undergo any further change but become extinct without leaving modified descendants; and the periods, during which species have undergone modification, though long as measured by years, have probably been short in comparison with the periods during which they retain the same form. It is the dominant and widely ranging species which vary most frequently and vary most, and varieties are often at first local—both causes rendering the discovery of intermediate links in any one formation less likely. Local varieties will not spread into other and distant regions until they are considerably modified and improved; and when they have spread, and are discovered in a geological formation, they appear as if suddenly created there, and will be simply classed as new species. Most formations have been intermittent in their accumulation; and their duration has probably been shorter than the average duration of specific forms. Successive formations are in most cases separated from each other by blank intervals of time of great length; for fossiliferous formations thick enough to resist future degradation can as a general rule be accumulated only where much sediment is deposited on the subsiding bed of the sea. During the alternate periods of elevation and of stationary level the record will generally be blank. During these latter periods there will probably be more variability in the forms of life; during periods of subsidence, more extinction. . . .

That the geological record is imperfect all will admit; but that it is imperfect to the degree required by our theory, few will be inclined to admit. If we look to long enough intervals of time, geology plainly declares that species have all changed; and they have changed in the manner required by the theory, for they have changed slowly and in a graduated manner. We clearly see this in the fossil remains from consecutive formations invariably being much more closely related to each other, than are the fossils from widely separated formations. . . .

Under domestication we see much variability, caused, or at least excited, by changed conditions of life; but often in so obscure a manner, that we are tempted to consider the variations as spontaneous. Variability is governed by many complex laws,—by correlated growth, compensation, the increased use and disuse of parts, and the definite action of the surrounding conditions. There is much difficulty in ascertaining how largely our domestic productions have been modified; but we may safely infer that the amount has been large, and that modifications can be inherited for long periods. As long as the conditions of life remain the same, we have reason to believe that a modification, which has already been inherited for many generations, may continue to be inherited for an almost infinite number of generations. On the other hand, we have evidence that variability when it has once come into play, does not cease under domestication for a very long period; nor do we know that it ever ceases, for new varieties are still occasionally produced by our oldest domesticated productions.

Variability is not actually caused by man; he only unintentionally exposes organic beings to new conditions of life, and then nature acts on the organization and causes it to vary. But man can and does select the variations given to him by nature, and thus accumulates them in any desired manner. He thus adapts animals and plants for his own benefit or pleasure. He may do this methodically, or he may do it unconsciously by preserving the individuals most useful or pleasing to him without any intention of altering the breed. It is certain that he can largely influence the character of a breed by selecting, in each successive generation, individual differences so slight as to be inappreciable except by an educated eye. This unconscious process of selection has been the great agency in the formation of the most distinct and useful domestic breeds. That many breeds produced by man have to a large extent the character of natural species, is shown by the inextricable doubts whether many of them are varieties or aboriginally distinct species.

There is no reason why the principles which have acted so efficiently under domestication should not have acted under nature. In the survival of favored individuals and races, during the constantly recurrent Struggle for Existence, we see a powerful and everacting form of Selection. The struggle for existence inevitably follows from the high geometrical ratio of increase which is common to all organic beings. This high rate of increase is proved by calculation,—by the rapid increase of many animals and plants during a succession of peculiar seasons, and when naturalized in new countries. More individuals are born than can possibly survive. A grain in the balance may determine which individuals shall live and which shall die,—which variety or species shall increase in number, and which shall decrease, or finally become extinct. As the individuals of the same species come in all respects into the closest competition with each other, the struggle will generally be most severe between them; it will be almost equally severe between the varieties of the same species, and next in severity between the species of the same genus. On the other hand the struggle will often be severe between beings remote in the scale of nature. The slightest advantage in certain individuals, at any age or during any season, over those with which they come into competition, or better adaptation in however slight a degree to the surrounding physical conditions, will, in the long run, turn the balance.

With animals having separated sexes, there will be in most cases a struggle between the males for the possession of the females. The most vigorous males, or those which have most successfully struggled with their conditions of life, will generally leave most progeny. But success will often depend on the males having special weapons, or means of defense, or charms; and a slight advantage will lead to victory.

As geology plainly proclaims that each land has undergone great physical changes, we might have expected to find that organic beings have varied under nature, in the same way as they have varied under domestication. And if there has been any variability under nature, it would be an unaccountable fact if natural selection had not come into play. It has often been asserted, but the assertion is incapable of proof, that the amount of variation under nature is a strictly limited quantity. Man, though acting on external characters alone and often capriciously, can produce within a short period a great result by adding up mere individual differences in his domestic productions; and every one admits that species present individual differences. But, besides such differences, all naturalists admit that natural varieties exist, which are considered sufficiently distinct to be worthy of record in systematic works. No one has drawn any clear distinction between individual differences and slight varieties; or between more plainly marked varieties and sub-species, and species. On separate continents, and on different parts of the same continent when divided by barriers of any kind, and on outlying islands, what a multitude of forms exist, which some experienced naturalists rank as varieties, others as geographical races or sub-species, and others as distinct, though closely allied species!

If, then, animals and plants do vary, let it be ever so slightly or slowly, why should not variations or individual differences, which are in any way beneficial, be preserved and accumulated through natural selection, or the survival of the fittest? If man can by patience select variations useful to him, why, under changing and complex conditions of life, should not variations useful to nature's living products often arise, and be preserved or selected? What limit can be put to this power, acting during long ages and rigidly scrutinizing the whole constitution, structure, and habits of each creature,—favoring the good and rejecting the bad? I can see no limit to this power, in slowly and beautifully adapting each form to the most complex relations of life. The theory of natural selection, even if we look no farther than this, seems to be in the highest degree probable. I have already recapitulated, as fairly as I could, the opposed difficulties and objections: now let us turn to the special facts and arguments in favor of the theory. ⟍ Starts direct argument

On the view that species are only strongly marked and permanent varieties, and that each species first existed as a variety, we can see why it is that no line of demarcation can be drawn between species, commonly supposed to have been produced by special acts of creation, and varieties which are acknowledged to have been produced by secondary laws. On this same view we can understand how it is that in a region where many species of a genus have been produced, and where they now flourish, these same species should present many varieties; for where the production of species has been active, we might expect, as a general rule, to find it still in action; and this is the case if varieties be incipient species. Moreover, the species of the larger genera, which afford the greater number of varieties or incipient species, retain to a certain degree the character of varieties; for they differ from each other by a less amount of difference than do the species of smaller genera. The closely allied species also of the larger genera apparently have restricted ranges, and in their affinities they are clustered in little groups round other species—in both respects resembling varieties. These are strange relations on the view that each species was independently created, but are intelligible if each existed first as a variety . . .

As natural selection acts solely by accumulating slight, successive, favorable variations, it can produce no great or sudden modifications; it can act only by short and slow steps. Hence, the canon of "Natura non facit saltum," which every fresh addition to our knowledge tends to confirm, is on this theory intelligible. We can see why throughout nature the same general end is gained by an almost infinite diversity of means, for every peculiarity when once acquired is long inherited, and structures already modified in many different ways have to be adapted for the same general purpose. We can, in short, see why nature is prodigal in variety, though stingy in innovation. But why this should be a law of nature if each species has been independently created, no man can explain. . . .

The fact, as we have seen, that all past and present organic beings can be arranged within a few great classes, in groups subordinate to groups, and with the extinct groups often falling in between the recent groups, is intelligible on the theory of natural selection with its contingencies of extinction and divergence of character. On these same principles we see how it is, that the mutual affinities of the forms within each class are so complex. We see why certain characters are far more serviceable than others for classification;—why adaptive characters, though of paramount importance to the beings, are of hardly any importance in classification; why characters derived from rudimentary parts, though of no service to the beings, are often of high classificatory value; and why embryological characters are often the most valuable of all. The real affinities of all organic beings, in contradistinction to their adaptive resemblances, are due to inheritance or community of descent. The Natural System is a genealogical arrangement, with the acquired grades of difference, marked by the terms, varieties, species, genera, families, and so forth; and we have to discover the lines of descent by the most permanent characters whatever they may be and of however slight vital importance.

The similar framework of bones in the hand of a man, wing of a bat, fin of the porpoise, and leg of the horse,—the same number of vertebrae forming the neck of the giraffe and of the elephant,—and innumerable other such facts, at once explain themselves on the theory of descent with slow and slight successive modifications. The similarity of pattern in the wing and in the leg of a bat, though used for such different purpose,—in the jaws and legs of a crab,—in the petals, stamens, and pistils of a flower, is likewise, to a large extent, intelligible on the view of the gradual modification of parts or organs which were aboriginally alike in an early progenitor in each of these classes. On the principle of successive variations not always appearing at an early age, and being inherited at a corresponding not early period of life, we clearly see why the embryos of mammals, birds, reptiles, and fishes should be so closely similar, and so unlike the adult forms. We may cease marvelling at the embryo of an air-breathing mammal or bird having branchial slits and arteries running in loops, like those of a fish which has to breathe the air dissolved in water by the aid of well-developed branchiae.

Disuse, aided sometimes by natural selection, will often have reduced organs when rendered useless under changed habits or conditions of life; and we can understand on this view the meaning of rudimentary organs. But disuse and selection will generally act on each creature, when it has come to maturity and has to play its full part in the struggle for existence, and will thus have little power on an organ during early life; hence the organ will not be reduced or rendered rudimentary at this early age. The calf, for instance, has inherited teeth, which never cut through the gums of the upper jaw, from an early progenitor having well-developed teeth; and we may believe that the teeth in the mature animal were formerly reduced by disuse, owing to the tongue and palate, or lips, having become excellently fitted through natural selection to browse without their aid; whereas in the calf, the teeth have been left unaffected, and on the principle of inheritance at corresponding ages have been inherited from a remote period to the present day. On the view of each organism with all its separate parts having been specially created, how utterly inexplicable is it that organs bearing the plain stamp of inutility, such as the teeth in the embryonic calf or the shriveled wings under the soldered wingcovers of many beetles, should so frequently occur. Nature may be said to have taken pains to reveal her scheme of modification by means of rudimentary organs, of embryological and homologous structures, but we are too blind to understand her meaning.

Summary !!

I have now recapitulated the facts and considerations which have thoroughly convinced me that species have been modified, during a long course of descent. This has been effected chiefly through the natural selection of numerous successive, slight, favorable variations aided in an important manner by the inherited effects of the use and disuse of parts; and in an unimportant manner, that is in relation to adaptive structures, whether past or present, by the direct action of external conditions, and by variations which seem to us in our ignorance to arise spontaneously. It appears that I formerly underrated the frequency and value of these latter forms of variation, as leading to permanent modifications of structure independently of natural selection. But as my conclusions have lately been much misrepresented, and it has been stated that I attribute the modification of species exclusively to natural selection, I may be permitted to remark that in the first edition of this work, and subsequently, I placed in a most conspicuous position—namely, at the close of the Introduction—the following words: "I am convinced that natural selection has been the main but not the exclusive means of modification." This has been of no avail. Great is the power of steady misrepresentation; but the history of science shows that fortunately this power does not long endure. . . .

I see no good reason why the views given in this volume should shock the religious feelings of any one. It is satisfactory, as showing how transient such impressions are, to remember that the greatest discovery ever made by man, namely the law of the attraction of gravity, was also attacked by Leibnitz,[1] "as subversive of natural, and inferentially of revealed, religion." A celebrated author and divine has written to me that "he has gradually learned to see that it is just as noble a conception of the Deity to believe that He created a few original forms capable of self-development into other and needful forms, as to believe that He required a fresh act of creation to supply the voids caused by the action of His laws."

Why, it may be asked, until recently did nearly all the most eminent living naturalists and geologists disbelieve in the mutability of species. It cannot be asserted that organic beings in a state of nature are subject to no variation; it cannot be proved that the amount of variation in the course of long ages is a limited quantity; no clear distinction has been, or can be, drawn between species and well-marked varieties. It cannot be maintained that species when intercrossed are invariably sterile, and varieties invariably fertile; or that sterility is a special endowment and sign of creation. The belief that species were immutable productions was almost unavoidable as long as the history of the world was thought to be of short duration; and now that we have acquired some idea of the lapse of time, we are too apt to assume, without proof, that the geological record is so perfect that it would have afforded us plain evidence of the mutation of species, if they had undergone mutation.

But the chief cause of our natural unwillingness to admit that one species has given birth to other and distinct species, is that we are always slow in admitting great changes of which we do not see the steps. The difficulty is the same as that felt by so many geologists, when Lyell[2] first insisted that long lines of inland cliffs had been formed, and great valleys excavated, by the force which we see still at work. The mind cannot possibly grasp the full meaning of the term of even a million years; it cannot add up and perceive the full effects of many slight variations, accumulated during an almost infinite number of generations. . . .

It may be asked how far I extend the doctrine of the modification of species. The question is difficult to answer, because the more distinct the forms are which we consider, by so much the arguments in favor of community of descent become fewer in number and less in force. But some arguments of the greatest weight extend very far. All the members of whole classes are connected together by a chain of affinities, and all can be classed on the same principle, in groups subordinate to groups. Fossil remains sometimes tend to fill up very wide intervals between existing orders.

Organs in a rudimentary condition plainly show that an early progenitor had the organ in a fully developed condition; and this in some cases implies an enormous amount of modification in the descendants. Throughout whole classes various structures are formed on the same pattern, and at a very early age the embryos closely resemble each other. Therefore I cannot doubt that the theory of descent with modification embraces all the members of the same great class or kingdom. I believe that animals are descended from at most only four or five progenitors, and plants from an equal or lesser number.

Analogy would lead me one step farther, namely, to the belief that all animals and plants are descended from some one prototype. But analogy may be a deceitful guide. Nevertheless all living things have much in common, in their chemical composition, their cellular structure, their laws of growth, and their liability to injurious influences. We see this even in so trifling a fact as that the same poison often similarly affects plants and animals; or that the poison secreted by the gall-fly produces monstrous growths on the wild rose or oak-tree. With all organic beings, excepting perhaps some of the very lowest, sexual reproduction seems to be essentially similar. With all, as far as is at present known, the germinal vesicle is the same; so that all organisms start from a common origin. If we look even to the two main divisions—namely, to the animal and vegetable kingdoms—certain low forms are so far intermediate in character that naturalists have disputed to which kingdom they should be referred. As Professor Asa Gray has remarked, "the spores and other reproductive bodies of many of the lower algae may claim to have first a characteristically animal, and then an unequivocally vegetable existence." Therefore, on the principle of natural selection with divergence of character, it does not seem incredible that, from some such low and intermediate form, both animals and plants may have been developed; and, if we admit this, we must likewise admit that all the organic beings which have ever lived on this earth may be descended from some one primordial form. But this inference is chiefly grounded on analogy, and it is immaterial whether or not it be accepted. No doubt it is possible, as Mr. G. H. Lewes has urged, that at the first commencement of life many different forms were evolved; but if so, we may conclude that only a very few have left modified descendants. For, as I have recently remarked in regard to the members of each great kingdom, such as the Vertebrata, Articulata, and so forth, we have distinct evidence in their embryological, homologous, and rudimentary structures, that within each kingdom all the members are descended from a single progenitor.

When the views advanced by me in this volume, and by Mr. Wallace,[3] or when analogous views on the origin of species are generally admitted, we can dimly foresee that there will be a considerable revolution in natural history. Systematists will be able to pursue their labors as at present; but they will not be incessantly haunted by the shadowy doubt whether this or that form be a true species. This, I feel sure and I speak after experience, will be no slight relief. The endless disputes whether or not some fifty species of British brambles are good species will cease. Systematists will have only to decide (not that this will be easy) whether any form be sufficiently constant and distinct from other forms, to be capable of definition; and if definable, whether the differences be sufficiently important to deserve a specific name. This latter point will become a far more essential consideration than it is at present; for differences, however slight, between any two forms, if not blended by intermediate gradations, are looked at by most naturalists as sufficient to raise both forms to the rank of species.

Hereafter we shall be compelled to acknowledge that the only distinction between species and well-marked varieties is, that the latter are known, or believed, to be connected at the present day by intermediate gradations, whereas species were formerly thus connected. Hence, without rejecting the consideration of the present existence of intermediate gradations between any two forms, we shall be led to weigh more carefully and to value higher the actual amount of difference between them. It is quite possible that forms now generally acknowledged to be merely varieties may hereafter be thought worthy of specific names; and in this case scientific and common language will come into accordance. In short, we shall have to treat species in the same manner as those naturalists treat genera, who admit that genera are merely artificial combinations made for convenience. This may not be a cheering prospect; but we shall at least be free from the vain search for the undiscovered and undiscoverable essence of the term species. . . .

Authors of the highest eminence seem to be fully satisfied with the view that each species has been independently created. To my mind it accords better with what we know of the laws impressed on matter by the Creator, that the production and extinction of the past and present inhabitants of the world should have been due to secondary causes, like those determining the birth and death of the individual. When I view all beings not as special creations, but as the lineal descendants of some few beings which lived long before the first bed of the Cambrian system was deposited, they seem to me to become ennobled. Judging from the past, we may safely infer that not one living species will transmit its unaltered likeness to a distant future. And of the species now living very few will transmit progeny of any kind to a far distant future; for the manner in which all organic beings are grouped, shows that the greater number of species in each genus, and all the species in many genera, have left no descendants, but have become utterly extinct. We can so far take a prophetic glance into the future as to foretell that it will be the common and widely-spread species, belonging to the larger and dominant groups within each class, which will ultimately prevail and procreate new and dominant species. As all the living forms of life are the lineal descendants of those which lived long before the Cambrian epoch, we may feel certain that the ordinary succession by generation has never once been broken, and that no cataclysm has desolated the whole world. Hence we may look with some confidence to a secure future of great length. And as natural selection works solely by and for the good of each being, all corporeal and mental endowments will tend to progress toward perfection.

It is interesting to contemplate a tangled bank, clothed with many plants of many kinds, with birds singing in the bushes, with various insects flitting about, and with worms crawling through the damp earth, and to reflect that these elaborately constructed forms, so different from each other, and dependent upon each other in so complex a manner, have all been produced by laws acting around us. These laws, taken in the largest sense, being Growth with Reproduction; Inheritance which is almost implied by reproduction; Variability from the indirect and direct action of the conditions of life, and from use and disuse: a Ratio of Increase so high as to lead to a Struggle for Life, and as a consequence to Natural Selection, entailing Divergence of Character and the Extinction of less-improved forms. Thus, from the war of nature, from famine and death, the most exalted object which we are capable of conceiving, namely, the production of the higher animals, directly follows. There is grandeur in this view of life, with its several powers, having been originally breathed by the Creator into a few forms or into one; and that, while this planet has gone cycling on according to the fixed law of gravity, from so simple a beginning endless forms most beautiful and most wonderful have been, and are being evolved.

from THE DESCENT OF MAN

Man, like every other animal, has no doubt advanced to his present high condition through a struggle for existence resulting from his rapid multiplication; and if he is to advance still higher, it is to be feared that he must remain subject to a severe struggle. Otherwise he would sink into indolence, and the more gifted men would not be more successful in the battle of life than the less gifted. Hence our natural rate of increase, though leading to many and obvious evils, must not be greatly diminished by any means. There should be open competition for all men; and the most able should not be prevented by laws or customs from succeeding best and rearing the largest number of offspring. Important as the struggle for existence has been and even still is, yet as far as the highest part of man's nature is concerned there are other factors more important. For the moral qualities are advanced, either directly or indirectly, much more through the effects of habit, the reasoning powers, instruction, religion, and so forth, than through natural selection. . . .

The main conclusion arrived at in this work, namely that man is descended from some lowly organized form, will, I regret to think, be highly distasteful to many. But there can hardly be a doubt that we are descended from barbarians. The astonishment which I felt on first seeing a group of Fuegians on a wild and broken shore will never be forgotten by me, for the thought at once rushed into my mind—such were our ancestors. These men were absolutely naked and smeared with paint, their long hair was tangled, their mouths frothed with excitement, and their expression was wild, startled, and distrustful. They possessed hardly any skills, and like wild animals lived on what they could catch; they had no government, and were merciless to everyone not of their own small tribe. He who has seen a savage . . . will not feel much shame, if forced to acknowledge that the blood of some more humble creature flows in his veins. For my own part I would as soon be descended from that heroic little monkey, who braved his dreaded enemy in order to save the life of his keeper, or from that old baboon, who descending from the mountains, carried away in triumph his young comrade from a crowd of astonished dogs—as from a savage who delights to torture his enemies, offers up bloody sacrifices, practices infanticide without remorse, treats his wives like slaves, knows no decency, and is haunted by the grossest superstitions.

Man may be excused for feeling some pride at having risen, though not through his own exertions, to the very summit of the organic scale; and the fact of his having thus risen, instead of having been simply placed there, may give him hope for a still higher destiny in the distant future. But we are not here concerned with hopes or fears, only with the truth as far as our reason permits us to discover it; and I have given the evidence to the best of my ability. We must, however, acknowledge, as it seems to me, that man with all his noble qualities, with sympathy which feels for the most debased, with benevolence which extends not only to other men but to the humblest living creature, with his god-like intellect which has penetrated into the movements and make-up of the solar system—with all these exalted powers—Man still bears in his bodily frame the indelible stamp of his lowly origin.

Notes

1 German philosopher Gottfried Wilhelm Leibnitz (1646–1716), satirized as Dr. Pangloss in Voltaire's novel *Candide*, who fought any changes to the social order or even to scientific knowledge. He believed that man should accept his

lot in life and not try to change it, because this was "the best of all possible worlds." Curiously, the Leibnizian paradigm has been used to explain Darwin's theory that all species evolve as part of a larger scheme in which they consistently become stronger and fitter.

2   Sir Charles Lyell (1797–1879) was an English geologist whose watershed book *Principles of Geology* (1830–1833) Darwin read on board the *Beagle*. After this work geological changes were no longer thought of solely as being created instantly by a great catastrophe but as developing over a long period of time, as Darwin theorizes happened in the evolution of species.

3   Alfred Russel Wallace (1823–1913), British naturalist, humanist, and geographer who became a public figure in England during the second half of the 19th century for his views on scientific and social topics. With Darwin he published the article "On the Tendency of Species to Form Varieties; and on the Perpetuation of Varieties and Species by Natural Means of Selection" in 1858. Wallace's private collection of animal specimens numbered over 125,000.

23

"The Dangers of Intervention" *from*
Man versus the State (1884)

Herbert Spencer

(1820–1903)

*L*ike Thomas Aquinas or Francis Bacon, Herbert Spencer was one of those rare
intellects who sought to synthesize all knowledge under the operation of a
single set of natural laws. The son of an English schoolmaster, Spencer turned
down the offer of a university education and was largely self-taught. After a few
years spent as a railway civil engineer, inventor of hapless gadgets (including a
proposed flying machine), and part-time essayist, he became in 1848 the subedi-
tor of the influential journal The Economist. Five years later an inheritance
allowed him to devote all his time to writing, which resulted in, among many
others, his extraordinary Synthetic Philosophy—a ten-volume overview of
biology, psychology, sociology, and ethics written over four decades—and several political and social commentaries, including Man versus the State (1884).

Spencer was hugely influential in his own time. His outlook was rigidly scientific
and materialistic, yet he borrowed part of his analytic principles from Jeremy
Bentham, the English proponent of utilitarianism, a philosophy of "the greatest
happiness for the greatest number." But where Bentham anticipated the creation
of the welfare state, Spencer moved to the opposite stance of extreme laissez-faire.
A full decade before Darwin issued The Origin of Species, Spencer had already
developed a full-blown theory of social evolution which included the term "survival of the fittest." Spencer's evolutionary scheme hinged on inherited character-
istics, however, while Darwin's turned on natural selection. Conceiving of society
as an organism, Spencer argued that simple, undifferentiated cultures responded
to challenges by becoming more complex and diversified—or else they died. The
free competition of individuals was central to this evolution, and the role of government was accordingly limited.

The extension of this policy . . . [of government legislation] fosters everywhere the tacit assumption that Government should step in whenever anything is not going right. "Surely you would not have this misery continue!"

exclaims someone, if you hint . . . [an objection] to much that is now being said and done. Observe what is implied by this exclamation. It takes for granted . . . that every evil can be removed: the truth being that with the existing defects of human nature, many evils can only be thrust out of one place or form into another place or form—often being increased by the change. The exclamation also implies the unhesitating belief, here especially concerning us, that evils of all kinds should be dealt with by the State. . . . Obviously, the more numerous governmental interventions become, the more confirmed does this habit of thought grow, and the more loud and perpetual the demands for intervention.

Every extension of the regulative policy involves an addition to the regulative agents—a further growth of officialism and an increasing power of the organization formed of officials. . . .

. . . Moreover, every additional State-interference strengthens the tacit assumption that it is the duty of the State to deal with all evils and secure all benefits. Increasing power of a growing administrative organization is accompanied by decreasing power of the rest of the society to resist its further growth and control. . . .

"But why is this change described as 'the coming-slavery'?" is a question which many will still ask. The reply is simple. All socialism involves slavery. . . .

Evidently then, the changes made, the changes in progress, and the changes urged, will carry us not only towards State-ownership of land and dwellings and means of communication, all to be administered and worked by State-agents, but towards State-usurpation of all industries: the private forms of which, disadvantaged more and more in competition with the State, which can arrange everything for its own convenience, will more and more die away, just as many voluntary schools have, in presence of Board-schools.[1] And so will be brought about the desired ideal of the socialists. . . .

. . . It is a matter of common remark, often made when a marriage is impending, that those possessed by strong hopes habitually dwell on the promised pleasures and think nothing of the accompanying pains. A further exemplification of this truth is supplied by these political enthusiasts and fanatical revolutionists. Impressed with the miseries existing under our present social arrangements, and not regarding these miseries as caused by the ill-working of a human nature but partially adapted to the social state, they imagine them to be forthwith curable by this or that rearrangement. Yet, even did their plans succeed it could only be by substituting one kind of evil for another. A little deliberate thought would show that under their proposed arrangements, their liberties must be surrendered in proportion as their material welfares were cared for.

For no form of co-operation, small or great, can be carried on without regulation, and an implied submission to the regulating agencies. . . .

. . . So that each [individual] would stand toward the governing agency in the relation of slave to master.

"But the governing agency would be a master which he and others made and kept constantly in check; and one which therefore would not control him or others more than was needful for the benefit of each and all."

To which reply the first rejoinder is that, even if so, each member of the community as an individual would be a slave to the community as a whole. Such a relation has habitually existed in militant communities, even under quasi-popular forms of government. In ancient Greece the accepted principle was that the citizen belonged neither to himself nor to his family, but belonged to his city—the city being with the Greek equivalent to the community. And this doctrine, proper to a state of constant warfare, is a doctrine which socialism unawares reintroduces into a state intended to be purely industrial. The services of each will belong to the aggregate of all; and for these services, such returns will be given as the authorities think proper. So that even if the administration is of the beneficent kind intended to be secured, slavery, however mild, must be the outcome of the arrangement. . . .

The function of Liberalism in the past was that of putting a limit to the powers of kings. The function of true Liberalism in the future will be that of putting a limit to the powers of Parliaments.

• First sentence references Locke's classical liberalism.

Note

[1] Roughly equivalent to American public schools.

24

Life in the Iron Mills

Rebecca Harding Davis

(1831–1910)

L ife in the Iron Mills *first appeared anonymously in 1861 in the prestigious* Atlantic Monthly. *It was a tumultuous time in American history. Revolutionary ideas and social change tore at the social fabric of the country: abolition, women's suffrage, new religious movements, utopian experiments, and increasing industrialism—and of course the dawn of the Civil War. Yet the reading public still expected literary works to be romances, a genre which softened the edges of harsh truths with imaginative distancing devices, such as the Puritan past in* The Scarlet Letter, *the whaling voyage in* Moby Dick, *and even the patriarchal South in* Uncle Tom's Cabin. *Davis's story about the plight of industrial workers startled the American reading public with its stark realism which borders on naturalism. This work by an unknown writer from the backwoods of Wheeling, Virginia (soon to be West Virginia) was simply unprecedented.*

As in all of Rebecca Harding Davis's work, the theme of this story is social justice. Written just 12 years after Marx and Engels published their Communist Manifesto *that probes class warfare between bourgeoisie and proletarians,* Life in the Iron Mills *explores the oppression of the working class by the middle class. The narrator states her aim to make real "a secret down here, in this nightmare fog, that has lain dumb for centuries." Just what that secret is becomes the reader's challenge. The impassioned narrator declares, "I want you to hear this story" about "the reality of soul starvation" in "a world gone wrong," a story about people whose desperate lives lead them to desperate acts—thievery and suicide. Replete with appeals to Holy Scripture, the story indicts the socioeconomic circumstances at work in capitalist America. Davis focuses particular attention on the Protestant church's utter failure to fulfill its own mission. The secret for breaking this stranglehold of power may well be a precursor to a force that takes shape in the early twentieth century—the Social Gospel.*

"Is this the end?
O Life, as futile, then, as frail!
What hope of answer of redress?"

A cloudy day: do you know what that is in a town of iron-works? The sky sank down before dawn, muddy, flat, immovable. The air is thick, clammy with the breath of crowded human beings. It stifles me. I open the window, and, looking out, can scarcely see through the rain the grocer's shop opposite, where a crowd of drunken Irishmen are puffing Lynchburg tobacco in their pipes. I can detect the scent through all the foul smells ranging loose in the air.

The idiosyncrasy of this town is smoke. It rolls sullenly in slow folds from the great chimneys of the iron-foundries, and settles down in black, slimy pools on the muddy streets. Smoke on the wharves, smoke on the dingy boats, on the yellow river,—clinging in a coating of greasy soot to the house-front, the two faded poplars, the faces of the passers-by. The long train of mules, dragging masses of pig-iron through the narrow street, have a foul vapor hanging to their reeking sides. Here, inside, is a little broken figure of an angel pointing upward from the mantel-shelf; but even its wings are covered with smoke, clotted and black. Smoke everywhere! A dirty canary chirps desolately in a cage beside me. Its dream of green fields and sunshine is a very old dream,—almost worn out, I think.

From the back-window I can see a narrow brick-yard sloping down to the river-side, strewed with rain-butts and tubs. The river, dull and tawny-colored, *(la belle riviére!)* drags itself sluggishly along, tired of the heavy weight of boats and coal-barges. What wonder? When I was a child, I used to fancy a look of weary, dumb appeal upon the face of the negro-like river slavishly bearing its burden day after day. Something of the same idle notion comes to me to-day, when from the street-window I look on the slow stream of human life creeping past, night and morning, to the great mills. Masses of men, with dull, besotted faces bent to the ground, sharpened here and there by pain or cunning; skin and muscle and flesh begrimed with smoke and ashes; stooping all night over boiling caldrons of metal, laired by day in dens of drunkenness and infamy; breathing from infancy to death an air saturated with fog and grease and soot, vileness for soul and body. What do you make of a case like that, amateur psychologist? You call it an altogether serious thing to be alive: to these men it is a drunken jest, a joke,—horrible to angels perhaps, to them commonplace enough. My fancy about the river was an idle one: it is no type of such a life. What if it be stagnant and slimy here? It knows that beyond there waits for it odorous sunlight,—quaint old gardens, dusky with soft, green foliage of apple-trees, and flushing crimson with roses,—air, and fields, and mountains. The future of the Welsh puddler passing just now is not so pleasant. To be stowed away, after his grimy work is done, in a hole in the muddy graveyard, and after that,—*not* air, nor green fields, nor curious roses.

Can you see how foggy the day is? As I stand here, idly tapping the window-pane, and looking out through the rain at the dirty back-yard and the coal-boats below, fragments of an old story float up before me,—a story of this old house into which I happened to come to-day. You may think it a tiresome story enough, as foggy as the day, sharpened by no sudden flashes of pain or pleasure.—I know: only the outline of a dull life, that long since, with thousands of dull lives like its own, was vainly lived and lost: thousands of them,—massed, vile, slimy lives, like those of the torpid lizards in yonder stagnant water-butt.—Lost? There is a curious point for you to settle, my friend, who study psychology in a lazy, *dilettante* way. Stop a moment. I am going to be honest. This is what I want you to do. I want you to hide your disgust, take no heed to your clean clothes, and come right down with me,—here, into the thickest of the fog and mud and foul effluvia. I want you to hear this story. There is a secret down here, in this nightmare fog, that has lain dumb for centuries: I want to make it a real thing to you. You, Egoist, or Pantheist, or Arminian, busy in making straight paths for your feet on the hills, do not see it clearly,—this terrible question which men here have gone mad and died trying to answer. I dare not put this secret into words. I told you it was dumb. These men, going by with drunken faces, and brains full of unawakened power, do not ask it of Society or of God. Their lives ask it; their deaths ask it. There is no reply. I will tell you plainly that I have a great hope; and I bring it to you to be tested. It is this: that this terrible dumb question is its own reply; that it is not the sentence of death we think it, but, from the very extremity of its darkness, the most solemn prophecy which the world has known of the Hope to come. I dare make my meaning no clearer, but will only tell my story. It will, perhaps, seem to you as foul and dark as this thick vapor about us, and as pregnant with death; but if your eyes are free as mine are to look deeper, no perfume-tinted dawn will be so fair with promise of the day that shall surely come.

My story is very simple,—only what I remember of the life of one of these men,—a furnace-tender in one of Kirby & John's rolling-mills,— Hugh Wolfe. You know the mills? They took the great order for the lower

Virginia railroads there last winter; run usually with about a thousand men. I cannot tell why I choose the half-forgotten story of this Wolfe more than that of myriads of these furnace-hands. Perhaps because there is a secret underlying sympathy between that story and this day with its impure fog and thwarted sunshine,—or perhaps simply for the reason that this house is the one where the Wolfes lived. There were the father and son,—both hands, as I said, in one of Kirby & John's mills for making railroad-iron,—and Deborah, their cousin, a picker in some of the cotton-mills. The house was rented then to half a dozen families. The Wolfes had two of the cellar-rooms. The old man, like many of the puddlers and feeders of the mills, was Welsh,—had spent half of his life in the Cornish tin-mines. You may pick the Welsh emigrants, Cornish miners, out of the throng passing the windows, any day. They are a trifle more filthy; their muscles are not so brawny; they stoop more. When they are drunk, they neither yell, nor shout, nor stagger, but skulk along like beaten hounds. A pure, unmixed blood, I fancy: shows itself in the slight angular bodies and sharply-cut facial lines. It is nearly thirty years since the Wolfes lived here. Their lives were like those of their class: incessant labor, sleeping in kennel-like rooms, eating rank pork and molasses, drinking—God and the distillers only know what; with an occasional night in jail, to atone for some drunken excess. Is that all of their lives?—of the portion given to them and these their duplicates swarming the streets to-day?—nothing beneath?—all? So many a political reformer will tell you,—and many a private reformer, too, who has gone among them with a heart tender with Christ's charity, and come out outraged, hardened.

One rainy night, about eleven o'clock, a crowd of half-clothed women stopped outside of the cellar-door. They were going home from the cotton-mill.

"Good-night, Deb," said one, a mulatto, steadying herself against the gas-post. She needed the post to steady her. So did more than one of them.

"Dah's a ball to Miss Potts' to-night. Ye'd best come."

"Inteet, Deb, if hur'll come, hur'll hef fun," said a shrill Welsh voice in the crowd.

Two or three dirty hands were thrust out to catch the gown of the woman, who was groping for the latch of the door.

"No."

"No? Where's Kit Small, then?"

"Begorra! on the spools. Alleys behint, though we helped her, we dud. An wid ye! Let Deb alone! It's ondacent frettin' a quite body. Be the powers, an' we'll have a night of it! there'll be lashin's o' drink,—the Vargent be blessed and praised for't!"

They went on, the mulatto inclining for a moment to show fight, and drag the woman Wolfe off with them; but, being pacified, she staggered away.

Deborah groped her way into the cellar, and, after considerable stumbling, kindled a match, and lighted a tallow dip, that sent a yellow glimmer over the room. It was low, damp,—the earthen floor covered with a green, slimy moss,—a fetid air smothering the breath. Old Wolfe lay asleep on a heap of straw, wrapped in a torn horse-blanket. He was a pale, meek little man, with a white face and red rabbit-eyes. The woman Deborah was like him; only her face was even more ghastly, her lips bluer, her eyes more watery. She wore a faded cotton gown and a slouching bonnet. When she walked, one could see that she was deformed, almost a hunchback. She trod softly, so as not to waken him, and went through into the room beyond. There she found by the half-extinguished fire an iron saucepan filled with cold boiled potatoes, which she put upon a broken chair with a pint-cup of ale. Placing the old candlestick beside this dainty repast, she untied her bonnet, which hung limp and wet over her face, and prepared to eat her supper. It was the first food that had touched her lips since morning. There was enough of it, however: there is not always. She was hungry,—one could see that easily enough,—and not drunk, as most of her companions would have been found at this hour. She did not drink, this woman,—her face told that, too,—nothing stronger than ale. Perhaps the weak, flaccid wretch had some stimulant in her pale life to keep her up,—some love or hope, it might be, or urgent need. When that stimulant was gone, she would take to whiskey. Man cannot live by work alone. While she was skinning the potatoes, and munching them, a noise behind her made her stop.

"Janey!" she called, lifting the candle and peering into the darkness. "Janey, are you there?"

A heap of ragged coats was heaved up, and the face of a young girl emerged, staring sleepily at the woman.

"Deborah," she said, at last, "I'm here the night."

"Yes, child. Hur's welcome," she said, quietly eating on.

The girl's face was haggard and sickly; her eyes were heavy with sleep and hunger: real Milesian eyes they were, dark, delicate blue, glooming out from black shadows with a pitiful fright.

"I was alone," she said, timidly.

"Where's the father?" asked Deborah, holding out a potato, which the girl greedily seized.

"He's beyant,—wid Haley,—in the stone house." (Did you ever hear the word *jail* from an Irish mouth?) "I came here. Hugh told me never to stay me-lone."

"Hugh?"

"Yes."

A vexed frown crossed her face. The girl saw it, and added quickly,

"I have not seen Hugh the day, Deb. The old man says his watch lasts till the mornin'."

The woman sprang up, and hastily began to arrange some bread and flitch in a tin pail, and to pour her own measure of ale into a bottle. Tying on her bonnet, she blew out the candle.

"Lay ye down, Janey dear," she said, gently, covering her with the old rags. "Hur can eat the potatoes, if hur's hungry."

"Where are ye goin', Deb? The rain's sharp."

"To the mill, with Hughs supper."

"Let him bide till th' morn. Sit ye down."

"No, no,"—sharply pushing her off. "The boy'll starve."

She hurried from the cellar, while the child wearily coiled herself up for sleep. The rain was falling heavily, as the woman, pail in hand, emerged from the mouth of the alley, and turned down the narrow street, that stretched out, long and black, miles before her. Here and there a flicker of gas lighted an uncertain space of muddy footwalk and gutter; the long rows of houses, except an occasional lagerbier shop, were closed; now and then she met a band of millhands skulking to or from their work.

Not many even of the inhabitants of a manufacturing town know the vast machinery of system by which the bodies of workmen are governed, that goes on unceasingly from year to year. The hands of each mill are divided into watches that relieve each other as regularly as the sentinels of an army. By night and day the work goes on, the unsleeping engines groan and shriek, the fiery pools of metal boil and surge. Only for a day in the week, in half-courtesy to public censure, the fires are partially veiled; but as soon as the clock strikes midnight, the great furnaces break forth with renewed fury, the clamor begins with fresh, breathless vigor, the engines sob and shriek like "gods in pain."

As Deborah hurried down through the heavy rain, the noise of these thousand engines sounded through the sleep and shadow of the city like far-off thunder. The mill to which she was going lay on the river, a mile below the city-limits. It was far, and she was weak, aching from standing twelve hours at the spools. Yet it was her almost nightly walk to take this man his supper, though at every square she sat down to rest, and she knew she should receive small word of thanks.

Perhaps, if she had possessed an artist's eye, the picturesque oddity of the scene might have made her step stagger less, and the path seem shorter; but to her the mills were only "summat deilish to look at by night."

The road leading to the mills had been quarried from the solid rock, which rose abrupt and bare on one side of the cinder-covered road, while the river, sluggish and black, crept past on the other. The mills for rolling iron are simply immense tent-like roofs, covering acres of ground, open on every side. Beneath these roofs Deborah looked in on a city of fires, that burned hot and fiercely in the night. Fire in every horrible form: pits of flame waving in the wind; liquid metal-flames writhing in tortuous streams through the sand; wide caldrons filled with boiling fire, over which bent ghastly wretches stirring the strange brewing; and through all, crowds of half-clad men, looking like revengeful ghosts in the red light, hurried, throwing masses of glittering fire. It was like a street in Hell. Even Deborah muttered, as she crept through, "'T looks like t' Devil's place!" It did,—in more ways than one.

She found the man she was looking for, at last, heaping coal on a furnace. He had not time to eat his supper; so she went behind the furnace, and waited. Only a few men were with him, and they noticed her only by a "Hyur comes t' hunchback, Wolfe."

Deborah was stupid with sleep; her back pained her sharply; and her teeth chattered with cold, with the rain that soaked her clothes and dripped from her at every step. She stood, however, patiently holding the pail, and waiting.

"Hour, woman! ye look like a drowned cat. Come near to the fire,"said one of the men, approaching to scrape away the ashes.

She shook her head. Wolfe had forgotten her. He turned, hearing the man, and came closer.

"I did no' think, gi' me my supper, woman."

She watched him eat with a painful eagerness. With a woman's quick instinct, she saw that he was not hungry,—was eating to please her. Her pale, watery eyes began to gather a strange light.

"Is't good, Hugh? T'ale was a bit sour, I feared."

"No, good enough." He hesitated a moment. "Ye're tired, poor lass! Bide here till I go. Lay down there on that heap of ash, and go to sleep."

He threw her an old coat for a pillow, and turned to his work. The heap was the refuse of the burnt iron, and was not a hard bed; the half-smothered warmth, too, penetrated her limbs, dulling their pain and cold shiver.

Miserable enough she looked, lying there on the ashes like a limp, dirty rag,—yet not an unfitting figure to crown the scene of hopeless discomfort and veiled crime: more fitting, if one looked deeper into the heart of things,—at her thwarted woman's form, her colorless life, her waking stupor that smothered pain and hunger,—even more fit to be a type of her class. Deeper yet if one could look, was there nothing worth reading in this wet, faded thing, half-covered with ashes? no story of a soul filled with groping passionate love, heroic unselfishness, fierce jealousy? of years of weary trying to please the one human being whom she loved, to gain one look of real heart-kindness from him? If anything like this were hidden beneath the pale, bleared eyes, and dull, washed-out-looking face, no one had ever taken the trouble to read its faint signs: not the half-clothed furnace-tender, Wolfe, certainly. Yet he was kind to her: it was his nature to be kind, even to the very rats that swarmed in the cellar; kind to her in just the same way. She knew that. And it might be that very knowledge had given to her face its apathy and vacancy more than her low, torpid life. One sees that dead, vacant look steal sometimes over the rarest, finest of women's faces,—in the very midst, it may be, of their warmest summer's day; and then one can guess at the secret of intolerable solitude that lies hid beneath the delicate laces and brilliant smile.

There was no warmth, no brilliancy, no summer for this woman; so the stupor and vacancy had time to gnaw into her face perpetually. She was young, too, though no one guessed it; so the gnawing was the fiercer.

She lay quiet in the dark corner, listening, through the monotonous din and uncertain glare of the works, to the dull plash of the rain in the far distance,—shrinking back whenever the man Wolfe happened to look towards her. She knew, in spite of all his kindness, that there was that in her face and form which made him loathe the sight of her. She felt by instinct, although she could not comprehend it, the finer nature of the man, which made him among his fellow-workmen something unique, set apart. She knew, that, down under all the vileness and coarseness of his life, there was a groping passion for whatever was beautiful and pure,— that his soul sickened with disgust at her deformity, even when his words were kindest. Through this dull consciousness, which never left her, came, like a sting, the recollection of the dark blue eyes and lithe figure of the little Irish girl she had left in the cellar. The recollection struck through even her stupid intellect with a vivid glow of beauty and of grace. Little Janey, timid, helpless, clinging to Hugh as her only friend: that was the sharp thought, the bitter thought, that drove into the glazed eyes a fierce light of pain. You laugh at it? Are pain and jealousy less savage realities down here in this place I am taking you to than in your own house or your own heart,—your heart, which they clutch at sometimes? The note is the same, I fancy, be the octave high or low.

If you could go into this mill where Deborah lay, and drag out from the hearts of these men the terrible tragedy of their lives, taking it as a symptom of the disease of their class, no ghost Horror would terrify you more. A reality of soul-starvation, of living death, that meets you every day under the besotted faces on the street,—I can paint nothing of this, only give you the outside outlines of a night, a crisis in the life of one man: whatever muddy depth of soul-history lies beneath you can read according to the eyes God has given you.

Wolfe, while Deborah watched him as a spaniel its master, bent over the furnace with his iron pole, unconscious of her scrutiny, only stopping to receive orders. Physically, Nature had promised the man but little. He had already lost the strength and instinct vigor of a man, his muscles were thin, his nerves weak, his face (a meek, woman's face) haggard, yellow with consumption. In the mill he was known as one of the girl-men: "Molly Wolfe" was his *sobriquet*. He was never seen in the cockpit, did not own a terrier, drank but seldom; when he did, desperately. He fought sometimes, but was always thrashed, pommelled to a jelly. The man was game enough, when his blood was up: but he was no favorite in the mill; he had the taint of school-learning on him,—not to a dangerous extent, only a quarter or so in the free-school in fact, but enough to ruin him as a good hand in a fight.

For other reasons, too, he was not popular. Not one of themselves, they felt that, though outwardly as filthy and ash-covered; silent, with foreign thoughts and longings breaking out through his quietness in innumerable curious ways: this one, for instance. In the neighboring furnace-buildings lay great heaps of the refuse from the ore after the pig-metal is run. *Korl* we call it here: a light, porous substance, of a delicate, waxen, flesh-colored tinge. Out of the blocks of this korl, Wolfe, in his off-hours from the furnace, had a habit of chipping and moulding figures,—hideous, fantastic enough, but sometimes strangely beautiful: even the mill-men saw that, while they jeered at him. It was a curious fancy in the man, almost a passion. The few hours for rest he spent hewing and hacking with his blunt knife, never speaking, until his watch came again,—working at one figure for months, and, when it was finished, breaking it to pieces perhaps, in a fit of disappointment. A morbid, gloomy man, untaught, unled, left to feed his soul in grossness and crime, and hard, grinding labor.

I want you to come down and look at this Wolfe, standing there among the lowest of his kind, and see him just as he is, that you may judge him justly when you hear the story of this night. I want you to look back, as he does every day, at his birth in vice, his starved infancy; to remember the heavy years he has groped through as boy and man,—the slow, heavy years of constant, hot work. So long ago he began, that he thinks sometimes he has worked there for ages. There is no hope that it will ever end. Think that God put into this man's soul a fierce thirst for beauty,—to know it, to create it; to *be*—something, he knows not what,—other than he is. There are moments when a passing cloud, the sun glinting on the purple thistles, a kindly smile, a child's face, will rouse him to a passion of pain,—when his nature starts up with a mad cry of rage against God, man, whoever it is that has forced this vile, slimy life upon him. With all this groping, this mad desire, a great blind intellect stumbling through wrong, a loving poet's heart, the man was by habit only a coarse, vulgar taborer, familiar with sights and words you would blush to name. Be just: when I tell you about this night, see him as he is. Be just,—not like man's law, which seizes on one isolated fact, but like God's judging angel, whose clear, sad eye saw all the countless cankering days of this man's life, all the countless nights, when, sick with starving, his soul fainted in him, before it judged him for this night, the saddest of all.

I called this night the crisis of his life. If it was, it stole on him unawares. These great turning-days of life cast no shadow before, slip by unconsciously. Only a trifle, a little turn of the rudder, and the ship goes to heaven or hell.

Wolfe, while Deborah watched him, dug into the furnace of melting iron with his pole, dully thinking only how many rails the lump would yield. It was late,—nearly Sunday morning; another hour, and the heavy work would be done,—only the furnaces to replenish and cover for the next day. The workmen were growing more noisy, shouting, as they had to do, to be heard over the deep clamor of the mills. Suddenly they grew less boisterous,—at the far end, entirely silent. Something unusual had happened. After a moment, the silence came nearer; the men stopped their jeers and drunken choruses. Deborah, stupidly lifting up her head, saw the cause of the quiet. A group of five or six men were slowly approaching, stopping to examine each furnace as they came. Visitors often came to see the mills after night: except by growing less noisy, the men took no notice of them. The furnace where Wolfe worked was near the bounds of the works; they halted there hot and tired: a walk over one of these great foundries is no trifling task. The woman, drawing out of sight, turned over to sleep. Wolfe, seeing them stop, suddenly roused from his indifferent stupor, and watched them keenly. He knew some of them: the overseer, Clarke,—a son of Kirby, one of the mill-owners,—and a Doctor May, one of the town-physicians. The other two were strangers. Wolfe came closer. He seized eagerly every chance that brought him into contact with this mysterious class that shone down on him perpetually with the glamour of another order of being. What made the difference between them? That was the mystery of his life. He had a vague notion that perhaps to-night he could find it out. One of the strangers sat down on a pile of bricks, and beckoned young Kirby to his side.

"This *is* hot, with a vengeance. A match, please?"—lighting his cigar. "But the walk is worth the trouble. If it were not that you must have heard it so often, Kirby, I would tell you that your works look like Dante's Inferno."

Kirby laughed.

"Yes. Yonder is Farinata himself in the burning tomb,"—pointing to some figure in the shimmering shadows.

"Judging from some of the faces of your men," said the other, "they bid fair to try the reality of Dante's vision, some day."

Young Kirby looked curiously around, as if seeing the faces of his hands for the first time.

"They're bad enough, that's true. A desperate set, I fancy. Eh, Clarke?"

The overseer did not hear him. He was talking of net profits just then,— giving, in fact, a schedule of the annual business of the firm to a sharp peering little Yankee, who jotted down notes on a paper laid on the crown of his hat: a reporter for one of the city papers, getting up a series of reviews of the leading manufactories. The other gentlemen had accompanied them merely for amusement. They were silent until the notes were finished, drying their feet at the furnaces, and sheltering their faces from the intolerable heat. At last the overseer concluded with—

"I believe that is a pretty fair estimate, Captain."

"Here, some of you men!" said Kirby, "bring up those boards. We may as well sit down, gentlemen, until the rain is over. It cannot last much longer at this rate."

"Pig-metal,"—mumbled the reporter,—"um!—coal facilities,—um!— hands employed, twelve hundred,—bitumen,—um!—all right, I believe, Mr. Clarke,—sinking-fund,—what did you say was your sinking-fund?"

"Twelve hundred hands?" said the stranger, the young man who had first spoken. "Do you control their votes, Kirby?"

"Control? No." The young man smiled complacently. "But my father brought seven hundred votes to the polls for his candidate last November. No force-work, you understand,—only a speech or two, a hint to form themselves into a society, and a bit of red and blue bunting to make them a flag. The Invincible Roughs,—I believe that is their name. I forget the motto: 'Our country's hope,' I think."

There was a laugh. The young man talking to Kirby sat with an amused light in his cool gray eye, surveying critically the half-clothed figures of the puddlers, and the slow swing of their brawny muscles. He was a stranger in the city,—spending a couple of months in the borders of a Slave State, to study the institutions of the South,—a brother-in-law of

Kirby's,—Mitchell. He was an amateur gymnast,—hence his anatomical eye; a patron, in a *blasé* way, of the prize-ring; a man who sucked the essence out of a science or philosophy in an indifferent, gentlemanly way; who took Kant, Novalis, Humboldt, for what they were worth in his own scales; accepting all, despising nothing, in heaven, earth, or hell, but one-idead men; with a temper yielding and brilliant as summer water, until his Self was touched, when it was ice, though brilliant still. Such men are not rare in the States.

As he knocked the ashes from his cigar, Wolfe caught with a quick plea-sure the contour of the white hand, the blood-glow of a red ring he wore. His voice, too, and that of Kirby's, touched him like music,—low, even, with chording cadences. About this man Mitchell hung the impalpable atmosphere belonging to the thoroughbred gentleman. Wolfe, scraping away the ashes beside him, was conscious of it, did obeisance to it with his artist sense, unconscious that he did so.

The rain did not cease. Clark and the reporter left the mills; the others, comfortably seated near the furnace, lingered, smoking and talking in a desultory way. Greek would not have been more unintelligible to the fur-nace-tenders, whose presence they soon forgot entirely. Kirby drew out a newspaper from his pocket and read aloud some article, which they dis-cussed eagerly. At every sentence, Wolfe listened more and more like a dumb, hopeless animal, with a duller, more stolid look creeping over his face, glancing now and then at Mitchell, marking acutely every smallest sign of refinement, then back to himself, seeing as in a mirror his filthy body, his more stained soul.

Never! He had no words for such a thought, but he knew now, in all the sharpness of the bitter certainty, that between them there was a great gulf never to be passed. Never!

The bells of the mills rang for midnight. Sunday morning had dawned. Whatever hidden message lay in the tolling bells floated past these men unknown. Yet it was there. Veiled in the solemn music ushering the risen saviour was a key-note to solve the darkest secrets of a world gone wrong,—even this social riddle which the brain of the grimy puddler grappled with madly to-night.

The men began to withdraw the metal from the caldrons. The mills were deserted on Sundays, except by the hands who fed the fires, and those who had no lodgings and slept usually on the ash-heaps. The three strangers sat still during the next hour, watching the men cover the furnaces, laughing now and then at some jest of Kirby's.

"Do you know," said Mitchell, I like this view of the works better than when the glare was fiercest? These heavy shadows and the amphitheatre of smothered fires are ghostly, unreal. One could fancy these red smouldering lights to be the half-shut eyes of wild beasts, and the spectral figures their victims in the den."

Kirby laughed. "You are fanciful. Come, let us get out of the den. The spectral figures, as you call them, are a little too real for me to fancy a close proximity in the darkness,—unarmed, too."

The others rose, buttoning their over-coats, and lighting cigars.

"Raining, still," said Doctor May, "and hard. Where did we leave the coach, Mitchell?"

"At the other side of the works.—Kirby, what's that?"

Mitchell started back, half-frightened, as, suddenly turning a corner, the white figure of a woman faced him in the darkness,—a woman, white, of giant proportions, crouching on the ground, her arms flung out in some wild gesture of warning.

"Stop! Make that fire burn there!" cried Kirby, stopping short.

The flame burst out, flashing the gaunt figure into bold relief.

Mitchell drew a long breath.

"I thought it was alive," he said, going up curiously.

The others followed.

"Not marble, eh?" asked Kirby, touching it.

One of the lower overseers stopped.

"Korl, Sir."

"Who did it?"

"Can't say. Some of the hands; chipped it out in off-hours."

"Chipped to some purpose, I should say. What a flesh-tint the stuff has! Do you see, Mitchell?"

"I see."

He had stepped aside where the light fell boldest on the figure, looking at it in silence. There was not one line of beauty or grace in it: a nude woman's form, muscular, grown coarse with labor, the powerful limbs instinct with some one poignant longing. One idea: there it was in the tense, rigid muscles, the clutching hands, the wild, eager face, like that of a starving wolf's. Kirby and Doctor May walked around it, critical, curious. Mitchell stood aloof, silent. The figure touched him strangely.

"Not badly done," said Doctor May. "Where did the fellow learn that sweep of the muscles in the arm and hand? Look at them! They are groping,—do you see?—clutching: the peculiar action of a man dying of thirst."

"They have ample facilities for studying anatomy," sneered Kirby, glancing at the half-naked figures.

"Look," continued the Doctor, "at this bony wrist, and the strained sinews of the instep! A working-woman,—the very type of her class."

"God forbid!" muttered Mitchell.

"Why?" demanded May. "What does the fellow intend by the figure? I cannot catch the meaning."

"Ask him," said the other, dryly. "There he stands,"—pointing to Wolfe, who stood with a group of men, leaning on his ash-rake.

The Doctor beckoned him with the affable smile which kind-hearted men put on, when talking with these people.

"Mr. Mitchell has picked you out as the man who did this,—I'm sure I don't know why. But what did you mean by it?"

"She be hungry."

Wolfe's eyes answered Mitchell, not the Doctor.

"Oh-h! But what a mistake you have made, my fine fellow! You have given no sign of starvation to the body. It is strong,—terribly strong. It has the mad, half-despairing gesture of drowning."

Wolfe stammered, glanced appealingly at Mitchell, who saw the soul of the thing, he knew. But the cool, probing eyes were turned on himself now,—mocking, cruel, relentless.

"Not hungry for meat," the furnace-tender said at last.

"What then? Whiskey?" jeered Kirby, with a coarse laugh.

Wolfe was silent a moment, thinking.

"I dunno," he said, with a bewildered look. "It mebbe. Summat to make her live, I think,—like you. Whiskey ull do it, in a way."

The young man laughed again. Mitchell flashed a look of disgust some-where,—not at Wolfe.

"May," he broke out impatiently, "are you blind? Look at that woman's face! It asks questions of God, and says, 'I have a right to know.' Good God, how hungry it is!"

They looked a moment; then May turned to the mill-owner:—

"Have you many such hands as this? What are you going to do with them? Keep them at puddling iron?"

Kirby shrugged his shoulders. Mitchell's look had irritated him.

"*Ce nést pas mon affaire.* I have no fancy for nursing infant geniuses. I sup-pose there are some stray gleams of mind and soul among these wretch-es. The Lord will take care of his own; or else they can work out their own salvation. I have heard you call our American system a ladder which any man can scale. Do you doubt it? Or perhaps you want to banish all social ladders, and put us all on a flat table-land,—eh, May?"

The Doctor looked vexed, puzzled. Some terrible problem lay hid in this woman's face, and troubled these men. Kirby waited for an answer, and, receiving none, went on, warming with his subject.

"I tell you, there's something wrong that no talk of '*Liberté* or '*Egalité* will do away. If I had the making of men, these men who do the lowest part of the world's work should be machines,—nothing more,—hands. It would be kindness. God help them! What are taste, reason, to creatures who must live such lives as that?" He pointed to Deborah, sleeping on the ash-heap. "So many nerves to sting them to pain. What if God had put your brain, with all its agony of touch, into your fingers, and bid you work and strike with that?"

"You think you could govern the world better?" laughed the Doctor.

"I do not think at all."

"That is true philosophy. Drift with the stream, because you cannot dive deep enough to find bottom, eh?"

"Exactly," rejoined Kirby. "I do not think. I wash my hands of all social problems,—slavery, caste, white or black. My duty to my operatives has a narrow limit,—the pay-hour on Saturday night. Outside of that, if they cut korl, or cut each other's throats, (the more popular amusement of the two,) I am not responsible."

The Doctor sighed,—a good honest sigh, from the depths of his stomach.

"God help us! Who is responsible?"

"Not I, I tell you," said Kirby, testily. "What has the man who pays them money to do with their souls' concerns, more than the grocer or butcher who takes it?"

"And yet," said Mitchell's cynical voice, "look at her! How hungry she is!"

Kirby tapped his boot with his cane. No one spoke. Only the dumb face of the rough image looking into their faces with the awful question, "What shall we do to be saved?" Only Wolfe's face, with its heavy weight of brain, its weak, uncertain mouth, its desperate eyes, out of which looked the soul of his class,—only Wolfe's face turned towards Kirby's. Mitchell laughed,—a cool, musical laugh.

"Money has spoken!" he said, seating himself lightly on a stone with the air of an amused spectator at a play. "Are you answered?"—turning to Wolfe his clear, magnetic face.

Bright and deep and cold as Arctic air, the soul of the man lay tranquil beneath. He looked at the furnace-tender as he had looked at a rare mosaic in the morning; only the man was the more amusing study of the two.

"Are you answered? Why, May, look at him! *'De profundis clamavi.'* Or, to quote in English, 'Hungry and thirsty, his soul faints in him.' And so Money sends back its answer into the depths through you, Kirby! Very clear the answer, too!—I think I remember reading the same words somewhere:—washing your hands in Eau de Cologne, and saying, 'I am innocent of the blood of this man. See ye to it!'"

Kirby flushed angrily.

"You quote Scripture freely."

"Do I not quote correctly? I think I remember another line, which may amend my meaning: 'Inasmuch as ye did it unto one of the least of these, ye did it unto me.' Deist? Bless you, man, I was raised on the milk of the Word. Now, Doctor, the pocket of the world having uttered its voice, what has the heart to say? You are a philanthropist, in a small way,—*n'est ce pas?* Here, boy, this gentleman can show you how to cut korl better,—or your destiny. Go on, May!"

"I think a mocking devil possesses you to-night," rejoined the Doctor, seriously.

He went to Wolfe and put his hand kindly on his arm. Something of a vague idea possessed the Doctor's brain that much good was to be done here by a friendly word or two: a latent genius to be warmed into life by a waited-for sunbeam. Here it was: he had brought it. So he went on complacently:—

"Do you know, boy, you have it in you to be a great sculptor, a great man?—do you understand?" (talking down to the capacity of his hearer: it is a way people have with children, and men like Wolfe)—"to live a better, stronger life than I, or Mr. Kirby here? A man may make himself anything he chooses. God has given you stronger powers than many men,—me, for instance."

May stopped, heated, glowing with his own magnanimity. And it was magnanimous. The puddler had drunk in every word, looking through the Doctor's flurry, and generous heat, and self-approval, into his will, with those slow, absorbing eyes of his.

"Make yourself what you will. It is your right."

"I know," quietly. "Will you help me?"

Mitchell laughed again. The Doctor turned now, in a passion,—

"You know, Mitchell, I have not the means. You know, if I had, it is in my heart to take this boy and educate him for"—

"The glory of God, and the glory of John May."

May did not speak for a moment; then, controlled, he said,

"Why should one be raised, when myriads are left?—I have not the money, boy," to Wolfe, shortly.

"Money?" He said it over slowly, as one repeats the guessed answer to a riddle, doubtfully. "That is it? Money?"

"Yes, money,—that is it," said Mitchell, rising, and drawing his furred coat about him. "You've found the cure for all the world's diseases.— Come May, find your good-humor, and come home. This damp wind chills my very bones. Come and preach your Saint-Simonian doctrines to-morrow to Kirby's hands. Let them have a clear idea of the rights of the soul, and I'll venture next week they'll strike for higher wages. That will be the end of it."

"Will you send the coach-driver to this side of the mills?" asked Kirby, turning to Wolfe.

He spoke kindly: it was his habit to do so. Deborah, seeing the puddler go, crept after him. The three men waited outside. Doctor May walked up and down, chafed. Suddenly he stopped.

"Go back, Mitchell! You say the pocket and the heart of the world speak without meaning to these people. What has its head to say? Taste, culture, refinement? Go!"

Mitchell was leaning against a brick wall. He turned his head indolently, and looked into the mills. There hung about the place a thick, unclean odor. The slightest motion of his hand marked that he perceived it, and his insufferable disgust. That was all. May said nothing, only quickened his angry tramp.

"Besides," added Mitchell, giving a corollary to his answer, "it would be of no use. I am not one of them."

"You do not mean"—said May, facing him.

"Yes, I mean just that. Reform is born of need, not pity. No vital movement of the people's has worked down, for good or evil; fermented, instead, car-ried up the heaving, cloggy mass. Think back through history, and you will know it. What will this lowest deep—thieves, Magdalens, negroes do with the light filtered through ponderous Church creeds, Baconian theo-ries, Goethe schemes? Some day, out of their bitter need will be thrown up their own light-bringer,—their Jean Paul, their Cromwell, their Messiah."

"Bah!" was the Doctor's inward criticism. However, in practice, he adopt-ed the theory; for, when, night and morning, afterwards, he prayed that power might be given these degraded souls to rise, he glowed at heart, recognizing an accomplished duty.

Wolfe and the woman had stood in the shadow of the works as the coach drove off. The Doctor had held out his hand in a frank, generous way, telling him to "take care of himself, and to remember it was his right to rise." Mitchell had simply touched his hat, as to an equal, with a quiet look of thorough recognition. Kirby had thrown Deborah some money, which she found, and clutched eagerly enough. They were gone now, all of them. The man sat down on the cinder-road, looking up into the murky sky.

"'T be late, Hugh. Wunnot hur come?"

He shook his head doggedly, and the woman crouched out of his sight against the wall. Do you remember rare moments when a sudden light flashed over yourself, your world, God? when you stood on a mountain-peak, seeing your life as it might have been, as it is? one quick instant, when custom lost its force and every-day usage? when your friend, wife, brother, stood in a new light? your soul was bared, and the grave,—a fore-taste of the nakedness of the Judgment-Day? So it came before him, his life, that night. The slow tides of pain he had borne gathered themselves up and surged against his soul. His squalid daily life, the brutal coarseness eating into his brain, as the ashes into his skin: before, these things had been a dull aching into his consciousness; to-night, they were reality. He gripped the filthy red shirt that clung, stiff with soot, about him, and tore it savagely from his arm. The flesh beneath was muddy with grease and ashes,—and the heart beneath that! And the soul? God knows.

Then flashed before his vivid poetic sense the man who had left him,—the pure face, the delicate, sinewy limbs, in harmony with all he knew of beauty or truth. In his cloudy fancy he had pictured a Something like this. He had found it in this Mitchell, even when he idly scoffed at his pain: a Man all-knowing, all-seeing, crowned by Nature, reigning,—the keen glance of his eye falling like a sceptre on other men. And yet his instinct taught him that he too—He! He looked at himself with sudden loathing, sick, wrung his hands with a cry, and then was silent. With all the phantoms of his heated, ignorant fancy, Wolfe had not been vague in his ambitions. They were practical, slowly built up before him out of his knowledge of what he could do. Through years he had day by day made this hope a real thing to himself,—a clear, projected figure of himself, as he might become.

Able to speak, to know what was best, to raise these men and women working at his side up with him: sometimes he forgot this defined hope in the frantic anguish to escape,—only to escape,—out of the wet, the pain, the ashes, somewhere, anywhere,—only for one moment of free air on a hill-side, to lie down and let his sick soul throb itself out in the sunshine. But to-night he panted for life. The savage strength of his nature was roused; his cry was fierce to God for justice.

"Look at me!" he said to Deborah, with a low, bitter laugh, striking his puny chest savagely. "What am I worth, Deb? Is it my fault that I am no better? My fault? My fault?"

He stopped, stung with a sudden remorse, seeing her hunchback shape writhing with sobs. For Deborah was crying thankless tears, according to the fashion of women.

"God forgi' me, woman! Things go harder wi' you nor me. It's a worse share."

He got up and helped her to rise; and they went doggedly down the muddy street, side by side.

"It's all wrong," he muttered, slowly,—"all wrong! I dunnot understan'. But it'll end some day."

"Come home, Hugh!" she said, coaxingly; for he had stopped, looking around bewildered.

"Home,—and back to the mill!" He went on saying this over to himself, as if he would mutter down every pain in this dull despair.

She followed him through the fog, her blue lips chattering with cold. They reached the cellar at last. Old Wolfe had been drinking since she went out, and had crept nearer the door. The girl Janey slept heavily in the corner. He went up to her, touching softly the worn white arm with his fingers. Some bitterer thought stung him, as he stood there. He wiped the drops from his forehead, and went into the room beyond, livid, trembling. A hope, trifling, perhaps, but very dear, had died just then out of the poor puddler's life, as he looked at the sleeping, innocent girl,—some plan for the future, in which she had borne a part. He gave it up that moment, then and forever. Only a trifle, perhaps, to us: his face grew a shade paler,—that was all. But, somehow, the man's soul, as God and the angels looked down on it, never was the same afterwards.

Deborah followed him into the inner room. She carried a candle, which she placed on the floor, closing the door after her. She had seen the look on his face, as he turned away: her own grew deadly. Yet, as she came up to him her eyes glowed. He was seated on an old chest, quiet, holding his face in his hands.

"Hugh!" she said, softly.

He did not speak.

"Hugh, did hur hear what the man said,—him with the clear voice? Did hur hear? Money, money,—that it wud do all?"

He pushed her away,—gently, but he was worn out; her rasping tone fretted him.

"Hugh!"

The candle flared a pale yellow light over the cobwebbed brick walls, and the woman standing there. He looked at her. She was young, in deadly earnest; her faded eyes, and wet, ragged figure caught from their frantic eagerness a power akin to beauty.

"Hugh, it is true! Money ull do it! Oh, Hugh, boy, listen till me! He said it true! It is money!"

"I know. Go back! I do not want you here."

"Hugh, it is t' last time. I'll never worrit hur again."

There were tears in her voice now, but she choked them back.

"Hear till me only to-night! If one of t' witch people wud come, them we heard of t' home, and gif hur all hur wants, what then? Say, Hugh!"

"What do you mean?"

"I mean money."

Her whisper shrilled through his brain.

"If one of t' witch dwarfs wud come from t' lane moors to-night, and gif hur money, to go out,—out, I say,—out, lad, where t' sun shines, and t' heath grows, and t' ladies walk in silken gownds, and God stays all t' time,—where t' man lives that talked to us to-night,—Hugh knows, Hugh could walk there like a king!"

He thought the woman mad, tried to check her, but she went on, fierce in her eager haste.

"If I were t' witch dwarf, if I had t' money, wud hur thank me? Wud hur take me out o' this place wid hur and Janey? I wud not come into the gran' house hur wud build, to vex hur wid t' hunch,—only at night, when t' shadows were dark, stand far off to see hur."

Mad? Yes! Are many of us mad in this way?

"Poor Deb! poor Deb!" he said, soothingly.

"It is here," she said, suddenly jerking into his hand a small roll. "I took it! I did it! Me, me!—not hur! I shall be hanged, I shall be burnt in hell, if anybody knows I took it! Out of his pocket, as he leaned against t' bricks. Hur knows?"

She thrust it into his hand, and then, her errand done, began to gather chips together to make a fire, choking down hysteric sobs.

"Has it come to this?"

That was all he said. The Welsh Wolfe blood was honest. The roll was a small green pocket-book containing one or two gold pieces, and a check for an incredible amount, as it seemed to the poor puddler. He laid it down, hiding his face again in his hands.

"Hugh, don't be angry wud me! It's only poor Deb,—hur knows?"

He took the long skinny fingers kindly in his.

"Angry? God help me, no! Let me sleep. I am tired."

He threw himself heavily down on the wooden bench, stunned with pain and weariness. She brought some old rags to cover him.

It was late on Sunday evening before he awoke. I tell God's truth, when I say he had then no thought of keeping this money. Deborah had hid it in his pocket. He found it there. She watched him eagerly, as he took it out.

"I must gif it to him," he said, reading her face.

"Hur knows," she said with a bitter sigh of disappointment. "But it is hur right to keep it."

His right! The word struck him. Doctor May had used the same. He washed himself, and went out to find this man Mitchell. His right! Why did this chance word cling to him so obstinately? Do you hear the fierce devils whisper in his ear, as he went slowly down the darkening street?

The evening came on, slow and calm. He seated himself at the end of an alley leading into one of the larger streets. His brain was clear to-night, keen, intent, mastering. It would not start back, cowardly, from any hell-ish temptation, but meet it face to face. Therefore the great temptation of his life came to him veiled by no sophistry, but bold, defiant, owning its own vile name, trusting to one bold blow for victory.

He did not deceive himself. Theft! That was it. At first the word sickened him; then he grappled with it. Sitting there on a broken cart-wheel, the fading day, the noisy groups, the church-bells' tolling passed before him like a panorama, while the sharp struggle went on within. This money! He took it out, and looked at it. If he gave it back, what then? He was going to be cool about it.

People going by to church saw only a sickly mill-boy watching them qui-etly at the alley's mouth. They did not know that he was mad, or they would not have gone by so quietly: mad with hunger; stretching out his hands to the world, that had given so much to them, for leave to live the life God meant him to live. His soul within him was smothering to death; he wanted so much, thought so much, and *knew*—nothing. There was nothing of which he was certain, except the mill and things there. Of God and heaven he had heard so little, that they were to him what fairy-land is to a child: something real, but not here; very far off. His brain, greedy, dwarfed, full of thwarted energy and unused powers, questioned these men and women going by, coldly, bitterly, that night. Was it not his right to live as they,—a pure life, a good, true-hearted life, full of beauty and kind words? He only wanted to know how to use the strength within him. His heart warmed, as he thought of it. He suffered himself to think of it longer. If he took the money?

Then he saw himself as he might be, strong, helpful, kindly. The night crept on, as this one image slowly evolved itself from the crowd of other thoughts and stood triumphant. He looked at it. As he might be! What wonder, if it blinded him to delirium,—the madness that underlies all rev-olution, all progress, and all fall?

You laugh at the shallow temptation? You see the error underlying its argument so clearly,—that to him a true life was one of full development rather than self-restraint? that he was deaf to the higher tone in a cry of voluntary suffering for truth's sake than in the fullest flow of sponta-neous harmony? I do not plead his cause. I only want to show you the mote in my brother's eye: then you can see clearly to take it out.

The money,—there it lay on his knee, a little blotted slip of paper, nothing in itself, used to raise him out of the pit; something straight from God's hand. A thief! Well, what was it to be a thief? He met the question at last, face to face, wiping the clammy drops of sweat from his forehead. God made this money—the fresh air, too—for his children's use. He never made the difference between poor and rich. The Something who looked down on him that moment through the cool gray sky had a kindly face, he knew,—loved his children alike. Oh, he knew that!

There were times when the soft floods of color in the crimson and purple flames, or the clear depth of amber in the water below the bridge, had somehow given him a glimpse of another world than this,—of an infinite depth of beauty and of quiet somewhere,—somewhere,—a depth of quiet and rest and love. Looking up now, it became strangely real. The sun had sunk quite below the hills, but his last rays struck upward, touching the zenith. The fog had risen, and the town and river were steeped in its thick, gray damp; but overhead, the sun-touched smoke-clouds opened like a cleft ocean,—shifting, rolling seas of crimson mist, waves of billowy silver veined with blood-scarlet, inner depths unfathomable of glancing light. Wolfe's artist-eye grew drunk with color. The gates of that other world! Fading, flashing before him now. What, in that world of Beauty, Content, and Right, were the petty laws, the mine and thine, of mill-owners and mill-hands?

A consciousness of power stirred within him. He stood up. A man, he thought, stretching out his hands,—free to work, to live, to love! Free! His right! He folded the scrap of paper in his hand. As his nervous fingers took it in, limp and blotted, so his soul took in the mean temptation, lapped it in fancied rights, in dreams of improved existences, drifting and endless as the cloud-seas of color. Clutching it, as if the tightness of his hold would strengthen his sense of possession, he went aimlessly down the street. It was his watch at the mill. He need not go, need never go again, thank God!—shaking off the thought with unspeakable loathing.

Shall I go over the history of the hours of that night? how the man wandered from one to another of his old haunts, with a half-consciousness of bidding them farewell,—lanes and alleys and back-yards where the mill-hands lodged,—noting, with a new eagerness, the filth and drunkenness, the pig-pens, the ash-heaps covered with potato-skins, the bloated, pimpled women at the doors,—with a new disgust, a new sense of sudden triumph, and, under all, a new, vague dread, unknown before, smothered down, kept under, but still there? It left him but once during the night, when, for the second time in his life, he entered a church. It was a sombre Gothic pile, where the stained light lost itself in far-retreating arches; built to meet the requirements and sympathies of a far other class than Wolfe's. Yet it touched, moved him uncontrollably. The distances, the shadows, the still, marble figures, the mass of silent kneeling worshippers, the mysterious music, thrilled, lifted his soul with a wonderful pain. Wolfe forgot himself, forgot the new life he was going to live, the mean terror gnawing underneath. The voice of the speaker strengthened the charm; it was clear, feeling, full, strong. An old man, who had lived much, suffered much; whose brain was keenly alive, dominant; whose heart was summer-warm with charity. He taught it to-night. He held up Humanity in its grand total; showed the great world-cancer to his people. Who could show it better? He was a Christian reformer; he had studied the age thoroughly; his outlook at man had been free, world-wide, over all time. His faith stood sublime upon the Rock of Ages; his fiery zeal guided vast schemes by which the gospel was to be preached to all nations. How did he preach it tonight? In burning, light-laden words he painted the incarnate Life, Love, the universal Man: words that became reality in the lives of these people—that lived again in beautiful words and actions, trifling, but heroic. Sin, as he defined it, was a real foe to them; their trials, temptations, were his. His words passed far over the furnace-tender's grasp, toned to suit another class of culture; they sounded in his ears a very pleasant song in an unknown tongue. He meant to cure this world-cancer with a steady eye that had never glared with hunger, and a hand that neither poverty nor strychnine-whiskey had taught to shake. In this morbid, distorted heart of the Welsh puddler he had failed.

Wolfe rose at last, and turned from the church down the street. He looked up; the night had come on foggy, damp; the golden mists had vanished, and the sky lay dull and ash-colored. He wandered again aimlessly down the street, idly wondering what had become of the cloud-sea of crimson and scarlet. The trial-day of this man's life was over, and he had lost the victory. What followed was mere drifting circumstance,—a quicker walking over the path,—that was all. Do you want to hear the end of it? You wish me to make a tragic story out of it? Why, in the police-reports of the morning paper you can find a dozen such tragedies: hints of shipwrecks unlike any that ever befell on the high seas; hints that here a power was lost to heaven,—that there a soul went down where no tide can ebb or flow. Commonplace enough the hints are,—jocose sometimes, done up in rhyme.

Doctor May, a month after the night I have told you of, was reading to his wife at breakfast from this fourth column of the morning-paper: an unusual thing,—these police-reports not being, in general, choice reading for ladies; but it was only one item he read.

"Oh, my dear! You remember that man I told you of, that we saw at Kirby's mill?—that was arrested for robbing Mitchell? Here he is; just listen:—'Circuit Court. Judge Day. Hugh Wolfe, operative in Kirby & John's Loudon Mills. Charge, grand larceny. Sentence, nineteen years hard labor in penitentiary.'—Scoundrel! Serves him right! After all our kindness that night! Picking Mitchell's pocket at the very time!"

His wife said something about the ingratitude of that kind of people, and then they began to talk of something else.

Nineteen years! How easy that was to read! What a simple word for Judge Day to utter! Nineteen years! Half a lifetime!

Hugh Wolfe sat on the window-ledge of his cell, looking out. His ankles were ironed. Not usual in such cases; but he had made two desperate efforts to escape. "Well," as Haley, the jailer, said, "small blame to him! Nineteen years' imprisonment was not a pleasant thing to look forward to." Haley was very good-natured about it, though Wolfe had fought him savagely.

"When he was first caught," the jailer said afterwards, in telling the story, "before the trial, the fellow was cut down at once,—laid there on that pallet like a dead man, with his hands over his eyes. Never saw a man so cut down in my life. Time of the trial, too, came the queerest dodge of any customer I ever had. Would choose no lawyer. Judge gave him one, of course. Gibson it was. He tried to prove the fellow crazy; but it wouldn't go. Thing was plain as day-light: money found on him. 'Twas a hard sentence,—all the law allows; but it was for 'xample's sake. These millhands are gettin' onbearable. When the sentence was read, he just looked up, and said the money was his by rights, and that all the world had gone wrong. That night, after the trial, a gentleman came to see him here, name of Mitchell,—him as he stole from. Talked to him for an hour. Thought he came for curiosity, like. After he was gone, thought Wolfe was remarkable quiet, and went into his cell. Found him very low; bed all bloody. Doctor said he had been bleeding at the lungs. He was as weak as a cat; yet, if ye'll b'lieve me, he tried to get a-past me and get out. I just carried him like a baby, and threw him on the pallet. Three days after, he tried it again:

that time reached the wall. Lord help you! he fought like a tiger,—giv' some terrible blows. Fightin' for life, you see; for he can't live long, shut up in the stone crib down yonder. Got a death-cough now. 'T took two of us to bring him down that day; so I just put the irons on his feet. There he sits, in there. Goin' to-morrow, with a batch more of 'em. That woman, hunchback, tried with him,—you remember?—she's only got three years. 'Complice. But *she's* a woman, you know. He's been quiet ever since I put on irons: giv' up, I suppose. Looks white, sick-lookin'. It acts different on 'em, bein' sentenced. Most of 'em gets reckless, devilish-like. Some prays awful, and sings them vile songs of the mills, all in a breath. That woman, now, she's desper't'. Been beggin' to see Hugh, as she calls him, for three days. I'm a-goin' to let her in. She don't go with him. Here she is in this next cell. I'm a-goin' now to let her in."

He let her in. Wolfe did not see her. She crept into a corner of the cell, and stood watching him. He was scratching the iron bars of the window with a piece of tin which he had picked up, with an idle, uncertain, vacant stare, just as a child or idiot would do.

"Tryin' to get out, old boy?" laughed Haley. "Them irons will need a crow-bar beside your tin, before you can open 'em."

Wolfe laughed, too, in a senseless way.

"I think I'll get out," he said.

"I believe his brain's touched," said Haley, when he came out.

The puddler scraped away with the tin for half an hour. Still Deborah did not speak. At last she ventured nearer, and touched his arm.

"Blood?" she said, looking at some spots on his coat with a shudder.

He looked up at her. "Why, Deb!" he said, smiling,—such a bright, boy-ish smile, that it went to poor Deborahs heart directly, and she sobbed and cried out loud.

"Oh, Hugh, lad! Hugh! dunnot look at me, when it wur my fault! To think I brought hur to it! And I loved hur so! Oh, lad, I dud!"

The confession, even in this wretch, came with the woman's blush through the sharp cry.

He did not seem to hear her, scraping away diligently at the bars with the bit of tin.

Was he going mad? She peered closely into his face. Something she saw there made her draw suddenly back,—something which Haley had not seen, that lay beneath the pinched, vacant look it had caught since the trial, or the curious gray shadow that rested on it. That gray shadow,— yes, she knew what that meant. She had often seen it creeping over women's faces for months, who died at last of slow hunger or consumption. That meant death, distant, lingering: but this—Whatever it was the woman saw, or thought she saw, used as she was to crime and misery, seemed to make her sick with a new horror. Forgetting her fear of him, she caught his shoulders, and looked keenly, steadily, into his eyes.

"Hugh!" she cried, in a desperate whisper,—"oh, boy, not that! for God's sake, not *that!*"

The vacant laugh went off his face, and he answered her in a muttered word or two that drove her away. Yet the words were kindly enough. Sitting there on his pallet, she cried silently a hopeless sort of tears, but did not speak again. The man looked up furtively at her now and then. Whatever his own trouble was, her distress vexed him with a momentary sting.

It was market-day. The narrow window of the jail looked down directly on the carts and wagons drawn up in a long line, where they had unloaded. He could see, too, and hear distinctly the clink of money as it changed hands, the busy crowd of whites and blacks shoving, pushing one another, and the chaffering and swearing at the stalls. Somehow, the sound, more than anything else had done, wakened him up,—made the whole real to him. He was done with the world and the business of it. He let the tin fall, and looked out, pressing his face close to the rusty bars. How they crowded and pushed! And he,—he should never walk that pavement again! There came Neff Sanders, one of the feeders at the mill, with a basket on his arm. Sure enough, Neff was married the other week. He whistled, hoping he would look up; but he did not. He wondered if Neff remembered he was there,—if any of the boys thought of him up there, and thought that he never was to go down that old cinder-road again. Never again! He had not quite understood it before; but now he did. Not for days or years, but never!—that was it.

How clear the light fell on that stall in front of the market! and how like a picture it was, the dark-green heaps of corn, and the crimson beets, and golden melons! There was another with game: how the light flickered on that pheasant's breast, with the purplish blood dripping over the brown feathers! He could see the red shining of the drops, it was so near. In one minute he could be down there. It was just a step. So easy, as it seemed, so natural to go! Yet it could never be—not in all the thousands of years to come—that he should put his foot on that street again! He thought of himself with a sorrowful pity, as of some one else. There was a dog down in the market, walking after his master with such a stately, grave look!— only a dog, yet he could go backwards and forwards just as he pleased: he had good luck! Why, the very vilest cur, yelping there in the gutter, had not lived his life, had been free to act out whatever thought God had put into his brain; while he—No, he would not think of that! He tried to put the thought away, and to listen to a dispute between a countryman and a woman about some meat; but it would come back. He, what had he done to bear this?

Then came the sudden picture of what might have been, and now. He knew what it was to be in the penitentiary,—how it went with men there. He knew how in these long years he should slowly die, but not until soul and body had become corrupt and rotten,—how, when he came out, if he lived to come, even the lowest of the mill-hands would jeer him,—how his hands would be weak, and his brain senseless and stupid. He believed he was almost that now. He put his hand to his head, with a puzzled, weary look. It ached, his head, with thinking. He tried to quiet himself. It was only right, perhaps; he had done wrong. But was there right or wrong for such as he? What was right? And who had ever taught him? He thrust the whole matter away. A dark, cold quiet crept through his brain. It was all wrong; but let it be! It was nothing to him more than the others. Let it be!

The door grated, as Haley opened it.

"Come, my woman! Must lock up for t' night. Come, stir yerself!"

She went up and took Hugh's hand.

"Good-night, Deb," he said, carelessly.

She had not hoped he would say more; but the tired pain on her mouth just then was bitterer than death. She took his passive hand and kissed it.

"Hur'll never see Deb again!" she ventured, her lips growing colder and more bloodless.

What did she say that for? Did he not know it? Yet he would not be impatient with poor old Deb. She had trouble of her own, as well as he.

"No, never again," he said, trying to be cheerful.

She stood just a moment, looking at him. Do you laugh at her, standing there, with her hunchback, her rags, her bleared, withered face, and the great despised love tugging at her heart?

"Come, you!" called Haley, impatiently.

She did not move.

"Hugh!" she whispered.

It was to be her last word. What was it?

"Hugh, boy, not THAT!"

He did not answer. She wrung her hands, trying to be silent, looking in his face in an agony of entreaty. He smiled again, kindly.

"It is best, Deb. I cannot bear to be hurted any more."

"Hur knows," she said, humbly.

"Tell my father good-bye; and—and kiss little Janey."

She nodded, saying nothing, looked in his face again, and went out of the door. As she went, she staggered.

"Drinkin' to-day?" broke out Haley, pushing her before him. "Where the Devil did you get it? Here, in with ye!" and he shoved her into her cell, next to Wolfe's, and shut the door.

Along the wall of her cell there was a crack low down by the floor, through which she could see the light from Wolfe's. She had discovered it days before. She hurried in now, and, kneeling down by it, listened, hoping to hear some sound. Nothing but the rasping of the tin on the bars. He was at his old amusement again. Something in the noise jarred on her ear, for she shivered as she heard it. Hugh rasped away at the bars. A dull old bit of tin, not fit to cut korl with.

He looked out of the window again. People were leaving the market now. A tall mulatto girl, following her mistress, her basket on her head, crossed the street just below, and looked up. She was laughing; but, when she caught sight of the haggard face peering out through the bars, suddenly grew grave, and hurried by. A free, firm step, a clear-cut olive face, with a scarlet turban tied on one side, dark, shining eyes, and on the head the basket poised, filled with fruit and flowers, under which the scarlet turban and bright eyes looked out half-shadowed. The picture caught his eye. It was good to see a face like that. He would try to-morrow, and cut one like it. *To-morrow!* He threw down the tin, trembling, and covered his face with his hands. When he looked up again, the daylight was gone.

Deborah, crouching near by on the other side of the wall, heard no noise. He sat on the side of the low pallet, thinking. Whatever was the mystery which the woman had seen on his face, it came out now slowly, in the dark there, and became fixed,—a something never seen on his face before. The evening was darkening fast. The market had been over for an hour; the rumbling of the carts over the pavement grew more infrequent: he listened to each, as it passed, because he thought it was to be for the last time. For the same reason, it was, I suppose, that he strained his eyes to catch a glimpse of each passer-by, wondering who they were, what kind of homes they were going to, if they had children,—listening eagerly to every chance word in the street, as if—(God be merciful to the man! what strange fancy was this?)—as if he never should hear human voices again.

It was quite dark at last. The street was a lonely one. The last passenger, he thought, was gone. No,—there was a quick step: Joe Hill, lighting the lamps. Joe was a good old chap; never passed a fellow without some joke or other. He remembered once seeing the place where he lived with his wife. "Granny Hill" the boys called her. Bedridden she was; but so kind as Joe was to her! kept the room so clean!—and the old woman, when he was there, was laughing at "some of t' lad's foolishness." The step was far down the street; but he could see him place the ladder, run up, and light the gas. A longing seized him to be spoken to once more.

"Joe!" he called, out of the grating. "Good-bye, Joe!"

The old man stopped a moment, listening uncertainly; then hurried on. The prisoner thrust his hand out of the window, and called again, louder; but Joe was too far down the street. It was a little thing; but it hurt him,—this disappointment.

"Good-bye, Joe!" he called, sorrowfully enough.

"Be quiet!" said one of the jailers, passing the door, striking on it with his club.

Oh, that was the last, was it?

There was an inexpressible bitterness on his face, as he lay down on the bed, taking the bit of tin, which he had rasped to a tolerable degree of sharpness, in his hand,—to play with, it may be. He bared his arms, looking intently at their corded veins and sinews. Deborah, listening in the next cell, heard a slight clicking sound, often repeated. She shut her lips tightly, that she might not scream; the cold drops of sweat broke over her, in her dumb agony.

"Hur knows best," she muttered at last, fiercely clutching the boards where she lay.

If she could have seen Wolfe, there was nothing about him to frighten her. He lay quite still, his arms outstretched, looking at the pearly stream of moonlight coming into the window. I think in that one hour that came then he lived back over all the years that had gone before. I think that all the low, vile life, all his wrongs, all his starved hopes, came then, and stung him with a farewell poison that made him sick unto death. He made neither moan nor cry, only turned his worn face now and then to the pure light, that seemed so far off, as one that said, "How long, O Lord? how long?"

The hour was over at last. The moon, passing over her nightly path, slowly came nearer, and threw the light across his bed on his feet. He watched it steadily, as it crept up, inch by inch, slowly. It seemed to him to carry with it a great silence. He had been so hot and tired there always in the mills! The years had been so fierce and cruel! There was coming now quiet and coolness and sleep. His tense limbs relaxed, and settled in a calm languor. The blood ran fainter and slow from his heart. He did not think now with a savage anger of what might be and was not; he was conscious only of deep stillness creeping over him. At first he saw a sea of faces: the mill-men,—women he had known, drunken and bloated,—Janey's timid and pitiful, poor old Debs: then they floated together like a mist, and faded away, leaving only the clear, pearly moonlight.

Whether, as the pure light crept up the stretched-out figure, it brought with it calm and peace, who shall say? His dumb soul was alone with God in judgment. A Voice may have spoken for it from far-off Calvary, "Father, forgive them, for they know not what they do!" Who dare say? Fainter and fainter the heart rose and fell, slower and slower the moon floated from behind a cloud, until, when at last its full tide of white splendor swept over the cell, it seemed to wrap and fold into a deeper stillness the dead figure that never should move again. Silence deeper than the Night! Nothing that moved, save the black nauseous stream of blood dripping slowly from the pallet to the floor!

There was outcry and crowd enough in the cell the next day. The coroner
and his jury, the local editors, Kirby himself, and boys with their hands
thrust knowingly into their pockets and heads on one side, jammed into
the corners. Coming and going all day. Only one woman. She came late,
and outstayed them all. A Quaker, or Friend, as they call themselves. I
think this woman was known by that name in heaven. A homely body,
coarsely dressed in gray and white. Deborah (for Haley had let her in)
took notice of her. She watched them all—sitting on the end of the pallet,
holding his head in her arms—with the ferocity of a watch-dog, if any of
them touched the body. There was no meekness, or sorrow, in her face; the
stuff out of which murderers are made, instead. All the time Haley and the
woman were laying straight the limbs and cleaning the cell, Deborah sat
still, keenly watching the Quaker's face. Of all the crowd there that day,
this woman alone had not spoken to her,—only once or twice had put
some cordial to her lips. After they all were gone, the woman, in the same
still, gentle way, brought a vase of wood-leaves and berries, and placed it
by the pallet, then opened the narrow window. The fresh air blew in, and
swept the woody fragrance over the dead face. Deborah looked up with
a quick wonder.

"Did hur know my boy wud like it? Did hur know Hugh?"

"I know Hugh now."

The white fingers passed in a slow, pitiful way over the dead, worn face.
There was a heavy shadow in the quiet eyes.

"Did hur know where they'll bury Hugh?" said Deborah in a shrill tone,
catching her arm.

This had been the question hanging on her lips all day.

"In t' town-yard? Under t' mud and ash? T' lad'll smother, woman! He
wur born on t' lane moor, where t' air is frick and strong. Take hur out,
for God's sake, take hur out where t' air blows!"

The Quaker hesitated, but only for a moment. She put her strong arm
around Deborah and led her to the window.

"Thee sees the hills, friend, over the river? Thee sees how the light lies
warm there, and the winds of God blow all the day? I live there,—where
the blue smoke is, by the trees. Look at me." She turned Deborah's face to
her own, clear and earnest. "Thee will believe me? I will take Hugh and
bury him there to-morrow."

Deborah did not doubt her. As the evening wore on, she leaned against the iron bars, looking at the hills that rose far off, through the thick sodden clouds, like a bright, unattainable calm. As she looked, a shadow of their solemn repose fell on her face: its fierce discontent faded into a pitiful, humble quiet. Slow, solemn tears gathered in her eyes: the poor weak eyes turned so hopelessly to the place where Hugh was to rest, the grave heights looking higher and brighter and more solemn than ever before. The Quaker watched her keenly. She came to her at last, and touched her arm.

"When thee comes back," she said, in a low, sorrowful tone, like one who speaks from a strong heart deeply moved with remorse or pity, "thee shall begin thy life again,—there on the hills. I came too late; but not for thee,—by God's help, it may be."

Not too late. Three years after, the Quaker began her work. I end my story here. At evening-time it was light. There is no need to tire you with the long years of sunshine, and fresh air, and slow, patient Christ-love, need-ed to make healthy and hopeful this impure body and soul. There is a homely pine house, on one of these hills, whose windows overlook broad, wooded slopes and clover-crimsoned meadows,—niched into the very place where the light is warmest, the air freest. It is the Friends' meetinghouse. Once a week they sit there, in their grave, earnest way, waiting for the Spirit of Love to speak, opening their simple hearts to receive His words. There is a woman, old, deformed, who takes a humble place among them: waiting like them: in her gray dress, her worn face, pure and meek, turned now and then to the sky. A woman much loved by these silent, restful people; more silent than they, more humble, more loving. Waiting: with her eyes turned to hills higher and purer than these on which she lives,—dim and far off now, but to be reached some day. There may be in her heart some latent hope to meet there the love denied her here,—that she shall find him whom she lost, and that then she will not be all-unworthy. Who blames her? Something is lost in the passage of every soul from one eternity to the other,—something pure and beautiful, which might have been and was not: a hope, a talent, a love, over which the soul mourns, like Esau deprived of his birthright. What blame to the meek Quaker, if she took her lost hope to make the hills of heaven more fair?

Nothing remains to tell that the poor Welsh puddler once lived, but this figure of the mill-woman cut in korl. I have it here in a corner of my library. I keep it hid behind a curtain,—it is such a rough, ungainly thing. Yet there are about it touches, grand sweeps of outline, that show a master's hand.

Sometimes,—to-night, for instance,—the curtain is accidentally drawn back, and I see a bare arm stretched out imploringly in the darkness, and an eager, wolfish face watching mine: a wan, woeful face, through which the spirit of the dead korl-cutter looks out, with its thwarted life, its mighty hunger, its unfinished work. Its pale, vague lips seem to tremble with a terrible question. "Is this the End?" they say,—"nothing beyond?—no more?" Why, you tell me you have seen that look in the eyes of dumb brutes,—horses dying under the lash. I know.

The deep of the night is passing while I write. The gas-light wakens from the shadows here and there the objects which lie scattered through the room: only faintly, though; for they belong to the open sunlight. As I glance at them, they each recall some task or pleasure of the coming day. A half-moulded child's head; Aphrodite; a bough of forest-leaves; music; work; homely fragments, in which lie the secrets of all eternal truth and beauty. Prophetic all! Only this dumb, woful face seems to belong to and end with the night. I turn to look at it. Has the power of its desperate need commanded the darkness away? While the room is yet steeped in heavy shadow, a cool, gray light suddenly touches its head like a blessing hand, and its groping arm points through the broken cloud to the far East, where, in the flickering, nebulous crimson, God has set the promise of the Dawn.

25

Good and Evil; Good and Bad

Friedrich Nietzsche

(1844–1900)

*F*riedrich Nietzsche was one of the most influential thinkers of the modern era. Born in Germany to a strict Lutheran family (his father was a minister), Nietzsche attended various schools and graduated with highest honors from the University of Liepzig. Tutors there secured him a professorship at the University of Basel, in Switzerland, where he taught for ten years before ill health forced him into seclusion. Although wracked by constant pain and increasing mental instability, Nietzsche poured out book after book, none of which received much attention in his lifetime. After his death, however, thinkers as diverse as Sigmund Freud and Carl Jung (psychology), Martin Heidegger and Jean-Paul Sartre (Philosophy), Jacques Derrida (linguistics and literary theory), Paul Tillich and Martin Buber (theology), and a host of poets, playwrights, and novelists acknowledged a profound debt to him. Ironically his name is often linked to German Nazism, although Nietzsche himself detested statism and anti-Semitism.

Nietzsche's beliefs are hard to encapsulate. His earliest works explored the Apollonian-Dyonisian dichotomy, the tension in Greek tragedy between reason and passion. Later in life he became absorbed in human values. In a sweeping analysis of history, he traced the transformation of terms such as "good" and "evil" from their origins as simple distinctions between rulers and ruled, to the emergence of a "slave" morality that turned suffering into a virtue, promised rewards in another world, and reduced all that was excellent and pure to a common level of mediocrity. Thus he was critical of the leveling tendencies of both Christianity and democracy and at the same time turned Darwinism on its head: evolution was a decline into sameness and meaninglessness. In response, Nietzsche urged humanity to free itself from sentimentalism and the supposition that the meek are fit to inherit the earth. He longed instead for men of will—supermen—who would acknowledge the pain and suffering of existence and then lead humanity to a new morality that would unite passion and reason in a celebration of life.

First Essay

I

THE ENGLISH psychologists to whom we owe the only attempts that have thus far been made to write a genealogy of morals are by no means posers of riddles, but the riddles they pose are themselves, and being incarnate have one advantage over their books—they are interesting. What are these English psychologists really after? One finds them always, whether intentionally or not, engaged in the same task of pushing into the foreground the nasty part of the psyche, looking for the effective motive forces of human development in the very last place we would wish to have them found, *e.g.*, in the inertia of habit, in forgetfulness, in the blind and fortuitous association of ideas; always in something that is purely passive, automatic, reflexive, molecular, and moreover, profoundly stupid. What drives these psychologists forever in the same direction? A secret, malicious desire to belittle humanity, which they do not acknowledge even to themselves? A pessimistic distrust, the suspiciousness of the soured idealist? Some petty resentment of Christianity (and Plato) which does not rise above the threshold of consciousness? Or could it be a prurient taste for whatever is embarrassing, painfully paradoxical, dubious and absurd in existence? Or is it, perhaps, a kind of stew—a little meanness, a little bitterness, a bit of anti-Christianity, a touch of prurience and desire for condiments? . . . But again, people tell me that these men are simply dull old frogs who hop and creep in and around man as in their own element—as though man were a bog. However, I am reluctant to listen to this, in fact I refuse to believe it; and if I may express a wish where I cannot express a conviction, I do wish wholeheartedly that things may be otherwise with these men—that these microscopic examiners of the soul may be really courageous, magnanimous, and proud animals, who know how to contain their emotions and have trained themselves to subordinate all wishful thinking to the truth—any truth, even a homespun, severe, ugly, obnoxious, un-Christian, unmoral truth. For such truths do exist. . . .

II

. . . Now it is obvious to me, first of all, that their theory looks for the genesis of the concept *good* in the wrong place: the judgment *good* does not originate with those to whom the *good* has been done. Rather it was the "good" themselves, that is to say the noble, mighty, highly placed, and high-minded who decreed themselves and their actions to be good, *i.e.*, belonging to the highest rank, in contradistinction to all that was base, low-minded and plebeian. It was only this *pathos of distance* that authorized them to create values and name them—what was utility to them? The notion of utility seems singularly inept to account for such a quick jetting forth of supreme value judgments. Here we come face to face with the exact opposite of that lukewarmness which every scheming prudence, every utilitarian calculus presupposes—and not for a time only, for the rare, exceptional hour, but permanently. The origin of the opposites *good* and *bad* is to be found in the pathos of nobility and distance, representing the dominant temper of a higher, ruling class in relation to a lower, dependent one. (The lordly right of bestowing names is such that one would almost be justified in seeing the origin of language itself as an expression of the rulers' power. They say, "This *is* that or that"; they seal off each thing and action with a sound and thereby take symbolic possession of it.) Such an origin would suggest that there is no *a priori* necessity for associating the word *good* with altruistic deeds, as those moral psychologists are fond of claiming. In fact, it is only after aristocratic values have begun to decline that the egotism-altruism dichotomy takes possession of the human conscience; to use my own terms, it is the herd instinct that now asserts itself. Yet it takes quite a while for this instinct to assume such sway that it can reduce all moral valuations to that dichotomy—as is currently happening throughout Europe, where the prejudice equating the *moral, altruistic* and *disinterested* has assumed the obsessive force of an *idée fixe.*

III

Quite apart from the fact that this hypothesis about the origin of the value judgment *good* is historically untenable, its psychology is intrinsically unsound. Altruistic deeds were originally commended for their usefulness, but this original reason has now been forgotten—so the claim goes. How is such a forgetting conceivable? Has there ever been a point in history at which such deeds lost their usefulness? Quite the contrary, this usefulness has been apparent to every age, a thing that has been emphasized over and over again. Therefore, instead of being forgotten, it must have impressed itself on the consciousness with ever increasing clearness. The opposite theory is far more sensible, though this does not necessarily make it any the truer—the theory held by Herbert Spencer, for example, who considers the concept *good* qualitatively the same as the concepts *useful* or *practical*, so that in the judgments *good* and *bad*, humanity is said to have summed up and sanctioned precisely its unforgotten and unforgettable experiences of the *useful practical* and the *harmful impractical*. According to this theory, the *good* is that which all along, has proved itself useful and which therefore may lay the highest claim to be considered valuable. As I have said, the derivation of this theory is suspect, but at least the explanation is self-consistent and psychologically tenable within its limits.

IV

The clue to the correct explanation was furnished me by the question "What does the etymology of the terms for good in various languages tell us?" I discovered that all these terms lead us back to the same conceptual transformation. The basic concept is always *noble* in the hierarchical, class sense, and from this has developed, by historical necessity, the concept *good* embracing nobility of mind, spiritual distinction. This development is strictly parallel to that other which eventually converted the notions *common, plebeian, base* into the notion *bad*. Here we have an important clue to the actual genealogy of morals; that it has not been hit upon earlier is due to the retarding influence which democratic prejudice has had upon all investigation of origins. This holds equally true with regard to the seemingly quite objective areas of natural science and physiology, though I cannot enlarge upon the question now. The amount of damage such prejudice is capable of doing in ethics and history, once it becomes inflamed with hatred, is clearly shown by the case of Buckle. Here we see the plebeian bias of the modern mind, which stems from England, erupt once again on its native soil with all the violence of a muddy volcano and all the vulgar and oversalted eloquence characteristic of volcanoes.

· · ·

VI

Granting that political supremacy always gives rise to notions of spiritual supremacy, it at first creates no difficulties (though difficulties might arise later) if the ruling caste is also the priestly caste and elects to characterize itself by a term which reminds us of its priestly function. In this context we encounter for the first time concepts of *pure* and *impure* opposing each other as signs of class, and here, too, *good* and *bad* as terms no longer referring to class, develop before long. The reader should be cautioned, however, against taking pure and impure in too large or profound or symbolic a sense: all the ideas of ancient man were understood in a sense much more crude, narrow, superficial and non-symbolic than we are able to imagine today. The pure man was originally one who washed himself, who refused to eat certain foods entailing skin diseases, who did not sleep with the unwashed plebeian women, who held blood in abomination—hardly more than that. At the same time, given the peculiar nature of a priestly aristocracy, it becomes clear why the value opposites would early turn inward and become dangerously exacerbated; and in fact the tension between such opposites has opened abysses between man and man, over which not even an Achilles of free thought would leap without a shudder. There is from the very start something unwholesome about such priestly aristocracies, about their way of life, which is turned away from action and swings between brooding and emotional explosions: a way of life which may be seen as responsible for the morbidity and neurasthenia of priests of all periods. Yet are we not right in maintaining that the cures which they have developed for their morbidities have proved a hundred times more dangerous than the ills themselves? Humanity is still suffering from the aftereffects of those priestly cures. Think, for example, of certain forms of diet (abstinence from meat), fasting, sexual continence, escape "into the desert"; think further of the whole anti-sensual metaphysics of the priests, conducive to inertia and false refinement; of the self-hypnosis encouraged by the example of fakirs and Brahmans, where a glass knob and an *idée fixe* take the place of the god. And at last, supervening on all this, comes utter satiety, together with its radical remedy, nothingness—or God, for the desire for a mystical union with God is nothing other than the Buddhist's desire to sink himself in nirvana. Among the priests everything becomes more dangerous, not cures and specifics alone but also arrogance, vindictiveness, acumen, profligacy, love, the desire for power, disease. In all fairness it should be added, however, that only on this soil, the precarious soil of priestly existence, has man been able to develop into an interesting creature; that only here has the human mind grown both profound and evil; and it is in these two respects, after all, that man has proved his superiority over the rest of creation. . . .

VII

. . . Human history would be a dull and stupid thing without the intelligence furnished by its impotents. Let us begin with the most striking example. Whatever else has been done to damage the powerful and great of this earth seems trivial compared with what the Jews have done, that priestly people who succeeded in avenging themselves on their enemies and oppressors by radically inverting all their values, that is, by an act of the most spiritual vengeance. This was a strategy entirely appropriate to a priestly people in whom vindictiveness had gone most deeply underground. It was the Jew who, with frightening consistency, dared to invert the aristocratic value equations good/noble/powerful/beautiful/happy/favored-of-the-gods and maintain, with the furious hatred of the underprivileged and impotent, that "only the poor, the powerless, are good; only the suffering, sick, and ugly, truly blessed. But you noble and mighty ones of the earth will be, to all eternity, the evil, the cruel, the avaricious, the godless, and thus the cursed and damned!". . . We know who has fallen heir to this Jewish inversion of values. . . . In reference to the grand and unspeakably disastrous initiative which the Jews have launched by this most radical of all declarations of war, I wish to repeat a statement I made in a different context (*Beyond Good and Evil*), to wit, that it was the Jews who started the slave revolt in morals; a revolt with two millennia of history behind it, which we have lost sight of today simply because it has triumphed so completely.

• • •

X

The slave revolt in morals begins by rancor turning creative and giving birth to values—the rancor of beings who, deprived of the direct outlet of action, compensate by an imaginary vengeance. All truly noble morality grows out of triumphant self-affirmation. Slave ethics, on the other hand, begins by saying *no* to an "outside," an "other," a non-self, and that *no* is its creative act. This reversal of direction of the evaluating look, this invariable looking outward instead of inward, is a fundamental feature of rancor. Slave ethics requires for its inception a sphere different from and hostile to its own. Physiologically speaking, it requires an outside stimulus in order to act at all; all its action is reaction. The opposite is true of aristocratic valuations: such values grow and act spontaneously, seeking out their contraries only in order to affirm themselves even more gratefully and delightedly. Here the negative concepts, *humble, base, bad,* are late, pallid counterparts of the positive, intense and passionate credo, "We noble, good, beautiful, happy ones." Aristocratic valuations may go amiss and do violence to reality, but this happens only with regard to spheres which they do not know well, or from the knowledge of which they austerely guard themselves: the aristocrat will, on occasion, misjudge a sphere which he holds in contempt, the sphere of the common man, the people. On the other hand we should remember that the emotion of contempt, of looking down, provided that it falsifies at all, is as nothing compared with the falsification which suppressed hatred, impotent vindictiveness, effects upon its opponent, though only in effigy. There is in all contempt too much casualness and nonchalance, too much blinking of facts and impatience, and too much inborn gaiety for it ever to make of its object a downright caricature and monster. . . .

Second Essay

VI

It is in the sphere of contracts and legal obligations that the moral universe of guilt, conscience, and duty ("sacred" duty) took its inception. Those beginnings were liberally sprinkled with blood, as are the beginnings of everything great on earth. (And may we not say that ethics has never lost its reek of blood and torture—not even in Kant, whose categorical imperative smacks of cruelty?) It was then that the sinister knitting together of the two ideas *guilt* and *pain* first occurred, which by now have become quite inextricable. Let us ask once more: in what sense could pain constitute repayment of a debt? In the sense that to make someone suffer was a supreme pleasure. In exchange for the damage he had incurred, including his displeasure, the creditor received an extraordinary amount of pleasure; something which he prized the more highly the more it disaccorded with his social rank. I am merely throwing this out as a suggestion, for it is difficult, and embarrassing as well, to get to the bottom of such underground developments. To introduce crudely the concept of vengeance at this point would obscure matters rather than clarify them, since the idea of vengeance leads us straight back to our original problem: how can the infliction of pain provide satisfaction? The delicacy—even more, the *tartufferie*—of domestic animals like ourselves shrinks from imagining clearly to what extent cruelty constituted the collective delight of older mankind, how much it was an ingredient of all their joys, or how naïvely they manifested their cruelty, how they considered disinterested malevolence (Spinoza's *sympathia malevolens*) a normal trait, something to which one's conscience could assent heartily. Close observation will spot numerous survivals of this oldest and most thorough human delight in our own culture. In both *Daybreak* and *Beyond Good and Evil* I have pointed to that progressive sublimation and apotheosis of cruelty which not only characterizes the whole history of higher culture, but in a sense constitutes it. Not so very long ago, a royal wedding or great public celebration would have been incomplete without executions, tortures, or *autos da fé*; a noble household without some person whose office it was to serve as a butt for everyone's malice and cruel teasing. (Perhaps the reader will recall Don Quixote's sojourn at the court of the Duchess. *Don Quixote* leaves a bitter taste in our mouths today; we almost quail in reading it. This would have seemed very strange to Cervantes and to his contemporaries, who read the work with the clearest conscience in the world, thought it the funniest of books, and almost died laughing over it.) To behold suffering gives pleasure, but to cause another to suffer affords an even greater pleasure. This severe statement expresses an old, powerful, human, all too human sentiment—though the monkeys too might endorse it, for it is reported that they heralded and preluded man in the devising of bizarre cruelties. There is no feast without cruelty, as man's entire history attests. Punishment, too, has its festive features. . . .

XVI

I can no longer postpone giving tentative expression to my own hypothesis concerning the origin of "bad conscience." It is one that may fall rather strangely on our ears and that requires close meditation. I take bad conscience to be a deep-seated malady to which man succumbed under the pressure of the most profound transformation he ever underwent—the one that made him once and for all a sociable and pacific creature. Just as happened in the case of those sea creatures who were forced to become land animals in order to survive, these semi-animals, happily adapted to the wilderness, to war, free roaming, and adventure, were forced to change their nature. Of a sudden they found all their instincts devalued, unhinged. They must walk on legs and carry themselves, where before the water had carried them: a terrible heaviness weighed upon them. They felt inapt for the simplest manipulations, for in this new, unknown world they could no longer count on the guidance of their unconscious drives. They were forced to think, deduce, calculate, weigh cause and effect—unhappy people, reduced to their weakest, most fallible organ, their consciousness! I doubt that there has ever been on earth such a feeling of misery, such a leaden discomfort. It was not that those old instincts had abruptly ceased making their demands; but now their satisfaction was rare and difficult. For the most part they had to depend on new, covert satisfactions. All instincts that are not allowed free play turn inward. This is what I call man's interiorization; it alone provides the soil for the growth of what is later called man's *soul*. Man's interior world, originally meager and tenuous, was expanding in every dimension, in proportion as the outward discharge of his feelings was curtailed. The formidable bulwarks by means of which the polity protected itself against the ancient instincts of freedom (punishment was one of the strongest of these bulwarks), caused those wild, extravagant instincts to turn in upon man. Hostility, cruelty, the delight in persecution, raids, excitement, destruction all turned against their begetter. Lacking external enemies and resistances, and confined within an oppressive narrowness and regularity, man began rending, persecuting, terrifying himself, like a wild beast hurling itself against the bars of its cage. This languisher, devoured by nostalgia for the desert, who had to turn *himself* into an adventure, a torture chamber, an insecure and dangerous wilderness— this fool, this pining and desperate prisoner, became the inventor of "bad conscience." Also the generator of the greatest and most disastrous of maladies, of which humanity has not to this day been cured: his sickness of himself, brought on by the violent severance from his animal past, by his sudden leap and fall into new layers and conditions of existence, by his declaration of war against the old instincts that had hitherto been the foundation of his power, his joy, and his awesomeness. Let me hasten to add that the phenomenon of an animal soul turning in upon itself, taking arms against itself, was so novel, profound, mysterious, contradictory, and pregnant with possibility, that the whole complexion of the universe was changed thereby. This spectacle (and the end of it is not yet in sight) required a divine audience to do it justice. It was a spectacle too sublime and paradoxical to pass unnoticed on some trivial planet. Henceforth man was to figure among the most unexpected and breathtaking throws in the game of dice played by Heraclitus' great "child," be he called Zeus or chance. Man now aroused an interest, a suspense, a hope, almost a conviction—as though in him something were heralded, as though he were not a goal but a way, an interlude, a bridge, a great promise. . . .

XVIII

We should guard against taking too dim a view of this phenomenon simply because it is both ugly and painful. After all, the same will to power which in those violent artists and organizers created polities, in the "labyrinth of the heart"—more pettily, to be sure, and in inverse direction—created negative ideals and humanity's bad conscience. Except that now the material upon which this great natural force was employed was man himself, his old animal self—and not, as in that grander and more spectacular phenomenon—his fellow man. This secret violation of the self, this artist's cruelty, this urge to impose on recalcitrant matter a form, a will, a distinction, a feeling of contradiction and contempt, this sinister task of a soul divided against itself, which makes itself suffer for the pleasure of suffering, this most energetic "bad conscience"—has it not given birth to a wealth of strange beauty and affirmation? Has it not given birth to beauty itself? Would beauty exist if ugliness had not first taken cognizance of itself, not said to itself, "I am ugly?" This hint will serve, at any rate, to solve the riddle of why contradictory terms such as *selflessness, self-denial, self-sacrifice* may intimate an ideal, a beauty. Nor will the reader doubt henceforth that the *joy* felt by the self-denying, self-sacrificing, selfless person was from the very start a *cruel* joy. So much for the origin of altruism as a moral value. Bad conscience, the desire for self-mortification, is the wellspring of all altruistic values. . . .

XXII

By now the reader will have guessed what has really been happening behind all these facades. Man, with his need for self-torture, his sublimated cruelty resulting from the cooping up of his animal nature within a polity, invented bad conscience in order to hurt himself, after the blocking of the more natural outlet of his cruelty. Then this guilt-ridden man seized upon religion in order to exacerbate his self-torment to the utmost. The thought of being in God's debt became his new instrument of torture. He focused in God the last of the opposites he could find to his true and inveterate animal instincts, making these a sin against God (hostility, rebellion against the "Lord," the "Father," the "Creator"). He stretched himself upon the contradiction "God" and "Devil" as on a rack. He projected all his denials of self, nature, naturalness out of himself as affirmations, as true being, embodiment, reality, as God (the divine Judge and Executioner), as transcendence, as eternity, as endless torture, as hell, as the infinitude of guilt and punishment. In such psychological cruelty we see an insanity of the *will* that is without parallel: man's will to find himself guilty, and unredeemably so; his will to believe that he might be punished to all eternity without ever expunging his guilt; his will to poison the very foundation of things with the problem of guilt and punishment and thus to cut off once and for all his escape from this labyrinth of obsession; his will to erect an ideal (God's holiness) in order to assure himself of his own absolute unworthiness. What a mad, unhappy animal is man! What strange notions occur to him; what perversities, what paroxysms of non-sense, what bestialities of idea burst from him, the moment he is prevent-ed ever so little from being a beast of action! . . . All this is exceedingly curi-ous and interesting, but dyed with such a dark, somber, enervating sadness that one must resolutely tear away one's gaze. Here, no doubt, is sickness, the most terrible sickness that has wasted man thus far. And if one is still able to hear—but how few these days have ears to hear it!—in this night of torment and absurdity the cry *love* rings out, the cry of rapt longing, of redemption in love, he must turn away with a shudder of invincible hor-ror. . . . Man harbors too much horror; the earth has been a lunatic asylum for too long. . . .

XXIV

It is clear that I am concluding this essay with three unanswered ques-tions. It may occur to some reader to ask me, "Are you constructing an ideal or destroying one?" I would ask him, in turn, whether he ever reflected upon the price that had to be paid for the introduction of every new ideal on earth? On how much of reality, in each instance, had to be slandered and misconceived, how much of falsehood ennobled, how many consciences disturbed, how many gods sacrificed? For the raising of an altar requires the breaking of an altar: this is a law—let anyone who can prove me wrong. We moderns have a millennial heritage of con-science-vivisection and cruelty to the animals in ourselves. This is our most ancient habit, our most consummate artistry perhaps, in any case our greatest refinement, our special fare. Man has looked for so long with an evil eye upon his natural inclinations that they have finally become inseparable from "bad conscience." A converse effort can be imagined, but who has the strength for it? It would consist of associating all the *unnatural* inclinations—the longing for what is unworldly, opposed to the senses, to instinct, to nature, to the animal in us, all the anti-biological and earth-calumniating ideals—with bad conscience. To whom, today, may such hopes and pretensions address themselves? The *good* man, in par-ticular, would be on the other side; and of course all the comfortable, resigned, vain, moony, weary people. Does anything give greater offense and separate one more thoroughly from others than to betray something of the strictness and dignity with which one treats oneself? But how kind and accommodating the world becomes the moment we act like all the rest and let ourselves go! To accomplish that aim, different minds are needed than are likely to appear in this age of ours: minds strengthened by struggles and victories, for whom conquest, adventure, danger, even pain, have become second nature. Minds accustomed to the keen atmosphere of high altitudes, to wintry walks, to ice and mountains in every sense. Minds possessed of a sublime kind of malice, of that self-assured recklessness which is a sign of strong health. What is needed, in short, is just superb health. Is such health still possible today?

But at some future time, a time stronger than our effete, self-doubting present, the true Redeemer will come, whose surging creativity will not let him rest in any shelter or hiding place, whose solitude will be misinterpreted as a flight from reality, whereas it will in fact be a dwelling *on*, a dwelling *in* reality—so that when he comes forth into the light he may bring with him the redemption of that reality from the curse placed upon it by a lapsed ideal. This man of the future, who will deliver us both from a lapsed ideal and from all that this ideal has spawned—violent loathing, the will to extinction, nihilism—this great and decisive stroke of midday, who will make the will free once more and restore to the earth its aim, and to man his hope; this anti-Christ and anti-nihilist, conqueror of both God and Unbeing—*one day he must come. . . .*

26

from Civilization and Its Discontents

Sigmund Freud

(1856–1939)

*O*ne of the great creative minds of the modern era, Sigmund Freud was born to a large and very poor family in Freiberg (now in the Czech Republic). His family fled anti-Semitic persecution there and settled in Vienna. As a medical student at the University of Vienna, he concentrated on neurological disorders, first from a physiological perspective, then from a psychological one. In 1895 Freud published (with Josef Brauer) Studies in Hysteria, a book that marks the beginning of Freudian psychoanalysis.

Freud's critical break with the accepted scientific tradition lay in his emphasis on the subconscious. The traditional view portrayed the human self as a conscious entity, reasoning and self-aware. Freud emphasized instead human instincts, notably ones of sexuality and aggressiveness, which drove individuals and which, if left unchecked, could and would destroy societies. To neutralize and/or redirect these basic instincts, individuals developed subconscious means of repressing and resisting them, yet they could reappear at any time. Healthy individuals maintained the balance; disturbed ones did not. The same applied to whole societies. The Interpretation of Dreams (1902) helped crystallize not only Freud's theories but his investigative techniques. Other notable works—among many—were Jokes and Their Relation to the Unconscious (1905), Totem and Taboo (1913), *and* Civilization and Its Discontents (1929), *an almost ruminative work on social aggression and war from which the following excerpt is taken.*

For all his inquiries into the irrational, the taboo, and the violent, Freud himself appears to have been a rather happy man, devoted to his wife, delighting in children, and dedicated to world peace. Stricken with cancer of the jaw in 1923, he endured over thirty operations with few complaints. In 1938 he fled Austria to avoid the inevitable fate of Jews under the Nazi regime; he died of cancer in London the following year.

Psycho-analytic work has shown us that it is precisely these frustrations of sexual life which people known as neurotics cannot tolerate. The neurotic creates substitutive satisfactions for himself in his symptoms, and these either cause him suffering in themselves or become sources of suffering for him by raising difficulties in his relations with his environment and the society he belongs to. The latter fact is easy to understand; the former presents us with a new problem. But civilization demands other sacrifices besides that of sexual satisfaction.

We have treated the difficulty of cultural development as a general difficulty of development by tracing it to the inertia of the libido, to its disinclination to give up an old position for a new one. We are saying much the same thing when we derive the antithesis between civilization and sexuality from the circumstances that sexual love is a relationship between two individuals in which a third can only be superfluous or disturbing, whereas civilization depends on relationships between a considerable number of individuals. When a love-relationship is at its height there is no room left for any interest in the environment; a pair of lovers are sufficient to themselves, and do not even need the child they have in common to make them happy. In no other case does Eros so clearly betray the core of his being, his purpose of making one out of more than one; but when he has achieved this in the proverbial way through the love of two human beings, he refuses to go further.

So far, we can quite well imagine a cultural community consisting of double individuals like this, who, libidinally satisfied in themselves, are connected with one another through the bonds of common work and common interests. If this were so, civilization would not have to withdraw any energy from sexuality. But this desirable state of things does not, and never did, exist. Reality shows us that civilization is not content with the ties we have so far allowed it. It aims at binding the members of the community together in a libidinal way as well and employs every means to that end. It favours every path by which strong identifications can be established between the members of the community, and it summons up aim-inhibited libido on the largest scale so as to strengthen the communal bond by relations of friendship. In order for these aims to be fulfilled, a restriction upon sexual life is unavoidable. But we are unable to understand what the necessity is which forces civilization along this path and which causes its antagonism to sexuality. There must be some disturbing factor which we have not yet discovered.

The clue may be supplied by one of the ideal demands, as we have called them, of civilized society. It runs: "Thou shalt love thy neighbour as thyself." It is known throughout the world and is undoubtedly older than Christianity, which puts it forward as its proudest claim. Yet it is certainly not very old; even in historical times it was still strange to mankind. Let us adopt a naïve attitude towards it, as though we were hearing it for the first time; we shall be unable then to suppress a feeling of surprise and bewilderment. Why should we do it? What good will it do us? But, above all, how shall we achieve it? How can it be possible? My love is something valuable to me which I ought not to throw away without reflection. It imposes duties on me for whose fulfilment I must be ready to make sacrifices. If I love someone he must deserve it in some way. (I leave out of account the use he may be to me, and also his possible significance for me as a sexual object, for neither of these two kinds of relationship comes into question where the precept to love my neighbor is concerned.) He deserves it if he is so like me in important ways that I can love myself in him; and he deserves it if he is so much more perfect than myself that I can love my ideal of my own self in him. Again, I have to love him if he is my friend's son, since the pain my friend would feel if any harm came to him would be my pain too—I should have to share it. But if he is a stranger to me and if he cannot attract me by any worth of his own or any significance that he may already have acquired for my emotional life, it will be hard for me to love him. Indeed, I should be wrong to do so, for my love is valued by all my own people as a sign of my preferring them, and it is an injustice to them if I put a stranger on a par with them. But if I am to love him (with this universal love) merely because he, too, is an inhabitant of this earth, like an insect, an earthworm, or a grass-snake, then I fear that only a small modicum of my love will fall to his share—not by any possibility as much as, by the judgement of my reason, I am entitled to retain for myself. What is the point of a precept enunciated with so much solemnity if its fulfilment cannot be recommended as reasonable?

On closer inspection, I find still further difficulties. Not merely is this stranger in general unworthy of my love; I must honestly confess that he has more claim to my hostility and even my hatred. He seems not to have the least trace of love for me and shows me not the slightest consideration. If it will do him any good he has no hesitation in injuring me, nor does he ask himself whether the amount of advantage he gains bears any proportion to the extent of the harm he does to me. Indeed, he need not even obtain an advantage; if he can satisfy any sort of desire by it, he thinks nothing of jeering at me, insulting me, slandering me and showing his superior power; and the more secure he feels and the more helpless I am, the more certainly I can expect him to behave like this to me. If he behaves differently, if he shows me consideration and forbearance as a stranger, I am ready to treat him in the same way, in any case and quite apart from any precept. Indeed, if this grandiose commandment had run "Love thy neighbor as thy neighbor loves thee," I should not take exception to it. And there is a second commandment, which seems to me even more incomprehensible and arouses still stronger opposition in me. It is "Love thine enemies." If I think it over, however, I see that I am wrong in treating it as a greater imposition. At bottom it is the same thing.[1]

I think I can now hear a dignified voice admonishing me: "It is precisely because your neighbour is not worthy of love, and is on the contrary your enemy, that you should love him as yourself." I then understand that the case is one like that of *Credo quia absurdum*.

I believe it b/c it is absurd.

Now it is very probable that my neighbour, where he is enjoined to love me as himself, will answer exactly as I have done and will repel me for the same reasons. I hope he will not have the same objective grounds for doing so, but he will have the same idea as I have. Even so, the behaviour of human beings shows differences, which ethics, disregarding the fact that such differences are determined, classifies as "good" or "bad." So long as these undeniable differences have not been removed, obedience to high ethical demands entails damage to the aims of civilization, for it puts a positive premium on being bad. One is irresistibly reminded of an incident in the French Chamber when capital punishment was being debated. A member had been passionately supporting its abolition and his speech was being received with tumultuous applause, when a voice from the hall called out: *"Que messieurs les assassins commencent!"*[2]

The element of truth behind all this, which people are so ready to disavow, is that men are not gentle creatures who want to be loved, and who at the most can defend themselves if they are attacked; they are, on the contrary, creatures among whose instinctual endowments is to be reckoned a powerful share of aggressiveness. As a result, their neighbour is for them not only a potential helper or sexual object, but also someone who tempts them to satisfy their aggressiveness on him, to exploit his capacity for work without compensation, to use him sexually without his consent, to seize his possessions, to humiliate him, to cause him pain, to torture and to kill him. *Homo homini lupus*.[3] Who, in the face of all his experience of life and of history, will have the courage to dispute this assertion? As a rule this cruel aggressiveness waits for some provocation or puts itself at the service of some other purpose, whose goal might also have been reached by milder measures. In circumstances that are favourable to it, when the mental counter-forces which ordinarily inhibit it are out of action, it also manifests itself spontaneously and reveals man as a savage beast to whom consideration towards his own kind is something alien. Anyone who calls to mind the atrocities committed during the racial migrations or the invasions of the Huns, or by the people known as Mongols under Jenghiz Khan and Tamerlane, or at the capture of Jerusalem by the pious Crusaders, or even, indeed, the horrors of the recent World War— anyone who calls these things to mind will have to bow humbly before the truth of this view.

The existence of this inclination to aggression, which we can detect in ourselves and justly assume to be present in others, is the factor which disturbs our relations with our neighbour and which forces civilization into such a high expenditure [of energy]. In consequence of this primary mutual hostility of human beings, civilized society is perpetually threatened with disintegration. The interest of work in common would not hold it together; instinctual passions are stronger than reasonable interests. Civilization has to use its utmost efforts in order to set limits to man's aggressive instincts and to hold the manifestations of them in check by psychical reaction-formations. Hence, therefore, the use of methods intended to incite people into identifications and aim-inhibited relationships of love, hence the restriction upon sexual life, and hence too the ideal's commandment to love one's neighbour as oneself—a commandment which is really justified by the fact that nothing else runs so strongly counter to the original nature of man. In spite of every effort, these endeavours of civilization have not so far achieved very much. It hopes to prevent the crudest excesses of brutal violence by itself assuming the right to use violence against criminals, but the law is not able to lay hold of the more cautious and refined manifestations of human aggressiveness. The time comes when each one of us has to give up as illusions the expectations which, in his youth, he pinned upon his fellowmen, and when he may learn how much difficulty and pain has been added to his life by their ill-will. At the same time, it would be unfair to reproach civilization with trying to eliminate strife and competition from human activity. These things are undoubtedly indispensable. But opposition is not necessarily enmity; it is merely misused and made an *occasion* for enmity.

The communists believe that they have found the path to deliverance from our evils. According to them, man is wholly good and is well-disposed to his neighbour; but the institution of private property has corrupted his nature. The ownership of private wealth gives the individual power, and with it the temptation to ill-treat his neighbour; while the man who is excluded from possession is bound to rebel in hostility against his oppressor. If private property were abolished, all wealth held in common, and everyone allowed to share in the enjoyment of it, ill-will and hostility would disappear among men. Since everyone's needs would be satisfied, no one would have any reason to regard another as his enemy; all would willingly undertake the work that was necessary. I have no concern with any economic criticisms of the communist system; I cannot enquire into whether the abolition of private property is expedient or advantageous.[4] But I am able to recognize that the psychological premises on which the system is based are an untenable illusion. In abolishing private property we deprive the human love of aggression of one of its instruments, certainly a strong one, though certainly not the strongest; but we have in no way altered the differences in power and influence which are misused by aggressiveness, nor have we altered anything in its nature. Aggressiveness was not created by property. It reigned almost without limit in primitive times, when property was still very scanty, and it already shows itself in the nursery almost before property has given up its primal, anal form; it forms the basis of every relation of affection and love among people (with the single exception, perhaps, of the mother's relation to her male child). If we do away with personal rights over material wealth, there still remains prerogative in the field of sexual relationships, which is bound to become the source of the strongest dislike and the most violent hostility among men who in other respects are on an equal footing. If we were to remove this factor, too, by allowing complete freedom of sexual life and thus abolishing the family, the germ-cell of civilization, we cannot, it is true, easily foresee what new paths the development of civilization could take; but one thing we can expect, and that is that this indestructible feature of human nature will follow it there.

It is clearly not easy for men to give up the satisfaction of this inclination to aggression. They do not feel comfortable without it. The advantage which a comparatively small cultural group offers of allowing this instinct an outlet in the form of hostility against intruders is not to be despised. It is always possible to bind together a considerable number of people in love, so long as there are other people left over to receive the manifestations of their aggressiveness. I once discussed the phenomenon that it is precisely communities with adjoining territories, and related to each other in other ways as well, who are engaged in constant feuds and in ridiculing each other—like the Spaniards and Portuguese, for instance, the North Germans and South Germans, the English and Scotch, and so on. I gave this phenomenon the name of "the narcissism of minor differences," a name which does not do much to explain it. We can now see that it is a convenient and relatively harmless satisfaction of the inclination to aggression, by means of which cohesion between the members of the community is made easier. In this respect the Jewish people, scattered everywhere, have rendered most useful services to the civilizations of the countries that have been their hosts; but unfortunately all the massacres of the Jews in the Middle Ages did not suffice to make that period more peaceful and secure for their Christian fellows. When once the Apostle Paul had posited universal love between men as the foundation of his Christian community, extreme intolerance on the part of Christendom towards those who remained outside it became the inevitable consequence. To the Romans, who had not founded their communal life as a State upon love, religious intolerance was something foreign, although with them religion was a concern of the State and the State was permeated by religion. Neither was it an unaccountable chance that the dream of a Germanic world-dominion called for anti-Semitism as its complement; and it is intelligible that the attempt to establish a new, communist civilization in Russia should find its psychological support in the persecution of the bourgeois. One only wonders, with concern, what the Soviets will do after they have wiped out their bourgeois.

If civilization imposes such great sacrifices not only on man's sexuality but on his aggressivity, we can understand better why it is hard for him to be happy in that civilization. In fact, primitive man was better off in knowing no restrictions of instinct. To counterbalance this, his prospects of enjoying this happiness for any length of time were very slender. Civilized man has exchanged a portion of his possibilities of happiness for a portion of security. We must not forget, however, that in the primal family only the head of it enjoyed this instinctual freedom; the rest lived in slavish suppression. In that primal period of civilization, the contrast between a minority who enjoyed the advantages of civilization and a majority who were robbed of those advantages was, therefore, carried to extremes. As regards the primitive peoples who exist to-day, careful researches have shown that their instinctual life is by no means to be envied for its freedom. It is subject to restrictions of a different kind but perhaps of greater severity than those attaching to modern civilized man.

When we justly find fault with the present state of our civilization for so inadequately fulfilling our demands for a plan of life that shall make us happy, and for allowing the existence of so much suffering which could probably be avoided—when, with unsparing criticism, we try to uncover the roots of its imperfection, we are undoubtedly exercising a proper right and are not showing ourselves enemies of civilization. We may expect gradually to carry through such alterations in our civilization as will better satisfy our needs and will escape our criticisms. But perhaps we may also familiarize ourselves with the idea that there are difficulties attaching to the nature of civilization which will not yield to any attempt at reform. Over and above the tasks of restricting the instincts, which we are prepared for, there forces itself on our notice the danger of a state of things which might be termed "the psychological poverty of groups."[5] This danger is most threatening where the bonds of a society are chiefly constituted by the identification of its members with one another, while individuals of the leader type do not acquire the importance that should fall to them in the formation of a group. The present cultural state of America would give us a good opportunity for studying the damage to civilization which is thus to be feared. But I shall avoid the temptation of entering upon a critique of American civilization; I do not wish to give an impression of wanting myself to employ American methods.

Notes

(All notes belong to Freud.)

1   A great imaginative writer may permit himself to give expression—jokingly, at all events—to psychological truths that are severely proscribed. Thus Heine confesses: "Mine is a most peaceable disposition. My wishes are: a humble cottage with a thatched roof, but a good bed, good food, the freshest milk and butter, flowers before my window, and a few fine trees before my door; and if God wants to make my happiness complete, he will grant me the joy of seeing some

six or seven of my enemies hanging from those trees. Before their death I shall, moved in my heart, forgive them all the wrong they did me in their lifetime. One must, it is true, forgive one's enemies—but not before they have been hanged!" (*Gedanken Und Einfale* [Section 1]).

2 "It's the murderers who should make the first move."

3 "Man is a wolf to man." Derived from Plautus, *Asinaria* II, iv, 88.

4 Anyone who has tasted the miseries of poverty in his own youth and has experienced the indifference and arrogance of the well-to-do, should be safe from the suspicion of having no understanding or goodwill towards endeavours to fight against the inequality of wealth among men and all that it leads to. To be sure, if an attempt is made to base this fight upon an abstract demand, in the name of justice, for equality for all men, there is a very obvious objection to be made—that nature, by endowing individuals with extremely unequal physical attributes and mental capacities, has introduced injustices against which there is no remedy.

5 The German "*psychologisches Elend*" seems to be a version of Janet's expression "*misére psychologique*" applied by him to describe the incapacity for mental synthesis which he attributes to neurotics.

27

from A Room of One's Own

Virginia Woolf

(1882–1941)

Virginia Woolf's name has become synonymous with literary modernism, for her life was characterized by prolific artistic experimentation and a personal search for meaning that ended in suicide. Woolf had familial ties to many strands of Victorian culture. Her father, Leslie Stephen, was a prominent editor known largely for his massive Dictionary of National Biography *that ranked important persons in British life over several centuries. Virginia's novel* Orlando: A Biography *(1928) spoofed her father's massive enterprise of collecting great men in print by having her great man, Orlando, unexpectedly turn into a woman halfway through the novel. Likewise, her novel* To the Lighthouse *(1927) treated the tensions in a tortured patriarchal family upon the sudden death of the mother, tensions Virginia herself had experienced at age thirteen when she lost her mother and suffered the first of many mental breakdowns. Despite the Woolf family's upper class status, Virginia and her sisters were not given a formal education. Not surprisingly, death and education (always pervaded with a sense of loss) serve as key themes in her fiction. Together with her siblings she established the Bloomsbury group, a gathering of novelists, art critics, and economists devoted to weekly discussions of* avant-garde *art, freedom of expression, and sexual tolerance. In 1912 she married a fellow member of this group, Leonard Woolf, and together they established the Hogarth Press and devoted themselves to writing careers. In 1928 she spoke to audiences at two women's colleges—Newnham and Girton College, Cambridge University—and later published her talk in the lengthy essay* A Room of One's Own, *excerpted below.*

But, you may say, we asked you to speak about women and fiction—what has that got to do with a room of one's own? I will try to explain. When you asked me to speak about women and fiction I sat down on the banks of a river and began to wonder what the words meant. They might mean simply a few remarks about Fanny Burney; a few more about Jane Austen; a tribute to the Brontës and a sketch of Haworth Parsonage under snow; some witticisms if possible about Miss Mitford; a respectful allusion to George Eliot; a reference to Mrs. Gaskell and one would have done.[1] But at second sight the words seemed not so simple. The title women and fiction might mean, and you may have meant it to mean, women and what they are like; or it might mean women and the fiction that they write; or it might mean women and the fiction that is written about them; or it might mean that somehow all three are inextricably mixed together and you want me to consider them in that light. But when I began to consider the subject in this last way, which seemed the most interesting, I soon saw that it had one fatal drawback. I should never be able to come to a conclusion. I should never be able to fulfil what is, I understand, the first duty of a lecturer—to hand you after an hour's discourse a nugget of pure truth to wrap up between the pages of your notebooks and keep on the mantelpiece for ever. All I could do was to offer you an opinion upon one minor point—a woman must have money and a room of her own if she is to write fiction; and that, as you will see, leaves the great problem of the true nature of woman and the true nature of fiction unsolved. I have shirked the duty of coming to a conclusion upon these two questions—women and fiction remain, so far as I am concerned, unsolved problems. But in order to make some amends I am going to do what I can to show you how I arrived at this opinion about the room and the money. I am going to develop in your presence as fully and freely as I can the train of thought which led me to think this. Perhaps if I lay bare the ideas, the prejudices, that lie behind this statement you will find that they have some bearing upon women and some upon fiction. At any rate, when a subject is highly controversial—and any question about sex is that—one cannot hope to tell the truth. One can only show how one came to hold whatever opinion one does hold. One can only give one's audience the chance of drawing their own conclusions as they observe the limitations, the prejudices, the idiosyncracies of the speaker. Fiction here is likely to contain more truth than fact. Therefore I propose, making use of all the liberties and licenses of a novelist, to tell you the story of the two days that preceded my coming here—how, bowed down by the weight of the subject which you have laid upon my shoulders, I pondered it, and made it work in and out of my daily life. I need not say that what I am about to describe has no existence; Oxbridge[2] is an invention; so is Fernham; "I" is only a convenient term for somebody who has no real being. Lies will flow from my lips, but there may perhaps be some truth mixed up with them; it is for you to seek out this truth and to decide whether any part of it is worth keeping. If not, you will of course throw the whole of it into the wastepaper basket and forget all about it.

• • •

I went, therefore, to the shelf where the histories stand and took down one of the latest, Professor [George] Trevelyan's *History of England*. Once more I looked up Women, found "position of," and turned to the pages indicated. "Wife-beating," I read, "was a recognized right of man, and was practiced without shame by high as well as low. . . . Similarly," the historian goes on, "the daughter who refused to marry the gentleman of her parents' choice was liable to be locked up, beaten and flung about the room, without any shock being inflicted on public opinion. Marriage was not an affair of personal affection, but of family avarice, particularly in the 'chivalrous' upper classes. . . . Betrothal often took place while one or both of the parties was in the cradle, and marriage when they were scarcely out of the nurses' charge." That was about 1470, soon after Chaucer's time. The next reference to the position of women is some two hundred years later, in the time of the Stuarts. "It was still the exception for women of the upper and middle class to choose their own husbands, and when the husband had been assigned, he was lord and master, so far at least as law and custom could make him. Yet even so," Professor Trevelyan concludes, "neither Shakespeare's women nor those of authentic seventeenth-century memoirs, like the Verneys and the Hutchinsons, seem lacking in personality and character." Certainly, if we consider it, Cleopatra must have had a way with her; Lady Macbeth, one would suppose, had a will of her own; Rosalind, one might conclude, was an attractive girl. Professor Trevelyan is speaking no more than the truth when he remarks that Shakespeare's women do not seem wanting in personality and character. Not being a historian, one might go even further and say that women have burned like beacons in all the works of all the poets from the beginning of time—Clytemnestra, Antigone, Cleopatra, Lady Macbeth, Phèdre, Cressida, Rosalind, Desdemona, the Duchess of Malfi, among the dramatists; then among the prose writers: Millamant, Clarissa, Becky Sharp, Anna Karenina, Emma Bovary, Madame de Guermantes— the names flock to mind, nor do they recall women "lacking in personality and character." Indeed, if woman had no existence save in the fiction written by men, one would imagine her a person of the utmost importance; very various; heroic and mean; splendid and sordid; infinitely beautiful and hideous in the extreme; as great as a man, some think even greater. But this is woman in fiction. In fact, as Professor Trevelyan points out, she was locked up, beaten and flung about the room.

A very queer, composite being thus emerges. Imaginatively she is of the highest importance; practically she is completely insignificant. She pervades poetry from cover to cover; she is all but absent from history. She dominates the lives of kings and conquerors in fiction; in fact she was the slave of any boy whose parents forced a ring upon her finger. Some of the most inspired words, some of the most profound thoughts in literature fall from her lips; in real life she could hardly read, could scarcely spell, and was the property of her husband.

It was certainly an odd monster that one made up by reading the historians first and the poets afterward—a worm winged like an eagle; the spirit of life and beauty in a kitchen chopping up suet. But these monsters, however amusing to the imagination, have no existence in fact. What one must do to bring her to life was to think poetically and prosaically at one and the same moment, thus keeping in touch with fact—that she is Mrs. Martin, aged thirty-six, dressed in blue, wearing a black hat and brown shoes; but not losing sight of fiction either—that she is a vessel in which all sorts of spirits and forces are coursing and flashing perpetually. The moment, however, that one tries this method with the Elizabethan woman, one branch of illumination fails; one is held up by the scarcity of facts. One knows nothing detailed, nothing perfectly true and substantial about her. History scarcely mentions her. And I turned to Professor Trevelyan again to see what history meant to him. I found by looking at his chapter headings that it meant—

"The Manor Court and the Methods of Open-field Agriculture . . . The Cistercians and Sheep-farming . . . The Crusades . . . The University . . . The House of Commons . . . The Hundred Years' War . . . The Wars of the Roses . . . The Renaissance Scholars . . . The Dissolution of the Monasteries . . . Agrarian and Religious Strife . . . The Origin of English Sea-power . . . The Armada . . ." and so on. Occasionally an individual woman is mentioned, an Elizabeth, or a Mary; a queen or a great lady. But by no possible means could middle-class women with nothing but brains and character at their command have taken part in any one of the great movements which, brought together, constitute the historian's view of the past. Nor shall we find her in any collection of anecdotes. Aubrey hardly mentions her. She never writes her own life and scarcely keeps a diary; there are only a handful of her letters in existence. She left no plays or poems by which we can judge her. What one wants, I thought—and why does not some brilliant student at Newnham or Girton supply it?—is a mass of information; at what age did she marry; how many children had she as a rule;

what was her house like; had she a room to herself, did she do the cooking; would she be likely to have a servant? All these facts lie somewhere, presumably, in parish registers and account books; the life of the average Elizabethan woman must be scattered about somewhere, could one collect it and make a book of it. It would be ambitious beyond my daring, I thought, looking about the shelves for books that were not there, to suggest to the students of those famous colleges that they should re-write history, though I acknowledge that it often seems a little queer as it is, unreal, lop-sided; but why should they not add a supplement to history? calling it, of course, by some inconspicuous name so that women might figure there without impropriety? For one often catches a glimpse of them in the lives of the great, whisking away into the background, concealing, I sometimes think, a wink, a laugh, perhaps a tear. And, after all, we have lives enough of Jane Austen; it scarcely seems necessary to consider again the influence of the tragedies of Joanna Baillie upon the poetry of Edgar Allan Poe; as for myself, I should not mind if the homes and haunts of Mary Russell Mitford were closed to the public for a century at least. But what I find deplorable, I continued, looking about the book-shelves again, is that nothing is known about women before the eighteenth century. I have no model in my mind to turn about this way and that. Here am I asking why women did not write poetry in the Elizabethan age, and I am not sure how they were educated; whether they were taught to write; whether they had sitting-rooms to themselves; how many women had children before they were twenty-one; what, in short, they did from eight in the morning till eight at night. They had no money evidently; according to Professor Trevelyan they were married whether they liked it or not before they were out of the nursery, at fifteen or sixteen very likely. It would have been extremely odd, even upon this showing, had one of them suddenly written the plays of Shakespeare, I concluded, and I thought of that old gentleman, who is dead now, but was a bishop, I think, who declared that it was impossible for any woman, past, present, or to come, to have the genius of Shakespeare. He wrote to the papers about it. He also told a lady who applied to him for information that cats do not as a matter of fact go to heaven, though they have, he added, souls of a sort. How much thinking those old gentlemen used to save one! How the borders of ignorance shrank back at their approach! Cats do not go to heaven. Women cannot write the plays of Shakespeare.

Be that as it may, I could not help thinking, as I looked at the works of Shakespeare on the shelf, that the bishop was right at least in this; it would have been impossible, completely and entirely, for any woman to have written the plays of Shakespeare in the age of Shakespeare. Let me imagine, since facts are so hard to come by, what would have happened had Shakespeare had a wonderfully gifted sister, called Judith, let us say. Shakespeare himself went, very probably—his mother was an heiress—to the grammar school, where he may have learned Latin—Ovid, Virgil and Horace—and the elements of grammar and logic. He was, it is well known, a wild boy who poached rabbits, perhaps shot a deer, and had, rather sooner than he should have done, to marry a woman in the neighbourhood, who bore him a child rather quicker than was right. That escapade sent him to seek his fortune in London. He had, it seemed, a taste for the theatre; he began by holding horses at the stage door. Very soon he got work in the theater, became a successful actor, and lived at the hub of the universe, meeting everybody, knowing everybody, practicing his art on the stage, exercising his wits in the streets, and even getting access to the palace of the queen. Meanwhile his extraordinarily gifted sister, let us suppose, remained at home. She was as adventurous, as imaginative, as agog to see the world as he was. But she was not sent to school. She had no chance of learning grammar and logic, let alone of reading Horace and Virgil. She picked up a book now and then, one of her brother's perhaps, and read a few pages. But then her parents came in and told her to mend the stockings or mind the stew and not moon about with books and papers. They would have spoken sharply but kindly, for they were substantial people who knew the conditions of life for a woman and loved their daughter—indeed, more likely than not she was the apple of her father's eye. Perhaps she scribbled some pages up in an apple loft on the sly, but was careful to hide them or set fire to them. Soon, however, before she was out of her teens, she was to be betrothed to the son of a neighbouring wool-stapler. She cried out that marriage was hateful to her, and for that she was severely beaten by her father. Then he ceased to scold her. He begged her instead not to hurt him, not to shame him in this matter of her marriage. He would give her a chain of beads or a fine petticoat, he said; and there were tears in his eyes. How could she disobey him? How could she break his heart? The force of her own gift alone drove her to it. She made up a small parcel of her belongings, let herself down by a rope one summer's night and took the road to London. She was not seventeen. The birds that sang in the hedge were not more musical than she was. She had the quickest fancy, a gift like her brother's, for the tune of words. Like him, she had a taste for the theatre. She stood at the stage door; she wanted to act, she said. Men laughed in her face. The manager—a fat, loose-lipped man—guffawed. He bellowed something about poodles dancing and women acting—no woman, he said, could possibly be an actress. He hinted—you can imagine what. She could get no training in her craft. Could she even seek her dinner in a tavern or roam the streets at midnight? Yet her genius was for fiction and lusted to feed abundantly upon the lives of men and women and the study of their ways. At last—for she was very young, oddly like Shakespeare the poet in her face, with the same grey eyes and rounded brows—at last Nick Greene the actor-manager took pity on her; she found herself with child by that gentleman and so—who shall measure the heat and violence of the poet's heart when caught and tangled in a woman's body?—killed herself one winter's night and lies buried at some cross-roads where the omnibuses now stop outside the Elephant and Castle.[3]

That, more or less, is how the story would run, I think, if a woman in Shakespeare's day had had Shakespeare's genius. But for my part, I agree with the deceased bishop, if such he was—it is unthinkable that any woman in Shakespeare's day should have had Shakespeare's genius. For genius like Shakespeare's is not born among labouring, uneducated, servile people. It was not born in England among the Saxons and the Britons. It is not born today among the working classes. How, then, could it have been born among women whose work began, according to Professor Trevelyan, almost before they were out of the nursery, who were forced to it by their parents and held to it by all the power of law and custom? Yet genius of a sort must have existed among women as it must have existed among the working classes. Now and again an Emily Brontë or a Robert Burns blazes out and proves its presence. But certainly it never got itself on to paper. When, however, one reads of a witch being dunked, of a woman possessed by devils, of a wise woman selling herbs, or even of a very remarkable man who had a mother, then I think we are on the track of a lost novelist, a suppressed poet, of some mute and inglorious Jane Austen, some Emily Brontë who dashed her brains out on the moor or mopped and mowed about the highways crazed with the torture that her gift had put her to. Indeed, I would venture to guess that Anon, who wrote so many poems without signing them, was often a woman. It was a woman Edward Fitzgerald [1809–1883], I think, suggested who made the ballads and the folk-songs, crooning them to her children, beguiling her spinning with them, or the length of the winter's night.

This may be true or it may be false—who can say?—but what is true in it, so it seemed to me, reviewing the story of Shakespeare's sister as I had made it, is that any woman born with a great gift in the sixteenth century would certainly have gone crazed, shot herself, or ended her days in some lonely cottage outside the village, half witch, half wizard, feared and mocked at. For it needs little skill in psychology to be sure that a highly gifted girl who had tried to use her gift for poetry would have been so thwarted and hindered by other people, so tortured and pulled asunder by her own contrary instincts, that she must have lost her health and sanity to a certainty. No girl could have walked to London and stood at a stage door and forced her way into the presence of actor-managers without doing herself a violence and suffering an anguish which may have been irra-tional—-for chastity may be a fetish invented by certain societies for unknown reasons—but were none the less inevitable. Chastity had then, it has even now, a religious importance in a woman's life, and has so wrapped itself round with nerves and instincts that to cut it free and bring it to the light of day demands courage of the rarest. To have lived a free life in London in the sixteenth century would have meant for a woman who was poet and playwright a nervous stress and dilemma which might well have killed her. Had she survived, whatever she had written would have been twisted and deformed, issuing from a strained and morbid imagination. And undoubtedly, I thought, looking at the shelf where there are no plays by women, her work would have gone unsigned. That refuge she would have sought certainly. It was the relic of the sense of chastity that dictated anonymity to women even so late as the nineteenth century. Currer Bell, George Eliot, George Sand,[4] all the victims of inner strife as their writings prove, sought ineffectively to veil themselves by using the name of a man. Thus they did homage to the convention, which if not implanted by the other sex was liberally encouraged by them (the chief glory of a woman is not to be talked of, said Pericles, himself a much-talked-of man), that publicity in women is detestable. Anonymity runs in their blood. The desire to be veiled still possesses them. They are not even now as concerned about the health of their fame as men are, and, speak-ing generally, will pass a tombstone or a signpost without feeling an irre-sistible desire to cut their names on it, as Alf, Bert or Chas. must do in obe-dience to their instinct . . . .

. . . [I]t is fairly evident that even in the nineteenth century a woman was not encouraged to be an artist. On the contrary, she was snubbed, slapped, lectured and exhorted. Her mind must have been strained and her vitality lowered by the need of opposing this, of disproving that. For here again we come within range of that very interesting and obscure masculine complex which has had so much influence upon the woman's movement; that deep-seated desire, not so much that *she* shall be inferior as that *he* shall be superior, which plants him wherever one looks, not only in front of the arts, but barring the way to politics too, even when the risk to himself seems infinitesimal and the suppliant humble and devoted. Even Lady Bessborough, I remembered, with all her passion for politics, must humbly bow herself and write to Lord Granville Leveson-Gower: ". . . notwithstanding all my violence in politics and talking so much on that subject, I perfectly agree with you that no woman has any business to meddle with that or any other serious business, farther than giving her opinion (if she is asked)." And so she goes on to spend her enthusiasm where it meets with no obstacle whatsoever upon that immensely important subject, Lord Granville's maiden speech in the House of Commons. The spectacle is certainly a strange one, I thought. The history of men's opposition to women's emancipation is more interesting perhaps than the story of that emancipation itself. An amusing book might be made of it if some young student at Girton or Newnham would collect examples and deduce a theory—but she would need thick gloves on her hands, and bars to protect her of solid gold.

. . . [T]he pressure of convention decrees that every speech must end with a peroration. And a peroration addressed to women should have something, you will agree, particularly exalting and ennobling about it. I should implore you to remember your responsibilities, to be higher, more spiritual; I should remind you how much depends upon you, and what an influence you can exert upon the future. But those exhortations can safely, I think, be left to the other sex, who will put them, and indeed have put them, with far greater eloquence than I can compass. When I rummage in my own mind I find no noble sentiments about being companions and equals and influencing the world to higher ends. I find myself saying briefly and prosaically that it is much more important to be oneself than anything else. Do not dream of influencing other people, I would say, if I knew how to make it sound exalted. Think of things in themselves.

And again I am reminded by dipping into newspapers and novels and biographies that when a woman speaks to women she should have something very unpleasant up her sleeve. Women are hard on women. Women dislike women. Women—but are you not sick to death of the word? I can assure you that I am. Let us agree, then, that a paper read by a woman to women should end with something particularly disagreeable.

But how does it go? What can I think of? The truth is, I often like women. I like their unconventionality. I like their subtlety. I like their anonymity. I like—but I must not run on in this way. . . . Let me then adopt a sterner tone. Have I, in the preceding words, conveyed to you sufficiently the warnings and reprobation of mankind? I have told you the very low opinion in which you were held by Mr. Oscar Browning. I have indicated what Napoleon once thought of you and what Mussolini thinks now. Then, in case any of you aspire to fiction, I have copied out for your benefit the advice of the critic about courageously acknowledging the limitations of your sex. I have referred to Professor X and given prominence to his statement that women are intellectually, morally and physically inferior to men. I have handed on all that has come my way without going in search of it, and here is a final warning—from Mr. John Langdon Davies.[5] Mr. John Langdon Davies warns women "that when children cease to be altogether desirable, women cease to be altogether necessary." I hope you will make a note of it.

How can I further encourage you to go about the business of life? Young women, I would say, and please listen, for the peroration is beginning, you are, in my opinion, disgracefully ignorant. You have never made a discovery of any sort of importance. You have never shaken an empire or led an army into battle. The plays of Shakespeare are not by you, and you have never introduced a barbarous race to the blessings of civilization. What is your excuse? It is all very well for you to say, pointing to the streets and squares and forests of the globe swarming with black and white and coffee-coloured inhabitants, all busily engaged in traffic and enterprise and love-making, we have had other work on our hands. Without our doing, those seas would be unsailed and those fertile lands a desert. We have borne and bred and washed and taught, perhaps to the age of six or seven years, the one thousand six hundred and twenty-three million human beings who are, according to statistics, at present in existence, and that, allowing that some had help, takes time.

There is truth in what you say—I will not deny it. But at the same time may I remind you that there have been at least two colleges for women in existence in England since the year 1866; that after the year 1880 a married woman was allowed by law to possess her own property; and that in

1919—which is a whole nine years ago—she was given a vote? May I also remind you that most of the professions have been open to you for close to ten years now? When you reflect upon these immense privileges and the length of time during which they have been enjoyed, and the fact that there must be at this moment some two thousand women capable of earning over five hundred a year in one way or another, you will agree that the excuse of lack of opportunity, training, encouragement, leisure and money no longer holds true. Moreover, the economists are telling us that Mrs. Seton has had too many children. You must, of course, go on bearing children, but, so they say, in twos and threes, not in tens and twelves.

Thus, with some time on your hands and with some book learning in your brains—you have had enough of the other kind, and are sent to college partly, I suspect, to be uneducated—surely you should embark upon another stage of your very long, very laborious and highly obscure career. A thousand pens are ready to suggest what you should do and what effect you will have. My own suggestion is a little fantastic, I admit; I prefer, therefore, to put it in the form of fiction.

I told you in the course of this paper that Shakespeare had a sister; but do not look for her in Sir Sidney Lee's life of the poet. She died young—alas, she never wrote a word. She lies buried where the omnibuses now stop, opposite the Elephant and Castle. Now my belief is that this poet who never wrote a word and was buried at the crossroads still lives. She lives in you and in me, and in many other women who are not here tonight, for they are washing up the dishes and putting the children to bed. But she lives; for great poets do not die; they are continuing presences; they need only the opportunity to walk among us in the flesh. This opportunity, as I think, it is now coming within your power to give her. For my belief is that if we live another century or so—I am talking of the common life which is the real life and not of the little separate lives which we live as individuals—and have five hundred a year each of us and rooms of our own; if we have the habit of freedom and the courage to write exactly what we think; if we escape a little from the common sitting-room and see human beings not always in their relation to each other but in relation to reality; and the sky, too, and the trees or whatever it may be in themselves; if we look past Milton's bogey, for no human being should shut out the view; if we face the fact, for it is a fact, that there is no arm to cling to, but that we go alone and that our relation is to the world of reality and not only to the world of men and women, then the opportunity will come and the dead poet who was Shakespeare's sister will put on the body which she has so often laid down. Drawing her life from the lives of the unknown who were her forerunners, as her brother did before her, she will be born. As for her coming without that preparation, without that effort on our part, without that determination that when she is born again she shall find it possible to live and write her poetry, that we cannot expect, for that would be impossible. But I maintain that she would come if we worked for her, and that so to work, even in poverty and obscurity, is worth while.

Notes

1   Important 19th-century novelists.

2   Slang term for Oxford and Cambridge universities.

3   A tavern on the outskirts of South London.

4   Pennames of Charlotte Brontë, Mary Ann Evans, and Amandine Dupin, respectively.

5   Author of *A Short History of Women*.

28

from Existentialism

Jean-Paul Sartre

(1905–1980)

*E*xistentialism is perhaps the most widely discussed philosophical movement of
the post-World War II era, and Jean-Paul Sartre was its leading spokesman.
*Born in Paris, Sartre graduated from the prestigious École Normale Supérieure
in 1929 and taught in French provincial schools. In 1938 he published his first
novel,* La Nausée (Nausea), *a bleak exploration of human meaninglessness.
When the war broke out, he joined the army, got captured and spent a year in a
Nazi prison, then escaped and joined the Resistance. After the war, Sartre wrote
plays, novels, short stories, biographies, and works of philosophy, notably* Being
and Nothingness *(1943). He took up communism, then got discouraged with it
after the Soviet invasion of Hungary in 1956 and tried to redefine it along existentialist lines.*

*Historically, existentialism had roots in the thought of Danish philosopher Søren
Kierkegaard, the Russian novelist Fyodor Dostoevsky, and the German philosopher
Friedrich Nietzsche. In the 20th century thinkers as diverse as Martin Heidegger
(who joined the Nazi party) and Martin Buber (a Jewish religious philosopher
who fled Germany) developed and expanded it. One of the best-known Christian
existentialists was Gabriel Marcel, a French Catholic; one of the best-known
atheist existentialists was Albert Camus. Common to its many varieties is the
belief that every human being must define his or her purpose in life without
recourse to preconceived Aristotelian notions of being, and then must act. The
selection below is taken from a series of lectures Sartre delivered at the end of
World War II and is unusually (for Sartre) optimistic about human potential.*

The Accusations

. . . [W]hat can be said from the very beginning is that by existentialism
we mean a doctrine which makes human life possible and, in addition,
declares that every truth and every action implies a human setting and a
human subjectivity. . . .

. . . What complicates matters is that there are two kinds of existentialist; first, those who are Christian, among whom I would include Jaspers[1] and Gabriel Marcel,[2] both Catholic; and on the other hand the atheistic existentialists, among whom I class Heidegger,[3] and then the French existentialists and myself. What they have in common is that they think that existence precedes essence, or, if you prefer, that subjectivity must be the starting point.

Just what does that mean? Let us consider some object that is manufactured, for example, a book or a paper-cutter: here is an object which has been made by an artisan whose inspiration came from a concept. He referred to the concept of what a paper-cutter is and likewise to a known method of production, which is part of the concept, something which is, by and large, a routine. Thus, the paper-cutter is at once an object produced in a certain way and, on the other hand, one having a specific use; and one can not postulate a man who produces a paper-cutter but does not know what it is used for. Therefore, let us say that, for the paper-cutter, essence— that is, the ensemble of both the production routines and the properties which enable it to be both produced and defined—precedes existence. Thus, the presence of the paper-cutter or book in front of me is determined. Therefore, we have here a technical view of the world whereby it can be said that production precedes existence.

When we conceive God as the Creator, He is generally thought of as a superior sort of artisan. Whatever doctrine we may be considering, whether one like that of Descartes or that of Leibnitz,[4] we always grant that will more or less follows understanding or, at the very least, accompanies it, and that when God creates He knows exactly what He is creating. Thus, the concept of man in the mind of God is comparable to the concept of paper-cutter in the mind of the manufacturer, and, following certain techniques and a conception, God produces man, just as the artisan, following a definition and a technique, makes a paper-cutter. Thus, the individual man is the realization of a certain concept in the divine intelligence.

In the eighteenth century, the atheism of the *philosophes* discarded the idea of God, but not so much the notion that essence precedes existence. To a certain extent, this idea is found everywhere; we find it in Diderot,[5] in Voltaire, and even in Kant.[6] Man has a human nature; this human nature, which is the concept of the human, is found in all men, which means that each man is a particular example of a universal concept, man. In Kant, the result of this universality is that the wild-man, the natural man, as well as the bourgeois, are circumscribed by the same definition and have the same basic qualities. Thus, here too the essence of man precedes the historical existence that we find in nature.

Atheistic existentialism, which I represent, is more coherent. It states that if God does not exist, there is at least one being in whom existence precedes essence, a being who exists before he can be defined by any concept, and that this being is man, or, as Heidegger says, human reality. What is meant here by saying that existence precedes essence? It means that, first of all, man exists, turns up, appears on the scene, and, only afterward, defines himself. If man, as the existentialist conceives him, is indefinable, it is because at first he is nothing. Only afterward will he be something, and he himself will have made what he will be. Thus, there is no human nature, since there is no God to conceive it. Not only is man what he conceives himself to be, but he is also only what he wills himself to be after this thrust toward existence.

Subjectivity and Responsibility

Man is nothing else but what he makes of himself. Such is the first principle of existentialism. It is also what is called subjectivity, the name we are labeled with when charges are brought against us. But what do we mean by this, if not that man has a greater dignity than a stone or table? For we mean that man first exists, that is, that man first of all is the being who hurls himself toward a future and who is conscious of imagining himself as being in the future. Man is at the start a plan which is aware of itself, rather than a patch of moss, a piece of garbage, or a cauliflower; nothing exists prior to this plan; there is nothing in heaven; man will be what he will have planned to be. Not what he will want to be. Because by the word "will" we generally mean a conscious decision, which is subsequent to what we have already made of ourselves. I may want to belong to a political party, write a book, get married; but all that is only a manifestation of an earlier, more spontaneous choice that is called "will." But if existence really does precede essence, man is responsible for what he is. Thus, existentialism's first move is to make every man aware of what he is and to make the full responsibility of his existence rest on him. And when we say that a man is responsible for himself, we do not only mean that he is responsible for his own individuality, but that he is responsible for all men.

The word subjectivism has two meanings, and our opponents play on the two. Subjectivism means, on the one hand, that an individual chooses and makes himself; and, on the other, that it is impossible for man to transcend human subjectivity. The second of these is the essential meaning of existentialism. When we say that man chooses his own self, we mean that every one of us does likewise; but we also mean by that in making this choice he also chooses all men. In fact, in creating the man that we want to be, there is not a single one of our acts which does not at the same time create an image of man as we think he ought to be. To choose to be this or that is to affirm at the same time the value of what we choose, because we can never choose evil. We always choose the good, and nothing can be good for us without being good for all.

If, on the other hand, existence precedes essence, and if we grant that we exist and fashion our image at one and the same time, the image is valid for everybody and for our whole age. Thus, our responsibility is much greater than we might have supposed, because it involves all mankind. If I am a workingman and choose to join a Christian trade-union rather than be a communist, and if by being a member I want to show that the best thing for man is resignation, that the kingdom of man is not of this world, I am not only involving my own case—I want to be resigned for everyone. As a result, my action has involved all humanity. To take a more individual matter, if I want to marry, to have children; even if this marriage depends solely on my own circumstances or passion or wish, I am involving all humanity in monogamy and not merely myself. Therefore, I am responsible for myself and for everyone else. I am creating a certain image of man of my own choosing. In choosing myself, I choose man.

This helps us understand what the actual content is of such rather grandiloquent words as anguish, forlornness, despair. As you will see, it's all quite simple.

Anguish

First, what is meant by anguish? The existentialists say at once that man is anguish. What that means is this: the man who involves himself and who realizes that he is not only the person he chooses to be, but also a lawmaker who is, at the same time, choosing all mankind as well as himself, can not help escape the feeling of his total and deep responsibility. Of course, there are many people who are not anxious; but we claim that they are hiding their anxiety, that they are fleeing from it. Certainly, many people believe that when they do something, they themselves are the only ones involved, and when someone says to them, "What if everyone acted that way?" they shrug their shoulders and answer, "Everyone doesn't act that way." But really, one should always ask himself, "What would happen if everybody looked at things that way?" There is no escaping this disturbing thought except by a kind of double-dealing. A man who lies and makes excuses for himself by saying "not everybody does that" is someone with an uneasy conscience, because the act of lying implies that a universal value is conferred upon the lie.

Anguish is evident even when it conceals itself. This is the anguish that Kierkegaard[7] called the anguish of Abraham. You know the story: an angel has ordered Abraham to sacrifice his son; if it really were an angel who has come and said, "You are Abraham, you shall sacrifice your son," everything would be all right. But everyone might first wonder, "Is it really an angel, and am I really Abraham? What proof do I have?"

There was a madwoman who had hallucinations; someone used to speak to her on the telephone and give her orders. Her doctor asked her, "Who is it who talks to you?" She answered, "He says it's God." What proof did she really have that it was God? If an angel comes to me, what proof is there that it's an angel? And if I hear voices, what proof is there that they come from heaven and not from hell, or from the subconscious, or a pathological condition? What proves that they are addressed to me? What proof is there that I have been appointed to impose my choice and my conception of man on humanity? I'll never find any proof or sign to convince me of that. If a voice addresses me, it is always for me to decide that this is the angel's voice; if I consider that such an act is a good one, it is I who will choose to say that it is good rather than bad.

Now, I'm not being singled out as an Abraham, and yet at every moment I'm obliged to perform exemplary acts. For every man, everything happens as if all mankind had its eyes fixed on him and were guiding itself by what he does. And every man ought to say to himself, "Am I really the kind of man who has the right to act in such a way that humanity might guide itself by my actions?" And if he does not say that to himself he is masking his anguish.

There is no question here of the kind of anguish which would lead to quietism, to inaction. It is a matter of a simple sort of anguish that anybody who has had responsibilities is familiar with. For example, when a military officer takes the responsibility for an attack and sends a certain number of men to death, he chooses to do so, and in the main he alone makes the choice. Doubtless, orders come from above, but they are too broad; he interprets them, and on this interpretation depend the lives of ten or fourteen or twenty men. In making a decision he can not help having a certain anguish. All leaders know this anguish. That doesn't keep them from acting; on the contrary, it is the very condition of their action. For it implies that they envisage a number of possibilities, and when they choose one, they realize that it has value only because it is chosen. We shall see that this kind of anguish, which is the kind that existentialism describes, is explained, in addition, by a direct responsibility to the other men whom it involves. It is not a curtain separating us from action, but is part of action itself.

Forlornness

When we speak of forlornness, a term Heidegger was fond of, we mean only that God does not exist and that we have to face all the consequences of this. The existentialist is strongly opposed to a certain kind of secular ethics which would like to abolish God with the least possible expense. About 1880, some French teachers tried to set up a secular ethics which went something like this: God is a useless and costly hypothesis; we are discarding it; but, meanwhile, in order for there to be an ethics, a society, a civilization, it is essential that certain values be taken seriously and that they be considered as having an *a priori* existence. It must be obligatory, *a priori*, to be honest, not to lie, not to beat your wife, to have children, and so forth. So we're going to try a little device which will make it possible to show that values exist all the same, inscribed in a heaven of ideas, though otherwise God does not exist. In other words—and this, I believe, is the tendency of everything called reformism in France—nothing will be changed if God does not exist. We shall find ourselves with the same norms of honesty, progress, and humanism, and will have made of God an outdated hypothesis which will peacefully die off by itself.

The existentialist, on the contrary, thinks it very distressing that God does not exist, because all possibility of finding values in a heaven of ideas disappears along with Him; there can no longer be an *a priori* Good, since there is no infinite and perfect consciousness to think it. Nowhere is it written that the Good exists, that we must be honest, that we must not lie because the fact is we are on a plane where there are only men. Dostoevsky[8] said, "If God didn't exist, everything would be possible." That is the very starting point of existentialism. Indeed, everything is permissible if God does not exist, and as a result man is forlorn, because neither within him nor without does he find anything to cling to. He can't start making excuses for himself.

If existence really does precede essence, there is no explaining things away by reference to a fixed and given human nature. In other words, there is no determinism, man is free, man is freedom. On the other hand, if God does not exist, we find no values or commands to turn to which legitimize our conduct. So, in the bright realm of values, we have no excuse behind us, nor justification before us. We are alone, with no excuses.

That is the idea I shall try to convey when I say that man is condemned to be free. Condemned, because he did not create himself, yet, in other respects is free; because, once thrown into the world, he is responsible for everything he does. The existentialist does not believe in the power of passion. He will never agree that a sweeping passion is a ravaging torrent which fatally leads a man to certain acts and is therefore an excuse. He thinks that man is responsible for his passion.

The existentialist does not think that man is going to help himself by finding in the world some omen by which to orient himself. Because he thinks that man will interpret the omen to suit himself. Therefore, he thinks that man, with no support and no aid, is condemned every moment to invent man. Ponge, in a very fine article, has said, "Man is the future of man." That's exactly it. But if it is taken to mean that this future is recorded in heaven, that God sees it, then it is false, because it would really no longer be a future. If it is taken to mean that, whatever a man may be, there is a future to be forged, a virgin future before him, then this remark is sound. But then we are forlorn.

To give you an example which will enable you to understand forlornness better, I shall cite the case of one of my students who came to see me under the following circumstances: his father was on bad terms with his mother, and, moreover, was inclined to be a collaborationist;[9] his older brother had been killed in the German offensive of 1940, and the young man, with somewhat immature but generous feelings, wanted to avenge him. His mother lived alone with him, very much upset by the half-treason of her husband and the death of her older son; the boy was her only consolation.

The boy was faced with the choice of leaving for England and joining the Free French Forces—that is, leaving his mother behind—or remaining with his mother and helping her to carry on. He was fully aware that the woman lived only for him and that his going-off—and perhaps his death—would plunge her into despair. He was also aware that every act that he did for his mother's sake was a sure thing, in the sense that it was helping her to carry on, whereas every effort he made toward going off and fighting was an uncertain move which might run aground and prove completely useless; for example, on his way to England he might, while passing through Spain, be detained indefinitely in a Spanish camp; he might reach England or Algiers and be stuck in an office at a desk job. As a result, he was faced with two very different kinds of action: one, concrete, immediate, but concerning only one individual; the other concerned an incomparably vaster group, a national collectivity, but for that very reason was dubious, and might be interrupted en route. And, at the same time, he was wavering between two kinds of ethics. On the one hand, an ethics of sympathy, of personal devotion; on the other, a broader ethics, but one whose efficacy was more dubious. He had to choose between the two.

Who could help him choose? Christian doctrine? No. Christian doctrine says, "Be charitable, love your neighbor, take the more rugged path, and so forth." But which is the more rugged path? Whom should he love as a brother? The fighting man or his mother? Which does the greater good, the vague act of fighting in a group, or the concrete one of helping a particular human being to go on living? Who can decide *a priori?* Nobody. No book of ethics can tell him. The Kantian ethics says, "Never treat any person as a means, but as an end." Very well, if I stay with my mother, I'll treat her as an end and not as a means; but by virtue of this very fact, I'm running the risk of treating the people around me who are fighting, as means; and, conversely, if I go to join those who are fighting, I'll be treating them as an end, and, by doing that, I run the risk of treating my mother as a means.

If values are vague, and if they are always too broad for the concrete and specific case that we are considering, the only thing left for us is to trust our instincts. That's what this young man tried to do; and when I saw him, he said, "in the end, feeling is what counts. I ought to choose whichever pushes me in one direction. If I feel that I love my mother enough to sacrifice everything else for her—my desire for vengeance, for action, for adventure—then I'll stay with her. If, on the contrary, I feel that my love for my mother isn't enough, I'll leave."

But how is the value of a feeling determined? What gives his feeling for his mother value? Precisely the fact that he remained with her. I may say that

I like so-and-so well enough to sacrifice a certain amount of money for him, but I may say so only if I've done it. I may say "I love my mother well enough to remain with her" if I have remained with her. The only way to determine the value of this affection is, precisely, to perform an act which confirms and defines it. But, since I require this affection to justify my act, I find myself caught in a vicious circle.

On the other hand, Gide[10] has well said that a mock feeling and a true feeling are almost indistinguishable; to decide that I love my mother and will remain with her, or to remain with her by putting on an act, amount somewhat to the same thing. In other words, the feeling is formed by the acts one performs; so, I can not refer to it in order to act upon it. Which means that I can neither seek within myself the true condition which will impel me to act, nor apply to a system of ethics for concepts which will permit me to act. You will say, "At least, he did go to a teacher for advice." But if you seek advice from a priest, for example, you have chosen this priest; you already knew, more or less, just about what advice he was going to give you. In other words, choosing your adviser is involving yourself. The proof of this is that if you are a Christian, you will say, "Consult a priest:" But some priests are collaborating, some are just marking time, some are resisting. Which to choose? If the young man chooses a priest who is resisting or collaborating, he has already decided on the kind of advice he's going to get. Therefore, in coming to see me he knew the answer I was going to give him, and I had only one answer to give: "You're free, choose, that is, invent." No general ethics can show you what is to be done; there are no omens in the world. The Catholics will reply, "But there are." Granted—but, in any case, I myself choose the meaning they have.

When I was a prisoner, I knew a rather remarkable young man who was a Jesuit. He had entered the Jesuit order in the following way: he had had a number of very bad breaks; in childhood, his father died, leaving him in poverty, and he was a scholarship student at a religious institution where he was constantly made to feel that he was being kept out of charity; then, he failed to get any of the honors and distinctions that children like; later on, at about eighteen, he bungled a love affair; finally, at twenty-two, he failed in military training, a childish enough matter, but it was the last straw.

This young fellow might well have felt that he had botched everything. It was a sign of something, but of what? He might have taken refuge in bitterness or despair. But he very wisely looked upon all this as a sign that he was not made for secular triumphs, and that only the triumphs of religion, holiness, and faith were open to him. He saw the hand of God in all this, and so he entered the order. Who can help seeing that he alone decided what the sign meant?

Some other interpretation might have been drawn from this series of setbacks; for example, that he might have done better to turn carpenter or revolutionist. Therefore, he is fully responsible for the interpretation. Forlornness implies that we ourselves choose our being. Forlornness and anguish go together.

Despair

As for despair, the term has a very simple meaning. It means that we shall confine ourselves to reckoning only with what depends upon our will, or on the ensemble of probabilities which make our action possible. When we want something, we always have to reckon with probabilities. I may be counting on the arrival of a friend. The friend is coming by rail or street-car; this supposes that the train will arrive on schedule, or that the street-car will not jump the track. I am left in the realm of possibility; but possibilities are to be reckoned with only to the point where my action comports with the ensemble of these possibilities, and no further. The moment the possibilities I am considering are not rigorously involved by my action, I ought to disengage myself from them, because no God, no scheme, can adapt the world and its possibilities to my will. When Descartes said, "Conquer yourself rather than the world," he meant essentially the same thing.

The Marxists to whom I have spoken reply, "You can rely on the support of others in your action, which obviously has certain limits because you're not going to live forever. That means: rely on both what others are doing elsewhere to help you in China, in Russia, and what they will do later on, after your death, to carry on the action and lead it to its fulfillment, which will be the revolution. You even *have* to rely upon that, otherwise you're immoral." I reply at once that I will always rely on fellow-fighters insofar as these comrades are involved with me in a common struggle, in the unity of a party or a group in which I can more or less make my weight felt; that is, one whose ranks I am in as a fighter and whose movements I am aware of at every moment. In such a situation, relying on the unity and will of the party is exactly like counting on the fact that the train will arrive on time or that the car won't jump the track. But, given that man is free and that there is no human nature for me to depend on, I can not count on men whom I do not know by relying on human goodness or man's concern for the good of society. I don't know what will become of the Russian revolution; I may make an example of it to the extent that at the present time it is apparent that the proletariat plays a part in Russia that it plays in no other nation. But I can't swear that this will inevitably lead to a triumph of the proletariat. I've got to limit myself to what I see.

Given that men are free and that tomorrow they will freely decide what man will be, I can not be sure that, after my death, fellow-fighters will carry on my work to bring it to its maximum perfection. Tomorrow, after my death, some men may decide to set up Fascism, and the others may be cowardly and muddled enough to let them do it. Fascism will then be the human reality, so much the worse for us.

Actually, things will be as man will have decided they are to be. Does that mean that I should abandon myself to quietism? No. First, I should involve myself, then, act on the old saw, "Nothing ventured, nothing gained." Nor does it mean that I shouldn't belong to a party, but rather that I shall have no illusions and shall do what I can. For example, suppose I ask myself, "Will socialization, as such, ever come about?" I know nothing about it. All I know is that I'm going to do everything in my power to bring it about. Beyond that, I can't count on anything. Quietism is the attitude of people who say, "Let others do what I can't do." The doctrine I am presenting is the very opposite of quietism, since it declares, "There is no reality except in action." Moreover, it goes further, since it adds, "Man is nothing else than his plan; he exists only to the extent that he fulfills himself; he is therefore nothing else than the ensemble of his acts, nothing else than his life."

Bad Faith

According to this, we can understand why our doctrine horrifies certain people. Because often the only way they can bear their wretchedness is to think, "Circumstances have been against me. What I've been and done doesn't show my true worth. To be sure, I've had no great love, no great friendship, but that's because I haven't met a man or woman who was worthy. The books I've written haven't been very good because I haven't had the proper leisure. I haven't had children to devote myself to because I didn't find a man with whom I could have spent my life. So there remains within me, unused and quite viable, a host of propensities, inclinations, possibilities, that one wouldn't guess from the mere series of things I've done."

Now, for the existentialist there is really no love other than one which manifests itself in a person's being in love. There is no genius other than one which is expressed in works of art; the genius of Proust[11] is the sum of Proust's works; the genius of Racine[12] is his series of tragedies. Outside of that, there is nothing. Why say that Racine could have written another tragedy, when he didn't write it? A man is involved in life, leaves his impress on it, and outside of that there is nothing. To be sure, this may seem a harsh thought to someone whose life hasn't been a success. But, on the other hand, it prompts people to understand that reality alone is what counts, that dreams, expectations, and hopes warrant no more than to define a man as a disappointed dream, as miscarried hopes, as vain expectations. In other words, to define him negatively and not positively. However, when we say, "You are nothing else than your life," that does not imply that the artist will be judged solely on the basis of his works of art; a thousand other things will contribute toward summing him up. What we mean is that a man is nothing else than a series of undertakings, that he is the sum, the organization, the ensemble of the relationships which make up these undertakings.

When all is said and done, what we are accused of, at bottom, is not our pessimism, but an optimistic toughness. If people throw up to us our works of fiction in which we write about people who are soft, weak, cowardly, and sometimes even downright bad, it's not because these people are soft, weak, cowardly, or bad; because if we were to say, as Zola[13] did, that they are that way because of heredity, the workings of environment, society, because of biological or psychological determinism, people would be reassured. They would say, "Well, that's what we're like, no one can do anything about it." But when the existentialist writes about a coward, he says that this coward is responsible for his cowardice. He's not like that because he has a cowardly heart or lung or brain; he's not like that on account of his physiological make-up; but he's like that because he has made himself a coward by his acts. There's no such thing as a cowardly constitution; there are nervous constitutions; there is poor blood, as the common people say, or strong constitutions. But the man whose blood is poor is not a coward on that account, for what makes cowardice is the act of renouncing or yielding. A constitution is not an act; the coward is defined on the basis of the acts he performs. People feel, in a vague sort of way, that this coward we're talking about is guilty of being a coward, and the thought frightens them. What people would like is that a coward or a hero be born that way.

One of the complaints most frequently made about *The Ways of Freedom* can be summed up as follows: "After all, these people are so spineless, how are you going to make heroes out of them?" This objection almost makes me laugh, for it assumes that people are born heroes. That's what people really want to think. If you're born cowardly, you may set your mind perfectly at rest; there's nothing you can do about it; you'll be cowardly all your life, whatever you may do. If you're born a hero, you may set your mind just as much at rest; you'll be a hero all your life; you'll drink like a hero and eat like a hero. What the existentialist says is that the coward makes himself cowardly, that the hero makes himself heroic. There's always a possibility for the coward not to be cowardly any more and for the hero to stop being heroic. What counts is total involvement; some one particular action or set of circumstances is not total involvement.

Thus, I think we have answered a number of the charges concerning existentialism. You see that it can not be taken for a philosophy of quietism, since it defines man in terms of action; nor for a pessimistic description of man—there is no doctrine more optimistic, since man's destiny is within himself, nor for an attempt to discourage man from acting, since it tells him that the only hope is in his acting and that action is the only thing that enables a man to live. Consequently, we are dealing here with an ethics of action and involvement.

Is Existentialism Too Subjective?

Nevertheless, on the basis of a few notions like these, we are still charged with immuring man in his private subjectivity. There again we're very much misunderstood. Subjectivity of the individual is indeed our point of departure, and this for strictly philosophic reasons. Not because we are bourgeois, but because we want a doctrine based on truth and not a lot of fine theories, full of hope but with no real basis. There can be no other truth to take off from than this: *I think; therefore, I exist.* There we have the absolute truth of consciousness becoming aware of itself. Every theory which takes man out of the moment in which he becomes aware of himself is, at its very beginning, a theory which confounds truth, for outside the Cartesian *cogito*, all views are only probable, and a doctrine of probability which is not bound to a truth dissolves into thin air. In order to describe the probable, you must have a firm hold on the true. Therefore, before there can be any truth whatsoever, there must be an absolute truth; and this one is simple and easily arrived at; it's on everyone's doorstep; it's a matter of grasping it directly.

Secondly, this theory is the only one which gives man dignity, the only one which does not reduce him to an object. The effect of all materialism is to treat all men, including the one philosophizing, as objects, that is, as an ensemble of determined reactions in no way distinguished from the ensemble of qualities and phenomena which constitute a table or a chair or a stone. We definitely wish to establish the human realm as an ensemble of values distinct from the material realm. But the subjectivity that we have thus arrived at, and which we have claimed to be truth, is not a strictly individual subjectivity, for we have demonstrated that one discovers in the *cogito* not only himself, but others as well.

The philosophies of Descartes and Kant to the contrary, through the *I think* we reach our own self in the presence of others, and the others are just as real to us as our own self. Thus, the man who becomes aware of himself through the *cogito* also perceives all others, and he perceives them as the condition of his own existence. He realizes that he can not be anything (in the sense that we say that someone is witty or nasty or jealous) unless others recognize it as such. In order to get any truth about myself, I must have contact with another person. The other is indispensable to my own existence, as well as to my knowledge about myself. This being so, in discovering my inner being I discover the other person at the same time, like a freedom placed in front of me which thinks and wills only for or against me. Hence, let us at once announce the discovery of a world which we shall call intersubjectivity; this is the world in which man decides what he is and what others are.

Besides, if it is impossible to find in every man some universal essence which would be human nature, yet there does exist a universal human condition. It's not by chance that today's thinkers speak more readily of man's condition than of his nature. By condition they mean, more or less definitely, the *a priori* limits which outline man's fundamental situation in the universe. Historical situations vary; a man may be born a slave in a pagan society or a feudal lord or a proletarian. What does not vary is the necessity for him to exist in the world, to be at work there, to be there in the midst of other people, and to be mortal there. The limits are neither subjective nor objective, or, rather, they have an objective and a subjective side. Objective because they are to be found everywhere and are recognizable everywhere; subjective because they are *lived* and are nothing if man does not live them, that is, freely determine his existence with reference to them. And though the configurations may differ, at least none of them are completely strange to me, because they all appear as attempts either to pass beyond these limits or recede from them or deny them or adapt to them. Consequently, every configuration, however individual it may be, has a universal value. Every configuration, even the Chinese, the Indian, or the Negro, can be understood by a Westerner. "Can be understood" means that by virtue of a situation that he can imagine, a European of 1945 can, in like manner, push himself to his limits and reconstitute within himself the configuration of the Chinese, the Indian, or the African. Every configuration has universality in the sense that every configuration can be understood by every man. This does not at all mean that this configuration defines man forever, but that it can be met with again. There is always a way to understand the idiot, the child, the savage, the foreigner, provided one has the necessary information.

In this sense we may say that there is a universality of man; but it is not given, it is perpetually being made. I build the universal in choosing myself; I build it in understanding the configuration of every other man, whatever age he might have lived in. This absoluteness of choice does not do away with the relativeness of each epoch. At heart, what existentialism shows is the connection between the absolute character of free involvement, by virtue of which every man remakes himself in realizing a type of mankind, an involvement always comprehensible in any age whatsoever and by any person whosoever, and the relativeness of the cultural ensemble which may result from such a choice; it must be stressed that the relativity of Cartesianism and the absolute character of Cartesian involvement go together. In this sense, you may, if you like, say that each of us performs an absolute act in breathing, eating, sleeping, or behaving in any way whatever. There is no difference between being free, like a configuration, like an existence which chooses its essence, and being absolute. There is no difference between being an absolute temporarily localized, that is, localized in history, and being universally comprehensible. . . .

Can Values 'Created' by Humans Be Taken Seriously?

. . . I've been reproached for asking whether existentialism is humanistic. It's been said, "But you said in *Nausea* that the humanists were all wrong. You made fun of a certain kind of humanist. Why come back to it now?"

Actually, the word humanism has two very different meanings. By humanism one can mean a theory which takes man as an end and as a higher value. Humanism in this sense can be found in Cocteau's tale *Around the World in Eighty Hours* when a character, because he is flying over some mountains in an airplane, declares, "Man is simply amazing!" That means that I, who did not build the airplanes, shall personally benefit from these particular inventions, and that I, as man, shall personally consider myself responsible for, and honored by, acts of a few particular men. This would imply that we ascribe a value to man on the basis of the highest deeds of certain men. This humanism is absurd, because only the dog or the horse would be able to make such an over-all judgment about man, which they are careful not to do, at least to my knowledge.

But it can not be granted that a man may make a judgment about man. Existentialism spares him from any such judgment. The existentialist will never consider man as an end because he is always in the making. Nor should we believe that there is a mankind to which we might set up a cult in the manner of Auguste Comte.[14] The cult of mankind ends in the self-enclosed humanism of Comte, and, let it be said, of fascism. This kind of humanism we can do without.

Existential Humanism

But there is another meaning of humanism. Fundamentally, it is this: man is constantly outside of himself, in projecting himself, in losing himself outside of himself, he makes for man's existing; and, on the other hand, it is by pursuing transcendent goals that he is able to exist; man, being in this state of passing-beyond, and seizing upon things only as they bear upon this passing-beyond, is at the heart, at the center of this passing-beyond. There is no universe other than a human universe, the universe of human subjectivity. This connection between transcendency, as a constituent element of man—not in the sense that God is transcendent, but in the sense of passing beyond—and subjectivity, in the sense that man is not closed in on himself but is always present in a human universe, is what we call existentialist humanism. Humanism, because we remind man that there is no law-maker other than himself, and that in his forlornness he will decide by himself; because we point out that man will fulfill himself as man, not in turning toward himself, but in seeking outside of himself a goal which is just this liberation, just this particular fulfillment.

From these few reflections it is evident that nothing is more unjust than the objections that have been raised against us. Existentialism is nothing else than an attempt to draw all the consequences of a coherent atheistic position. It isn't trying to plunge man into despair at all. But if one calls every attitude of unbelief despair, like the Christians, then the word is not being used in its original sense. Existentialism isn't so atheistic that it wears itself out showing that God doesn't exist. Rather, it declares that even if God did exist, that would change nothing. There you've got our point of view. Not that we believe that God exists, but we think that the problem of His existence is not the issue; [what man needs is to find himself again, and to understand that nothing can save him from himself, not even a valid proof of the existence of God]. In this sense existentialism is optimistic, a doctrine of action, and it is plain dishonesty for Christians to make no distinction between their own despair and ours and then to call us despairing.

Notes

1 Karl Jaspers (1883–1969) was a German psychiatrist who turned to philosophy. He was not so thoroughly Catholic as Sartre implies here, but argued that a "Transcendence" existed that could neither be visualized or intellectually grasped but whom humans must encounter.

2 Gabriel Marcel (1889–1973) was a French Catholic who worked with the Red Cross during World War I. His experiences there led him to rethink the mystery of existence, which he combined with Christianity to argue for a life of service and love for others.

3 Martin Heidegger (1889–1976) was a German philosopher who set down many of the basic tenets of existentialism even though he personally rejected the label. He is often regarded as the central figure in 20th century existentialist thought.

4 René Descartes and Gottfried Wilhelm von Leibnitz were 17th century mathematicians and philosophers.

5 Denis Diderot (1713–1784), a French skeptic who challenged common notions of the origins of morality.

6 Immanuel Kant (1724–1804) was a pivotal German philosopher who challenged Locke's idea that the mind was a *tabula rasa* and postulated instead that the human mind had its own inherent logic, an *a priori* ability to systematize and understand.

7 Søren Kiekegaard (1813–1855) was a Danish philosopher and a Lutheran minister. He rejected the idea that God could be understood by reason and argued that humans must take a leap of faith into what is logically often absurd in order to overcome despair.

8　Fyodor Dostoevsky (1821–1881) was a Russian novelist and essayist. He rejected notions that human beings were innately good and rational and instead characterized them as depraved, mindlessly submissive to authority, and resentful.

9　A French citizen who cooperated with the Nazis during the German occupation of France in World War II.

10　André Gide (1869–1951) was a French novelist, essayist, and social critic.

11　Marcel Proust (1871–1922) was a French novelist best known for his work *Remembrance of Things Past.*

12　Jean Baptiste Racine (1639–1699) was a French dramatist.

13　Emile Zola (1840–1902), a French novelist and master of "naturalist" fiction.

14　Auguste Comte (1798–1857), the leading proponent of positivism, a philosophy that calls for a purely scientific, empirical approach to history and society.

29

The Myth of Sisyphus

Albert Camus

(1913–1960)

Born in Algeria and educated at the University of Algiers, Albert Camus was a French writer trained in philosophy. Poor health prevented him from entering a military or teaching career, but he found success as a journalist working in both Paris and Algeria during the German occupation of 1940–1944. His philosophical novel The Stranger *in 1940 introduced the theme of the absurd that would frame his repeated question: How does humankind live in an absurd world? In 1942* The Myth of Sisyphus, *excerpted below, placed the classical allegory of Sisyphus in the context of a modern philosophical essay on suicide and the absurd. Camus received the Nobel Prize for Literature in 1957.*

The gods had condemned Sisyphus to ceaselessly rolling a rock to the top of a mountain, whence the stone would fall back of its own weight. They had thought with some reason that there is no more dreadful punishment than futile and hopeless labor.

If one believes Homer, Sisyphus was the wisest and most prudent of mortals. According to another tradition, however, he was disposed to practice the profession of highwayman. I see no contradiction in this. Opinions differ as to the reasons why he became the futile laborer of the underworld. To begin with, he is accused of certain levity in regard to the gods. He stole their secrets. Ægina, the daughter of Æsopus, was carried off by Jupiter. The father was shocked by that disappearance and complained to Sisyphus. He, who knew of the abduction, offered to tell about it on condition that Æsopus would give water to the citadel of Corinth. To the celestial thunderbolts he preferred the benediction of water. He was punished for this in the underworld. Homer tells us also that Sisyphus had put Death in chains. Pluto could not endure the sight of his deserted, silent empire. He dispatched the god of war who liberated Death from the hands of her conqueror.

It is said also that Sisyphus, being near to death, rashly wanted to test his wife's love. He ordered her to cast his unburied body into the middle of the public square. Sisyphus woke up in the underworld. And there, annoyed by obedience so contrary to human love, he obtained from Pluto permission to return to earth in order to chastise his wife. But when he had seen again the face of this world, enjoyed water and sun, warm stones and the sea, he no longer wanted to go back to the infernal darkness. Recalls, signs of anger, warnings were of no avail. Many years more he lived facing the curve of the gulf, the sparkling sea, and the smiles of earth. A decree of the gods was necessary. Mercury came and seized the impudent man by the collar and, snatching him from his joys, led him forcibly back to the underworld, where his rock was ready for him.

You have already grasped that Sisyphus is the absurd hero. He is, as much through his passions as through his torture. His scorn of the gods, his hatred of death, and his passion for life won him that unspeakable penalty in which the whole being is exerted toward accomplishing nothing. This is the price that must be paid for the passions of this earth. Nothing is told us about Sisyphus in the underworld. Myths are made for the imagination to breathe life into them. As for this myth, one sees merely the whole effort of a body straining to raise the huge stone, to roll it and push it up a slope a hundred times over; one sees the face screwed up, the cheek tight against the stone, the shoulder bracing the clay-covered mass, the foot wedging it, the fresh start with arms outstretched, the wholly human security of two earth-clotted hands. At the very end of his long effort measured by skyless space and time without depth, the purpose is achieved. Then Sisyphus watches the stone rush down in a few moments toward that lower world whence he will have to push it up again toward the summit. He goes back down to the plain.

It is during that return, that pause, that Sisyphus interests me. A face that toils so close to stones is already stone itself! I see that man going back down with a heavy yet measured step toward the torment of which he will never know the end. That hour like a breathing-space which returns as surely as his suffering, that is the hour of consciousness. At each of those moments when he leaves the heights and gradually sinks toward the lairs of the gods, he is superior to his fate. He is stronger than his rock.

If this myth is tragic, that is because its hero is conscious. Where would his torture be, indeed, if at every step the hope of succeeding upheld him? The workman of today works every day in his life at the same tasks, and this fate is no less absurd. But it is tragic only at the rare moments when it becomes conscious. Sisyphus, proletarian of the gods, powerless and rebellious, knows the whole extent of his wretched condition: it is what he thinks of during his descent. The lucidity that was to constitute his torture at the same time crowns his victory. There is no fate that cannot be surmounted by scorn.

If the descent is thus sometimes performed in sorrow, it can also take place in joy. This word is not too much. Again I fancy Sisyphus returning toward his rock, and the sorrow was in the beginning. When the images of earth cling too tightly to memory, when the call of happiness becomes too insistent, it happens that melancholy rises in man's heart: this is the rock's victory, this is the rock itself. The boundless grief is too heavy to bear. These are our nights of Gethsemane. But crushing truths perish from being acknowledged. Thus, Œdipus at the outset obeys fate without knowing it. But from the moment he knows, his tragedy begins. Yet at the same moment, blind and desperate, he realizes that the only bond linking him to the world is the cool hand of a girl. Then a tremendous remark rings out: "Despite so many ordeals, my advanced age and the nobility of my soul make me conclude that all is well." Sophocles' Œdipus, like Dostoevsky's Kirilov, thus gives the recipe for the absurd victory. Ancient wisdom confirms modern heroism.

One does not discover the absurd without being tempted to write a manual of happiness. "What! by such narrow ways—?" There is but one world, however. Happiness and the absurd are two sons of the same earth. They are inseparable. It would be a mistake to say that happiness necessarily springs from the absurd discovery. It happens as well that the feeling of the absurd springs from happiness. "I conclude that all is well," says Œdipus, and that remark is sacred. It echoes in the wild and limited universe of man. It teaches that all is not, has not been, exhausted. It drives out of this world a god who had come into it with dissatisfaction and a preference for futile sufferings. It makes of fate a human matter, which must be settled among men.

All Sisyphus' silent joy is contained therein. His fate belongs to him. His rock is his thing. Likewise, the absurd man, when he contemplates his torment, silences all the idols. In the universe suddenly restored to its silence, the myriad wondering little voices of the earth rise up. Unconscious, secret calls, invitations from all the faces, they are the necessary reverse and price of victory. There is no sun without shadow, and it is essential to know the night. The absurd man says yes and his effort will henceforth be unceasing. If there is a personal fate, there is no higher destiny, or at least there is but one which he concludes is inevitable and despicable. For the rest, he knows himself to be the master of his days. At that subtle moment when man glances backward over his life, Sisyphus returning toward his rock, in that slight pivoting he contemplates that series of unrelated actions which becomes his fate, created by him, combined under his memory's eye and soon sealed by his death. Thus, convinced of the wholly human origin of all that is human, a blind man eager to see who knows that the night has no end, he is still on the go. The rock is still rolling.

I leave Sisyphus at the foot of the mountain! One always finds one's burden again. But Sisyphus teaches the higher fidelity that negates the gods and raises rocks. He too concludes that all is well. This universe henceforth without a master seems to him neither sterile nor futile. Each atom of that stone, each mineral flake of that night-filled mountain, in itself forms a world. The struggle itself toward the heights is enough to fill a man's heart. One must imagine Sisyphus happy.

30

Universal Declaration of Human Rights

The United Nations

(1948)

The Charter of the United Nations, established at the San Francisco Conference of 1945, begins by reaffirming a "faith in fundamental human rights, in the dignity and worth of the human person, in the equal rights of men and women and of nations large and small." The intentions of the participants sparked immediate legal and political controversy, however, because they explicitly rejected a proposal to ensure the protection as well as the promotion of human rights. Given the absence of a supranational authority and the presence of divisive power politics, the best the Charter could attempt was to create a moral statement that would aid representatives of the General Assembly in investigating and evaluating specific human rights abuses. On December 10, 1948, the General Assembly adopted without dissent the Universal Declaration of Human Rights. *While not a treaty with enforceable legal obligations, it makes explicit "a common standard of achievement for all peoples and all nations." The Declaration played a key role in 1977 when the Security Council imposed a mandatory arms embargo against South Africa as a response to the Apartheid government's continued record of human rights abuses. The international organization Amnesty International plays a key role in bringing specific cases to the attention of the Commission on Human Rights, a subsidiary body of the General Assembly.*

Preamble

WHEREAS recognition of the inherent dignity and of the equal and inalienable rights of all members of the human family is the foundation of freedom, justice and peace in the world,

WHEREAS disregard and contempt for human rights have resulted in barbarous acts which have outraged the conscience of mankind, and the advent of a world in which human beings shall enjoy freedom of speech and belief and freedom from fear and want has been proclaimed as the highest aspiration of the common people,

WHEREAS it is essential, if man is not to be compelled to have recourse, as a last resort, to rebellion against tyranny and oppression, that human rights should be protected by the rule of law,

WHEREAS it is essential to promote the development of friendly relations between nations,

WHEREAS the people of the United Nations have in the Charter reaffirmed their faith in fundamental human rights, in the dignity and worth of the human person and in the equal rights of men and women and have determined to promote social progress and better standards of life in larger freedom,

WHEREAS Member States have pledged themselves to achieve, in co-operation with the United Nations, the promotion of universal respect for and observance of human rights and fundamental freedoms,

WHEREAS a common understanding of these rights and freedoms is of the greatest importance for the full realization of this pledge,

Now, Therefore,

The General Assembly Proclaims

This Universal Declaration of Human Rights as a common standard of achievement for all peoples and all nations, to the end that every individual and every organ of society, keeping this Declaration constantly in mind, shall strive by teaching and education to promote respect for these rights and freedoms and by progressive measures, national and international, to secure their universal and effective recognition and observance, both among the peoples of Member States themselves and among the peoples of territories under their jurisdiction.

Article 1.

All human beings are born free and equal in dignity and rights. They are endowed with reason and conscience and should act towards one another in a spirit of brotherhood.

Article 2.

Everyone is entitled to all the rights and freedoms set forth in this Declaration, without distinction of any kind, such as race, colour, sex, language, religion, political or other opinion, national or social origin, property, birth or other status.

Furthermore, no distinction shall be made on the basis of the political, jurisdictional or international status of the country or territory to which a person belongs, whether it be independent, trust, non-self-governing or under any other limitation of sovereignty.

Article 3.

Everyone has the right to life, liberty and security of person.

Article 4.

No one shall be held in slavery or servitude; slavery and the slave trade shall be prohibited in all their forms.

Article 5.

No one shall be subjected to torture or to cruel, inhuman or degrading treatment or punishment.

Article 6.

Everyone has the right to recognition everywhere as a person before the law.

Article 7.

All are equal before the law and are entitled without any discrimination to equal protection of the law. All are entitled to equal protection against any discrimination in violation of this Declaration and against any incitement to such discrimination.

Article 8.

Everyone has the right to an effective remedy by the competent national tribunals for acts violating the fundamental rights granted him by the Constitution or by law.

Article 9.

No one shall be subjected to arbitrary arrest, detention or exile.

Article 10.

Everyone is entitled in full equality to a fair and public hearing by an independent and impartial tribunal, in the determination of his rights and obligations and of any criminal charge against him.

Article 11.

1. Everyone charged with a penal offence has the right to be presumed innocent until proved guilty according to law in a public trial at which he has had all the guarantees necessary for his defense.

2. No one shall be held guilty of any penal offense on account of any act or omission which did not constitute a penal offence, under national or international law, at the time when it was committed. Nor shall a heavier penalty be imposed than the one that was applicable at the time the penal offence was committed.

Article 12.

No one shall be subjected to arbitrary interference with his privacy, family, home or correspondence, nor to attacks upon his honour and reputation. Everyone has the right to the protection of the law against such interference or attacks.

Article 13.

1. Everyone has the right to freedom of movement and residence within the borders of each state.

2. Everyone has the right to leave any country, including his own, and to return to his country.

Article 14.

1. Everyone has the right to seek and to enjoy in other countries asylum from persecution.

2. This right may not be invoked in the case of prosecutions genuinely arising from nonpolitical crimes or from acts contrary to the purposes and principles of the United Nations.

Article 15.

1. Everyone has the right to a nationality.

2. No one shall be arbitrarily deprived of his nationality nor denied the right to change his nationality.

Article 16.

1. Men and women of full age, without any limitation due to race, nationality or religion, have the right to marry and to found a family. They are entitled to equal rights as to marriage, during marriage and at its dissolution.

2. Marriage shall be entered into only with the free and full consent of the intending spouses.

3. The family is the natural and fundamental group unit of society and is entitled to protection by society and the State.

Article 17.

1. Everyone has the right to own property alone as well as in association with others.

2. No one shall be arbitrarily deprived of his property.

Article 18.

Everyone has the right to freedom of thought, conscience and religion; this right includes freedom to change his religion or belief, and freedom, either alone or in community with others and in public or private, to manifest his religion or belief in teaching, practice, worship and observance.

Article 19.

Everyone has the right to freedom of opinion and expression; this right includes freedom to hold opinions without interference and to seek, receive and impart information and ideas through any media and regardless of frontiers.

Article 20.

1. Everyone has the right to freedom of peaceful assembly and association.

2. No one may be compelled to belong to an association.

Article 21.

1. Everyone has the right to take part in the government of his country, directly or through freely chosen representatives.

2. Everyone has the right of equal access to public service in his country.

3. The will of the people shall be the basis of the authority of government; this will shall be expressed in periodic and genuine elections which shall be by universal and equal suffrage and shall be held by secret vote or by equivalent free voting procedures.

Article 22.

Everyone, as a member of society, has the right to social security and is entitled to realization, through national effort and international co-operation and in accordance with the organization and resources of each State, of the economic, social and cultural rights indispensable for his dignity and the free development of his personality.

Article 23.

1. Everyone has the right to work, to free choice of employment, to just and favourable conditions of work and to protection against unemployment.

2. Everyone, without any discrimination, has the right to equal pay for equal work.

3. Everyone who works has the right to just and favorable remuneration insuring for himself and his family an existence worthy of human dignity, and supplemented, if necessary, by other means of social protection.

4. Everyone has the right to form and to join trade unions for the protection of his interests.

Article 24.

Everyone has the right to rest and leisure, including reasonable limitation of working hours and periodic holidays with pay.

Article 25.

1. Everyone has the right to a standard of living adequate for the health and well-being of himself and of his family, including food, clothing, housing and medical care and necessary social services, and the right to security in the event of unemployment, sickness, disability, widowhood, old age or other lack of livelihood in circumstances beyond his control.

2. Motherhood and childhood are entitled to special care and assistance. All children, whether born in or out of wedlock, shall enjoy the same social protection.

Article 26.

1. Everyone has the right to education. Education shall be free, at least in the elementary and fundamental stages. Elementary education shall be compulsory. Technical and professional education shall be made generally available and higher education shall be equally accessible to all on the basis of merit.

2. Education shall be directed to the full development of the human personality and to the strengthening of respect for human rights and fundamental freedoms. It shall promote understanding, tolerance and friendship among all nations, racial or religious groups, and shall further the activities of the United Nations for the maintenance of peace.

3. Parents have a prior right to choose the kind of education that shall be given to their children.

Article 27.

1. Everyone has the right freely to participate in the cultural life of the community, to enjoy the arts and to share in scientific advancement and its benefits.

2. Everyone has the right to the protection of the moral and material interests resulting from any scientific, literary or artistic production of which he is the author.

Article 28.

Everyone is entitled to a social and international order in which the rights and freedoms set forth in this Declaration can be fully realized.

Article 29.

1. Everyone has duties to the community in which alone the free and full development of his personality is possible.

2. In the exercise of his rights and freedoms, everyone shall be subjected only to such limitations as are determined by law solely for the purpose of securing due recognition and respect for the rights and freedom of others and of meeting the just requirements of morality, public order and the general welfare in a democratic society.

3. These rights and freedoms may in no case be exercised contrary to the purposes and principles of the United Nations.

Article 30.

Nothing in this Declaration may be interpreted as implying for any State, group or person any right to engage in any activity or to perform any act aimed at the destruction of any of the rights and freedoms set forth herein.

31

Selected Writings

Mohandas K. Gandhi

(1869–1948)

*R*evered *throughout the world as Mahatma ("the Great-Souled"), Mohandas Gandhi became one of the most influential figures of the twentieth century. Gandhi's nonviolent resistance to British imperialism in his native India finally succeeded in 1947 when India won independence from British rule. Gandhi's method of "satyagraha," usually translated as "passive resistance," repudiated the use of violence in any form. The term literally means "insistence on truth," and Gandhi himself used it in connection with phrases such as "truth-force" or "soul-force." A deeply religious man, Gandhi drew his faith not only from his native Hindu religion but from ideas gleaned when he was a law student in London, notably the Christianity of the Sermon on the Mount and the pacifistic anarchism of the Russian Peter Kropotkin (1842–1921). Gandhi also was strongly opposed to the materialism of modern Western civilization and worked to return India to a simpler mode of life centered on the village economy and Hindu reverence for life. Caught between warring Hindu and Muslim elements in Indian society, Gandhi was assassinated by a young Hindu zealot who opposed his generosity towards Muslims.*

The Doctrine of the Sword

(11 August 1920)

In this age of the rule of brute-force, it is almost impossible for anyone to believe that anyone else could possibly reject the law of the final supremacy of brute force. And so I receive anonymous letters advising me that I must not interfere with the progress of non-co-operation even though popular violence may break out. Others come to me and assuming that secretly I must be plotting violence, enquire when the happy moment for declaring open violence will arrive. They assure me that the English will never yield to anything but violence secret or open. Yet others, I am informed, believe that I am the most rascally person living in India because I never give out my real intention and that they have not a shadow of a doubt that I believe in violence just as much as most people do.

Such being the hold that the doctrine of the sword has on the majority of mankind, and as success of non-co-operation depends principally on absence of violence during its pendency and as my views in this matter affect the conduct of a large number of people, I am anxious to state them as clearly as possible.

I do believe that where there is only a choice between cowardice and violence I would advise violence. Thus when my eldest son asked me what he should have done, had he been present when I was almost fatally assaulted in 1908, whether he should have run away and seen me killed or whether he should have used his physical force which he could and wanted to use, and defended me, I told him that it was his duty to defend me even by using violence. Hence it was that I took part in the Boer War, the so-called Zulu rebellion and the late War. Hence also do I advocate training in arms for those who believe in the method of violence. I would rather have India resort to arms in order to defend her honour than that she should in a cowardly manner become or remain a helpless witness to her own dishonour.

But I believe that non-violence is infinitely superior to violence, forgiveness is more manly than punishment. *Kshama virasya bhushanam.* "Forgiveness adorns a soldier." But abstinence is forgiveness only when there is the power to punish; it is meaningless when it pretends to proceed from a helpless creature. A mouse hardly forgives a cat when it allows itself to be torn to pieces by her. I, therefore, appreciate the sentiment of those who cry out for the condign punishment of General Dyer[1] and his ilk. They would tear him to pieces if they could. But I do not believe India to be helpless. I do not believe myself to be a helpless creature. Only I want to use India's and my strength for a better purpose.

Let me not be misunderstood. Strength does not come from physical capacity. It comes from an indomitable will. An average Zulu is any way more than a match for an average Englishman in bodily capacity. But he flees from an English boy, because he fears the boy's revolver or those who will use it for him. He fears death and is nerveless in spite of his burly figure. We in India may in a moment realize that one hundred thousand Englishmen need not frighten three hundred million human beings. A definite forgiveness would therefore mean a definite recognition of our strength. With enlightened forgiveness must come a mighty wave of strength in us, which would make it impossible for a Dyer and a Frank Johnson to heap affront upon India's devoted head. It matters little to me that for the moment I do not drive my point home. We feel too down-trodden not to be angry and revengeful. But I must not refrain from saying that India can gain more by waiving the right of punishment. We have better work to do, a better mission to deliver to the world.

I am not a visionary. I claim to be a practical idealist. The religion of non-violence is not meant merely for the *rishis* and saints. It is meant for the common people as well. Non-violence is the law of our species as violence is the law of the brute. The spirit lies dormant in the brute and he knows no law but that of physical might. The dignity of man requires obedience to a higher law—to the strength of the spirit.

I have therefore ventured to place before India the ancient law of self-sacrifice. For satyagraha and its off-shoots, non-co-operation and civil resistance, are nothing but new names for the law of suffering. The *rishis*, who discovered the law of non-violence in the midst of violence, were greater geniuses than Newton. They were themselves greater warriors than Wellington. Having themselves known the use of arms, they realized their uselessness and taught a weary world that its salvation lay not through violence but through non-violence.

Non-violence in its dynamic condition means conscious suffering. It does not mean meek submission to the will of the evil-doer, but it means the putting of one's whole soul against the will of the tyrant. Working under this law of our being, it is possible for a single individual to defy the whole might of an unjust empire to save his honour, his religion, his soul and lay the foundation for that empire's fall or its regeneration.

And so I am not pleading for India to practise non-violence because it is weak. I want her to practise non-violence being conscious of her strength and power. No training in arms is required for realization of her strength. We seem to need it because we seem to think that we are but a lump of flesh. I want India to recognize that she has a soul that cannot perish and that can rise triumphant above every physical weakness and defy the physical combination of a whole world. What is the meaning of Rama, a mere human being, with his host of monkeys, pitting himself against the insolent strength of ten-headed Ravana surrounded in supposed safety by the raging waters on all sides of Lanka? Does it not mean the conquest of physical might by spiritual strength? However, being a practical man, I do not wait till India recognizes the practicability of the spiritual life in the political world. India considers herself to be powerless and paralyzed before the machine-guns, the tanks and the aeroplanes of the English. And she takes up non-co-operation out of her weakness. It must still serve the same purpose, namely, bring her delivery from the crushing weight of British injustice if a sufficient number of people practise it.

I isolate this non-co-operation from Sinn Feinism,[2] for, it is so conceived as to be incapable of being offered side by side with violence. But I invite even the school of violence to give this peaceful non-co-operation a trial. It will not fail through its inherent weakness. It may fail because of poverty of response. Then will be the time for real danger. The high-souled men, who are unable to suffer national humiliation any longer, will want to vent their wrath. They will take to violence. So far as I know, they must perish without delivering themselves or their country from the wrong. If India takes up the doctrine of the sword; she may gain momentary victory. Then India will cease to be the pride of my heart. I am wedded to India because I owe my all to her. I believe absolutely that she has a mission for the world. She is not to copy Europe blindly; India's acceptance of the doctrine of the sword will be the hour of my trial. I hope I shall not be found wanting. My religion has no geographical limits. If I have a living faith in it, it will transcend my love for India herself. My life is dedicated to service of India through the religion of non-violence which I believe to be the root of Hinduism. . . .

Excerpt from a Letter to Narandas Gandhi

(28–31 July 1930)

The commencement of this discourse is both comic and painful. We two had a discussion on how to economize in the use of cloth-lined envelopes and save the same envelopes for use again and again. The question was whether to paste a blank sheet on the whole side of the envelope or paste only slips over portions where something was written. This was a futile discussion. We wasted on it fifteen minutes of beautiful time after prayers, demonstrating our foolishness thereby. In doing this we violated truth and ahimsa and displayed lack of discrimination. Truth was violated, because the discussion was not inspired by an ardent desire for its search. Ahimsa was shamed, because I, who ought to give every moment of my time to discover the sufferings of the people and in thinking about the ways of ending them, wasted fifteen priceless minutes in a futile discussion. We displayed lack of discrimination, because if we had thought about the utility of the discussion, it would not have lasted even a minute. After we had stolen fifteen minutes from people's time, we realized our foolishness and thanked God for opening our eyes.

I have purposely given this introduction.

The path of Truth is as narrow as it is straight. Even so is that of ahimsa. It is like balancing oneself on the edge of a sword. By concentration an acrobat can walk on a rope. But the concentration required to tread the path of Truth and ahimsa is far greater. The slightest inattention brings one tumbling to the ground. One can realize Truth and ahimsa only by ceaseless striving.

But it is impossible for us to realize perfect truth so long as we are imprisoned in this mortal frame. We can only visualize it in our imagination. We cannot, through the instrumentality of this ephemeral body, see face to face truth which is eternal. That is why in the last resort we must depend on faith.

It appears that the impossibility of full realization of truth in this mortal body led some ancient seeker after truth to the appreciation of ahimsa. The question which confronted him was: 'Shall I bear with those who create difficulties for me, or shall I destroy them?' The seeker realized that he who went on destroying others did not make headway but simply stayed where he was, while the man who suffered those who created difficulties marched ahead and at times even took the others with him. The first act of destruction taught him that the truth which was the object of his quest was not outside himself but within. Hence the more he took to violence; the more he receded from truth. For in fighting the imagined enemy without, he neglected the enemy within.

We punish thieves because we think they harass us. They may leave us alone; but they will only transfer their attentions to another victim. This other victim, however, is also a human being, ourselves in a different form, and so we are caught in a vicious circle. The trouble from thieves continues to increase, as they think it is their business to steal. In the end we see that it is better to tolerate the thieves than to punish them. The forbearance may even bring them to their senses. By tolerating them we realize that thieves are not different from ourselves, they are our brethren, our friends, and may not be punished. But whilst we may bear with the thieves, we may not endure the infliction. That would only induce cowardice. So we realize a further duty. Since we regard the thieves as our kith and kin, they must be made to realize the kinship. And so we must take pains to devise ways and means of winning them over. This is the path of ahimsa. It may entail continuous suffering and the cultivation of endless patience. Given these two conditions, the thief is bound in the end to turn away from his evil ways and we shall get a clearer vision of truth. Thus step by step we learn how to make friends with all the world; we realize their greatness of God, of Truth. Our peace of mind increases in spite of suffering; we become braver and more enterprising; we understand more clearly the difference between what is everlasting and what is not; we learn how to distinguish between what is our duty and what is not. Our worldly attachments diminish and likewise the evil within us diminishes from day to day.

Ahimsa is not the crude thing it has been made to appear. Not to hurt any living thing is no doubt a part of ahimsa. But it is its least expression. The principle of ahimsa is hurt by every evil thought, by undue haste, by lying, by hatred, by wishing ill of anybody. It is also violated by our holding on to what the world needs. But the world needs even what we eat day by day. In the place where we stand there are millions of micro-organisms to whom the place belongs and who are hurt by our presence there. What should we do then? Should we commit suicide? Even that is no solution, if we believe, as we do, that so long as the spirit is attached to the flesh, on every destruction of the body it weaves for itself another. The body will cease to be only when we give up all attachment to it. This freedom from all attachment is the realization of God as Truth. Such realization cannot be attained in a hurry. Realizing that this body does not belong to us, that it is a trust handed over to our charge, we should make the right use of it and progress towards our goal.

I wished to write something which would be easy for all to understand, but I find that I have written a difficult discourse. However, no one who has thought even a little about ahimsa should find any difficulty in understanding what I have written.

It is perhaps clear from the foregoing that without ahimsa it is not possible to seek and find Truth. Ahimsa and Truth are so intertwined that it is practically impossible to disentangle and separate them. They are like the two sides of a coin, or rather of a smooth unstamped metallic disc. Who can say which is the obverse and which is the reverse? Nevertheless, ahimsa is the means and Truth is the end. Means to be means must always be within our reach, and so ahimsa becomes our supreme duty and Truth becomes God for us. If we take care of the means, we are bound to reach the end sooner or later. If we resolve to do this, we shall have won the battle. Whatever difficulties we encounter, whatever apparent reverses we sustain, we should not lose faith but should ever repeat one mantra: "Truth exists, it alone exists. It is the only God and there is but one way of realizing it; there is but one means and that is ahimsa. I will never give it up. May the God that is Truth, in whose name I have taken this pledge, give me the strength to keep it."

Indian Problems

Hinduism

I call myself a Sanatani Hindu because—

- I believe in the Vedas, the Upanishads, the Puranas, and all that goes by the name of Hindu Scriptures and therefore in Avataras (divine incarnations) and rebirth.
- I believe in Varnashrama Dharma in a sense strictly Vedic, but not in its present popular and crude sense.
- I believe in "Cow Protection" in a much larger sense than the popular belief.
- I do not disbelieve in "idol-worship."
- I believe implicitly in the Hindu aphorism that no one truly knows the Scriptures who has not renounced all acquisition or possession of wealth.
- I believe, along with every Hindu, in God and His Oneness, in rebirth and salvation.

That which distinguishes Hinduism from every other religion is its "Cow Protection," even more than its Varnashrama. Varnashrama is in my opinion inherent in human nature, and Hinduism has simply reduced it to a science. It attaches to birth. A man cannot change "Varna" by choice. Not to abide by Varna is to disregard the law of heredity.

I do *not* believe the Bible, the Koran, and the Zend Avesta to be as much divinely inspired as the Vedas. My belief in the Hindu Scriptures does not require me to accept every word and every sense as divinely inspired. Nor do I claim to have any first-hand knowledge of these wonderful books. But I do claim to know and feel the truths of the essential teaching of the Scriptures. I decline to be bound by any interpretation, however learned it may be, if it is repugnant to reason or moral sense.

I do *not* believe that interdining, or even intermarriage, necessarily deprives a man of the Caste status that his birth has given him. The four divisions, Brahmin, Kshattriya, Vaishya, Shudra, define a man's calling; they do not restrict or regulate social intercourse. The divisions define duties; they confer no privileges. It is, I hold, against the genius of Hinduism to arrogate to oneself a higher status, or assign to another a lower status. All are born to serve God's creation—a Brahmin with his knowledge, a Kshatriya with his power of protection, a Vaishya with his commercial ability, and a Shudra with his bodily labor.

This, however, does not mean that a Brahmin is absolved from bodily labor, or the duty of protecting himself and others. His birth makes a Brahmin predominantly a man of knowledge, the fittest by heredity and training to impart it to others. There is nothing, again, to prevent the Shudra from acquiring all the knowledge he wishes. Only he will best serve with his body, and need not envy others their special qualities for service. But a Brahmin who claims superiority by right of knowledge falls, and has no knowledge. And so with the others, who pride themselves upon their special qualities. Varnashrama implies self-restraint, conservation, and economy of energy.

Though, therefore, Varnashrama is not affected by interdining or intermarriage, Hinduism does most emphatically discourage these things.

Hinduism has reached the highest limit of self-restraint. It is undoubtedly a religion of renunciation of the flesh, so that the spirit may be set free. By restricting a Hindu's choice of a bride for his son to a particular group he exercises rare self-restraint.

Hinduism does not regard the married state as by any means essential for salvation. Marriage is a "fall" even as "birth" is a fall. Salvation is freedom from birth and hence from death also.

Prohibition against intermarriage and interdining is essential for a rapid evolution of the soul. But this self-denial is no test of Varna (Caste). A Brahmin may remain a Brahmin, though he may dine with his Shudra brother, provided he has not left off his duty of service by knowledge. It follows from what I have said above that restraint in matters of marriage and dining is not based upon notions of superiority. A Hindu who refuses to dine with another from a sense of superiority altogether misrepresents his Hindu religion.

Unfortunately, today Hinduism seems to consist merely in "eating" and "not eating." Hinduism is in danger of losing its substance; it is resolving itself into a matter of elaborate rules as to what and with whom to eat. Abstemiousness from meat is undoubtedly a great aid to the evolution of the spirit; but it is by no means an end in itself. Many a man eating meat and dining with everybody, but living in the fear of God, is nearer to his salvation than a man religiously abstaining from meat and many other things, but blaspheming God in every one of his acts.

The central fact of Hinduism, however, is "Cow Protection." "Cow Protection" to me is one of the most wonderful phenomena in all human evolution, for it takes the human being beyond his species. The cow to me means the entire sub-human world. Man through the cow in enjoined to realize his identity with all that lives. Why the cow was selected for apotheosis is obvious to me. The cow was in India the best companion. She was the giver of plenty. Not only did she give milk, but she also made agriculture possible. The cow is a poem of pity. One reads pity in the gentle animal. She is the "mother" to millions of Indian mankind. Protection of the cow means protection of the whole dumb creation of God. The ancient seer, whoever he was, began in India with the cow. The appeal of the lower order of creation is all the more forcible because it is speechless. "Cow Protection" is the gift of Hinduism to the world; and Hinduism will live so long as there are Hindus to protect the cow.

Hindus are enjoined to protect the cow by self-purification, by self-sacrifice. The present day "Cow Protection" has degenerated into a perpetual feud with the Mussalmans, whereas true cow protection means conquering the Mussalmans by our love.

A Mussalman friend sent me some time ago a book detailing the inhumanities practiced by us on the cow and her progeny, how we bleed her to take the last drop of milk from her; how we starve her to emaciation; how we ill-treat the calves; how we deprive them of their portion of milk; how cruelly we treat the oxen; how we castrate them; how cruelly we beat them; how we overload them. If they had speech they would bear witness to our crimes against them which would stagger the world. By every act of cruelty to our cattle we disown God and Hinduism; I do not know that the condition of the cattle in any other part of the world is so bad as in unhappy India. We may not blame the Englishman for this; we may not plead poverty in our defense. Criminal negligence is the only source of the miserable condition of our cattle. Our cow-shelters, though they are an answer to our instinct of mercy, are a clumsy demonstration of its execution. Instead of being model dairy farms and great profitable national institutions they are merely depots for receiving decrepit cattle.

Hindus will be judged, not by their correct chanting of sacred texts, not by their pilgrimages, not by their most punctilious observance of Caste rules, but by their ability to protect the cow. Whilst professing the religion of "Cow Protection" we have enslaved the cow and her progeny and have become slaves ourselves.

I can no more describe my feeling for Hinduism than for my own wife. She moves me as no other woman in the world can. Not that she has no faults; I dare say she has many more than I see myself. But the feeling of an indissoluble bond is there. Even so I feel for and about Hinduism with all its faults and limitations. Nothing elates me so much as the music of the Gita or Tulsidas's Ramayana, the only two books in Hinduism I may be said really to know. When on one occasion I fancied I was taking my last breath the Gita was my solace.

I know the vice that is going on today in all the great Hindu shrines, but I love them in spite of their unspeakable failings. There is an interest which I take in them and in no other. I am a reformer through and through. But my zeal never leads me to the rejection of any of the essential things of Hinduism.

I have said I do not disbelieve in idol-worship. An idol does not excite any feeling of veneration in me. But I think that idol-worship is part of human nature. We hanker after symbolism. Why should one be more composed in a church than elsewhere? Images are an aid to worship. No Hindu considers an image to be God. I do not consider idol-worship sin.

It is clear from the foregoing that Hinduism is not an exclusive religion. In it there is room for the worship of all the prophets of the world. It is not a missionary religion in the ordinary sense of the term. It has no doubt absorbed many tribes in its fold, but this absorption has been of an evolutionary, imperceptible character. Hinduism tells everyone to worship God according to his own faith, and so it lives at peace with all the religions. . . .

"Untouchability" is repugnant to reason and to the instinct of pity or love. A religion that establishes the worship of the cow cannot possibly countenance or warrant a cruel and unhuman boycott of human beings; and I should be content to be torn to pieces rather than disown the suppressed classes. Hindus will certainly never deserve freedom, nor get it, if they allow their noble religion to be disgraced by the retention of the taint of untouchability; and, as I love Hinduism dearer than life itself, the taint has become for me an intolerable burden. Let us not deny God by denying to a fifth of our race the right of association on equal footing.

Notes

1 Reginald Edward Harry Dyer, the British general remembered for his brutal handling of the riots at Amritsar, India, in 1919, where Dyer's troops killed 379 unarmed protesters.

2 Pronounced "shin fain": a political organization in Ireland in 1905 that advocated independence from Britain. Today Sinn Fein exists as the political wing of the Irish Republican Army.

32

Why the Rich Are Getting Richer and the Poor, Poorer

Robert B. Reich

(b. 1946)

Robert Reich has moved in many circles. A graduate of Yale Law School and former faculty member at the John F. Kennedy School of Government at Harvard, Reich also studied at Oxford University as a Rhodes Scholar where he became friends with Bill Clinton and other influential policymakers. Reich later served as Secretary of Labor during Clinton's first term as president. The 1990s saw a continuation of the rapid economic expansion of the '80s but with more transformative technologies, particularly the Internet and wireless communication. The essay below first appeared in 1991 in Reich's book The Work of Nations. *Its thesis—that the emerging multinational economic market will cause uncalculated disruptions in individual lives—has proven truer than anyone imagined just a decade ago.* The Work of Nations *echoes Adam Smith's economic treatise* The Wealth of Nations *(1776). But it also borrows from Karl Marx's use of class analysis. Reich's distinctions among different types of work have been an influential part of an emerging literature on "globalization," and his book has been translated into seventeen languages. Reich now serves on the faculty of Brandeis University as a specialist in policy studies.*

The division of labour is limited by the extent of the market.

—Adam Smith,
An Inquiry into the Nature and Causes of
the Wealth of Nations (1776)

Regardless of how your job is officially classified (manufacturing, service, managerial, technical, secretarial, and so on), or the industry in which you work (automotive, steel, computer, advertising, finance, food processing), your real competitive position in the world economy is coming to depend on the function you perform in it. Herein lies the basic reason why incomes are diverging. The fortunes of routine producers are declining. In-person servers are also becoming poorer, although their fates are less clear-cut. But symbolic analysts—who solve, identify, and broker new problems—are, by and large, succeeding in the world economy.

All Americans used to be in roughly the same economic boat. Most rose or fell together as the corporations in which they were employed, the industries comprising such corporations, and the national economy as a whole became more productive—or languished. But national borders no longer define our economic fates. We are now in different boats, one sinking rapidly, one sinking more slowly, and the third rising steadily.

The boat containing routine producers is sinking rapidly. Recall that by midcentury routine production workers in the United States were paid relatively well. The giant pyramidlike organizations at the core of each major industry coordinated their prices and investments—avoiding the harsh winds of competition and thus maintaining healthy earnings. Some of these earnings, in turn, were reinvested in new plant and equipment (yielding ever-larger-scale economies); another portion went to top managers and investors. But a large and increasing portion went to middle managers and production workers. Work stoppages posed such a threat to high-volume production that organized labor was able to exact an ever-larger premium for its cooperation. And the pattern of wages established within the core corporations influenced the pattern throughout the national economy. Thus the growth of a relatively affluent middle class, able to purchase all the wondrous things produced in high volume by the core corporations.

But, as has been observed, the core is rapidly breaking down into global webs which earn their largest profits from clever problem-solving, -identifying, and brokering. As the costs of transporting standard things and of communicating information about them continue to drop, profit margins on high-volume, standardized production are thinning, because there are few barriers to entry. Modern factories and state-of-the-art machinery can be installed almost anywhere on the globe. Routine producers in the United States, then, are in direct competition with millions of routine producers in other nations. Twelve thousand people are added to the world's population every hour, most of whom, eventually, will happily work for a small fraction of the wages of routine producers in America.[1]

The consequence is clearest in older, heavy industries, where high-volume, standardized production continues its ineluctable move to where labor is cheapest and most accessible around the world. Thus, for example, the Maquiladora factories cluttered along the Mexican side of the U.S. border in the sprawling shanty towns of Tijuana, Mexicali, Nogales, Agua Prieta, and Ciudad Juárez—factories owned mostly by Americans, but increasingly by Japanese—in which more than a half million routine producers assemble parts into finished goods to be shipped into the United States.

The same story is unfolding worldwide. Until the late 1970s, AT&T had depended on routine producers in Shreveport, Louisiana, to assemble standard telephones. It then discovered that routine producers in Singapore would perform the same tasks at a far lower cost. Facing intense competition from other global webs, AT&T's strategic brokers felt compelled to switch. So in the early 1980s they stopped hiring routine producers in Shreveport and began hiring cheaper routine producers in Singapore. But under this kind of pressure for ever lower high-volume production costs, today's Singaporean can easily end up as yesterday's Louisianan. By the late 1980s, AT&T's strategic brokers found that routine producers in Thailand were eager to assemble telephones for a small fraction of the wages of routine producers in Singapore. Thus, in 1989, AT&T stopped hiring Singaporeans to make telephones and began hiring even cheaper routine producers in Thailand.

The search for ever lower wages has not been confined to heavy industry. Routine data processing is equally footloose. Keypunch operators located anywhere around the world can enter data into computers, linked by satellite or transoceanic fiber-optic cable, and take it out again. As the rates charged by satellite networks continue to drop, and as more satellites and fiber-optic cables become available (reducing communication costs still further), routine data processors in the United States find themselves in ever more direct competition with their counterparts abroad, who are often eager to work for far less.

By 1990, keypunch operators in the United States were earning, at most, $6.50 per hour. But keypunch operators throughout the rest of the world were willing to work for a fraction of this. Thus, many potential American data-processing jobs were disappearing, and the wages and benefits of the remaining ones were in decline. Typical was Saztec International, a $20-million-a-year data-processing firm headquartered in Kansas City, whose American strategic brokers contracted with routine data processors in Manila and with American-owned firms that needed such data-processing services. Compared with the average Philippine income of

$1,700 per year, data-entry operators working for Saztec earn the prince-
ly sum of $2,650. The remainder of Saztec's employees were American
problem-solvers and -identifiers, searching for ways to improve the
worldwide system and find new uses to which it could be put.[2]

By 1990, American Airlines was employing over 1,000 data processors in
Barbados and the Dominican Republic to enter names and flight numbers
from used airline tickets (flown daily to Barbados from airports around
the United States) into a giant computer bank located in Dallas. Chicago
publisher R. R. Donnelley was sending entire manuscripts to Barbados
for entry into computers in preparation for printing. The New York Life
Insurance Company was dispatching insurance claims to Castleisland,
Ireland, where routine producers, guided by simple directions, entered
the claims and determined the amounts due, then instantly transmitted
the computations back to the United States. (When the firm advertised in
Ireland for twenty-five data-processing jobs, it received six hundred
applications.) And McGraw-Hill was processing subscription renewal
and marketing information for its magazines in nearby Galway. Indeed,
literally millions of routine workers around the world were receiving
information, converting it into computer-readable form, and then sending it back—at the speed of electronic impulses—whence it came.

The simple coding of computer software has also entered into world
commerce. India, with a large English-speaking population of technicians
happy to do routine programming cheaply, is proving to be particularly
attractive to global webs in need of this service. By 1990, Texas Instruments maintained a software development facility in Bangalore, linking
fifty Indian programmers by satellite to TI's Dallas headquarters. Spurred
by this and similar ventures, the Indian government was building a tele-
port in Poona, intended to make it easier and less expensive for many other
firms to send their routine software design specifications for coding.[3]

This shift of routine production jobs from advanced to developing
nations is a great boon to many workers in such nations who otherwise
would be jobless or working for much lower wages. These workers, in
turn, now have more money with which to purchase symbolic-analytic
services from advanced nations (often embedded within all sorts of complex products). The trend is also beneficial to everyone around the world
who can now obtain high-volume, standardized products (including
information and software) more cheaply than before.

But these benefits do not come without certain costs. In particular the burden is borne by those who no longer have good-paying routine production jobs within advanced economies like the United States. Many of these people used to belong to unions or at least benefited from prevailing wage rates established in collective bargaining agreements. But as the old corporate bureaucracies have flattened into global webs, bargaining leverage has been lost. Indeed, the tacit national bargain is no more.

Despite the growth in the number of new jobs in the United States, union membership has withered. In 1960, 35 percent of all nonagricultural workers in America belonged to a union. But by 1980 that portion had fallen to just under a quarter, and by 1989 to about 17 percent. Excluding government employees, union membership was down to 13.4 percent.[4] This was a smaller proportion even than in the early 1930s, before the National Labor Relations Act created a legally protected right to labor representation. The drop in membership has been accompanied by a growing number of collective bargaining agreements to freeze wages at current levels, reduce wage levels of entering workers, or reduce wages overall. This is an important reason why the long economic recovery that began in 1982 produced a smaller rise in unit labor costs than any of the eight recoveries since World War II—the low rate of unemployment during its course notwithstanding.

Routine production jobs have vanished fastest in traditional unionized industries (autos, steel, and rubber, for example), where average wages have kept up with inflation. This is because the jobs of older workers in such industries are protected by seniority, the youngest workers are the first to be laid off. Faced with a choice of cutting wages or cutting the number of jobs, a majority of union members (secure in the knowledge that there are many who are junior to them who will be laid off first) often have voted for the latter.

Thus the decline in union membership has been most striking among young men entering the work force without a college education. In the early 1950s, more than 40 percent of this group joined unions; by the late 1980s, less than 20 percent (if public employees are excluded, less than 10 percent).[5] In steelmaking, for example, although many older workers remained employed, almost half of all routine steelmaking jobs in America vanished between 1974 and 1988 (from 480,000 to 260,000). Similarly with automobiles: During the 1980s, the United Auto Workers lost 500,000 members—one-third of their total at the start of the decade. General Motors alone cut 150,000 American production jobs during the 1980s (even as it added employment abroad). Another consequence of the same phenomenon: the gap between the average wages of unionized and nonunionized workers widened dramatically—from 14.6 percent in 1973 to 20.4 percent by end of the 1980s.[6] The lesson is clear. If you drop out of high school or have no more than a high school diploma, do not expect a good routine production job to be awaiting you.

Also vanishing are lower- and middle-level management jobs involving routine production. Between 1981 and 1986, more than 780,000 foremen, supervisors, and section chiefs lost their jobs through plant closings and layoffs.[7] Large numbers of assistant division heads, assistant directors, assistant managers, and vice presidents also found themselves jobless. GM shed more than 40,000 white-collar employees and planned to eliminate another 25,000 by the mid-1990s.[8] As America's core pyramids metamorphosed into global webs, many middle-level routine producers were as obsolete as routine workers on the line.

As has been noted, foreign-owned webs are hiring some Americans to do routine production in the United States. Philips, Sony, and Toyota factories are popping up all over—to the self-congratulatory applause of the nation's governors and mayors, who have lured them with promises of tax abatements and new sewers, among other amenities. But as these ebullient politicians will soon discover, the foreign-owned factories are highly automated and will become far more so in years to come. Routine production jobs account for a small fraction of the cost of producing most items in the United States and other advanced nations, and this fraction will continue to decline sharply as computer-integrated robots take over. In 1977 it took routine producers thirty-five hours to assemble an automobile in the United States; it is estimated that by the mid-1990s, Japanese-owned factories in America will be producing finished automobiles using only eight hours of a routine producer's time.[9]

The productivity and resulting wages of American workers who run such robotic machinery may be relatively high, but there may not be many such jobs to go around. A case in point: in the late 1980s, Nippon Steel joined with America's ailing Inland Steel to build a new $400 million cold-rolling mill fifty miles west of Gary, Indiana. The mill was celebrated for its state-of-the-art technology, which cut the time to produce a coil of steel from twelve days to about one hour. In fact, the entire plant could be run by a small team of technicians, which became clear when Inland subsequently closed two of its old cold-rolling mills, laying off hundreds of routine workers. Governors and mayors take note: your much-bally-hooed foreign factories may end up employing distressingly few of your constituents.

Overall, the decline in routine jobs has hurt men more than women. This is because the routine production jobs held by men in high-volume metal-bending manufacturing industries had paid higher wages than the routine production jobs held by women in textiles and data processing. As both sets of jobs have been lost, American women in routine produc-tion have gained more equal footing with American men—equally poor footing, that is. This is a major reason why the gender gap between male and female wages began to close during the 1980s.

The second of the three boats, carrying in-person servers, is sinking as well, but somewhat more slowly and unevenly. Most in-person servers are paid at or just slightly above the minimum wage and many work only part-time, with the result that their take-home pay is modest, to say the least. Nor do they typically receive all the benefits (health care, life insur-ance, disability, and so forth) garnered by routine producers in large man-ufacturing corporations or by symbolic analysts affiliated with the more affluent threads of global webs.[10] In-person servers are sheltered from the direct effects of global competition and, like everyone else, benefit from access to lower-cost products from around the world. But they are not immune to its indirect effects.

For one thing, in-person servers increasingly compete with former rou-tine production workers, who, no longer able to find well-paying routine production jobs, have few alternatives but to seek in-person service jobs. The Bureau of Labor Statistice estimates that of the 2.8 million manufac-turing workers who lost their jobs during the early 1980s, fully one-third were rehired in service jobs paying at least 20 percent less.[11] In-person servers must also compete with high school graduates and dropouts who years before had moved easily into routine production jobs but no longer can. And if demographic predictions about the American work force in the first decades of the twenty-first century are correct (and they are like-ly to be, since most of the people who will comprise the work force are already identifiable), most new entrants into the job market will be black or Hispanic men, or women—groups that in years past have possessed relatively weak technical skills. This will result in an even larger number of people crowding into in-person services. Finally, in-person servers will be competing with growing numbers of immigrants, both legal and illegal, for whom in-person services will comprise the most accessible jobs. (It is estimated that between the mid-1980s and the end of the century, about a quarter of all workers entering the American labor force will be immigrants.[12])

Perhaps the fiercest competition that in-person servers face comes from labor-saving machinery (much of it invented, designed, fabricated, or assembled in other nations, of course). Automated tellers, computerized cashiers, automatic car washes, robotized vending machines, self-service gasoline pumps, and all similar gadgets substitute for the human beings that customers once encountered. Even telephone operators are fast disappearing, as electronic sensors and voice simulators become capable of carrying on conversations that are reasonably intelligent and always polite. Retail sales workers—among the largest groups of in-person servers—are similarly imperiled. Through personal computers linked to television screens, tomorrow's consumers will be able to buy furniture, appliances, and all sorts of electronic toys from their living rooms—examining the merchandise from all angles, selecting whatever color, size, special features, and price seem most appealing, and then transmitting the order instantly to warehouses from which the selections will be shipped directly to their homes. So, too, with financial transactions, airline and hotel reservations, rental car agreements, and similar contracts, which will be executed between consumers in their homes and computer banks somewhere else on the globe.[13]

Advanced economies like the United States will continue to generate sizable numbers of new in-person service jobs, of course, the automation of older ones notwithstanding. For every bank teller who loses her job to an automated teller, three new jobs open for aerobics instructors. Human beings, it seems, have an almost insatiable desire for personal attention. But the intense competition nevertheless ensures that the wages of in-person servers will remain relatively low. In-person servers—working on their own, or else dispersed widely amid many small establishments, filling all sorts of personal-care niches—cannot readily organize themselves into labor unions or create powerful lobbies to limit the impact of such competition.

In two respects, demographics will work in favor of in-person servers, buoying their collective boat slightly. First, as has been noted, the rate of growth of the American work force is slowing. In particular, the number of young workers is shrinking. Between 1985 and 1995, the number of the eighteen- to twenty-four-year-olds will have declined by 17.5 percent. Thus, employers will have more incentive to hire and train in-person servers whom they might previously have avoided. But this demographic relief from the competitive pressures will be only temporary. The cumulative procreative energies of the postwar baby-boomers (born between 1946 and 1964) will result in a new surge of workers by 2010 or thereabouts.[14] And immigration—both legal and illegal—shows every sign of increasing in years to come.

Next, by the second decade of the twenty-first century, the number of Americans aged sixty-five and over will be rising precipitously, as the baby-boomers reach retirement age and live longer. Their life expectancies will lengthen not just because fewer of them will have smoked their way to their graves and more will have eaten better than their parents, but also because they will receive all sorts of expensive drugs and therapies designed to keep them alive—barely. By 2035, twice as many Americans will be elderly as in 1988, and the number of octogenarians is expected to triple. As these decaying baby-boomers ingest all the chemicals and receive all the treatments, they will need a great deal of personal attention. Millions of deteriorating bodies will require nurses, nursing-home operators, hospital administrators, orderlies, home-care providers, hospice aides, and technicians to operate and maintain all the expensive machinery that will monitor and temporarily stave off final disintegration. There might even be a booming market for euthanasia specialists. In-person servers catering to the old and ailing will be in strong demand.[15]

One small problem: the decaying baby-boomers will not have enough money to pay for these services. They will have used up their personal savings years before. Their Social Security payments will, of course, have been used by the government to pay for the previous generation's retirement and to finance much of the budget deficits of the 1980s. Moreover, with relatively fewer young Americans in the population, the supply of housing will likely exceed the demand, with the result that the boomers' major investments—their homes—will be worth less (in inflation-adjusted dollars) when they retire than they planned for. In consequence, the huge cost of caring for the graying boomers will fall on many of the same people who will be paid to care for them. It will be like a great sump pump: in-person servers of the twenty-first century will have an abundance of health-care jobs, but a large portion of their earnings will be devoted to Social Security payments and income taxes, which will in turn be used to pay their salaries. The net result: no real improvement in their standard of living.

The standard of living of in-person servers also depends, indirectly, on the standard of living of the Americans they serve who are engaged in world commerce. To the extent that *these* Americans are richly rewarded by the rest of the world for what they contribute, they will have more money to lavish upon in-person services. Here we find the only form of "trickle-down" economics that has a basis in reality. A waitress in a town whose major factory has just been closed is unlikely to earn a high wage or enjoy much job security; in a swank resort populated by film producers and banking moguls, she is apt to do reasonably well. So, too, with nations. In-person servers in Bangladesh may spend their days performing roughly the same tasks as in-person servers in the United States, but have a far lower standard of living for their efforts. The difference comes in the value that their customers add to the world economy.

Unlike the boats of routine producers and in-person servers, however, the vessel containing America's symbolic analysts is rising. Worldwide demand for their insights is growing as the ease and speed of communicating them steadily increases. Not every symbolic analyst is rising as quickly or as dramatically as every other, of course; symbolic analysts at the low end are barely holding their own in the world economy. But symbolic analysts at the top are in such great demand worldwide that they have difficulty keeping track of all their earnings. Never before in history has opulence on such a scale been gained by people who have earned it, and done so legally.

Among symbolic analysts in the middle range are American scientists and researchers who are busily selling their discoveries to global enterprise webs. They are not limited to American customers. If the strategic brokers in General Motors' headquarters refuse to pay a high price for a new means of making high-strength ceramic engines dreamed up by a team of engineers affiliated with Carnegie Mellon University in Pittsburgh, the strategic brokers of Honda or Mercedes-Benz are likely to be more than willing.

So, too, with the insights of America's ubiquitous management consultants, which are being sold for large sums to eager entrepreneurs in Europe and Latin America. Also, the insights of America's energy consultants, sold for even larger sums to Arab sheikhs. American design engineers are providing insights to Olivetti, Mazda, Siemens, and other global webs; American marketers, techniques for learning what worldwide consumers will buy; American advertisers, ploys for ensuring that they actually do. American architects are issuing designs and blueprints for opera houses, art galleries, museums, luxury hotels, and residential complexes in the world's major cities; American commercial property developers, marketing these properties to worldwide investors and purchasers.

Americans who specialize in the gentle art of public relations are in demand by corporations, governments, and politicians in virtually every nation. So, too, are American political consultants, some of whom, at this writing, are advising the Hungarian Socialist Party, the remnant of Hungary's ruling Communists, on how to salvage a few parliamentary seats in the nation's first free election in more than forty years. Also at this writing, a team of American agricultural consultants is advising the managers of a Soviet farm collective employing 1,700 Russians eighty miles outside Moscow. As noted, American investment bankers and lawyers specializing in financial circumnavigations are selling their insights to Asians and Europeans who are eager to discover how to make large amounts of money by moving large amounts of money.

Developing nations, meanwhile, are hiring American civil engineers to advise on building roads and dams. The present thaw in the Cold War will no doubt expand these opportunities. American engineers from Bechtel (a global firm notable for having employed both Caspar Weinberger and George Shultz for much larger sums than either earned in the Reagan administration) have begun helping the Soviets design and install a new generation of nuclear reactors. Nations also are hiring American bankers and lawyers to help them renegotiate the terms of their loans with global banks, and Washington lobbyists to help them with Congress, the Treasury, the World Bank, the IMF, and other politically sensitive institutions. In fits of obvious desperation, several nations emerging from communism have even hired American economists to teach them about capitalism.

Almost everyone around the world is buying the skills and insights of Americans who manipulate oral and visual symbols—musicians, sound engineers, film producers, makeup artists, directors, cinematographers, actors and actresses, boxers, scriptwriters, songwriters, and set designers. Among the wealthiest of symbolic analysts are Steven Spielberg, Bill Cosby, Charles Schulz, Eddie Murphy, Sylvester Stallone, Madonna, and other star directors and performers—who are almost as well known on the streets of Dresden and Tokyo as in the Back Bay of Boston. Less well rewarded but no less renowned are the unctuous anchors on Turner Broadcasting's Cable News, who appear daily, via satellite, in places ranging from Vietnam to Nigeria. Vanna White is the world's most-watched game-show hostess. Behind each of these familiar faces is a collection of American problem-solvers, -identifiers, and brokers who train, coach, advise, promote, amplify, direct, groom, represent, and otherwise add value to their talents.[16]

There are also the insights of senior American executives who occupy the world headquarters of global "American" corporations and the national or regional headquarters of global "foreign" corporations. Their insights are duly exported to the rest of the world through the webs of global enterprise. IBM does not export many machines from the United States, for example. Big Blue makes machines all over the globe and services them on the spot. Its prime American exports are symbolic and analytic. From IBM's world headquarters in Armonk, New York, emanate strategic brokerage and related management services bound for the rest of the world. In return, IBM's top executives are generously rewarded.

The most important reason for this expanding world market and increasing global demand for the symbolic and analytic insights of Americans has been the dramatic improvement in worldwide communication and transportation technologies. Designs, instructions, advice, and visual and audio symbols can be communicated more and more rapidly around the globe, with ever-greater precision and at ever-lower cost. Madonna's voice can be transported to billions of listeners, with perfect clarity, on digital compact discs. A new invention emanating from engineers in Battelle's laboratory in Columbus, Ohio, can be sent almost anywhere via modem, in a form that will allow others to examine it in three dimensions through enhanced computer graphics. When face-to-face meetings are still required—and videoconferencing will not suffice—it is relatively easy for designers, consultants, advisers, artists, and executives to board supersonic jets and, in a matter of hours, meet directly with their worldwide clients, customers, audiences, and employees.

With rising demand comes rising compensation. Whether in the form of licensing fees, fees for service, salaries, or shares in final profits, the economic result is much the same. There are also nonpecuniary rewards. One of the best-kept secrets among symbolic analysts is that so many of them enjoy their work. In fact, much of it does not count as work at all, in the traditional sense. The work of routine producers and in-person servers is typically monotonous; it causes muscles to tire or weaken and involves little independence or discretion. The "work" of symbolic analysts, by contrast, often involves puzzles, experiments, games, a significant amount of chatter, and substantial discretion over what to do next. Few routine producers or in-person servers would "work" if they did not need to earn the money. Many symbolic analysts would "work" even if money were no object.

At midcentury, when America was a national market dominated by core pyramid-shaped corporations, there were constraints on the earnings of people at the highest rungs. First and most obviously, the market for their services was largely limited to the borders of the nation. In addition, whatever conceptual value they might contribute was small relative to the value gleaned from large scale—and it was dependent on large scale for whatever income it was to summon. Most of the problems to be identified and solved had to do with enhancing the efficiency of production and improving the flow of materials, parts, assembly, and distribution. Inventors searched for the rare breakthrough revealing an entirely new product to be made in high volume; management consultants, executives, and engineers thereafter tried to speed and synchronize its manufacture, to better achieve scale efficiencies; advertisers and marketers sought then to whet the public's appetite for the standard item that emerged. Since white-collar earnings increased with larger scale, there was considerable incentive to expand the firm; indeed, many of America's core corporations grew far larger than scale economies would appear to have justified.

By the 1990s, in contrast, the earnings of symbolic analysts were limited neither by the size of the national market nor by the volume of production of the firms with which they were affiliated. The marketplace was worldwide, and conceptual value was high relative to value added from scale efficiencies.

There had been another constraint on high earnings, which also gave way by the 1990s. At midcentury, the compensation awarded to top executives and advisers of the largest of America's core corporations could not be grossly out of proportion to that of low-level production workers. It would be unseemly for executives who engaged in highly visible rounds of bargaining with labor unions, and who routinely responded to government requests to moderate prices, to take home wages and benefits wildly in excess of what other Americans earned. Unless white-collar executives restrained themselves, moreover, blue-collar production workers could not be expected to restrain their own demands for higher wages. Unless both groups exercised restraint, the government could not be expected to forbear from imposing direct controls and regulations.

At the same time, the wages of production workers could not be allowed to sink too low, lest there be insufficient purchasing power in the economy. After all, who would buy all the goods flowing out of American factories if not American workers? This, too, was part of the tacit bargain struck between American managers and their workers.

Recall the oft-repeated corporate platitude of the era about the chief executive's responsibility to carefully weigh and balance the interests of the corporation's disparate stakeholders. Under the stewardship of the corporate statesman, no set of stakeholders—least of all white-collar executives—was to gain a disproportionately large share of the benefits of corporate activity; nor was any stakeholder—especially the average worker—to be left with a share that was disproportionately small. Banal though it was, this idea helped to maintain the legitimacy of the core American corporation in the eyes of most Americans, and to ensure continued economic growth.

But by the 1990s, these informal norms were evaporating, just as (and largely because) the core American corporation was vanishing. The links between top executives and the American production worker were fading: an ever-increasing number of subordinates and contractees were foreign, and a steadily growing number of American routine producers were working for foreign-owned firms. An entire cohort of middle-level managers, who had once been deemed "white collar," had disappeared; and, increasingly, American executives were exporting their insights to global enterprise webs.

As the American corporation itself became a global web almost indistinguishable from another, its stakeholders were turning into a large and diffuse group, spread over the world. Such global stakeholders were less visible, and far less noisy, than national stakeholders. And as the American corporation sold its goods and services all over the world, the purchasing power of American workers became far less relevant to its economic survival.

Thus have the inhibitions been removed. The salaries and benefits of America's top executives, and many of their advisers and consultants, have soared to what years before would have been unimaginable heights, even as those of other Americans have declined.

Notes

[All Notes belong to Reich.]

1 The reader should note, of course, that lower wages in other areas of the world are of no particular attraction to global capital unless workers there are sufficiently productive to make the labor cost of producing *each unit* lower there than in higher-wage regions. Productivity in many low-wage areas of the world has improved due to the ease with which state-of-the-art factories and equipment can be installed there.

2 John Maxwell Hamilton, "A Bit Player Buys into the Computer Age," *New York Times Business World*, December 3, 1989, p. 14.

3 Udayan Gupta, "U.S.–Indian Satellite Link Stands to Cut Software Costs," *Wall Street Journal*, March 6, 1989, p. B2.

4 *Statistical Abstract of the United States* (Washington, DC: U.S. Government Printing Office, 1989), p. 416, table 684.

5 Calculations from Current Population Surveys by L. Katz and A. Revenga, "Changes in the Structure of Wages: U.S. and Japan," National Bureau of Economic Research, September 1989.

6 U.S. Department of Commerce, Bureau of Labor Statistics, "Wages of Unionized and Non-Unionized Workers," various issues.

7 U.S. Department of Labor, Bureau of Labor Statistics, "Reemployment Increases Among Displaced Workers," *BLS News*, USDL 86–414, October 14, 1986, table 6.

8 *Wall Street Journal*, February 16, 1990, p. A5.

9 Figures from the International Motor Vehicles Program, Massachusetts Institute of Technology, 1989.

10 The growing portion of the American labor force engaged in in-person services, relative to routine production, thus helps explain why the number of Americans lacking health insurance increased by at least 6 million during the 1980s.

11 U.S. Department of Labor, Bureau of Labor Statistics, "Reemployment Increases Among Disabled Workers," *BLS News*, October 14, 1986.

[12] Federal Immigration and Naturalization Service, *Statistical Yearbook* (Washington, DC: U.S. Government Printing Office, 1986, 1987).

[13] See Claudia H. Deutsch, "The Powerful Push for Self-Service," *New York Times*, April 9, 1989, section 3, p. 1.

[14] U.S. Bureau of the Census, Current Population Reports, Series P-23, no. 138, tables 2-1, 4-6. See W. Johnson, A. Packer, et al., *Workforce 2000: Work and Workers for the 21st Century* (Indianapolis: Hudson Institute, 1987).

[15] The Census Bureau estimates that by the year 2000, at least 12 million Americans will work in health services—well over 6 percent of the total work force.

[16] In 1989, the entertainment business summoned to the United States $5.5 billion in foreign earnings—making it among the nation's largest export industries, just behind aerospace. U.S. Department of Commerce, International Trade Commission, "Composition of U.S. Exports," various issues.

33

20th-Century Poetry

Ezra Pound

(1885–1972)

*O*ne of the most controversial poets of the modern era, Ezra Pound was born in Idaho and educated at the University of Pennsylvania but soon left for Europe to pursue his poetic calling. In reaction to the excesses of the so-called decadent poetry that espoused art for art's sake, Pound campaigned for "imagism," his term for a new kind of poetry that attempted to present the object directly rather than describe it and then generalize about it. Imagistic poetry tends to work in nonsyntactical fragments that force the reader or listener to connect them for meaning. Although the formal movement of Imagism lasted only briefly, most twentieth-century poetry reveals its influence.

IN A STATION OF THE METRO

The apparition of these faces in the crowd;
Petals on a wet, black bough.

1916

A RETROSPECT

There has been so much scribbling about a new fashion in poetry, that I may perhaps be pardoned this brief recapitulation and retrospect.

In the spring or early summer of 1912, "H. D.," Richard Aldington, and myself decided that we were agreed upon the three principles following:

1. Direct treatment of the "thing" whether subjective or objective.

2. To use absolutely no word that does not contribute to the presentation.

3. As regarding rhythm: to compose in the sequence of the musical phrase, not in sequence of a metronome.

341

Upon many points of taste and of predilection we differed, but agreeing upon these three positions we thought we had as much right to a group name, at least as much right, as a number of French "schools" proclaimed by Mr. Flint in the August number of Harold Monro's magazine for 1911.

This school has since been "joined" or "followed" by numerous people who, whatever their merits, do not show any signs of agreeing with the second specification. Indeed *vers libre* has become as prolix and as verbose as any of the flaccid varieties that preceded it. It has brought faults of its own. The actual language and phrasing is often as bad as that of our elders without even the excuse that the words are shovelled in to fill a metric pattern or to complete the noise of a rhyme-sound. Whether or no the phrases followed by the followers are musical must be left to the reader's decision. At times I can find a marked metre in "*vers libres*," as stale and hackneyed as any pseudo-Swinburnian, at times the writers seem to follow no musical structure whatever. But it is, on the whole, good that the field should be ploughed. Perhaps a few good poems have come from the new method, and if so it is justified.

Criticism is not a circumscription or a set of prohibitions. It provides fixed points of departure. It may startle a dull reader into alertness. That little of it which is good is mostly in stray phrases; or if it be an older artist helping a younger it is in great measure but rules of thumb, cautions gained by experience.

I set together a few phrases on practical working about the time the first remarks on imagism were published. The first use of the word "Imagiste" was in my note to T. E. Hulmes five poems, printed at the end of my "Ripostes" in the autumn of 1912. I reprint my cautions from *Poetry* for March, 1913.

A Few Don'ts

An "Image" is that which presents an intellectual and emotional complex in an instant of time. I use the term "complex" rather in the technical sense employed by the newer psychologists, such as Hart, though we might not agree absolutely in our application.

It is the presentation of such a "complex" instantaneously which gives that sense of sudden liberation; that sense of freedom from time limits and space limits; that sense of sudden growth, which we experience in the presence of the greatest works of art.

It is better to present one Image in a lifetime than to produce voluminous works.

All this, however, some may consider open to debate. The immediate necessity, is to tabulate A LIST OF DON'TS for those beginning to write verses. I can not put all of them into Mosaic negative.

To begin with, consider the three propositions (demanding direct treatment, economy of words, and the sequence of the musical phrase), not as dogma—never consider anything as dogma—but as the result of long contemplation, which, even if it is some one else's contemplation, may be worth consideration.

Pay no attention to the criticism of men who have never themselves written a notable work. Consider the discrepancies between the actual writing of the Greek poets and dramatists, and the theories of the Graeco-Roman grammarians, concocted to explain their metres.

1918

T. S. Eliot

(1888–1965)

Born in St. Louis and educated at Harvard University, T. S. Eliot moved to Europe to continue his studies at the Sorbonne in Paris and then at Oxford. His elitist social and educational views not surprisingly influenced his demanding poetry, which is full of scholarly allusions, myths, and the splintered images encouraged by close friend and editor Ezra Pound. Eliot's publication of the fragmented poem The Waste Land *in 1922 remains a key cultural event of the post-World War I generation, for it reflects the poet's attempt to regain meaning in a shattered world. In the poem below, Prufrock exemplifies the Modernist tradition of boredom and despair, but with moments of meaning that exist only in glimpses from fleeting symbols and images.*

THE LOVE SONG OF J. ALFRED PRUFROCK

S'io credessi che mia risposta fosse
a persona che mai tornasse al mondo,
questa fiamma staria senza più scosse.
Ma per ciò che giammai di questo fondo
non tornò vivo alcun, s'i'odo il vero,
senza tema d'infamia ti rispondo.

Let us go then, you and I,
When the evening is spread out against the sky
Like a patient etherised upon a table;
Let us go, through certain half-deserted streets,
The muttering retreats
Of restless nights in one-night cheap hotels
And sawdust restaurants with oyster-shells:
Streets that follow like a tedious argument
Of insidious intent
To lead you to an overwhelming question . . .
Oh, do not ask, "What is it?"
Let us go and make our visit.

In the room the women come and go
Talking of Michelangelo.

The yellow fog that rubs its back upon the window-panes,
The yellow smoke that rubs its muzzle on the window-panes,
Licked its tongue into the corners of the evening,
Lingered upon the pools that stand in drains,
Let fall upon its back the soot that falls from chimneys,
Slipped by the terrace, made a sudden leap,
And seeing that it was a soft October night,
Curled once about the house, and fell asleep.

And indeed there will be time
For the yellow smoke that slides along the street
Rubbing its back upon the window-panes;
There will be time, there will be time
To prepare a face to meet the faces that you meet;
There will be time to murder and create,
And time for all the works and days of hands
That lift and drop a question on your plate;
Time for you and time for me,
And time yet for a hundred indecisions,
And for a hundred visions and revisions,
Before the taking of a toast and tea.

In the room the women come and go
Talking of Michelangelo.

And indeed there will be time
To wonder, "Do I dare?" and, "Do I dare?"
Time to turn back and descend the stair,
With a bald spot in the middle of my hair—
(They will say: "How his hair is growing thin!")
My morning coat, my collar mounting firmly to the chin,
My necktie rich and modest, but asserted by a simple pin—
(They will say: "But how his arms and legs are thin!")
Do I dare
Disturb the universe?

In a minute there is time
For decisions and revisions which a minute will reverse.

For I have known them all already, known them all—
Have known the evenings, mornings, afternoons,

I have measured out my life with coffee spoons;
I know the voices dying with a dying fall
Beneath the music from a farther room.
        So how should I presume?

And I have known the eyes already, known them all—
The eyes that fix you in a formulated phrase,
And when I am formulated, sprawling on a pin,
When I am pinned and wriggling on the wall,
Then how should I begin
To spit out all the butt-ends of my days and ways?
        And how should I presume?

And I have known the arms already, known them all—
Arms that are braceleted and white and bare
(But in the lamplight, downed with light brown hair!)
Is it perfume from a dress
That makes me so digress?
Arms that lie along a table, or wrap about a shawl.
        And should I then presume?
        And how should I begin?

                        •   •   •

Shall I say, I have gone at dusk through narrow streets
And watched the smoke that rises from the pipes
Of lonely men in shirt-sleeves, leaning out of windows? . . .

I should have been a pair of ragged claws
Scuttling across the floors of silent seas.

                        •   •   •

And the afternoon, the evening, sleeps so peacefully!
Smoothed by long fingers,
Asleep . . . tired . . . or it malingers,
Stretched on the floor, here beside you and me.
Should I, after tea and cakes and ices,
Have the strength to force the moment to its crisis?
But though I have wept and fasted, wept and prayed,
Though I have seen my head (grown slightly bald) brought in upon
        a platter,
I am no prophet—and here's no great matter;

I have seen the moment of my greatness flicker,
And I have seen the eternal Footman hold my coat, and snicker,
And in short, I was afraid.

And would it have been worth it, after all,
After the cups, the marmalade, the tea,
Among the porcelain, among some talk of you and me,
Would it have been worth while,
To have bitten off the matter with a smile,
To have squeezed the universe into a ball
To roll it towards some overwhelming question,
To say: "I am Lazarus, come from the dead,
Come back to tell you all, I shall tell you all"—
If one, settling a pillow by her head,
> Should say: "That is not what I meant at all.
> That is not it, at all."

And would it have been worth it, after all,
Would it have been worth while,
After the sunsets and the dooryards and the sprinkled streets,
After the novels, after the teacups, after the skirts that trail along
> the floor—
And this, and so much more?—
It is impossible to say just what I mean!
But as if a magic lantern threw the nerves in patterns on a screen:
Would it have been worth while
If one, settling a pillow or throwing off a shawl,
And turning toward the window, should say:
> "That is not it at all,
> That is not what I meant, at all."

• • •

No! I am not Prince Hamlet, nor was meant to be;
Am an attendant lord, one that will do
To swell a progress, start a scene or two,
Advise the prince; no doubt, an easy tool,
Deferential, glad to be of use,
Politic, cautious, and meticulous;
Full of high sentence, but a bit obtuse;
At times, indeed, almost ridiculous—

Almost, at times, the Fool.

I grow old . . . I grow old . . .
I shall wear the bottoms of my trousers rolled.

Shall I part my hair behind? Do I dare to eat a peach?
I shall wear white flannel trousers, and walk upon the beach.
I have heard the mermaids singing, each to each.

I do not think that they will sing to me.

I have seen them riding seaward on the waves
Combing the white hair of the waves blown back
When the wind blows the water white and black.

We have lingered in the chambers of the sea
By sea-girls wreathed with seaweed red and brown
Till human voices wake us, and we drown.

                                                      1915

Langston Hughes
(1902–1967)

*L*angston Hughes was one of the most popular and acclaimed writers connected with the Harlem Renaissance, an outpouring of artistic creativity by blacks
associated with the Harlem area of New York City in the 1930s. Hughes was born
in Joplin, Missouri, and studied a year at Columbia University before working as
a merchant seaman, a nightclub staffer in Paris, a busboy in Washington, DC—
all experiences which helped him understand the overwhelming difficulties facing
a young black man in white America. Beginning in the 1920s he steadily published poems that adapted everyday black speech to poetic lines and incorporated
the improvisational meters of jazz and blues music into stanza forms. In the
1930s Hughes was so central to racial politics that in 1953 he was called to testify before Senator Joseph McCarthy's committee on subversive activities connected to his 1930s radicalism. Hughes's long and productive literary career
reflected the shift of many blacks from the countryside to the industrial cities of
the north.

THE NEGRO SPEAKS OF RIVERS

I've known rivers:
I've known rivers ancient as the world and older than the flow of human
    blood in human veins.
My soul has grown deep like the rivers.

I bathed in the Euphrates when dawns were young.
I built my hut near the Congo and it lulled me to sleep.
I looked upon the Nile and raised the pyramids above it.
I heard the singing of the Mississippi when Abe Lincoln went down
    to New Orleans, and I've seen its muddy bosom turn all golden in
    the sunset.

I've known rivers:
Ancient, dusky rivers.

My soul has grown deep like the rivers.

1921

THE SAME

It is the same everywhere for me:
On the docks at Sierra Leone,
In the cotton fields of Alabama,
In the diamond mines of Kimberley,
On the coffee hills of Haiti,
The banana lands of Central America,
The streets of Harlem,
And the cities of Morocco and Tripoli.

Black:
Exploited, beaten, and robbed,
Shot and killed.
Blood running into

    DOLLARS
    POUNDS
    FRANCS
    PESETAS
    LIRE

For the wealth of the exploiters—
Blood that never comes back to me again.
Better that my blood
Runs into the deep channels of Revolution,
Runs into the strong hands of Revolution,
Stains all flags red,
Drives me away from

    SIERRA LEONE
    KIMBERLEY
    ALABAMA
    HAITI
    CENTRAL AMERICA
    HARLEM
    MOROCCO
    TRIPOLI

And all the black lands everywhere.
The force that kills,
The power that robs,

And the greed that does not care.
Better that my blood makes one with the blood
Of all the struggling workers in the world—
Till every land is free of

> DOLLAR ROBBERS
> POUND ROBBERS
> FRANC ROBBERS
> PESETA ROBBERS
> LIRE ROBBERS
> LIFE ROBBERS—

Until the Red Armies of the International Proletariat
Their faces, black, white, olive, yellow, brown,
Unite to raise the blood-red flag that
Never will come down!

1932

NEGRO

I am a Negro:
> Black as the night is black,
> Black like the depths of my Africa.

I've been a slave:
> Caesar told me to keep his door-steps clean.
> I brushed the boots of Washington.

I've been a worker:
> Under my hand the pyramids arose.
> I made mortar for the Woolworth Building.

I've been a singer:
> All the way from Africa to Georgia
> I carried my sorrow songs.
> I made ragtime.

I've been a victim:
> The Belgians cut off my hands in the Congo.
> They lynch me still in Mississippi.

I am a Negro:
    Black as the night is black,
    Black like the depths of my Africa.

1922

I, Too, Sing in America

I, too, sing America.

I am the darker brother.
They send me to eat in the kitchen
When company comes,
But I laugh,
And eat well,
And grow strong.

Tomorrow,
I'll be at the table
When company comes.
Nobody'll dare
Say to me,
"Eat in the kitchen,"
Then.

Besides,
They'll see how beautiful I am
And be ashamed—

I, too, am America.

1925

William Carlos Williams

(1883–1963)

William Carlos Williams once claimed that he had *"delivered more babies than any poet in America,"* for his primary career was as a rural physician in Rutherford, New Jersey. He saw his poetry as distinctive from the other modernists in its simplicity of verse forms and matter-of-factness about everyday life. Like his friend Ezra Pound he wanted to make a new kind of poetry, but with an American voice within an American context. Literary scholars see him as a bridge between the regional focus of Robert Frost and the European context of T. S. Eliot. Williams avoided the assumption shared by other modernist poets that Western civilization was in decline, preferring instead to avoid such generalizations and present instead concrete particulars of everyday life. He often advocated, *"No ideas but in things."*

THE GREAT FIGURE

Among the rain
and lights
I saw the figure 5
in gold,
on a red
firetruck
moving
tense
unheeded
to gong clangs
siren howls
and wheels rumbling
through the dark city.

1921

SPRING AND ALL

By the road to the contagious hospital
under the surge of the blue
mottled clouds driven from the
northeast—a cold wind. Beyond, the
waste of broad, muddy fields
brown with dried weeds, standing and fallen

patches of standing water
the scattering of tall trees

All along the road the reddish
purplish, forked, upstanding, twiggy
stuff of bushes and small trees
with dead, brown leaves under them
leafless vines—

Lifeless in appearance, sluggish
dazed spring approaches—

They enter the new world naked,
cold, uncertain of all
save that they enter. All about them
the cold, familiar wind—

Now the grass, tomorrow
the stiff curl of wildcarrot leaf

One by one objects are defined—
It quickens: clarity, outline of leaf

But now the stark dignity of
entrance—Still, the profound change
has come upon them: rooted, they
grip down and begin to awaken

1923

POEM (THE ROSE FADES)

The rose is obsolete
but each petal ends in
an edge, the double facet
cementing the grooved
columns of air—The edge
cuts without cutting
meets—nothing—renews
itself in metal or porcelain—

whither? It ends—

But if it ends
the start is begun
so that to engage roses
becomes a geometry—

Sharper, neater, more cutting
figured in majolica—
the broken plate
glazed with a rose

Somewhere the sense
makes copper roses
steel roses—

The rose carried weight of love
but love is at an end—of roses

It is at the edge of the
petal that love waits

Crisp, worked to defeat
laboredness—fragile
plucked, moist, half-raised
cold, precise, touching

What

The place between the petal's
edge and the

From the petal's edge a line starts
that being of steel
infinitely fine, infinitely
rigid penetrates
the Milky Way
without contact—lifting
from it—neither hanging
nor pushing—

The fragility of the flower
unbruised
penetrates space.

1923

TO ELSIE

The pure products of America
go crazy—
mountain folk from Kentucky

or the ribbed north end of
Jersey
with its isolate lakes and

valleys, its deaf-mutes, thieves
old names
and promiscuity between

devil-may-care men who have taken
to railroading
out of sheer lust of adventure—

and young slatterns, bathed
in filth
from Monday to Saturday

to be tricked out that night
with gauds

from imaginations which have no

peasant traditions to give them
character
but flutter and flaunt

sheer rags—succumbing without
emotion
save numbed terror

under some hedge of choke-cherry
or viburnum—
which they cannot express—

Unless it be that marriage
perhaps
with a dash of Indian blood

will throw up a girl so desolate
so hemmed round
with disease or murder

that she'll be rescued by an
agent—
reared by the state and

sent out at fifteen to work in
some hard-pressed
house in the suburbs—

some doctor's family, some Elsie
voluptuous water
expressing with broken

brain the truth about us—
her great
ungainly hips and flopping breasts

addressed to cheap
jewelry
and rich young men with fine eyes

as if the earth under our feet
were
an excrement of some sky

and we degraded prisoners
destined
to hunger until we eat filth

while the imagination strains
after deer
going by fields of goldenrod in

the stifling heat of September
somehow
it seems to destroy us

It is only in isolate flecks that
something
is given off

No one
to witness
and adjust, no one to drive the car

1923

THE RED WHEELBARROW

so much depends
upon

a red wheel
barrow

glazed with rain
water

beside the white
chickens.

1923

Gertrude Stein

(1874–1946)

*U*nusually cultured for a woman of her generation, Gertrude Stein had lived in Austria, France, and California and had studied psychology under the philosopher William James at Radcliffe College, and medicine at Johns Hopkins before she began her writing career in London and later Paris in the early 1900s. Her Paris home became a salon for the avante-garde, the leading writers and artists of the period between World Wars I and II including the American expatriates whom she named the "Lost Generation." Stein was among the first collectors of Picasso, Matisse, and the Cubists and in her own work attempted to parallel the theories of Cubism. Her poetry often illuminates the present moment by using abstraction, repetition with slight variations, fragmentation, and extreme simplification.

SUSIE ASADO

Sweet sweet sweet sweet sweet tea.
    Susie Asado.
Sweet sweet sweet sweet sweet tea.
    Susie Asado.
Susie Asado which is a told tray sure.
A lean on the shoe this means slips slips hers.
When the ancient light grey is clean it is yellow, it is a silver seller.
This is a please this is a please there are the saids to jelly. These
    are the wets these say the sets to leave a crown to Incy.
Incy is short for incubus.
A pot. A pot is a beginning of a rare bit of trees. Trees tremble,
    the old vats are in bobbles, bobbles which shade and shove
    and render clean, render clean must.
    Drink pups.
Drink pups drink pups lease a sash hold, see it shine and a
    bobolink has pins. It shows a nail.
What is a nail. A nail is unison.
Sweet sweet sweet sweet sweet tea.

1913

from THE GEOGRAPHICAL HISTORY OF AMERICA OR THE RELATION OF HUMAN NATURE TO THE HUMAN MIND

Page III

Human nature has nothing to do with it.
Human nature.
Has nothing to do with it.

Page IV

Emptying and filling an ocean has nothing to do with it because if
      it is full it is an ocean and if it is empty it is not an ocean.
Filling and emptying an ocean has nothing to do with it.

Page V

Nothing to do with war.

Page VI

War has nothing to do with master-pieces.
Who says it has.
Everybody says it has.
Does anybody say what a master-piece is.
No nobody does.

Page VIII

So then the important literary thinking is being done.
Who does it.
I do it.
Oh yes I do it.

Page XXI

Money one.
Romanticism one
Scenery one
Human nature not one.
Master-pieces.
Human nature never knows anything about one and one.

Page XXI

Storms.
Even a little one is not exciting.

Page XXI

Is there any difference between flat land and an ocean a big
        country and a little one.
Is there any difference between human nature and the human
        mind.
Poetry and prose is not interesting.
What is necessary now is not form but content.
That is why in this epoch a woman does the literary thinking.
Kindly learn everything please.

Page XXII

How ardently hurry comes too late.
That is what they used to say
Donald.
Donald and Dorothy Dora and Don Donald and Donald he comes
        when he can.
If he can when he can as he can nine.
Donald and Donald is all in one time.
To-morrow is as Donald would say twenty a day.
What does Donald do.
He does it all.
Of course what does Donald do.
Of course he does he does do it at all.
Donald dear.
Welcome here.
If he comes yes he comes.
Yes he comes.
If he comes.
Any Donald is not Donald there.
Donald there is not any Donald here.
But better here.
What if Donald may.
Not likely is not as different as very likely.
And very likely Donald is here.

Page XVIII

I may not be through with Donald.

Page XIX

Donald has nothing to do with romanticism.
Donald has nothing to do with money.
Donald has nothing to do with scenery.
Donald has nothing to do with human nature.
Donald has nothing to do.
Donald.
No one can reproach Donald.
Donald and Dorothy and once there was an ocean and they were
    not drowned.

Page III

Why should a woman do the literary important literary thinking of
    this epoch.

Page IV

Master-pieces are what they are.

Page V

There is no identity nor time in master-pieces even when they tell
    about that.

1935

Wallace Stevens

(1879–1955)

A vice president for the Hartford Accident and Indemnity Company, Wallace Stevens wrote poetry not as a career but to make meaning out of the modern world. His business travels to Florida offered a marked natural contrast between the climates of the tropics and his native New England, a useful metaphor for opposing ways of imagining the world. Stevens' poetic concern is with the role of the perceiver in creation, a modernist sense that the subjective vision makes its own reality within a world that is itself real but not necessarily guaranteed by God. This belief in the poet as the forger of a new faith links him with T. S. Eliot and Ezra Pound, although his subject matter reveals that he shared a love for the American landscape with his literary friends William Carlos Williams and Marianne Moore.

SUNDAY MORNING

I

Complacencies of the peignoir, and late
Coffee and oranges in a sunny chair,
And the green freedom of a cockatoo
Upon a rug mingle to dissipate
The holy hush of ancient sacrifice.
She dreams a little, and she feels the dark
Encroachment of that old catastrophe,
As a calm darkens among water-lights.
The pungent oranges and bright, green wings
Seem things in some procession of the dead,
Winding across wide water, without sound.
The day is like wide water without sound,
Stilled for the passing of her dreaming feet
Over the seas, to silent Palestine,
Dominion of the blood and sepulchre.

II

Why should she give her bounty to the dead?
What is divinity if it can come
Only in silent shadows and in dreams?

Shall she not find in comforts of the sun,
In pungent fruit and bright, green wings, or else
In any balm or beauty of the earth,
Things to be cherished like the thought of heaven?
Divinity must live within herself:
Passions of rain, or moods in falling snow;
Grievings in loneliness, or unsubdued
Elations when the forest blooms; gusty
Emotions on wet roads on autumn nights;
All pleasures and all pains, remembering
The bough of summer and the winter branch.
These are the measures destined for her soul.

III

Jove in the clouds had his inhuman birth.
No mother suckled him, no sweet land gave
Large-mannered motions to his mythy mind.
He moved among us, as a muttering king,
Magnificent, would move among his hinds,
Until our blood, commingling, virginal,
With heaven, brought such requital to desire
The very hinds discerned it, in a star.
Shall our blood fail? Or shall it come to be
The blood of paradise? And shall the earth
Seem all of paradise that we shall know?
The sky will be much friendlier then than now,
A part of labor and a part of pain,
And next in glory to enduring love,
Not this dividing and indifferent blue.

IV

She says, "I am content when wakened birds,
Before they fly, test the reality
Of misty fields, by their sweet questionings;
But when the birds are gone, and their warm fields
Return no more, where, then, is paradise?"
There is not any haunt of prophecy,
Nor any old chimera of the grave,

Neither the golden underground, nor isle
Melodious, where spirits gat them home,
Nor visionary south, nor cloudy palm
Remote on heaven's hill, that has endured
As April's green endures; or will endure
Like her remembrance of awakened birds,
Or her desire for June and evening, tipped
By the consummation of the swallow's wings.

V

She says, "But in contentment I still feel
The need of some imperishable bliss."
Death is the mother of beauty; hence from her,
Alone, shall come fulfilment to our dreams
And our desires. Although she strews the leaves
Of sure obliteration on our paths,
The path sick sorrow took, the many paths
Where triumph rang its brassy phrase, or love
Whispered a little out of tenderness,
She makes the willow shiver in the sun
For maidens who were wont to sit and gaze
Upon the grass, relinquished to their feet.
She causes boys to pile new plums and pears
On disregarded plate. The maidens taste
And stray impassioned in the littering leaves.

VI

Is there no change of death in paradise?
Does ripe fruit never fall? Or do the boughs
Hang always heavy in that perfect sky,
Unchanging, yet so like our perishing earth,
With rivers like our own that seek for seas
They never find, the same receding shores
That never touch with inarticulate pang?
Why set the pear upon those river-banks
Or spice the shores with odors of the plum?
Alas, that they should wear our colors there,
The silken weavings of our afternoons,

And pick the strings of our insipid lutes!
Death is the mother of beauty, mystical,
Within whose burning bosom we devise
Our earthly mothers waiting, sleeplessly.

VII

Supple and turbulent, a ring of men
Shall chant in orgy on a summer morn
Their boisterous devotion to the sun,
Not as a god, but as a god might be,
Naked among them, like a savage source.
Their chant shall be a chant of paradise,
Out of their blood, returning to the sky;
And in their chant shall enter, voice by voice,
The windy lake wherein their lord delights,
The trees, like serafin, and echoing hills,
That choir among themselves long afterward.
They shall know well the heavenly fellowship
Of men that perish and of summer morn.
And whence they came and whither they shall go
The dew upon their feet shall manifest.

VIII

She hears, upon that water without sound,
A voice that cries, "The tomb in Palestine
Is not the porch of spirits lingering.
It is the grave of Jesus, where he lay."
We live in an old chaos of the sun,
Or old dependency of day and night,
Or island solitude, unsponsored, free,
Of that wide water, inescapable.
Deer walk upon our mountains, and the quail
Whistle about us their spontaneous cries;
Sweet berries ripen in the wilderness;
And, in the isolation of the sky,
At evening, casual flocks of pigeons make
Ambiguous undulations as they sink,
Downward to darkness, on extended wings.

1915, 1923

Marianne Moore

(1887–1972)

*B*orn *in a suburb of St. Louis but later moving to Brooklyn, New York,
Marianne Moore never married but helped support her mother through jobs
in schools and libraries. Through work for* avant-garde *magazines in the 1920s,
she entered the modernist literary world as a poet and astute critic. Moore's private life reminded many of Emily Dickinson, for both created a protected space to
do her own work. But Moore was a deliberate professional who was famous for
her statement that poetry departs from the real world but then recreates that
world within its forms: poems were "imaginary gardens with real toads in
them." Like other modernists she wanted to break with tradition and connect
poetry to the world in a new way. As the editor for* Dial *magazine, Moore became
friends with T. S. Eliot, William Carlos Williams, and Ezra Pound. Her unique
technical contribution is her use of the stanza as the primary unit of poetry.
Moore's stanza is composed of regular lines counted by syllables, instead of by
metric stress, and connected by elaborate verse patterns and subtle rhymes. One
of her poetic ironies is the degree to which her poems attempt to draw the reader
from the page and into the world. Moore's service as a poet is the bringing together of the loose material of life into a specific way of seeing.*

POETRY

I, too, dislike it: there are things that are important beyond all this
        fiddle.
   Reading it, however, with a perfect contempt for it, one discovers in
   it after all, a place for the genuine.
      Hands that can grasp, eyes
      that can dilate, hair that can rise
           if it must, these things are important not because a

high-sounding interpretation can be put upon them but because they
      are
   useful. When they become so derivative as to become unintelligible,
   the same thing may be said for all of us, that we
      do not admire what
      we cannot understand: the bat
           holding on upside down or in quest of something to

eat, elephants pushing, a wild horse taking a roll, a tireless wolf under
    a tree, the immovable critic twitching his skin like a horse that feels
        a flea, the base-
  ball fan, the statistician—
      nor is it valid
         to discriminate against "business documents and

school-books"; all these phenomena are important. One must make a
    distinction
    however: when dragged into prominence by half poets, the result
      is not poetry,
  nor till the poets among us can be
      "literalists of
      the imagination"—above
         insolence and triviality and can present

for inspection, "imaginary gardens with real toads in them," shall we
    have
    it. In the meantime, if you demand on the one hand,
    the raw material of poetry in
      all its rawness and
      that which is on the other hand
        genuine, you are interested in poetry.

                    1921

THE STEEPLE-JACK

Dürer would have seen a reason for living
        in a town like this, with eight stranded whales
to look at; with the sweet sea air coming into your house
on a fine day, from water etched
        with waves as formal as the scales
on a fish.

One by one in two's and three's, the seagulls keep
        flying back and forth over the town clock,
or sailing around the lighthouse without moving their wings—
rising steadily with a slight
        quiver of the body—or flock
mewing where

a sea the purple of the peacock's neck is
	paled to greenish azure as Dürer changed
the pine green of the Tyrol to peacock blue and guinea
gray. You can see a twenty-five-
	pound lobster; and fish nets arranged
to dry. The

whirlwind fife-and-drum of the storm bends the salt
	marsh grass, disturbs stars in the sky and the
star on the steeple; it is a privilege to see so
much confusion. Disguised by what
	might seem the opposite, the sea-
side flowers and

trees are favored by the fog so that you have
	the tropics at first hand: the trumpet-vine,
fox-glove, giant snap-dragon, a salpiglossis that has
spots and stripes; morning-glories, gourds,
	or moon-vines trained on fishing-twine
at the back door;

cat-tails, flags, blueberries and spiderwort,
	striped grass, lichens, sunflowers, asters, daisies—
yellow and crab-claw ragged sailors with green bracts—toad-plant,
petunias, ferns; pink lilies, blue
	ones, tigers; poppies; black sweet-peas.
The climate

is not right for the banyan, frangipani, or
	jack-fruit trees; or for exotic serpent
life. Ring lizard and snake-skin for the foot, if you see fit;
but here they've cats, nor cobras, to
	keep down the rats. The diffident
little newt

with white pin-dots on black horizontal spaced-
	out bands lives here; yet there is nothing that
ambition can buy or take away. The college student
named Ambrose sits on the hillside
	with his not-native books and hat
and sees boats

at sea progress white and rigid as if in
        a groove. Liking an elegance of which
the source is not bravado, he knows by heart the antique
sugar-bowl shaped summer-house of
        interlacing slats, and the pitch
of the church

spire, not true, from which a man in scarlet lets
        down a rope as a spider spins a thread;
he might be part of a novel, but on the sidewalk a
sign says C. J. Poole, Steeple-Jack,
        in black and white; and one in red
and white says

Danger. The church portico has four fluted
        columns, each a single piece of stone, made
modester by white-wash. This would be a fit haven for
waifs, children, animals, prisoners,
        and presidents who have repaid
sin-driven

senators by not thinking about them. The
        place has a school-house, a post-office in a
store, fish-houses, hen-houses, a three-masted
        schooner on
the stocks. The hero, the student,
        the steeple-jack, each in his way,
is at home.

It could not be dangerous to be living
        in a town like this, of simple people,
who have a steeple-jack placing danger-signs by the church
while he is gilding the solid-
        pointed star, which on a steeple
stands for hope.

                                                    1932

Elizabeth Bishop
(1911–1979)

*N*ow considered a central figure in modernist poetry, Elizabeth Bishop wrote *relatively few poems and wasn't well known until after her death in 1979. An American poet, Bishop traveled extensively throughout Europe, and lived much of her adult life in New York, Key West, and Brazil until settling into a teaching position at Harvard. Bishop's poems tend to be lyrical, miniaturist, and meditative explorations of domesticity and nature. She has been credited with helping to revive some aspects of the formalist traditions after the early twentieth-century modernist rejections of the fixed form. "One Art," for example, is a nineteen-line French form called a villanelle, a form that obsessively repeats lines, forcing its reader to periodically reacquire a state of careful attention and meditative possibility. Like Marianne Moore's poems, Bishop's work encourages her readers to pay attention to the world, to celebrate the often overlooked. In short, her work attempts to restore the domestic and mundane to considerations of beauty. Consequently, her poems are filled with particulars and seemingly endless qualifiers, "the same sea, the same, / slightly, indifferently swinging above the stones, / icily free above the stones."*

ONE ART

The art of losing isn't hard to master;
so many things seem filled with the intent
to be lost that their loss is no disaster.

Lose something every day. Accept the fluster
of lost door keys, the hour badly spent.
The art of losing isn't hard to master.

Then practice losing farther, losing faster:
places, and names, and where it was you meant
to travel. None of these will bring disaster.

I lost my mother's watch. And look! my last, or
next-to-last, of three loved houses went.
The art of losing isn't hard to master.

I lost two cities, lovely ones. And, vaster,
some realms I owned, two rivers, a continent.
I miss them, but it wasn't a disaster.

—Even losing you (the joking voice, a gesture
I love) I shan't have lied. It's evident
the art of losing's not too hard to master
though it may look like (*Write* it!) like disaster.

1976

Philip Larkin
(1922–1985)

*B*orn in Coventry, England, Philip Larkin studied at Oxford University and became a professional librarian known better as a crotchety traditionalist poet. Larkin was influenced early by Thomas Hardy's bleak outlook on life but also could laugh at the world's and his own absurdist despair. He once told a reviewer that "deprivation is for me what daffodils were for Wordsworth." His subject matter is always decidedly English.

CHURCH GOING

Once I am sure there's nothing going on
I step inside, letting the door thud shut.
Another church: matting, seats, and stone,
And little books; sprawlings of flowers, cut
For Sunday, brownish now; some brass and stuff
Up at the holy end; the small neat organ;
And a tense, musty, unignorable silence,
Brewed God knows how long. Hatless, I take off
My cycle-clips in awkward reverence,

Move forward, run my hand around the font.
From where I stand, the roof looks almost new—
Cleaned, or restored? Someone would know: I don't.
Mounting the lectern, I peruse a few
Hectoring large-scale verses, and pronounce
"Here endeth" much more loudly than I'd meant.
The echoes snigger briefly. Back at the door
I sign the book, donate an Irish sixpence,
Reflect the place was not worth stopping for.

Yet stop I did: in fact I often do,
And always end much at a loss like this,
Wondering what to look for; wondering, too,
When churches fall completely out of use
What we shall turn them into, if we shall keep
A few cathedrals chronically on show,
Their parchment, plate and pyx in locked cases,
And let the rest rent-free to rain and sheep.

Shall we avoid them as unlucky places?

Or, after dark, will dubious women come
To make their children touch a particular stone;
Pick simples for a cancer; or on some
Advised night see walking a dead one?

Power of some sort or other will go on
In games, in riddles, seemingly at random;
But superstition, like belief, must die,
And what remains when disbelief has gone?
Grass, weedy pavement, brambles, buttress, sky,

A shape less recognizable each week,
A purpose more obscure. I wonder who
Will be the last, the very last, to seek
This place for what it was, one of the crew
That tap and jot and know what rood-lofts were?
Some ruin-bibber, randy for antique,
Or Christmas-addict, counting on a whiff
Of gown-and-bands and organ-pipes and myrrh?
Or will he be my representative,

Bored, uninformed, knowing the ghostly silt
Dispersed, yet tending to this cross of ground
Through suburb scrub because it held unspilt
So long and equably what since is found
Only in separation—marriage, and birth,
And death, and thoughts of these—for whom was built
This special shell? For, though I've no idea
What this accoutred frowsty barn is worth,
It pleases me to stand in silence here;

A serious house on serious earth it is,
In whose blent air all our compulsions meet,
Are recognised, and robed as destinies.
And that much never can be obsolete,
Since someone will forever be surprising
A hunger in himself to be more serious,
And gravitating with it to this ground,
Which, he once heard, was proper to grow wise in,
If only that so many dead lie round.

1955

Bruce Weigl

(b. 1947)

*B**ruce Weigl is one of the most acclaimed American poets to emerge from the
Vietnam War. A native of Lorain, Ohio—home of Nobel laureate Toni
Morrison—Weigl joined the U.S. Army after graduating from high school in
1967 and served a one-year tour in Vietnam. He then began university studies,
earned a Ph.D., and is currently professor of English at Pennsylvania State University. His poetry incorporates the best themes of romanticism—nature and the
self—but always within the context of his Vietnam experiences.*

SNOWY EGRET

My neighbor's boy has lifted his father's shotgun and stolen
down to the backwaters of the Elizabeth
and in the moon he's blasted a snowy egret
from the shallows it stalked for small fish.

Midnight. My wife wakes me. He's in the backyard
with a shovel so I go down half-drunk with pills
that let me sleep to see what I can see and if it's safe.
The boy doesn't hear me come across the dewy grass.
He says through tears he has to bury it,
he says his father will kill him
and he digs until the hole is deep enough and gathers
the egret carefully into his arms
as if not to harm the blood-splattered wings
gleaming in the flashlight beam.

His man's muscled shoulders
shake with the weight of what he can't set right no matter what,
but one last time he tries to stay a child, sobbing
please don't tell. . . .
He says he only meant to flush it from the shadows,
he only meant to watch it fly
but the shot spread too far
ripping into the white wings spanned awkwardly for a moment
until it glided into brackish death.

I want to grab his shoulders,
shake the lies loose from his lips but he hurts enough,
he burns with shame for what he's done,
with fear for his hard father's
fists I've seen crash down on him for so much less.
I don't know what to do but hold him.
If I let go he'll fly to pieces before me.
What a time we share, that can make a good boy steal away,
wiping out from the blue face of the pond
what he hadn't even known he loved, blasting
such beauty into nothing.

1984